Maids and Mistresses,
Cousins and Queens

Maids and Mistresses, Cousins and Queens

· · · · · · · · · · · · · · · · · · ·

Women's Alliances in Early Modern England

EDITED BY

Susan Frye

Karen Robertson

New York   Oxford

Oxford University Press

1999

Oxford University Press

Oxford   New York
Athens   Auckland   Bangkok   Bogotá   Buenos Aires   Calcutta
Cape Town   Chennai   Dar es Salaam   Delhi   Florence   Hong Kong   Istanbul
Karachi   Kuala Lumpur   Madrid   Melbourne   Mexico City   Mumbai
Nairobi   Paris   São Paulo   Singapore   Taipei   Tokyo   Toronto   Warsaw

and associated companies in
Berlin   Ibadan

Published by Oxford University Press, Inc.
198 Madison Avenue, New York, New York 10016

Oxford is a registered trademark of Oxford University Press

Helen Ostovich's "The Appropriation of Pleasure in
The *Magnetic Lady*" is reprinted by permission of *SEL:
Studies in English Literature 1500–1900* 34,
no. 2 (Spring 1994).

Library of Congress Cataloging-in-Publication Data
Maids and mistresses, cousins and queens : women's alliances in early
modern England / edited by Susan Frye and Karen Robertson.
p.   cm.
"Began as a seminar at the Shakespeare of America Association
Meeting of 1993 in Atlanta and the project continued to expand"—
Foreword.
Includes bibliographical references.
ISBN 0-19-511734-4; ISBN 0-19-511735-2 (pbk.)
1. Women—England—History.   2. Women—Social networks—England—
History.   3. Female friendship—England—History.   4. Women and
literature—England—History.   5. Women in literature.   I. Frye,
Susan, 1952– .   II. Robertson, Karen.   III. Shakespeare
Association of America. Meeting (1993 : Atlanta, Ga.)
HQ1599.E5M35   1998
305.4'0942—dc21   98-3448

1 3 5 7 9 8 6 4 2

Printed in the United States of America
on acid-free paper

for James Lewton-Brain,
husband and friend

and

for Eleanor Frye,
Ethel Harris, and Florence Coutant,
grandmother and great aunts

Preface

Women's Alliances in Early Modern England

THIS COLLECTION OF ESSAYS explores how early modern women associated with other women in a variety of roles, from alewives to midwives, prostitutes to pleasure seekers, slaves to queens, servingmaids to ladies in waiting, mothers to vagrants, and transvestites to authors. Bringing together a variety of literary and historic texts, material culture and social practice, these essays examine for the first time the complexity of the "alliances" or relationships among English women during the 250-year period between 1450 and 1700. In particularizing women's economic, intellectual, social, racial, political, and familial relations, the collection reveals the complexity of women's associations and the importance of men in mediating and disrupting these associations, as well as the frequency with which women were connected and separated by issues of race, class, and ethnicity.

This book's use of the term "alliances" is meant to signal women's deliberate associations. The study of men's alliances is far advanced, because male economic, political, intellectual, and military relationships constitute such well-known and well-studied institutions as guilds, parliament, the university, and the military. While the gap between the study of men in groups and women in groups is understandable because the activity of men has been so much more public and recorded, the need for the study of women's alliances has grown in proportion to our increasing awareness of and information about women's roles. Studying the subject of women's alliances is fundamental not only to the study of women but also to our emerging picture of early modern English society as a whole.

In juxtaposing the perspectives of feminism, historicism, Marxism, cultural theory, queer theory, and postcolonialism, the collection's scholars build on and revise the last decade's scholarship on women in the early modern period. Many compelling studies have pictured women as marginalized participants in English society, have focused on exceptional women, or have discussed women in groups without this collection's degree of awareness of the complexities surrounding the formation and inhibition of women's alliances. *Maids and Mistresses, Cousins and Queens: Women's Alliances in Early Modern England* grows out of the recognition of the emergent theoretical and historical interrogation of the category of "woman," providing an overview of women's activities that challenges prevalent conceptions of women's limitations within patriarchal society by confronting the differences that bind and divide women.

THIS VOLUME BEGAN as a seminar at the Shakespeare Association of America meeting of 1993 in Atlanta, and the project continued to expand in the following years as we added new contributors especially interested in our topic. Editing *Maids and Mistresses* has changed forever its editors' sense of the literary and historical past. We are grateful to each contributor for so carefully and energetically researching, writing, and meticulously recreating his or her particular alliance in so far as that is possible. We are grateful for the assistance of the librarians at the British Library, Stanford University, Vassar College, and the University of Wyoming, with particular thanks to Robin Harcourt Williams, Librarian at Hatfield House. In addition, we would like to thank a number of people for their help and suggestions: Jean Howard, Ann Rosalind Jones, Valerie Wayne, Alison Smith, and the members of the Second Attending to Women Conference Seminar, "Digging Out Our Sisters: Method and Theory Toward the Recovery of Women's Alliances in Primary Texts." Margaret Ferguson, Anthony Dawson, Nancy Dye, Benjamin Kohl, Paul Russell, Lowell Gallagher, Linda Woodbridge, Sara Mendelson, Patricia Crawford, Janet Constantinides, Susan Aronstein, Robert Torry, Lisa Shipley, Jennifer Munroe, and members of three graduate seminars at the University of Wyoming, as well as our Oxford editor, T. Susan Chang, have offered the support and encouragement that enabled this project to come into being. Colleen Cohen, Miriam Cohen, and members of the Women's Studies faculty at Vassar College offered insight and advice, and the Vassar student assistants, Jessica Houser, Damien Keane, Melissa Scardaville, and Jennifer Van Ore were cheerfully reliable, as was Ray Bruno. Ed Hudson and Daniel Kirkpatrick hospitably cheered and inspired us. Elizabeth Robertson provided advice and a space for work as well as a model of feminist connection.

Susan Frye wishes particularly to acknowledge the help, kindness, and support of her daughter Lizzie, and of her parents, Bruce and Caroline Frye, without whom her work would not be possible. Betty Hacker, grandmother, mother-in-law, and reference librarian, offered support and comfort in equal measure. The National Endowment for the Humanities and the University of Wyoming provided financial support and the University's Department of English offered many different forms of assistance while we were editing this collection. Sandra Schwartzkopf, whose death in 1997 during treatment for breast cancer took her from us, was also an important contributor to this volume as student, research assistant, colleague, and friend. To Karen Robertson, co-editor, friend, and collaborator in many ventures, she owes something beyond gratitude for the many pleasures involved in working together. Susan dedicates this work to a wonderful trio of women whose relationship as affectionate sisters has presided over her life and work: her grandmother, Eleanor Frye, who died in 1996 at the age of 98, and Eleanor's sisters, also deceased, Ethel Harris and Florence Coutant.

Any collaboration by midcareer professionals will be marked by transitions. This particular project has been a time of enormous pleasure and professional growth but also one marked by death. For Karen Robertson, these years have brought the death of a father whose own passion for science has set for her a standard for intellectual engagement and pleasure in collaborative work. They have also brought the death of her husband, James Lewton-Brain. These experiences brought to Karen a knowledge of the way sororal and maternal bonds can deepen through death, and she thanks her friend, Susan, her sister, Elizabeth, and her mother, Dody, for their love and the practical efficiency that made this volume possible. Both editors wish to acknowledge the support of Jim Brain, who sat by us as we planned this collection, whose advice (rooted in his own work in feminist anthropology) helped us to conceptualize the connections of women, and whose provision of fish stew and caffè lattes lifted the burden of domestic tasks and enabled our work together. Karen dedicates the volume to Jim, who, to our sorrow, will not be here to accept the volume from our hands and celebrate its completion with us.

Laramie, Wyoming   S. F.
Poughkeepsie, New York   K. R.
October 1998

Contents

Contributors

HARRIETTE ANDREADIS is an Associate Professor of English at Texas A&M University. Her published articles include "Sappho in Early Modern England: A Study in Sexual Reputation" in *Re-Reading Sappho: Reception and Transmission*, ed. Ellen Greene (University of California Press, 1996), and "Tribades, Tommies, Lollepots and . . . Romantic Friends?: Theorizing Early Modern Lesbianisms" in *Thymris* 3, no.1 (Spring 1996). She is currently working on a book-length study of the construction of lesbianism(s) in early modern England and a book-length compilation of private writings by nineteenth-century Texas women.

BARBARA BOWEN is an Associate Professor of English at Queens College and The Graduate Center at the City University of New York. Her recent publications include "Shakespeare and Sexuality: Current Questions in an International Frame" in *Queer Theater* (ed. Framji Minwalla and Alisa Solomon, forthcoming), *Gender in the Theater of War: Shakespeare's Troilus and Cressida* (Garland Publications, 1993), and "Writing Caliban: Anticolonial Appropriations of *The Tempest*," in *Current Writing* (Durban, South Africa) 5 (Fall 1993). She was also series editor for *Gender and Genre in World Literature* for Garland Publishing from 1991 to 1996, and wrote articles on African-American literature. She is currently working on *Caliban's Tempest: Revisions of Shakespeare's Play from a Century of Decolonization*, an edited collection and analysis of forty versions of *The Tempest* from the Americas, Asia, the Caribbean, and Europe. She works as a member of CUNY faculty union in the context of combating efforts to devalue scholarship in the humanities and underfund higher education nationwide. The chapter in this book is part of a larger, ongoing project on Lanyer.

ELIZABETH A. BROWN is an Associate Professor of English at the University of Rio Grande. She is currently continuing work on attendants in the courts of Elizabeth I and Anne of Denmark as well as research on the working lives of early modern women.

KATHLEEN BROWN is an Associate Professor in the Department of History at the University of Pennsylvania. She is the author of *Good Wives, Nasty Wenches, and Anxious Patriachs: Gender, Race, and Power in Colonial Virginia* (Chapel Hill, 1996) which won the American Historical Society's Dunning Prize for the best book by a younger scholar. Her current research is a history of cleanliness in early modern England and early America, 1500–1900.

SUSAN FRYE is Associate Professor of English and Women's Studies at the University of Wyoming. The author of *Elizabeth I: The Competition for Representation* (Oxford University Press, 1993, 1997) and articles on Elizabeth, Spenser, and Shakespeare; she is currently working on a book entitled *Women's Work and Women's Writing*, about the relation between women's domestic and literary production in the early modern period.

LOWELL GALLAGHER, Associate Professor of English at the University of California, Los Angeles, is the author of *Medusa's Gaze: Casuistry and Conscience in the Renaissance* (Stanford University Press, 1991), as well as articles on semiotics and narrative theory concerning early modern religious cultures. He is currently completing a book on the ethics of narrative and sacred corporeality and a book on opera and the politics of diva worship.

LISA GIM is Assistant Professor of English at Fordham University. She has published articles on Shakespeare and Puttenham. Her essay in this collection is drawn from her recently completed book, *(Re)presenting Regina: Literary Representations of Queen Elizabeth I by Women Writers of the Sixteenth and Seventeenth Centuries*.

MARGO HENDRICKS is an Assistant Professor of Literature at the University of California, Santa Cruz. Her writings include "Obscured by Dreams: Race, Desire and Empire in Shakespeare's *A Midsummer Night's Dream*," "Managing the Barbarian: *The Tragedy of Dido, Queen of Carthage*," and "The Moor of Venice: The Italian on the English Renaissance Stage" in *Shakespearean Tragedy and Gender* (ed. Shirley Nelson Garner and Madelon Sprengnether). She is co-editor of *Women, 'Race', and Writing in the Early Modern Period* and is finishing a book on Aphra Behn.

JEAN E. HOWARD is a Professor of English at Columbia University and the author of *The Stage and Social Struggle in Early Modern England* (Routledge, 1994). She is also co-editor with Phyllis Rackin of *Engendering a Nation* (Routledge, 1997) and co-editor, with S. Greenblatt, K. Mauss, and W. Cohen, of *The Norton Shakespeare* (Norton, 1997). She is completing a book entitled *Drama of a City*, which is a study of the dramatic genres that dominated the city theaters in the first two decades of the seventeenth century, with special attention to the social problems mediated by those genres.

ANN ROSALIND JONES is Esther Cloudman Dunn Professor of Comparative Literature at Smith College, where she directs the program in Comparative Literature. She has published on a range of Renaissance writers, including Maurice Sceve, Philip Sidney, and Thomas Nashe. Women writers are her main interest, eight of whom she discusses in *The Currency of Eros: Women's Love Lyric in Europe, 1540–1620* (1990). She has translated, with Margaret Rosenthal, *The Poems and Selected Letters of Veronica Franco*, and has recently completed, with Peter Stallybrass, *Worn Worlds: Clothes and The Fashioned Subject in Early Modern England and Europe*. She is now at work on a study of women's uses of dialogue form in the Querelle des Femmes.

JODI MIKALACHKI is an Assistant Professor of English at Wellesley College. Her published articles include "Gender, Cant and Cross-talking in *The Roaring Girl*" in *Renaissance Drama* (n.s. 25, 1996). She is currently working on a book, *Boadicea's Breasts: The Recovery of Native Origins in Early Modern England* as well as a book on thieves' cant and roguery in early modern England.

SIMON MORGAN-RUSSELL is an Assistant Professor of English and Adjunct Graduate Faculty Theater, at Bowling Green State University. He is continuing to examine urban discourses in the seventeenth century. His current work is primarily on Restoration drama.

HELEN OSTOVICH is an Associate Professor in the Department of English at McMaster University, Hamilton, Ontario. Her most recent publication is *Ben Jonson: Four Comedies*, a modern critical edition of *Volpone, Epicoene, The Alchemist*, and *Bartholomew Fair*, in the Longman Annotated Texts series (London: Addison Wesley Longman, 1997). Currently she is preparing a modern critical edition of Jonson's *Every Man Out of his Humour* for Revels Plays (Manchester: University of Manchester Press).

KAREN ROBERTSON is Adjunct Associate Professor of English and Women's Studies at Vassar College. She is co-editor with Carole Levin of *Sexuality and Politics in Renaissance Drama* (Lewiston, N.Y.: Edwin Mellen, 1991) and with J.-A. George of a student edition of John Pikering's *Horestes* (Galway: Galway University Press, 1996). Her publications include essays on Shakespeare, revenge tragedy, and women's letter writing. She is now expanding her essay, "Pocahontas at the Masque" *Signs: Journal of Women in Culture and Society* vol. 21 (1996): 3 into a book on Pocahontas and the Jacobeans.

JESSICA TVORDI is a Ph.D. candidate in literature at the University of Arizona. She is currently working on an article on the invention of heterosexuality in *Paradise Lost*, while completing her dissertation on religious conversion and erotic coercion in early modern devotional literature.

MARY WACK is currently Senior Fellow in the Center for Teaching and Learning at Washington State University. She has published on a variety of medieval topics. Her book, *Lovesickness in the Middle Ages*, won the 1990 Harry Levin prize from the American Comparative Literature Association.

VALERIE WAYNE is Professor of English at the University of Hawai'i at Manoa. She has edited *The Matter of Difference: Materialist Feminist Criticism of Shakespeare*, Edmund Tilney's *The Flower of Friendship: A Renaissance Dialogue Contesting Marriage*, and Thomas Middleton's *A Trick to Catch the Old One* (in the *Collected Works of Thomas Middleton*, for which she also serves as an Associate General Editor). Her future work includes an edition of *The Winter's Tale* in the Bedford Shakespeare Series and an edition of *Cymbeline* for the Arden Shakespeare, Third Series.

Maids and Mistresses,
Cousins and Queens

Introduction

. . . .

SUSAN FRYE AND KAREN ROBERTSON

WOMEN'S ALLIANCES IN EARLY modern England have tended to be obscured by the impressive body of scholarship devoted to male alliances, even though the connections of women were often constructed through and interactive with those of males. Men's alliances, formalized in such institutions as the guild, government, law, church, and university, left behind the records, architecture, and literature that have invited generations of scholars to codify them. As a result, entire libraries are filled with books analyzing men's connections. The relations among women, whether competitive or supportive, have proved not only less visible but also more difficult to reconstruct, often because women did not formally record their activities or seek memorialization in material structures.

Maids and Mistresses, Cousins and Queens: Women's Alliances in Early Modern England is the first volume to address the complex relations among English women between 1450 and 1700. The scholars in this collection recover many different forms of alliance among English women by using a variety of primary materials, including plays and poems, government documents, conduct manuals, letters, diaries, inventories, recipe books, wills, epitaphs, portraits, ecclesiastical records, court cases, and textiles. Their essays reveal the complex processes by which women mobilized existing channels of connection or conceptualized and materialized new communities of women. In the sexual economies of the city, court, household, colony, and school, women left traces of their engagement with one another. Our examination of the alliances in which historical women and female characters located their identity is designed to demonstrate how important such relationships were to early modern conceptions of community.

While the individual female subject remains of enduring concern in this volume, each subject came to consciousness and lived out her life within communities of interconnection and social interaction. Both men and women of the period condensed their understandings of community and relationship in the classical image of the beehive, an image which locates the individual subject within a matrix of interactions.[1] For early modern people the single individual invokes household, kin, and class, just as the bee invokes the hive. Women in particular appropriated the hive and the bee not only to validate the place of women within their own society, but also the connections between women themselves. Amelia Lanyer and Mary Sidney Wroth use the bee to describe aspects of their writing and their relation to patrons and reproduction.[2] Lanyer's bee offering honey to female aristocratic patrons and Wroth's bee describing the activity and vulnerability of the female lover both express perceived relations between the single female subject and a larger world. Women also repeatedly embroidered bees in textiles for household use and decoration, where the bee embroidered on a piece of cloth both asserts and memorializes the sewer's own productive industry. The hive worked by Mary Queen of Scots, for example, suggests both personal economy—the needleworker in captivity who keeps busy in the face of despair—and the possibility of political cabal. For women whose lives passed less in the political spotlight, the needleworked "hive" carries the meaning of "storehouse" and the bee implies their service and connection to a larger unity, the household located among all the other households constituting society.[3]

The many uses that these women made of the hive demonstrate that early modern women were conceptualizing themselves in groups. By tracing out the connections implicit in the single bee, women's communities can be recovered, or at least inferred, despite the fragmentary nature of their documentation. We summarize women's connections with the word "alliance," which denotes a formally recognized relationship, activated or chosen to the political advantage of its members. In the early modern period, "alliance" is most closely associated with women in the economic and diplomatic process called the "marriage alliance," a phrase that captures the extent to which women's connections to others depends on their bodies. In this collection our term "alliance" builds on this earlier usage by including any form of women's interrelationships while retaining its sense of the sexual politics of women's connections. The contributors to this volume understand "alliance" to signal a range of relationships: not only marriage and kinship, but also defensive and offensive unions, intellectual, educational, and religious connections, friendship, and same-sex love.

At the same time, we recognize the extent to which women's alliances were often temporary—and included conflict as well as union. Women in early modern England had few institutional structures beyond the family to guarantee continuity of connection, so that conflict may serve as useful evidence of association. Contention or competition rarely occurred among women who were strangers to one another. Simon Morgan-Russell points out in his essay that, on stage, city wives might work together with a bawd against their wandering husbands, but readily turn their backs on the disreputable woman when their marriages are restored. Other essays in this volume also examine points of rupture and connection among women, including Kathleen Brown's discussion of the mistress–slave–servant relationships in the controversy surrounding a stillbirth in Virginia; Susan Frye's examination of the alliance and disconnection of Mary Queen of Scots and Elizabeth Talbot, countess of Shrewsbury, through their textiles; Jessica Tvordi's demonstration of how class and politics affect female same-sex relations in Shakespeare's comedies; and Helen Ostovich's discussion of the staged male disruption of women's associations through birth and ambition.

While some alliances described in this collection study women divided by race or class, others examine women as united for protection. Ann Rosalind Jones, for example, describes the interconnections of London maid-servants, while Valerie Wayne discusses the allied response of "women" to the misogyny of Joseph Swetnam, and Harriette Andreadis considers the literary tradition of women's same-sex friendships. Further alliances were assembled for purposes of protection, support, education, and resistance. The alewives of Chester, writes Mary Wack, came under pressure to disassociate when male brewers began to form institutions excluding them. Lowell Gallagher casts light on the vigorous community of Catholic women founded by Mary Ward that emphasized the education of girls and women. The educational establishment advertised by Bathsua Makin, discussed by Lisa Gim, sought to found a community for the development of a particular group of women by drawing on the model of an exceptional intellectual woman from an earlier era, Elizabeth I; yet it also affirmed the intellectual potential in all women through that school. Women responded to the economic and social pressures of their time not only by conflict with one another, but by association against perceived oppression.

The contributors ground their work in the feminist scholarship of the last two decades, and particularly in three major developments of that scholarship. First, in response to the American feminist movement of the 1960s, scholars worked to recover women's voices by excavating women's experiences and texts. Second, beginning in the first half of the 1980s scholars confronted the issue of difference in ways that problematized the definitions of "voice" and "woman," a confrontation that caused feminists to turn in increasing numbers to postmodernist approaches. Third, in the second half of the 1980s and in the 1990s the challenge of women's studies to traditional disciplinary boundaries provided one model for reconfiguring the relationships among texts now loosely gathered under the rubric of cultural studies.[4] The practice of feminist cultural studies has led to a renewed search for women's historical and literary artifacts, energized the discussion of their theoretical relations, and provided an increasingly localized sense of women's connections to their culture and to one another that in turn enables reconceptualizations of larger social and literary patterns.

Although literary scholars, drawing on anthropology, sociology, and history,[5] have moved to recover the communities of early modern women, literary studies has been slower to take up women's alliances as an entire subject of study. In part this is because the disciplinary impetus in literary studies has traditionally led to the study of single authors or genres, a process reflected in much valuable feminist work on the early modern period. The preeminence of the canonical author, Shakespeare, in English Renaissance studies, legitimized feminist study that considered representations of women in his work and exposed contradictions and contestations in the construction of "woman" in his plays.[6] The masculinist concept of a stable "author" itself, however, blocked the consideration of works signed by women, as well as of anonymous and pseudonymous works that address their condition. Postmodernist analyses of the performance of gender have opened up such texts, as Valerie Wayne demonstrates in her essay in this volume "The Dearth of the Author: Anonymity's Allies in *Swetnam the Woman-hater*."

To date, the work on women in groups includes the essays of *Rewriting the Renaissance* (1986), edited by Margaret Ferguson, Maureen Quilligan, and Nancy J. Vickers, which articulated the growing concern with women as discreet entities and as members of the institution of the family.[7] Mary Ellen Lamb and Margaret Hannay have informed us of the Sidney patronage network, while Josephine Roberts's introduction to her edition of Mary Sidney Wroth's *Urania* emphasizes not only that Wroth herself "belonged to a circle of women writers of her own generation, many of them related by kinship" (Wroth 1983, p. xxxvii) but that in her *Urania* Wroth places "a network of women at the center of her fiction" (Wroth 1983, p. xxvi). The discussions of female homoerotics by Valerie Traub and Harriette Andreadis have drawn attention to the need to consider the significance of women's pleasure and the meanings of women's friendship.[8] Except for this work, the literary study of women's alliances has awaited an accumulation of theoretical understandings, archival research, and the editing of works by women from which this volume benefits. Much scholarship and many conferences have contributed to our growing understanding of the complexities involved in making women visible, of talking about the relation between female characters and historical women, of examining the problems of agency, subjectivity, and voice in relation to women's social, political, and intellectual history.[9] As Betty S. Travitsky pointed out in the introduction to the collection *Attending to Women in Early Modern England*, "Far from scrambling against one another to publish [a] few morsels" of information about women, "scholars have discovered that—while much in the female tradition has regrettably been lost—enormous amounts of materials survive."[10] We have headed for the archives to make discoveries, and have at times come away either empty-handed or with information on the edge of intelligibility, as shown in Karen Robertson's examination of the puzzle of eighteen women's names included with an Elizabeth Throckmorton letter to Robert Cecil. We have also learned how much harder we need to think about the racial and class discourses cutting across the definition of "woman" presupposed in our work,[11] as several essays in this volume demonstrate. They include Jodi Mikalachki's work on female vagrants; Kathleen Brown's consideration of the relations of a household including a mistress, a Native American servant, and a slave; Elizabeth Brown's elucidation of the political roles of ladies-in-waiting; Barbara Bowen's discussion of the relationship between Aemilia Lanyer's Jewish past and Christian present; and Margo Hendricks's exploration of Aphra Behn's racial identity.

The feminist interest in recovering women's cultural, social, and economic histories has led to an abundance of newly edited material neglected by previous generations of scholars. In particular, literary scholars and historians have benefited from the increasing availability of women's texts. Anthologies of essays on women in the Renaissance have provided a version of connection as women writers of the sixteenth and seventeenth centuries jostle one another within a simulacrum of connection.[12] A great deal of effort has been devoted to the editing of individual women writers. That effort has resulted in the publication of valuable individual editions, including the work of Elizabeth Cary, Mary Sidney Wroth, and Aemilia Lanyer,[13] which entered the canon of Renaissance literary study in advance of critical editions in large part because they were available in texts provided by the Brown Women Writers Project. Editions of other women writers are currently available, with more on the way: Mary Sidney Herbert, Isabella Whitney, Arbella Stuart, Anne Clifford, Martha Moulsworth, and Mary, Lady Chudleigh. These texts contribute to this volume's realization of women's interactions and have only begun to alter our sense of the lives of early modern women.[14]

The significance of these editions cannot be underestimated, both in themselves and for the perspective on early modern women that they grant us as their number increases. The works have been crucial to our examination of women's alliances because they offer more direct access to women's self-representation in the past and provide a ground from which to scrutinize male-authored texts and ideological constructions of femininity.[15] Readings of male authors, such as Valerie Wayne's edition of Edmund Tilney's *Flower of Friendship*, and the many analyses of Shakespeare, can now be set beside the writings of women themselves. Sara Jayne Steen and Elizabeth Hageman have carried this newly found ability to juxtapose male- and female-authored texts into the area of pedagogy with "Teaching Judith Shakespeare," their issue of *Shakespeare Quarterly* (47: Winter 1996). While early modern female authors partici- pated in the reiteration of hegemonic beliefs, by their very presence as writers they challenged the insistence on women's silence. Women writ- ers of the past, like female characters and historical women in a variety of relations to one another, offer present scholars purchase on the struc- ture of male-authored ideological systems that tends to deny or efface women's alliances.

This collection is divided into four areas of alliance: Alliances in the City, Alliances in the Household, Materializing Communities, and Emerging Alliances. The essays of the first part, Alliances in the City, focus on con- nections formed within London, Chester, Dorchester, and Brainford, be- cause considering cities provides an initial overview of the existence and multiplicity of connections formed across households or other collectivi- ties. These essays use a variety of techniques to recover connections that women formed in response to the market pressures of early modern cities. The legal regulation of women's behavior in cities provides access to alli- ances formed by women through churching, ale brewing, domestic ser- vice, and even vagabondage, while the construction of citizen wives in dramatic comedy stages their alliances against sexual predation.

This group of essays begins with Ann Rosalind Jones's "Maidservants of London: Sisterhoods of Kinship and Labor" (chapter 1), which shows us how the poems of Isabella Whitney not only articulate the difficul- ties and hardships of domestic service, but in addressing women simi- larly employed across the city of London, also create an alliance of both kin and service. Jones sets these poems beside the Tudor regulation of vagabondage, which forced any unemployed woman between the ages of fourteen and forty into service, in order to understand the compre- hensiveness of service in the lives of unmarried women. Whitney's poems make clear the difficulties and hardships of domestic service to suggest the necessity for female alliances within the labor economy of early modern London. Mary Wack's essay, "Women, Work, and Plays in an English Medieval Town" (chapter 2), provides a model of the process re- quired for the recovery of women's communities in male-authored texts. Her reading of two late Tudor interpolations in the Chester mystery plays—dismissed by earlier critics as comic intrusions on the aesthetic integrity of the cycle—offers access to an understanding of women's communities in Chester by its topical allusions to changes in legal and economic statutes that affected women. The interpolated scenes in the Harrowing of Hell and Noah plays speak to a heterogenous audience, and while they justify women's exclusion from larger communities according to the civic fathers, they also represent to Chester women the losses of economic opportunity as well as freedom of dress and female ritual. Wack's essay exposes the restrictions on the lives and livelihoods of a broad spectrum of city women who, while watching the plays, would have momentarily constituted a community focused on their loss.

The economic and sexual pressures on women servants, alluded to by Whitney, acquire particularity in the legal documents from the town of Dorchester used by Jodi Mikalachki in chapter 3, "Women's Networks and the Female Vagrant: A Hard Case." Mikalachki traces the unfortunate career of Alice Balstone, whose dismissal from service and illegitimate pregnancy precipitated her imprisonment, vagrancy, and early death. At the core of Balstone's story lies a scene of female advice given in prison, when the Widow Sacer counsels Balstone to name her master as the father of her illegitimate child during the birth. Although the story provided by the temporary network of women failed to prevail against the social and economic power of her former master, the incident provides a moment of feminine connection, one partially enabled by incarceration, though such connections could not be sustained for long against the instability and poverty of vagabondage.

Simon Morgan-Russell situates the regulation of female sexuality within the pressures of the urban London market in flesh, in order to read the alliances of city wives in a male-authored city comedy in chapter 4, "No good thing ever comes out of it": Male Expectation and Female Alliance in Dekker and Webster's *Westward Ho*." Morgan-Russell shows the way in which the pressure of the congested sexual economy of the city leads to male attempts to lure city wives away for adulterous assignations in the market town of Brentford, also known as Brainford, names that historically were synonymous with adultery. The city wives form an alliance for protection from their husbands, but their cross-class bond with a bawd fractures at the end of the play.

The essays in the second part, Alliances in the Household, consider the issues that arose for early modern women in constructing and maintaining a household, including relations with serving women and slaves, childbearing, and the difficulties of women forming and maintaining a household with or without men. Tensions across class and race are included in Kathleen Brown's discussion of Madame Anne Tayloe's household in "'A P[ar]cell of Murdereing Bitches': Female Relationships in an Eighteenth-Century Slaveholding Household" (chapter 5). Court records from the case of the unmarried Tayloe's alleged infanticide in early eighteenth-century Virginia reveal the politics of female relationships—which were formed from a mosaic of different interests among the white mistress, white hired woman, Native American hired woman, and enslaved woman of African descent—as well as the ways in which the complexities of this household conflict with men's perceptions of women's alliances.

Helen Ostovich also highlights childbirth in chapter 6, "The Appropriation of Pleasure in *The Magnetic Lady*." Her essay considers Ben

Jonson's staging of women's alliances by taking up the play's expression of anxieties toward and disruptions of these connections. Ostovich examines how Jonson uses *The Magnetic Lady* to play out a war between gender and class roles by demonizing an alliance of servingwomen who attempt to secure their own pleasure—defined as wealth and power— by taking over a widow's household and nominating their own heiress to the family fortune. They are defeated by an alliance of gentlemen who use the weapons of law and higher education to overcome female control of succession—clear evidence of the fear and contempt that dominated so many masculinist treatments of women's alliances in the period and that have helped until now to ensure their obscurity. Jessica Tvordi examines further aspects of the staged disruption and construction of women's alliances within households in chapter 7, "Female Alliance and the Construction of Homoeroticism in *As You Like It* and *Twelfth Night*." Tvordi discusses how in these plays Shakespeare provides two intersecting locales for the possibility of female homoeroticism between the couples Rosalind and Celia, and Olivia and Maria. While both couples experience the pressures of politics or class and the heterosexual imperative to marry, Olivia and Maria achieve a gynocentric household within marriage. Rosalind, on the other hand, abandons whatever relationship she and Celia had at court to enter the Forest of Arden's homoerotic exchanges that conclude in a series of heterosexual marriages.

The final essay in this part turns to the households of queens as Elizabeth Brown examines the relation between the serving women of Elizabeth I and Shakespeare's Cleopatra in chapter 8, "'Companion me with my mistress': Cleopatra, Elizabeth I, and Their Waiting Women." Brown compares the staged relationships among Cleopatra's attendants in Shakespeare's *Antony and Cleopatra* with the far richer historical kin and patronage system of Elizabeth I's ladies-in-waiting, demonstrating that much of Cleopatra's vulnerability on stage springs from the play's erasure of the complex female alliances that Elizabeth enjoyed. These essays on women's alliances within the household elucidate the often tenuous and tension-filled quality of women's relations across race and class, as well as the complex relationship between the experience of historical women and those of the "women" staged by male playwrights working with all-male companies.

The third group of essays, Materializing Communities, focuses on four instances in which women created or "materialized" other forms of community beyond the city and household in order to pursue their economic, political, educational, and religious aspirations. The first essay by Karen Robertson, "Tracing Women's Connections from a Letter by Elizabeth Ralegh" (chapter 9), functions as an introduction to this part by considering the obstacles to materializing the particulars of female support. When Elizabeth Throckmorton, the wife of Walter Ralegh, attempted after Ralegh's imprisonment for treason to obtain familial land and revenues from Robert Cecil, she was not alone in her struggles. One of her letters to Cecil includes a list of eighteen women's names, possible evidence of a bond of association on her behalf. Robertson's discussion of her difficulties in tracing these names and deducing the nature of their interconnection with Throckmorton highlights the challenges involved in recovering women's communities and reminds us of how many alliances beyond the scope of this collection we may only glimpse or never know.

In Susan Frye's "Sewing Connections: Elizabeth Tudor, Mary Stuart, Elizabeth Talbot, and Seventeenth-Century Anonymous Needleworkers" (chapter 10), the "material" in evidence is the domestic textiles produced by women as the means of articulating their place in the world through gift-giving, the production of large needlework hangings for the aristocratic spaces of New Hardwick Hall, or in the samplers and needlework pictures of women of the gentry and merchant classes. Needlework bookcovers, emblematic pieces, samplers, and pictures suggest the means to recover a number of women's communities, and conflicts within those communities, across a period of 150 years. Lisa Gim, in chapter 11, "Faire *Eliza*'s Chaine": Two Female Writers' Literary Links to Queen Elizabeth I," examines how two seventeenth-century women of intellect and resource sought to create both imagined and real communities of women through the figure of Elizabeth I, whom they interpreted as authorizing their activities as intellectual women. In the figure of Elizabeth, Bathsua Makin found grounds for her argument for the education of women in a school that she hoped to base in part on the humanist education that Elizabeth had received and in part on her experience as tutor to the children of Charles I; Diana Primrose also worked to make Elizabeth's virtue and intellect a resource from which women could draw the motivation to work and write in the public world.

The final essay in this part discusses the materialization of a women's community within the conservative institution of the Catholic Church. Lowell Gallagher's recovery of documents concerning the missionary community founded by Mary Ward (1585–1645) allows him to show in "Mary Ward's 'Jesuitresses' and the Construction of a Typological Community" (chapter 12) how this remarkable woman charted a path between a general ethos of subservience to patriarchal norms and a particular, radical critique of patriarchal authority in both the theological and social realms. Ward founded the School of Blessed Mary, a community of religious women whose mission included educating female students in a curriculum adapted from the Jesuits. Ward's movement expanded across Europe to found ten houses and schools also organized along Jesuitical models. Mary Ward's operations crossed class and gender expectations in ways that made her theological and social adversaries pronounce her a "scandal" and "holy amazon" while suggesting the emergence of a socially progressive ideology.

The essays in the final part, Emergent Alliances, trace the connections among women forming within the nexus of early modern colonialism, class, and desire. These essays participate in a process of reanimating the categories of gender, race, and sexuality, to make these familiar categories, in Barbara Bowen's words, "speak and deliver up their histories." Valerie Wayne, in chapter 13, "The Dearth of the Author: Anonymity's Allies in *Swetnam the Woman-hater*," considers the instability of gender as a category of authorship within a discussion of *Swetnam the Woman-hater*'s construction of a women's alliance formed to punish a misogynist. While our introduction has stressed the importance of female authorship in order to open ideological systems, Wayne reminds us that feminists must not recapitulate the rigidity of traditional gender divisions. By considering the impersonation of gender through a "character first presented as a man," her essay provides a model for the reading of cultural performance that avoids a static notion of originary gender as it searches out resistance in male- and female-authored texts.

Harriette Andreadis's "The Erotics of Female Friendship in Early Modern England" (chapter 14) takes up and complicates the issue of the erotics of women's alliances and traces their development into and through the eighteenth century. In the seventeenth century, the very acknowledgment of same-sex erotic behaviors brought with it an opprobrium evaded by women eager to maintain both their same-sex friendships and their class respectability. Andreadis traces the developing tradition of a poetry of female friendship through the seventeenth century, from Lanyer's dedications through Katharine Phillips's development of a "shadowed" discourse of eroticism. The exposure of this discourse both discloses women's alliances and demonstrates the problems of uncovering the relations which women poets so carefully veiled. Andreadis places the discourses of women's alliance within a historical continuum in order to document transgressive connections that are discursively shadowed within a variety of texts. In doing so, she demonstrates that these transgressive alliances, like the other alliances explored in this volume, are made visible by the analytical languages that simultaneously enable contemporary feminist understandings and issues and keep them open for reexamination.

The final two essays examine the ways in which communities of women in the early modern period lie embedded within the colonial enterprise by addressing the complex moment in the early modern period when communities of women necessarily constructed themselves through race. Margo Hendricks's and Barbara Bowen's essays reanimate the fluidity of categories of race in early modern writing emerging from the colonial economy of seventeenth-century England. In chapter 15, "Alliance and Exile: Aphra Behn's Racial Identity," Hendricks uses the sense of exile in Aphra Behn's work to reopen biographical assumptions about Behn's racial status, assumptions too readily presumed in a notoriously unstable biography. When considered from the perspective of the twentieth-century notion of "passing," Behn's repeated evocation of a lost community of women in lyric and pastoral can be described as saturated with the momentous pain of the absolute exile required of the "passing" individual. These insights lead to Hendricks's reading of the mirror of the racial other in *Oroonoko*. Her necessarily speculative exploration of "passing" in the early modern period exposes our tacit and unexamined presumptions about the racial identity of the unmarked racial subject. This essay, by evoking the mixed-race author haunted by separation and loss, revitalizes understandings made too fixed by a simple binarism of black and white.

In chapter 16, "Aemilia Lanyer and the Invention of White Womanhood," Bowen considers the women's community imagined in Lanyer's *Salve Deus Rex Judaeorum* as one constituted by a racialized outsider, Lanyer, who was the daughter of an Italian Jew. Alert to moments of syntactic slippage in the text, Bowen explores the complex status of the daughter of a Jew who rewrites Christianity from a female point of view that reveals the extent to which the definition of a collective is predicated on racial exclusion. Bowen's essay at the conclusion of the volume shows that relations among women in the early modern period are tempered by an awareness of race as well as kinship, friendship, and intellectual community. Even as Lanyer takes a deserved place in the early modern canon, the celebration of her poems' female communities, like this volume's celebration of women's alliances in general, must be tempered by the awareness that such associations are constructed in terms of gender, class, and race.

AS WOMEN'S ALLIANCES COME into scholarly view, it is our hope that a new or renewed sense of their existence will enter the always emerging picture of early modern English culture. We need to study not only exceptional or individual women, but also women in their dynamic relations with one another as they are represented in historical materials at court and in the courtroom, in palaces, prisons, birthing chambers, religious communities, and schools, as well as in poems or plays. To study women in groups is to gain a sense of women as productive and imaginative, interactive with even the most patriarchal injunctions to silence and domesticity, and, at times, resistant and even transformative of dominant discourses. This volume represents a preliminary attempt to discern the variety, complexity, and meaning of women's alliances, a foray into conceptualizing a culture in which women functioned fully because they lived, worked, and wrote together. As such, it is meant to be more suggestive than complete, to invite a reevaluation of women's roles within the social text.

NOTES

1. Many writers and artists appropriated Virgil's epic simile of the beehive in Book I of the *Aeneid*:

> It was like the work which keeps the bees hard at their tasks about the flowering countryside as the sun shines in the calm of early summer, when

they escort their new generation, now full grown, into the open air, or squeeze clear honey into bulging cells, packing them with sweet nectar; or else take over loads brought by their foragers; or sometimes form up to drive a flock of lazy drones from their farmstead. All is a ferment of activity; and the scent of honey rises with the perfume of thyme. (*Aeneid I.* 429–32)

2. Lanyer draws a distinction between the literary work of Mary Sidney's circle and her own poems by casting the circle's work as sugar "more finer, higher priz'd," while her own work is honey that in its sweetness is no less meritorious than theirs: "Yet is the painefull Bee no whit disgrace'd,/Nor her faire wax, or hony more despiz'd" (Lanyer, pp. 30–31). In Worth's Urania, the hive and the bee are located within the female body itself (Wroth 1983, p. 289).

3. Margaret Swain, *The Needlework of Mary Queen of Scots* (London: Van Nostrand Reinhold, 1973), p. 101, lists "Bees with beehive" as one of Mary's needlework pieces. For examples of bees in needlework, see Liz Arthur, *Embroidery 1600–1700 at the Burrell Collection* (London: John Murray, 1995), p. 106; see also in Janet Arnold, *Queen Elizabeth's Wardrobe Unlock'd* (London: Maney, 1988) the embroidered mirror case (p. 67) and the sampler (p. 62). See also the garments listed in the Stowe inventory, in Arnold, item 94, p. 294, and in the Folger Inventory, item 31, p. 342.

4. In an overview of feminist scholarship in anthropology, Pat Caplan, "Engendering Knowledge: The Politics of Ethnography Part 2," *Anthropology Today* 4 (1988) 6: 14–17 observes that English and American feminist challenges to foundationalist discourses of the 1970s, although contemporaneous with the work of poststructuralist philosophers, should not necessarily be attributed to French poststructuralist thought: "Second-wave feminism and postmodernism are contemporaneous, and share many of the same sources, yet they are seen as independent developments. However, as a number of scholars have noted, forms of feminist scholarship anticipate and in some ways go further than postmodernism." For a discussion of the connection in the discipline of history between feminism and poststructuralism see Kathleen Canning, "Feminist History after the Linguistic Turn: Historicizing Discourse and Experience" *Signs* 19 (1994): 368-404. For a recent discussion of the connections between feminism and postmodernism see Fran Mascia-Lees, Patricia Sharpe, and Colleen Ballerino Cohen, "The Postmodernist Turn in Modern Anthropology: Cautions from a Feminist Perspective" *Signs* 1 (1989): 7–33. On the development of cultural studies, see Cary Nelson, Paula A. Treichler, and Lawrence Grossberg's "Cultural Studies: An Introduction," *Cultural Studies*, ed. Lawrence Grossberg, Cary Nelson and Paula A. Treichler (New York: Routledge, 1992) pp. 1–16.

5. See, for example, Michelle Rosaldo and Louise Lamphere, *Women, Culture, and Society* (Stanford: Stanford University Press, 1974) and *Signs* 14 (1989); Judith M. Bennett, "Medieval Women, Modern Women: Across the Great Divide," in *Culture and History 1350–1600: Essays on English Communities, Identities, and Writing*, ed. David Aers (London: Harvester, 1992), pp. 147–75; Judith Brown, *Immodest Acts: The Life of a Lesbian Nun in Renaissance Italy* (New York: Oxford University Press, 1986); Barbara Hannawalt, "Lady Honor Lisle's Networks of Influence," in *Women and Power in the Middle Ages*, ed. Mary Erler and Maryanne Kowaleski (Athens: University of Georgia Press, 1988), pp. 188–212, and editor of *Women and Work in Pre-Industrial Europe* (Bloomington: University of Indiana Press, 1986); Barbara J. Harris, "Property, Power, and Personal Relations: Elite Mothers and Sons in Yorkist and Early Tudor England" *Signs* 15 (1990): 606-32; Merry Wiesner, *Working Women in Renaissance Germany* (New Brunswick, N.J.: Rutgers University Press, 1986). See also Renata Bridenthal, Claudia Koonz, and Susan Stuart, eds., *Becoming Visible: Women in*

European History (Boston: Houghton Mifflin, 1987); Margaret L. King, *Women of the Renaissance* (Chicago: University of Chicago Press, 1991); and *A History of Women: Renaissance and Enlightenment Paradoxes* (Cambridge, Mass.: Harvard University Press, 1993).

6. Early work by Juliet Dusinberre, *Shakespeare and the Nature of Women* (London: Macmillan, 1975) and Linda Bamber, *Comic Women, Tragic Men: A Study of Gender and Genre in Shakespeare* (Stanford: Stanford University Press, 1982) has been followed by a range of feminist work on Shakespeare. To mention only a few examples: Carol Neely Thomas, *Broken Nuptials in Shakespeare's Plays* (New Haven, Conn.: Yale University Press, 1985); Patricia Parker, *Literary Fat Ladies* (London: Methuen, 1987); Phyllis Rackin, *Stages of History: Shakespeare's English Chronicles* (Ithaca, N.Y.: Cornell University Press, 1990); Valerie Wayne, ed., *The Matter of Difference: Materialist Feminist Criticism of Shakespeare* (Ithaca, N.Y.: Cornell University Press, 1991); Janet Adelman, *Suffocating Mothers: Fantasies of Maternal Origin in Shakespeare's Plays, Hamlet to The Tempest* (New York: Routledge, 1992); Lynda Boose, "The Father and the Bride in Shakespeare," in *Ideological Approaches to Shakespeare: The Practice of Theory*, ed. Robert P. Merrix and Nicholas Ranson (Lewiston, N.Y.: Edwin Mellen, 1992), 3–38; Deborah E. Barker and Ivo Kamps, eds., *Shakespeare and Gender: A History* (New York: Verso, 1995); and Coppélia Kahn, *Roman Shakespeare: Warriors, Wounds, and Women* (London: Routledge, 1997); Frances Dolan, ed., *The Taming of the Shrew: Texts and Contexts* (Boston: St. Martin's Press, 1996); and Jean R. Howard and Phyllis Rackin, *Engendering a Nation: A Feminist Account of Shakespeare's English Histories* (London: Routledge, 1997).

7. See also Linda Woodbridge, *Women and the English Renaissance: Literature and the Nature of Womankind, 1540-1620* (Urbana: University of Illinois Press, 1984); Constance Jordan, *Renaissance Feminism: Literary Texts and Political Models* (Ithaca, N.Y.: Cornell University Press, 1990); and Karen Newman, *Fashioning Femininity and English Renaissance Drama* (Chicago: University of Chicago Press, 1991). As documentation of the growth of the field of Renaissance feminist studies, see also the special issues on women published by *English Literary Renaissance: Women in the Renaissance* II, 4, no. 3 (1984), II, 18, no. 1 (1988), and *Women in the Renaissance III: Studies in Honor of Ruth Mortimer* 24, no. 1 (1994), as well as the anthology *Women in the Renaissance: Selections from English Literary Renaissance*, ed. Kirby Farrell, Elizabeth H. Hageman, and Arthur F. Kinney (Amherst: University of Massachusetts Press, 1990).

8. Margaret L. Hannay, "'Your Vertuous and Learned Aunt': The Countess of Pembroke as Mentor to Mary Wroth" in *Reading Mary Wroth: Representing Alternatives in Early Modern England*, ed. Naomi J. Miller and Gary Waller (Knoxville: University of Tennessee Press, 1991), pp. 15–34; Mary Ellen Lamb, *Gender and Authorship in the Sidney Circle* (Madison: University of Wisconsin Press, 1990); Valerie Traub, *Desire and Anxiety: Circulations of Sexuality in Shakespearean Drama* (New York: Routledge, 1992); and Harriette Andreadis, "The Sapphic-Platonics of Katherine Philips, 1632-1664," *Signs* 15 (1989): 34–60.

9. For bibliographies of work on women in the Renaissance, see the three special issues of *English Literary Renaissance*, cited in note 7. Anthologies of critical studies include Margaret Hannay, *Silent but for the Word: Tudor Women as Patrons, Translators, and Writers of Religious Work* (Kent, Ohio: Kent State University Press, 1985); Mary Beth Rose, *Women in the Middle Ages and the Renaissance: Literary and Historical Perspectives* (Syracuse, N.Y.: Syracuse University Press, 1986); Carole Levin and Jeanie Watson, *Ambiguous Realities* (Detroit, Mich.: Wayne State University Press, 1987); Anne M. Haselkorn and Betty S. Travitsky, *The Renaissance Englishwoman in Print: Counterbalancing the Canon* (Amherst: University of Massachusetts Press, 1990); Ann Rosalind Jones and

Betty Travitsky, "Women in the Renaissance: An Interdisciplinary Forum," *Women's Studies* 19, no. 2 (1991); S. P. Cerasano and Marion Wynne-Davies, *Gloriana's Face: Women, Public and Private, in the English Renaissance* (Detroit, Mich.: Wayne State University Press, 1992); Jean R. Brink, Maryanne C. Horowitz, and Allison P. Coudert, "Privileging Gender in Early Modern England," *Sixteenth Century Essays and Studies* 23 (Kirksville, Miss.: Sixteenth Century Studies Press, 1993); Leslie C. Dunn and Nancy A. Jones, *Embodied Voices: Representing Female Vocality in Western Culture* (Cambridge: Cambridge University Press, 1994); Carole Levin and Karen Robertson, *Sexuality and Politics in Renaissance Drama* (Lewiston, N.Y.: Edwin Mellen, 1994); and Valerie Traub, M. Lindsay Kaplan, and Dympna Callahan, eds., *Feminist Readings of Early Modern Culture: Emerging Subjects* (New York: Cambridge University Press, 1996).

10. Betty S. Travitsky and Adele Seeff, *Attending to Women in Early Modern England* (Newark: University of Delaware Press, 1994), 16. The first Attending to Women Conference is summarized in this volume. That symposium was followed by second, and third multidisciplinary conferences, "Attending to Women in Early Modern Europe," held again at the University of Maryland in April 1994, and October 1997.

11. Studies that consider the representation of women in a variety of authors or dramatic genres include Lisa Jardine, *Still Harping on Daughters: Women and Drama in the Age of Shakespeare* (Brighton, Sussex: Harvester Press, 1983); Anthony Dawson, "Women Beware Women and the Economy of Rape," *Studies in English Literature* 27, no. 2 (1987): 303–20; Mary Beth Rose, *Expense of Spirit: Love and Sexuality in English Renaissance Drama* (Ithaca, N.Y.: Cornell University Press, 1988); Dympna Callaghan, *Women and Gender in Renaissance Tragedy: A Study of King Lear, Othello, The Duchess of Malfi, and The White Devil* (Atlantic Highlands, N.J.: Humanities Press International, 1989); Kate McCluskie, *Renaissance Dramatists* (Atlantic Highlands, N.J.: Humanities Press International, 1989); Barbara Hodgdon, *The End Crowns All: Closure and Contradiction in Shakespeare's History* (Princeton, N.J.: Princeton University Press, 1991); Coppélia Kahn, "Whores and Wives in Jacobean Drama," in *In Another Country: Feminist Perspectives on Renaissance Drama*, ed. Dorothea Kehler and Susan Baker (Methuen, N.J.: Scarecrow, 1991), pp. 246–60; Susan Frye, *Elizabeth I: The Competition for Representation* (New York: Oxford University Press, 1993); Jean E. Howard, *The Stage and Social Struggle in Early Modern England* (New York: Routledge, 1994); and Deborah Willis, *Malevolent Nurture: Witch-Hunting and Maternal Power in Early Modern England* (Ithaca, N.Y.: Cornell University Press, 1995). The collection edited by Margo Hendricks and Patricia Parker, *Women, "Race," and Writing in the Early Modern Period* (New York: Routledge, 1994) takes up questions of the inscription of racial as well as gender discourses. See also Ania Loomba, *Gender, Race, Renaissance Drama* (Manchester: Manchester University Press, 1989) and Kim Hall, *Things of Darkness: Economies of Race and Gender in Early Modern England* (Ithaca, N.Y.: Cornell University Press, 1995).

12. The early anthologies, Mary R. Mahl and Helen Koon, ed., *The Female Spectator: English Women Writers before 1800* (Bloomington: Indiana University Press, 1977) and Betty Travitsky, ed., *The Paradise of Women: Writings by Englishwomen of the Renaissance* (rpt. 1989; New York: Columbia University Press, 1991), were followed by anthologies compiled by Katharina M. Wilson, *Women Writers of the Renaissance and Reformation* (Athens: University of Georgia Press, 1984); Katharina M. Wilson and Frank J. Warnke, *Women Writers of the Seventeenth Century* (Athens: University of Georgia Press, 1989); and Louise Schleiner, *Tudor and Stuart Women Writers* (Bloomington: Indiana University Press, 1994). See also Elspeth Graham, Hilary Hinds, Elaine Hobby, and Helen

Wilcox, ed., *Her Own Life: Autobiographical Writings by Seventeenth-Century Englishwomen* (London: Routledge, 1989). These anthologies have provided a useful resource for courses that include Renaissance women writers, and courses using these materials have in turn fueled a demand for further editions. The Women Writers Database Project at Brown University first directed by Susanne Woods has provided invaluable copies of unedited facsimiles while scholarly editions are being prepared.

13. Elizabeth Cary's *The Tragedie of Mariam, Faire Queene of Jewery* (1613) is now available in three editions: *The Tragedy of Mariam, Fair Queen of Jewery*, ed. Barry Weller and Margaret F. Ferguson (Berkeley: University of California Press, 1994); in *Renaissance Women: The Plays of Elizabeth Cary, The Poems of Aemilia Lanyer*, ed. Diana Purkiss (London: Pickering and Chatto, 1994); and in *Renaissance Drama by Women: Texts and Documents*, ed. S. P. Cerasano and Marion Wynne-Davies (New York: Routledge, 1996). Also see Lady Mary Wroth, *The First Part of The Countess of Montgomery's Urania*, ed. Josephine A. Roberts, Renaissance English Text Society, seventh series, vol. 140 (Binghamton, N.Y.: Medieval & Renaissance Texts & Studies, 1995); Aemilia Lanyer, *The Poems of Aemilia Lanyer: Salve Deus Rex Judeorum*, ed. Susanne Woods (New York: Oxford University Press, 1993).

14. See *The Collected Works of Mary Sidney Herbert*, ed. Margaret Hannay, Noel Kinnamon, and Michael Brennan (Oxford: The Clarendon Press), forthcoming; Betty Travitsky, ed. "The 'Wyll and Testament' of Isabella Whitney," reprinted in *English Literary Renaissance* 10 (1980): 76–94; Sara Jayne Steen, ed., *The Letters of Arbella Stuart* (New York: Oxford University Press, 1994); Katherine O. Acheson, ed. *The Diary of Anne Clifford 1616–1619* (New York: Garland, 1995); Robert C. Evans and Barbara Wiedemann, eds., *"My Name Was Martha": A Renaissance Woman's Autobiographical Poem* (West Cornwall, Conn.: Locust Hill, 1993); and Margaret J. M. Ezell, ed. *The Poems and Prose of Mary, Lady Chudleigh* (New York: Oxford University Press, 1993).

15. For full-length studies of early modern women writers, see Elaine V. Beilin, *Redeeming Eve: Women Writers of the English Renaissance* (Princeton, N.J.: Princeton University Press, 1987); Ann Rosalind Jones, *The Currency of Eros: Women's Love Lyric in Europe, 1540–1620* (Bloomington: Indiana University Press, 1990); Tina Krontiris, *Oppositional Voices: Women as Writers and Translators of Literature in the English Renaissance* (New York: Routledge, 1992); and Barbara Kiefer Lewalski, *Writing Women in Jacobean England* (Cambridge, Mass.: Harvard University Press, 1993). For analysis of the theoretical problems engaged by women participating in print culture, see Wendy Wall, *The Imprint of Gender: Authorship and Publication in the English Renaissance* (Ithaca, N.Y.: Cornell University Press, 1993).

PART I

Alliances in the City

I

Maidservants of London

Sisterhoods of Kinship and Labor

. . . .

ANN ROSALIND JONES

MOST OF SHAKESPEARE'S PLAYS, comic and tragic, include ladies in waiting, often articulate ones such as Maria of *Twelfth Night*, who hatches a plot to protect her mistress against her steward's ambition to marry her. Othello's Emilia dies attempting to save her mistress' reputation; Cleopatra's Iras and Charmian, attendants so "conspicuously loyal" (as Elizabeth Brown reminds us in an essay in this volume) that they follow their queen in suicide. But ladies in waiting are gentlewomen, close in rank to the queens or aristocrats they serve. Companions to noblewomen in early modern courts and country estates historically constituted a very small percentage of women in service.

A far greater number of women in Shakespeare's time worked lower down the social scale, as housemaids in city or rural houses. In domestic employment, a frequently followed path led girls in their teens from gentry families in the countryside to large London households, via the "putting-out system" through which their parents hoped they would find long-term husbands as well as short-term employment in the city (Clark, 1919, p. 115 ff; Wiesner, 1993, pp. 50, 92–94; Pearson, 1957, pp. 430 ff; Elliott, 1982, pp. 92–96).[1] The writers of citizen comedy often assigned this category of servingwoman to a lower class so that she could be played as a comic figure: in Dekker's *The Shoemaker's Holiday*, Sibil, Rose Oateley's maid, in return for "a cambric apron . . . and a pair of purple stockings," promises to "go jiggy-joggy to London and be here in a trice" (I, ii, 54–5, 61–2). The city maid may also be assigned the role of managing plots whereby her young mistress succeeds in marrying the man she loves: an example is Middleton's laconic but effective Jugg, in *A Chaste Maid in Cheapside*. Such plays position female domestics as accomplices to citizen or aristocratic heroines: chambermaids work in the interests of their "betters." But outside dramatic scripts, how might women servants have sounded if they were working in their own interests?

To know this, we need to know how maidservants sounded when they were writing in their own interests, rather than operating as objects of representation in texts written by men. Limited literacy and limited leisure made such self-representation unlikely for this class of women. Yet two recently exhumed pamphlets from late sixteenth-century London suggest that urban housemaids had a good deal to say for themselves, and that they said it in a spirit of group solidarity that considerably enlarges our sense of women's alliances in early modern England. My analysis of Isabella Whitney's "A Modest meane for Maids" (1573) and the anonymous pamphlet "A Letter sent by the Maydens of London" (1567) is intended to suggest the advantages these writers gained by framing their complaints about a servingwoman's lot in a plural "we," a speaking position that united such women as a group and strengthened their defense of their usefulness to their city employers and to the commonwealth as a whole.

Isabella Whitney is perhaps best known for her "Wyll and Testament," a long poem written as a farewell to London, edited by Betty Travitsky in 1980. This detailed description and farewell to the city, R. J. Fehrenbach has suggested, may have been written as Whitney looked forward to a marriage that would take her back to the countryside (Fehrenbach, 1983). But it is clear from shorter poems in *A sweet nosegay or pleasant posye. Contayning a hundred and ten Phylosophicall flowers* that Whitney had spent considerable time in London, where her sisters also worked as domestic servants, and that she had thought critically about the circumstances of women workers like herself.

That situation was less than ideal. Serving in a London household was mandated for any unmarried woman from fourteen to forty years of age by a London statute passed in the fifth year of Elizabeth's reign, in an effort to cut down on vagabonds. The law empowered any two "Burgesses," or aldermen, to command any unemployed woman "to serve and be retained by yeare, weeke, or day, in such cost and for such wages as they shall thinke meete, and if she refuse, they may commit her to prison, till she shall be bound to serve" (T. E., 1632, p. 8). Such a law had particularly harsh effects in periods of low employment, when, through no fault of her own, a woman's failure to find work risked landing her in debtors' prison. If a woman did find work in a household, she made less money than a man in service; her wages were one-half to two-thirds of the average pay for a man. One to two pounds per year was all she could expect (Erikson, 1993, p. 85; Elliott, 1982, p. 95), and trial records show

that some servants had to sue to obtain wages withheld by their employers (Amussen, 1988, pp. 158–59). Still, many young women migrating
to the city found stable jobs, working for the same family for an average
of four years; they also found husbands through employment in large
households (Elliott, 1982, p. 90).

But others were seduced by male employers and fired as a result. Susan
Amussen points out, "Abuses were common even within families. . . .
Sexual relations between masters and servants involved a double exercise of power—as a master and a man" (p. 159).[2] She gives several instances in which women named their employers as the fathers of their
children but were silenced by counteraccusations of slander. One case
suggests that Londoners saw abortion as one way out of this master/ser-
vant predicament:

> Holme Hale . . . criticized Henry Eaton, who in 1622 was charged by his
> servant Marie Hubbert of fathering the child she was then carrying. Eaton
> sought to have Hubbert accuse others of paternity, and gave her savine
> [*Juniperus sabina*, shrub juniper] as an abortifacient, affirming . . . that
> it was a common thing in London, for such women, to use such practices
> in such cases. (Amussen, 1988, p. 167)

If a woman refused to shift the blame from her employer to some other
man and abortifacients failed, vagrancy was often the result, as Jodi
Mikalachki shows in this volume.

Even if a woman servant escaped sexual exploitation, she faced the
strict expectations of her mistress and the scrutiny of eligible men in the
house. Maids' attitudes, not only their actions, were critically observed,
Hannah Woolley warned in her manual for maids of various status, *The
Gentlewoman's Companion* (London: Edward Thomas, 1675):

> Be modest in your deportment, ready at her call, always diligent, answer-
> ing not again when reproved, but with pacifying words; . . . not gig-
> gling or idling out your time, nor wantoning in the society of men; you
> will find the benefit thereof, for an honest and sober man will sooner
> make that woman his wife whom he seeth continually imployed . . . than
> one who makes it her business to trifle away her own and others time;
> neither will a virtuous and understanding Mistress long entertain such
> a servant whom she finds of such a temper. (p. 207)

In contrast to Woolley's advice, given from a superior position outside domestic labor, Isabella Whitney's comments on her life in London
emphasize the economic instability of her career as a domestic servant.
And "A Modest meane for Maids," her poem to girls in the same situation as her own, implies that the power relations of master or mistress to
maid demand almost impossible patience and diplomacy from women
servants. What appears at first glance to be a pious rhymed homily advising her sisters on their duties to their employers reveals a darker side
of resentment and covert accusation against employers incapable of recognizing the merits—or even the humanity—of their maids.

In the "familiar Epistles and friendly Letters by the Auctor: with Replies," Whitney's autobiographical remarks, and the replies she includes from friends, suggest that she has lost a good job as a result of defamation. In "To her Brother" she explains that she is dedicating the *Nosegay* both to him and to a valued mistress who has fired her:

> Receave of me, and eke accept
> a simple token heare:
> A smell of such a Nosegay as
> I do for present beare
> Unto a vertuous Ladye, which
> tyll death I honour will:
> The losse I had of service hers,
> I languish for it styll.
>
> (C6v)

At other points in her fragmented epistolary dialogue, Whitney remarks on her poverty and illness, a combination she identifies as providing the enforced leisure that she used to educate herself above her status. In "The Auctor to the Reader," she begins:

> This Harvest tyme, I Harvestlesse
> and serviceless also:
> And subject unto sicknesse, that
> abrode I could not go
> Had leasure good (though learning lackt)
> some study to apply:
> To read such Bookes, wherby I thought
> my selfe to edyfye.
>
> (A5v)

Whitney's allusions to her loyal service and interrupted employment include the claim that her enemies' lies have been the cause of her bad fortune. In "Is. W to C. B.," she remarks "how some me spite," and she sets C. B.'s answer immediately after her complaint as an affirmation of her virtue against slanderers. He writes, chivalrously:

> The vertue that hath ever beene,
> within thy tender brest:
> Which I from yeare to yeare have seen
> in all thy deedes exprest:
> Doth me perswade thy enemies lye,
> And in that quarrell would I die.
>
> (D7)

Whitney's "servicelessness" also shadows "A Modest meane for Maides," whose genre and audience are defined in its subtitle: "An order prescribed by Is. W. to two of her younger sisters servinge in London" (C7v). Whitney claims authority in both private and public spheres by emphasizing her role as older sister and by entering the realm of print as the writer of a pamphlet. Both roles are evident in her rueful allusion

to her sisters' better fortune and to her own regret at losing a position
less dependable than theirs. But here the implicit complaint begins: she
refuses to accept blame for her misfortune. By pointing out that her sisters' jobs are worth holding onto because they work in decent households, she hints, by contrast, that other positions (perhaps including her
previous one) are less desirable:

> And sith that vertue guides,
>> where both of you do dwell:
> Give thanks to God, and painfull bee
>> to please your rulers well,
> For fleeting is a foe,
>> experience hath me taught:
> The rolling stone doth get no mosse
>> your selves have h[e]ard full oft.
>>> (C8v)

To publish such advice, framed in the language of proverbs (a discourse
more general than the domestic focus of family counsel), is to aim for an
audience beyond her sisters. This larger audience is also the target for
Whitney's list of practical tenets for success, throughout which she inter-
weaves oblique denunciations of employers' unreasonable judgments,
addressed to all maids who will encounter the kind of contradictory
expectations that makes such "A Modest meane" necessary.

Whitney frames "A Modest meane" with exhortations to prayer, establishing herself and her sisters as pious believers. But the center of the
poem has to do with sexual risk. By her third stanza, she is linking proper
labor with the banishment of erotic preoccupation: "Then justly do such
deeds as are to you assigned: / All wanton toys, good sisters, now exile
out of your mind." As she finishes the stanza, she shifts the responsibility for proper behavior from her sisters to other inhabitants of their
household, whom she labels as potential corruptors:

> I hope you give no cause
>> whereby I should suspect.
> But this I know: too many live
>> that would you soon infect,
> If God do not prevent
>> or with his grace expell.
> I cannot speak or write too much
>> because I love you well.

To readers besides Whitney's sisters, this is curiously unreassuring advice. Who are these "infectors"? Why can she not speak further? In the
context of the "wanton toys" she has just invoked, Whitney's nonspecifi-
cation of the risks her sisters face invites conjecture. Is she alluding to
the domestic discord caused by the seduction, impregnation, and firing
of maidservants, who finally appear in the historical record as vagrants?
Whitney's "infectors" may well be the fathers and sons of city house-

holds who exploit domestic servants as their sexual property; they may also be the gossips whose tales make a young woman unemployable elsewhere. Her final couplet in the next stanza points again to slander and sexual desire as enemies to the virtue and survival of maids: "God shield you from all such as would by word or Will / Procure your shame, or never cease / til they have wrought you ill."

Whitney invokes God as the main protection against such dangers, implying that maids themselves have limited power to resist the demands and criticism of their employers. What follows in "the Modest meane" confirms this warning. In her fourth stanza, she lays out a set of neither/nor alternatives that undercut their own practical sagacity. The maidservant is caught in a double bind. Whichever way she turns, she is likely to be judged wanting, and any complaint she makes will be held against her:

> See that you secrets seale,
>   tread trifles underground:
> If to rehearsall oft you come,
>   it will your quiet wound.
> Of laughter be not much,
>   nor over solemne seeme:
> For then be sure th'eyle coumpt you light
>   or proud will you esteeme.

In this context, Whitney's turn to God in her next lines sounds less like modest piety than an appeal for vengeance unavailable to maids from any earthly source:

> Though cause they give of contrary
>   yet be to wrath no thrall.
> Refer you all to hym
>   that sits above the skyes:
> Vengeance is his, he wil reveng[e],
>   you need it not devise.

Yet it is also possible to hear a threat in this conclusion, directed toward employers who deserve divine retribution.

The poem concludes with an image effectively aimed at masters: a concrete description of maids' role as the protectors of householders' goods. Whitney's vivid scene of her sisters closing up the house and bolting it against nocturnal thieves reminds her London readers of the urban dangers such workers labor to turn aside:

> Your Masters gone to Bed,
>   your Mistresses at rest.
> Their daughters all do hast[e] about
>   to get themselves undrest.
> See that their Plate be safe,
>   and that no Spoone do lacke,
> See Do[o]res and Windowes bolted fall
>   for fear of any wrack.

In this final stanza, Whitney invokes a concentric set of alliances. She advises her sisters; she aligns herself with all maids against those who would corrupt them by deed or word; and finally she celebrates the shared routine through which all of London's households are secured by servants against the dangers of the night.

Throughout these stanzas of advice, Whitney makes a point of not naming the city dwellers who have used their power to damage her reputation and her career in the city. Amussen cites a case, which, though drawn from village rather than city records, may clarify Whitney's reticence:

> Robert Dey, the Rector of Cranwich in the 1590's, seduced two of his servants; one, Elizabeth Purkey alias Bate, he married off when she became pregnant; the other, Agnes Greene, left his service. When Greene left, she began to talk about his behaviour, so he brought a defamation suit against her, which he dropped (at the instigation of a local justice of the peace) in return for her promise of silence. Neither Elizabeth Purkey nor Agnes Greene had much control over the outcome, and the class power of Dey made it very difficult to speak out against him. (1988, p. 159)

The fear of being accused of defamation may well be one of Whitney's motives for refraining from naming names.

She also establishes herself and her kin as a team of watchwomen with the power to preserve the goods and peace of the property owners of London. In establishing such a community of interests, "A Modest meane for Maids" is hardly revolutionary. But from stanza to stanza, Whitney's poem rebalances the social power of her two audiences. She addresses masters through her apostrophe to maids, pinpointing employers' abuses of power and reminding them of how much they need these nightly watchers. However indirectly, the poem implies, "We refrain from attacking you for your vices, even though you attribute all sorts to us." And this implication points the way to a next question: "You cannot do without us—so why don't you do better by us?"

Given the ways that Whitney builds on her particular experience in London to set up a model for better conduct by servants and masters alike, it is not surprising that "A Letter sent by Maydens of London" makes similar demands. This is a much more outspoken text, however. Its woman-to-woman alliances are dramatically clear, focused against a single historical opponent, Edward Hake. In 1567 Hake, a lawyer, moralist, and pamphleteer who later published the thunderous satire *A Touchstone for this Time Present* (1574), published an attack on the sloth and dishonesty of London maidservants in a lost pamphlet entitled "The Mery Meeting of Maydens in London." In the dynamic identified by Valerie Wayne in this volume, whereby misogyny in action or in print generated defenses against misogyny, stimulating feminist writing in early modern England, the moralizing lawyer's antiwoman tract galvanized resistance. "A Letter" has multiple speakers and addressees—six London maids, calling on "the vertuous Matrones and Mistresses of the same" city—and the united chorus it constructs exposes Hake's hostility to all women and deprives him of authority to judge London maidservants in particular. The pamphlet is signed "by us / Rose, Jane, Rachell, Sara, Philumias and Dorothie," and its speakers frequently appeal to the good judgment of their "right wise, sober and discrete Matrons and Mistresses" (title page), which they oppose to the intemperate errors of "the Author." R. J. Fehrenbach takes the specialized legal vocabulary of the pamphlet as proof that it must have been composed by a man (Fehrenbach, 1984, pp. 30–31). Its homely humor and command of domestic detail, however, convince me that a collaboration of women servants with a sympathetic man writing from the Inns of Court is equally plausible.

Whoever wrote the pamphlet, it departs radically from the conventional techniques of the gender debate in early modern England. The "Letter" shifts the usual logic-chopping debate over women's essential nature—good or evil—into a much more pragmatic framework in which the servants appeal not to abstract philosophical principles or to a male judge but to the facts of household life and to their female employers as codefendants. The pamphlet responds directly to three of Hake's points: maids have too much free time, they steal from their mistresses, and they go too often to public places such as the church and the theater because they hope to meet men and make their own independent matches there. But the "Maydens'" pamphlet directs its counterarguments not to Hake but to "most woorthie Matrones and Mistresses" (p. 36). That is, London housewives are interpellated by their "handmaydens and servants" (p. 47) in apostrophes that exclude the provoking man from the conversation. By attributing the response to Hake to a chorus of working women making their case to another group of women, the pamphlet constructs its "we" as a convincingly political plural, an alliance of women defending their common interests on the basis of habits and knowledge they share with the women who have power over them.

The pamphlet opens with a potent double language of solidarity and threat: it is lucky that no one has taken Hake seriously, for if the "Matrones" believed him to the extent of depriving maids of their free Sunday afternoons, they would find themselves bereft of domestic help. The maids present the following scenario:

> For if at his false surmise and suggestion . . . ye shoulde have forthwith condemned us of such things as he layeth unto our charges . . . and thereby also should have gone about immediatly to abridge us of our lawful libertie, such an inconvenience might have arisen and growne therby, that in a verie short time and space, ye shoulde have gotten very fewe or no servants at all, when such as are born in the countrey should choose rather to tarie at home, and remaine there to take paines for a small stipend or wages with libertie: and such as are Citizens borne, should repaire also to the country, or to other Cities where they might be free, than to abide as slaves and bondewomen in London. (p. 37)

The argument is not ethical but practical: "if you make our work circumstances intolerable, we will cease to work for you." The maids then
define their relationship to their mistresses in a metaphor that turns
contemporary representations of social order upside down. Domestic
servants are not the parasites of the commonwealth (the belly to the
monarch's head, the body to the ruler's heart) but the working limbs
that keep the polity from paralysis:

> For as there are divers and sundry membres in the body, the least wherof
> the body may not well want or spare; and when any one of them is hurt
> or greeved, the whole body suffreth smart therfore: Even so are we to
> you (good Mistresses) such as stande you in more steade, than some of
> the membres stand the body in, yea in as much steade we alone do stande
> you in, as divers membres of the body altogether do stande the body in.
> (p. 37)

As the metaphor is expanded, it becomes less emblematic and more concrete. The maids point out the physical debility and lack of skill of citizen housewives, which make their maidservants indispensable assistants:

> For one might live although he lacked one of his eyes, one of his hands,
> one of his legs, and might also see, or handle any thing, and walke abrode.
> But ye (good matrones and Mistresses) withoute your maides what coulde
> ye doe when now ye are paste paines taking youre selves, some by reson
> of age waxen unwieldie, some by the grossenesse of your bodies, some
> by lack of bringing up in paines taking . . . we are to you very eyes, hands,
> feete and altogether. (p. 37)

The pamphlet then shifts into a language of quasi-feudal mutual obligation (the maids' "merite" requires that their mistresses "cherish" them).
In these earlier lines, however, I hear something much more modern,
uncannily close to the language of collective bargaining: a discourse that
insists that those in power recognize the possibility that their employees
could withdraw their labor. Better the countryside with lower wages than
London with no days off. By suggesting that London servants as well as
rural ones will abandon employers who curtail their holidays, the "mayds"
confront their mistresses with the specter of something like a general
strike: no one available, anywhere, to keep the system running.

   This adversarial attitude is only one of the strategies of the pamphlet,
however. Another is to close ranks against the male critic—who, the maids
imply, knows nothing about the households and kitchens on which he
passes judgment. One of Hake's accusations is that maids steal from their
mistresses to give to "Mother B.," a "poore woman" whom his pamphlet
apparently represented as an employment agent and bawd, going from
house to house to offer jobs to maids who have been fired (Fehrenbach,
1984, p. 45 note 62, p. 46 note 69).[3] The response to this accusation makes
an appeal to two different kinds of alliances between women. At first the
maids deny Hake's accusations by complimenting their mistresses. They
are too sharp-eyed, too competent, to permit household theft:

> Ye your selves are farre better hable to answere for us, and to excuse us, than he is hable to accuse us. For why? Ye knowe that we admit no poore women . . . without your leave and licence; . . . your provisions also being dayly made in the shambles and markets, we cannot lightly be false in robbing your poudering tubbes; . . . ye are not so slender huswives, but ye would easily espie it, and quickly misse it. (p. 45)

The familiar language here, of butcher shops and pickling barrels, specifically names the work that maids and mistresses do together and banishes Hake from the domestic realm which he presumes to oversee.

The maids also declare and defend their solidarity with poor women hired as temporary help. By setting their modest gifts to "Mother B." against Hake's accusations, they represent him not only as ignorant of how households are actually run but as an enemy to women's charity:

> . . . a candles end is not so costly, that giving it to a poore woman to light hir home in a dark night for breaking hir face or shinnes, would undoe you, or greatly hinder you. But he is loth that poverty should have any relief at your handes. (p. 45)

The pamphlet further implies that the maids' accuser muddles the distinction between charity and earned wages, preferring generosity to the poor over fair payment to women who perform useful work:

> what think ye would he have you to give at your dores in almes to beggers that do nothing for it, when he is thus offended that poore women should have their hire for their paynes, a few scraps of broken bread meete for their toyle and travaile? (pp. 45–46)

Against their critic, the maids defend their mistresses' freedom to reward other women as they see fit.

But they then shift alliances to take a stand against unjust employers. They defend "Mother B.'s" propriety by pointing out that if employers break the year-long contracts they have signed, maidservants need "Mother B.'s" help to survive: "yet surely were it not amisse, if any such brokers were, then servants sodenly without warning to be put out of service, should not by any neccesitie be constrayned to live unhonestly" (p. 45). The need for solidarity among women at the mercy of unfair mistresses is reasserted in the maids' comment on a case heard by a London alderman, in which a maid defended her right to leave her employers. Hake apparently quoted the alderman's "stout" sermon to one "Dorothy," but the maids point out that the alderman finally affirmed her right to leave a household where her contract was up and she had been "overcharged with work" (p. 46). Here the pamphlet allies the maids of the city with its official authorities in a move that further disqualifies Hake's authority to judge women servants.

Another strategy the pamphlet uses to ally maids and mistresses is of interest to historians of the London theater. Hake's attack on their playgoing, the maids point out, is really an attack on their mistresses' right to attend public spectacles in general. Invoking the traditional defense of drama as a medium that teaches virtue—an argument that links plays to sermons—the maids challenge their employers to resist the moralist's sideways attack on them through their maids:

> Now in that he findeth fault for our going to plaies and enterludes, your wisdomes know well, that in a godly play or enterlude . . . may be much learning had; for so lively are in them set forth the vices and vertues before our eyes, that we can bothe take learning and pleasure in them. But as for you (right worthy and vertuous Matrons) many resort to sermons, also not so much for your pleasure (as we take it) as ye do for your good instruction and edifying. But herein the author playeth the crafty marchant, by casting that in our teeth for which he rather mysliketh you that are our mistresses, as who wold say he chastened the Lyon by the whelpe. (p. 44)

By exposing Hake as less hostile toward maidservants than toward their mistresses, this self-defense expands to include employers as a primary target of the moralist's attack.

In both London pamphlets, then, female speakers define themselves as members of an alliance of women at work, acknowledging a first-level opposition between themselves and their employers. But they also represent themselves as sharing the position of their employers. Maids, mistresses, and masters are united against an outside other—whether that other be the burglars bringing nocturnal "wrack" to householders' peace and prosperity, as in Whitney, or the misogynist enemy who attacks mistresses through their maidservants, as the "Letter's" speakers reveal the "Author" of "The Mery meeting of Maydens in London" to be. This shared defense against the alien intruder might appear to join women together in a unity that overcomes the divide separating employees and employers. But the realities of class difference are not effaced by an alliance among all women as women in these texts. Something more complex is accomplished by Whitney and the "Maydens" of London. Before the solidarity into which they invite their mistresses comes their consolidation of all maidservants as a group sharing vulnerability to masters and mistresses. Both pamphlets assert that maids are indispensable, crucial partners in the defense of London households against the burglars of the night and the interfering moralists of the day. And this argument is made in realistic economic terms that work toward a new balance of power:

> For as ye are they that care and provide for our meat, drinke and wages, so we are they that labor and take paines for you: so that your care for us, and our labor for you is so requisite, that they can not be separated: so needful that they may not be severed. (p. 38)

As the maid and "maydens" of London remind their employers of their common interests in the private household, they also affirm in public print the interests of all maids bound together in the kinship of labor.

NOTES

1. Women servants were called "maids" precisely because unmarried status was expected of them. Once married, they were likely to leave domestic employment to set up households of their own, back in the rural areas they had come from or under the roof of husbands in London.

2. On the subject of pregnancy as a risk run by maidservants, see also Merry Wiesner, *Women and Gender in Early Modern Europe* (Cambridge: Cambridge University Press, 1993), pp. 50–53.

3. Wiesner comments on the role of older women as legitimate employment agents in German and French cities (p. 93). The "Maydens'" "Mrs. B." is evidently a similar go-between for households needing maids and maids seeking work in new households.

2

Women, Work, and Plays in
an English Medieval Town

. . . .

MARY WACK

ALTHOUGH THE CHESTER mystery cycle has been called the most "medieval" and conservative of the great dramatic cycles, when viewed from
the perspective of women and work, it seems rather an uneasy negotiation
between past and present, between medieval traditions and sixteenth-
century social commentary.[1] Two scenes, often termed instances of
"comic realism" added late in the cycle's history and considered textu-
ally problematic, are powerful representations of change and loss in
women's lives that exemplify the liminal position of the Chester cycle.

In the Noah play, Noah's wife refuses to enter the ark when Noah
orders her to board the boat. Verbal and physical sparring follow; in
modern productions, this is usually played for comic effect.[2] She then
desires to join her friends and to divorce Noah. The passage concludes
with a "good gossips'" drinking song sung as the waters of the flood
rise and engulf the gossips before the eyes of Mrs. Noah and the audience (stanzas 25–31).

Like Mrs. Noah herself, the scene has been troublesome for critics in
a number of respects. First, whereas much of the Chester cycle reworks
earlier literary sources, this scene has no counterpart in the source
material that informs the play but draws rather upon a popular medieval legend that was used by other English Noah plays.[3] It thus does not
participate in large-scale unifying structures of the cycle, such as pro-

phetic parallels and evocations of authority that link one play to the next.[4] Furthermore, it violates the general tendency of the cycle to preserve historical patterning and not to mix Biblical time with contemporary references. Such structural anomalies, together with inconsistencies in the dramatic action and in the stage headings, suggest the presence of two compositional strata—earlier and later versions that have survived as the scene under discussion.[5] Critics generally accept that the material dealing with Mrs. Noah and the gossips appears to be an addition of the second half of the sixteenth century.[6]

The Chester play is also the only extant English Noah play in which the good gossips appear with a drinking song (stanzas 29–31). The passage is without analogues in the other Noah plays, and like the larger episode of which it is a part, it may involve two compositional layers. Moreover, it is one of the few places in the cycle where nonliturgical music is sung[7]: the tune is thus far unidentified, but was presumably a popular drinking song, perhaps of local interest in Chester. Critics have decided that the passage "remains something of an anomaly."[8] Peter Travis felt that the whole passage so greatly violated the dramatic vision of the Chester master that he excised it from his consideration of the plays by an act of what he terms "minor textual surgery."[9] Traditional critical and philological methods thus emphasize—from a medieval point of view—the scene's secondary, belated, indeed corrupt status. Like the unruly Mrs. Noah's disruption of divine order and the onward course of patriarchal history, the scene itself threatens the aesthetic order of the Chester master. And so, like the good gossips swept away by the flood, the intrusive scene must be amputated from the body of the text.

The second scene similarly dismissed in the criticism is the tapster scene from the Harrowing of Hell play, put on by the Cooks and Innkeepers of Chester. After all the souls in hell have been rescued by the triumphant resurrected Christ, "Mulier," who has been both a tapster (a retail seller of alcohol) and a brewer of ale and wine, is dragged back to hell for trade violations and is married to demons.[10] While she was a brewer, she adulterated "good malt" with hops, ashes, and herbs. She continues, describing the eternal punishments due tapsters who "break the statutes of this country":

> Tavernes, tapsters of this cittye
> shalbe promoted here with mee
> for breakinge statutes of this contrye,
> hurtinge the commonwealth,
> with all typpers-tappers that are cunninge,
> mispendinge muche malt, bruyinge so thinne,
> sellinge smale cuppes money to wynne,
> agaynst all trueth to deale. (stanza 39)

She concludes by addressing the audience directly, consigning other tapsters like herself to dwell with Satan: "Thus I betake you, more and lesse, / to my sweete mayster, syr Sathanas, / to dwell with him in his place / when hyt shall you please" (stanza 41). Satan welcomes his "dear daughter," a second demon welcomes his "sweet ladye" whom he will wed, while a third welcomes her to eternal suffering (stanzas 42–43). There the play ends—and there ended the second day's productions of the pageants. The scene thus occupies an emphatic concluding position, giving it particular prominence.[11]

Like the Mrs. Noah scene, this too has had a problematic textual and critical history. It is unique to the Chester cycle, and like the Noah scene also involves anachronisms linking the scene to contemporary Chester. One manuscript omits the scene, "perhaps" in the words of its most recent editors, "because it was felt to be unwarranted or inappropriate."[12] Lumiansky documents earlier discomfort with the scene, citing such comments as "irrelevant comic matter" or "the barmaid is an absurdity."[13] Like most subsequent critics, the cycle's earliest EETS editor, Deimling, believed it to be "a later appendix," and Travis predictably performs appendectomy on "the alewife epilogue." He believes it was "tacked on" in four manuscripts as a crypto-Protestant move "to leaven the seriousness and the importance of the entire pageant."[14]

These two passages, added to the cycle in ways that have disturbed critics of medieval drama seeking to describe the aesthetic integrity of the plays, share significant features: they embody a tension between women and/or women's communities and the patriarchal order of both Biblical history and the city of Chester. In both scenes this tension is expressed through references to communities of women structured around drink: the good gossips in the Noah play, and the tapsters in the Harrowing.

Reversing the usual critical perspective, we may ask: what is so important about the scenes that the Tudor playwright(s) felt they should be *added* to a cycle otherwise characterized by strong aesthetic integrity? If Travis is right in characterizing Chester as the most conservative of the English cycles, there must be extraordinary significance in those scenes worked into the fabric of the cycle in the middle of the sixteenth century. The fruitful question then becomes: How did a scene such as that of Mrs. Noah and the gossips complicate or enrich the sixteenth-century experience of the plays? What civic needs did such scenes meet?

The relevance of the scenes for a sixteenth-century audience can be glossed first, by outlining women's connections to the productions of the Chester plays; second, by examining several types of source material on alewives and women's drinking songs to suggest that drinking songs offer a model of community that challenges and inverts masculine marital and civic authority; and third, by discussing civic legislation of the 1530s that reshaped women's relation to the civic body in ways likely to produce anxieties needing collective staging and mediation. My rereadings of these scenes attempt to explain how they could speak through comedy and pathos to a heterogeneous audience and could mediate the divisive effects of legislation that changed women's lives and places in the civic body.

I cast the play's relation to its sixteenth-century audience in terms of *civic needs* because I adopt the social framework of Mervyn James, who argues that:

> in towns like York and Chester, characterized by numerous crafts and gild organizations which preserved their vitality far into the sixteenth and even the seventeenth centuries, the play cycles provided a mechanism . . . by which the tensions implicit in the diachronic rise and fall of occupational communities could be confronted and worked out. In addition, they made available a means by which visual and public recognition could be given to changes in the relationships of superiority, dependence, or cooperation which existed between occupations.[15]

The diachronic rise and fall of occupations at Chester, and their impact on the plays, is easily illustrated. In 1523, for example, the Cappers guild petitioned to be relieved of the burden of producing the play of Balaam and Balak because they had fallen on hard times and could no longer afford the expense.[16] Because the Chester plays were under central civic control, they were especially responsive to the changing contours of the social body. Though previous criticism has made little of this fact, preferring instead to stress Chester's conservatism, the cycle's capacity to challenge and negotiate local issues the way public theater was to do later in the sixteenth century is evident in such responsiveness to changing social conditions.[17]

The social body whose wholeness and differentiation was thus manifested through the drama was also a gendered body, and it is here that I wish to develop James's model. If we are to understand the drama in its relation to the social body, then we need to understand how that social body constructed its gender roles, especially in relation to work, and how it reflected and contested them. In the case of the Chester drama, it is not enough (though it is certainly relevant) to have recourse to medieval or Renaissance idealistic or misogynistic visions of women as an explanation of their representations in the plays. Ostensibly disruptive passages such as the Mrs. Noah scene are anchored in the city's construction of women's place within the social body at a particular moment in its history. For reasons noted later, I define a crucial time for Chester's (re-)construction of women's place within the social body as the period from Henry Gee's first mayoralty in 1532–33 to 1561–72, what Clopper calls the "final phase" of the plays' development.

While it is usually assumed that women had little involvement in medieval drama, their participation in Chester's production of the plays is well documented and signals one "place" occupied by women within the civic body.[18] The most celebrated instances are the records indicating that the "wives of the town" put on an Assumption play. Before the development of the plays as a three-day cycle in Whitsun week in the second and third decades of the sixteenth century, this pageant was staged before Lord Strange in the Bridgestrete (var.: High Crosse) in 1488, before Prince Arthur in 1498, and in 1515 at St. John's Churchyard. On the evidence of the early Banns, it was also incorporated into the Whitsun plays until about 1548:[19] "The wurshipffull Wyffys of this towne / fynd of our Lady th'Assumpcon; / it to bryng forth they be bowne, / and meytene with all theyre might." Used as a showcase piece for entertaining illustrious visitors, the wives' production of this play was thus deeply important to the town. As the guild records make clear, considerable resources were needed to mount a play, so the wives' longstanding production of the Assumption play bespeaks their economic prosperity in the late fifteenth and early sixteenth centuries. The playing of their pageant accorded them and their work an important public identity and status within the community of guilds and crafts, even if they themselves were categorized as "wives" rather than as a formal guild of work.

But women could also belong to guilds, and as guildsmembers of various crafts women contributed the mandatory "dues" that defrayed the costs of production. Surviving records indicate that tapsters were organized into a guild, and that they were allied with the Cooks and Hostlers for producing the Harrowing of Hell play.[20] The wives of John Harrison and Richard Barker contributed to the Smiths, Cutlers, and Plumbers in 1561.[21] Widow Percevall contributed 3 shillings to the "recets of the bretheren for the plays" in 1566–67 and again the following year, when she was joined by widow Robinson, the brethren in this case being the same group of guilds.[22]

Other evidence records women's participation in Chester's crafts, guilds, and occupational communities: we know that women were strongly represented in the retail food and drink trades, that they belonged to the bakers' guild, and that in 1575 (the last year in which the cycle was performed) five women blacksmiths could be found in the city.[23] As wives of guildsmembers, women provided food, drink, and cloth for rehearsals and performances, and they were paid for it. In 1567–68 the Painters, Glaziers, Embroiderers, and Stationers paid Richard Chalewodde's wife a total of more than 17 pence for haggis, bacon, a calf's head, bread, and ale for the Whitsun plays.[24] In the same year the Smiths paid Griff Yeuans' wife for washing the curtains (presumably those around the lower part of the pageant wagon).[25]

Women were also involved in procuring the performance scripts. In 1574–75 the Coopers spent 2 pence "on margery gybban to get our regynale" that is, to make a performance copy from the original or master text kept in the Pentice, Chester's central civic building.[26]

Finally, women even went to court to defend good seating for the plays. In 1568 a Mistress Webster was sued by a Mr. Whitmore to use a certain house for viewing the upcoming performance that she and others had previously rented for the purpose of watching the plays. She had seen the Whitsun performances from that presumably fine vantage point twice earlier; Whitmore now claimed that the space was rightfully his.[27] The case shows that good seats—that is, a privileged perspective on the shows—were valuable and contested. It also documents that Mistress Webster had money and was willing to spend it on performance seating. I take this case as emblematic of the existence of an involved female audience for whom the plays offered visual and public recognition of their complex relationships to community life. This overview of women's social and economic investments in the plays indicates that we must think of the plays' audiences as including women with strong ties to the performances and important roles in the community, women for whom the cycle would articulate a vision of the social body.

Women's complex relations to community life and to the plays are well represented in alewives. Judith Bennett has sketched how ale-brewing was the archetypal form of married women's participation in the local economy. The process of brewing lent itself to the structure of married women's lives: it used domestic implements; it took place in the home, so that it meshed with domestic responsibilities; and selling ale publicly lent itself to episodic participation, whenever production exceeded the needs of the household. In the English medieval town Bennett studied, most women at some time in their lives worked as alewives, and at Chester, by all indications, things were no different.[28] In fact, alewives in Chester took their place along with other crafts in the Corpus Christi procession.[29] Women's participation in the ale trades was thus a long-standing part of their identity in public life and in civic ritual. It formed a point of intersection between domestic and civic economies, and between private and public female identities.

In addition to their identity as "alewives," women's public identities were constructed in relation to alcohol in another way, through the genre of the "good gossips' song." There are roughly half a dozen examples of the genre, of which Skelton's "The Tunnyng of Eleanor Rummyng" is perhaps the most famous. The central feature of these poems is the depiction of "good gossips" drinking together, forming their own community around the bottle. What is interesting for the Noah play, and for the notion of "local reading" (developed later in this essay), is that many of the surviving examples refer to real people and places.[30] The genre, in other words, lends itself to topicality. If the good gossips song in the Noah play was meant to be recognized as an embedded set piece of this genre, it points us toward contemporary Chester as an important context for interpreting the scene. This supposition is further strengthened by the fact that one of the surviving gossips' songs is from the neighborhood of Chester, and contains local names that may refer to a street in Chester in the early 1540s.[31]

This song parallels the Noah passage in that the drinking women explicitly constitute themselves as a women's community contesting the authority of their husbands. "A strype or two God might send me if my husband might here see me," says one gossip. Alice replies: "She that is afeared, let her flee. . . . I dread no man, good gossips myn-a." When another is downcast because her husband beats her "like the devil of hell," Margaret responds: "So may I thrive, I know no man alive who gives me two strokes without getting five." The group of gossips in the song is also constituted by the "casting of the shot," throwing down the money on the table for payment. Somebody skips off without paying her full share, and is barred henceforth from the group: "Not but a penny?" says Eleanor, "She shall no more be of our lore." After the women break up to return home, the poet notes: "This is the thought that gossips take: Once in the week merry will they make, and all small drynkes forsake, but wine of the best shall have no rest."

The poetic version of casting the shot once a week had its real life counterpart in Chester civic practices. The weekly custom of the shot was an important one for the men who governed sixteenth-century Chester. The city fathers—mayor, aldermen, sheriffs, and other office-holders—would meet on Sunday mornings for a drink ("every man to spend a penny") in the Pentice (city hall). They would then process through the town to Mass in hierarchical order.[32] The weekly ritual thus asserted a fraternal bond through the drinking and also manifested distinctions of hierarchy and order in the procession to church. Like the drama, then, it expressed a desire for experiencing the social body as both a whole and as articulated into members. And it was enacted by the men who controlled the text of the plays, which was housed in the Pentice and altered only at the instance and under the supervision of the city fathers. In Chester, then, the poetic genre of the gossips' drinking songs offered an inverted mirror of a central civic practice, in which women both usurp and reject masculine civic authority, by casting the shot and by contesting their marriage vows.[33]

Thanks to the work of a nineteenth-century local historian, Rupert Morris, we also know that in the 1530s and after—when the cycle was assuming its final textual form—a series of laws was enacted concerning women, women's labor, and women's place in the social body. They represent, if they did not actually cause, the sorts of changes in civic life that prompted the added scenes and conditioned their meaningfulness to the Chester citizenry, male and female.

Because the laws involve women's marital status in some fashion or another, let me begin with a general observation on marriage in late medieval towns. The institution of marriage—the intersection of the private body and the social body—was the most important moment in the late medieval townsman's social, economic, and political advancement.[34] It made possible full participation in guild and civic life; that is, it allowed access to public authority. Symbolic threats to marriage, like those uttered by Mrs. Noah or in the gossips' drinking songs, are not simply, at the individual level, threats to the mastery of husbands over wives, or, at the theological level, reenactments of Luciferian or Eve-like insubordination to divine authority (i.e., what the audience has watched in the two previous plays on the first day of the cycle). They must also be understood at the social level to embody anxieties over access to and use of public authority, which authority was in practice available only to married guildsmen.

There was good reason for such anxiety in the 1530s, when a series of laws involving married or marriageable women attempted to refashion women's relation to public authority and the body politic.[35] Take, for example, the cap legislation of 1533. Because wives, widows, and maids had taken to wearing the same type of headgear, such that a single woman could not be known from a married, "which disordering and abusing of apparrell," says the legislation, "is not onely contrary to the good use and honest facion used in other good cities and places of the realme . . . but also is verrey costly more than necessary charges conveynyently requireth and ageynst the common welthe of this city." Henceforth, Chester women were to becap themselves such that marital status was immediately readable from their headgear. The law forced a rearticulation through dress of the social distinction between married and unmarried women, a distinction that had slipped into an undifferentiated vestimentary code.[36]

A second law, in the same mayoralty of Henry Gee, sprang from the impulse to protect the commonwealth against women's extravagance. By its provisions, women were no longer permitted to have their customary elaborate childbed or churching ceremonies because of the "gret excesse and superfluose costes and charges" that drew off money the poorer classes should have spent on "necessary charge." The law specifically forbade food and wine to be brought to the new mother in childbed or at churching and forbade all women to attend the laboring woman, except for her mother, sisters, and sisters-in-law and the midwife. The law thus privatized a woman's reproductive labor by excluding her friends' presence during birth (again dividing woman from woman). It furthermore withdrew public recognition of that labor's contribution to the community through restricting the money spent on ceremonial display.

To understand the powerful significance of this move, we need only recollect, with Adrian Wilson, that the ritual of childbirth "represented a successful form of women's *resistance* to patriarchal authority."[37] The process of lying-in, which constituted an exclusively female space and female community—the mother, the midwife, and the mother's gossips— reversed normal power relations between wives and husbands. The wife's bodily energies and sexuality belonged to herself for a month; she could "boss her husband around with impunity."[38] If the Corpus Christi processions and dramas were a way for the essentially masculine guild structure—a community of labor—to represent itself through public ceremony, the childbed and churching ceremonies could be viewed as women's counterpart: public rituals that marked the civic importance of women's reproductive labor. To restrict that customary usage—one that ritualized a powerful moment in individual, family, and civic life—would entail, I submit, profound consequences that may be inferred from public and symbolic projections of communal life such as the drama.

The final set of laws to be discussed also has important implications for women's place in the social body. The same activist mayor, Henry Gee, promulgated a series of ordinances controlling alcohol. The laws involved standardization of measures and prices and prohibition of adulteration, chiefly with hops.[39] In this same period, rules were promulgated against selling alcohol at night and on Sunday during mass. There were violators, including a former mayor who, in 1569, was fined for selling beer in his cellar during divine service. The most consequential of these laws for women's economic lives was the one that prohibited women between the ages of fourteen and forty from working as tapsters, under the rather staggering fine of 40 shillings (about a month's wages). The legislation reads, in part:

> Wher as all the taverns and alchouse of this citie have and be used to be kept by yong women otherwyse then is used in any other places of this relme wherof all strangers resorting hether greatly marvill and thinke it an unconvenyent use wherby not only grete slaunders and dishonest report of this citie hath and doth rune abroade in avoyding wherof and also to exchew as well such grete occasions and provocations of wantonny and braules frays and other inconvenyents. . . . It is ordered [etc] there shall no taverns nor alehouses be kept within the said citie by eny woman being between xiiii and xl yeres of ages under payne of xl s. to be forfyted. . . .[40]

In 1566 sixteen people were prosecuted for violating the statute and at least one other case is documented for the following year. The law significantly restricted women's access to a trade traditionally theirs. While evidence for alehouse regulation elsewhere in the region is scanty, some years after 1571 complaint was made of Lancashire and Cheshire that "Alehouses are innumerable and the law for suppressing them and keeping them in order is unexecuted whereby toleration of drunkenness, unlawful games and other great abuses follow."[41]

That this profound change in civic life registered itself in drama is apparent from the tapster scene added to the Harrowing play.[42] That a local reading is needed is clear from the scene's obvious fusion of theology and contemporary civic law.[43] The playwright casts the "sins" meriting eternal damnation as crimes against civic alcohol ordinances ("breakinge statutes of this contrye, hurting the commonwealth"—the language could be that of Henry Gee's ordinances). The urban worker's relation to civic order is thus not simply a question of obeying the law or not obeying it and accepting the appropriate civic penalties, such as paying the appropriate fines (as did, say, the former mayor William Ball). Instead, the civic infraction is repaid by salvation or damnation. While this may, at some level, be a dig at the medieval Catholic economy of salvation by a reformation playwright, it perhaps more importantly suggests deep anxieties over questions of order related to the alcohol ordinances.

Second, representing the play's one damned sinner as a woman, an alewife and tapster, suggests that the anxieties are specifically linked to gender issues. Civic records make clear that the abuses enumerated by the Tapster were practiced by both men and women in Chester, and indeed that men were beginning to outnumber women in the brewing trade.[44] But by selectively figuring women as the sinners in this matter, the scene becomes more than the "comic realism" of contemporary infractions like short measures and brewing with hops; rather, it is about justifying women's exclusion from larger communities. Mulier's exclusion from the community of the saved is, in the context of Henry Gee's legislation, a figure of women's exclusion from the alehouses and in a larger sense from the city's public economic life. But in sixteenth-century Chester, this figuration could have been interpreted in a number of ways, according to different life circumstances of those watching the play. For the city fathers, say, as well as for the guild of Cooks and Innkeepers who put on the play, the scene says: Men of Chester, you were correct in your legislation; these are the damnable abuses you have worked to correct and to forestall. For them, the scene both represents their accomplishment and justifies it, thus allaying any unease generated by the restriction—which would, in fact, have affected the ability of working women to support their families, which needed their supplementary income. The comedy of the scene—if it is such—would have an apotropaic function: warding off through laughter the divisive consequences of consigning to hell a figure who represents, after all, their wives, daughters, neighbors, and friends—for example, Mrs. Davison, at whose tavern the Smiths drank in 1554 after rehearsals, or Richard Halewood's wife, who together with her husband furnished food and drink at their establishment for the Painters and Glaziers in 1568.[45]

For the women of Chester, like Mrs. Davison and Mrs. Halewood, the scene is admonitory in two senses. As a kind of deterrent, it says: If you transgress economically like the tapster, you will be punished eternally. The scene also says something like this: look what you have been saved from—if you cannot work as alewives and tapsters, you won't be hauled off to hell and an unholy trinity like the unhappy Mulier, in an infernal parody of the Virgin's ascension. It thus works as an ideological justification of the restrictive legislation barring them from their customary trade. Perhaps it conveyed more than that as well. Beyond whatever putative comic realism it embodies, the scene may, for women, have also staged (if not exorcised) a kind of despair. Mulier's marriage to the demon is an ironic inversion of the urban guildsman's marriage, for whom it was the gateway to public advancement. It bespeaks a feeling of marriage as the foreclosure of opportunity, even of marriage as a hellish dead end. Such a feeling is understandable not only in light of the alehouse

legislation, but even more pertinently in light of the restrictions on customary childbed and churching rituals. Not only were women barred
from working in the alehouses during their procreative years, their procreative labor itself was privatized to a greater degree, and public recognition of its value diminished. The tapster's demonic marriage may have
represented and mediated Chester women's sense of lost economic opportunity and lost civic identity resulting from the legislation of the 1530s.[46]

These sixteenth-century economic and social relations in Chester shed
important light on Mrs. Noah and her rebellion. What makes her rebellion so striking in the Chester play is her earlier harmonious participation in the building of the ark (stanza 9, lines 65–69). In that scene, unlike in the parallel scenes in the other English Noah plays, everyone
pitches in to construct the ark: Mr. and Mrs. Noah, plus their sons and
their wives. What is represented is a community of work that calls attention to itself as an ideal image—not just of "the social ideal which
Adam's family had hoped to achieve" (so Travis, p. 100)—but more
specifically of Chester's occupational hierarchies and their stratification
by gender. In the scene, Noah's sons refer to their craft skill, and link
their skills to Chester by referring to the locus of their actions as "this
town." Thus Sem says: "an axe I have, by my crowne, as sharpe as any
in all thys towne" and Cam adds: "I have an hatchett wonder keene . . .
a better grownde, as I weene, is not in all this towne" (lines 53–60). The
deixis refers both to the "town" of Noah's kin and to the space compris-
ing audience and performers alike, namely, the port town of Chester in
which maritime crafts were important to the local economy.[47] The space
of the performance thus becomes coterminous with the space of the town.
This moment suggests that the sixteenth-century Chester audience, like
the London audiences that Leah Marcus studies, was invited to inter-
pret the drama not just as ritual action set *in illo tempore* of salvation
history, but as representative of local, contemporary issues as well.

Even the women pitch in to construct the ark, and this reflects the
actual labor situation in Chester as elsewhere in late medieval towns. In
contrast to the men, who perform the skilled and technological tasks with
axe, hatchet, and hammer, the women serve as unskilled laborers, bringing timber, chopping blocks, pitch, and gathering chips to light the fire
for dinner. This is a fair image of women's secondary status both within
the labor market and within the guild occupations. Although women
were admitted as members to many crafts, they were, by and large,
second-class members when they were allowed to join, not full participants in their economic and political advantages.[48]

The playwright, however, does not merely represent this secondary status but also feels compelled to rationalize it. This occurs when
Noah's Wife says: "Wee mon nothinge ells doe / women bynne weake
to underfoe any great travell." She rationalizes the stratification of labor
roles in terms of strength and weakness—the women can only gather
wood and light fires to cook—but in fact the realities of sixteenth-century

Chester's world of work contradicted this apportioning. In the 1550s, when the town walls were extensively repaired, women performed much of the backbreaking labor hauling the stones; five female blacksmiths are recorded in 1575—an occupation notorious for the strength required.[49] Thus, even as the scene projects an image of a harmonious community of work, it also declares that this community is stratified along gender lines.[50] Furthermore, women's secondary status is naturalized by reference to innate weakness. This rationalization, contradicted by the facts of daily life, reveals an unease over women's place in Chester's world of work. The terms of Mrs. Noah's later rebellion suggest further dimensions of this unease. Consider her refusal to enter the ark:

> Yea, syr, sett up your seale
> and rowe forthe with evell hayle;
> for withouten any fayle
> I will not owt of this towne.
>
> But I have my gossips everyechone,
> one foote further I will not gone.
> They shall not drowne, by sayncte John,
> and I may save there life.
>
> The loved me full well, by Christe.
> But thou wilte lett them into thy chiste,
> elles rowe forthe, Noe, when thy liste
> and gett thee a newe wyfe. (stanzas 25–27)

She rebels against Noah's authority in two ways. First, she will remain "in this town" in solidarity with her gossips who have loved her well and whom she wishes to save. "This town," as in the ark-building scene, is at once the space of salvation history and of contemporary Chester. And, as in the earlier scene, it points to a contemporary context for understanding the tension articulated here between women's community and patriarchal authority. The second aspect of her rebellion lies in her order to Noah to sail forth and get a new wife. Noah's wife repudiates his authority, and marriage itself, unless he accepts her gossips into the ark—that is, incorporates her community of women into the larger social body. In other words, in a salvific act she will form a new community, a women's community, outside the control of this aged patriarch, and she makes explicit that the formation of such a community involves denial of the hierarchical bond of marriage. It is a challenge to religious *and* civic authority, a challenge that expresses both a longing for community and a sense of community divided.

Consider now the nature and fate of the women's community thus briefly evoked. Terrified of drowning and denied entrance to the community within the ark (underscored by the pathos of a variant line in one manuscript: "let me in"), Mrs. Noah's friends, the good gossips, sing and drink one last time. Before the waves submerge them, they join together in a moment of fellowship around drink, as they have often done in the past ("oftetymes wee have done soe"). The women's community is thus formed onstage at this moment, constituted by the rejection of Noah's authority. Like the city fathers on Sunday morning, Mrs. Noah and her gossips form a sororal community around drink. But unlike the city fathers, this community is not incorporated into the hierarchical structures of the surrounding order. Whereas the city fathers entered church in a hierarchically arranged procession, the gossips in the Noah play suffer a different fate. Instead of processing into the ark—a traditional figure of the Church—with the community of the saved, they are swept away by the waters of the Flood and the onward course of patriarchal history.

The formation and dissolution of the gossips' community addresses ambivalent feelings about women's place within the social body. Though the normative hierarchy of male power is threatened, its authority is eventually reasserted: Mrs. Noah enters the ark "whether she will or not," woman is divided from woman, and the women not reincorporated into the larger community of the ark perish.[51]

The scene's available messages thus range from the triumph of challenged authority to an elegiac pathos for lost community. In a local, social reading, the first possibility would appeal to feelings of guilt or fear in the promulgators and beneficiaries of the laws restricting Chester women's opportunities for contributing to public life and restricting the public recognition given to their productive and reproductive labor. It is this dimension of the scene that yields to a typological reading of the gossips as sinful humanity before the flood and as the reprobate at Doomsday:

> Just as there were, in the days before the flood, those who drank and ate, married and gave in marriage, until that day when Noah entered the ark, and they did not take heed until the flood came and carried them all away, so will be the coming of the Son of Man.[52]

Seen thus as heedless sybarites, their drinking and drowning can be viewed as justified and as comic, as nearly all critics have termed the theatrical effect of the whole scene. But note the gender shift that makes the typological reading possible: the inclusive plurals of the Biblical passage indicate evildoing by both sexes. Just as the Harrowing play selectively figured the violators of the alcohol statutes as female, a typological reading of this passage in the Noah play selectively figures sinful humanity as female. Insofar as a typological reading functions as a justification of the destruction of this female community, it also reveals that justification was needed for gendering the ungendered Biblical statement of human sinfulness. Such an interpretation neutralizes the terror of their drowning and allows the scene to be played as "comic realism." Perhaps, insofar as it is comic, it is apotropaic—an attempt to ward off the specter of women's potential rebellion against masculine authority (as in the gossips' songs), a rebellion that would have had local impetus after the 1530s.

At the same time, to the extent that women in the audience identified with the female characters on stage—and the evidence of women's
involvement in the plays makes it likely—the coming of the Flood would
have been an intensely pathetic, even tragic, moment. Kolve senses the
elegiac strain in the scene, and claims that Mrs. Noah represents "natural man." Through her we are able to experience a sense of human loss
by "temporary participation through laughter in the corrupted world
at its last moment of being."[53] My claim is that, to a sixteenth-century
Chester audience, Mrs. Noah must also represent "Chester woman," who
had losses closer to home to mourn: loss of economic opportunity, of
economic freedom, of freedom of dress, of friends and community at
childbirth, of civic status. The power of those feelings of loss is commu-
nicated, I would suggest, by Mrs. Noah's anachronisms—"They shall
not drowne, by sayncte John, / and I may save there life" and "They
loved me full well, by Christe." They endow her with a salvific role, one
with strong and unmistakable positive religious resonances. Her community is one worth saving.[54] In the conflict between Mr. and Mrs. Noah,
then, the play dramatizes and thus publicly recognizes the value to
women both of community among themselves and of a secure place
within the social body. In this way, the scene gave Chester women an
opportunity to recognize and reaffirm their own solidarity, as well as to
confront the social forces that threatened or restricted it.

NOTES

Versions of this essay have been presented at Stanford, University of Illinois, Washington State University, and the Rocky Mountain Medieval and
Renaissance Association. I am grateful for thoughtful suggestions from these
audiences. In particular I would like to thank Susan Frye and Theodora Jankowski for their helpful suggestions.

1. Although the cycle's legendary origins reach back to the fourteenth century, the extant texts are a different matter. The five complete manuscripts and
some fragments "are versions performed in the final decades of the cycle's existence," around the middle of the sixteenth century. The last performance at
Midsummer 1575—in Elizabeth's reign—brings us within fifteen years of Shakespeare and Marlowe. The cycle *as we have it* is therefore a Tudor cycle. Lawrence
Clopper, "The History and Development of the Chester Cycle," *Modern Philology* 75 (1978): 219–46, and David Mills, "Theories and Practices in the Editing
of the Chester Cycle Play-manuscripts," in *The Chester Mystery Cycle: A Casebook*, ed. Kevin Harty (New York: Garland, 1993), pp. 3–17.

2. Quotations from the Chester plays are taken from R. M. Lumiansky and
D. Mills, *The Chester Mystery Cycle*, vol. 1: Text, EETS SS 3 (London: Oxford,
1974) and vol. 2: Commentary and Glossary, EETS SS 9 (London: Oxford, 1986).
On the "rough humor" of the scene with Noah's wife, see G. G. Coulton, *Medieval Panorama: The English Scene from Conquest to Reformation* (Cambridge: Cambridge University Press, 1938), pp. 604–7; Rosemary Woolf, *The English Mystery Plays* (Berkeley: University of California Press, 1972), pp. 138–44; Meg
Twycross, "'Transvestism' in the Mystery Plays," *Medieval English Theater*, 5,
no. 2 (1982): 162–72. On comedy's relation to inversion of social roles, see Bar-

bara A. Babcock, *The Reversible World: Symbolic Inversion in Art and Society* (Ithaca, N.Y.: Cornell University Press, 1978), p. 17, who cites Henri Bergson's "Le rire." Joy Wiltenburg, *Disorderly Women and Female Power in the Street Literature of Early Modern England and Germany* (Charlottesville: University Press of Virginia, 1992), p. 184, points out that "the comedy of female violence relies not only on the simple inversion of weak and strong, high and low, but also on the symbolic links between sexual relations and violence."

3. Katherine Garvin, "A Note on Noah's Wife," *Modern Language Notes* 49 (1934): 88–90; Anna Jean Mill, "Noah's Wife Again," *PMLA* 56 (1941): 613–26; Francis Lee Utley, "Noah, His Wife, and the Devil," *Studies in Biblical and Jewish Folklore*, ed. Raphael Patai, Francis Lee Utley, and Dov Noy (Bloomington: Indiana University Press, 1960), pp. 59–61; F. L. Utley, "The Devil in the Ark," *Internationaler Kongress der Volkserzählungsforscher in Kiel und Kopenhagen, Vorträge und Referate* (Berlin: de Gruyter, 1961), 446–63; M. D. Anderson, *Drama and Imagery in English Medieval Churches* (Cambridge: Cambridge University Press, 1963), pp. 107–8, 212; Valerie Wayne, "Refashioning the Shrew," *Shakespeare Studies* 17 (1985): 159–87; Sarah Sutherland, "'Not or I see more neede': The Wife of Noah in the Chester, York, and Towneley Cycles," in *Shakespeare and Dramatic Tradition: Essays in Honor of S. F. Johnson*, ed. W. R. Elton and William B. Long (Newark: University of Delaware Press, 1990), pp. 181–93.

4. Robert Lumiansky and David Mills, "Concerning Sources, Analogues, and Authorities," in *The Chester Mystery Cycle: Essays and Documents* (Chapel Hill: University of North Carolina Press, 1983), pp. 87–110; Kevin Harty, "The Unity and Structure of the Chester Mystery Cycle," *Mediaevalia* 2 (1976), 137–58; Kathleen Ashley, "Divine Power in the Chester Cycle and Late Medieval Thought," *Journal of the History of Ideas* 39 (1978): 387–404; Peter Travis, *Dramatic Design in the Chester Cycle* (Chicago: University of Chicago Press, 1982). David Mills, "The Chester Cycle," in *The Cambridge Companion to Medieval English Theatre*, ed. Richard Beadle (Cambridge: Cambridge University Press, 1994), pp. 109–33 omits any reference to Play 3 in his discussion of the typological and prophetic linkages among the plays.

5. See the textual notes by Lumiansky and Mills, *Chester Mystery Cycle*, vol. 2: 39–40, and vol. 1: xxviii for details of the changes and dislocations. The editors indicate that there may have been alternate stagings in the tradition. While Lumiansky and Mills indicate that the Noah play was part of the cycle by 1500, Clopper has also shown that the cycle was continuously revised during the sixteenth century. "The Development of the Cycle," in *The Chester Mystery Cycle: Essays*, p. 174, as well as Clopper, "History and Development."

6. Oscar Brownstein, "Revision in the 'Deluge' of the Chester Cycle," *Speech Monographs*, 36 (1968) 55–65; Lawrence Clopper, "Lay and Clerical Impact on Civic Religious Drama and Ceremony," in *Contexts for Early English Drama*, ed. Marianne Briscoe and John Coldewey (Bloomington: Indiana University Press, 1989), pp. 102–36.

7. Richard Rastall, "Music in the Cycle," in Lumiansky and Mills, *The Chester Mystery Cycle: Essays*, pp. 111–64.

8. Rastall, "Music," p. 116, points out that the Gossips' Song is an exception to the rule that humans' musicality in the plays "is often an indication that they are the chosen instruments of God's Will." Quotation is from p. 119.

9. Travis, *Dramatic Design*, p. 67.

10. "Sometyme I was a taverner, / a gentle gossipe and a tapster / of wyne and ale a trustie bruer, which woe hath me wrought. / Of kannes I kept no trewe measure. / My cuppes I sould at my pleasure, / deceavinge manye a creature, / thoe my ale were nought" (stanza 37).

11. Mills, "The Chester Cycle," p. 117.

12. Lumiansky and Mills, *Chester Mystery Cycle*, vol. 2, p. 274.

13. R. M. Lumiansky, "Comedy and Theme in the Chester Harrowing of Hell," *Tulane Studies in English,* 10 (1960): 5–12, notes 3, 7, and 8.

14. Hermann Deimling, ed., *The Chester Plays,* part 1, EETS ES 62 (London: Oxford University Press, 1892); Travis, *Dramatic Design,* pp. 67–68.

15. Mervyn James, "Ritual, Drama, and Social Body in the Late Medieval English Town," *Past and Present* 98 (1983): 3–28. Quotation is from p. 15.

16. Lumiansky and Mills, *Chester Mystery Cycle: Essays,* p. 212; see also John Coldewey, "Some Economic Aspects of the Late Medieval Drama," in *Contexts for Early English Drama,* ed. Briscoe and Coldewey, pp. 77–101.

17. Theodora Jankowski, "Historicizing and Legitimating Capitalism: Thomas Heywood's *Edward IV* and *If You Know Not Me, You Know Nobody,*" *Medieval and Renaissance Drama in England,* 7 (1995): 305–37.

18. The evidence for women's participation in medieval drama is contested. There are scattered references to their roles as actresses in Continental and English drama, for example, Glynne Wickham, *The Medieval Theatre,* 3rd ed. (Cambridge: Cambridge University Press, 1987), pp. 93–94; Elizabeth Howe, *The First English Actresses: Women and Drama, 1660–1700* (Cambridge: Cambridge University Press, 1992), p. 19; John Wesley Harris, *Medieval Theatre in Context: An Introduction* (London and New York: Routledge, 1992), p. 150. Others, however, believe that they did not appear on the stage, for example, Meg Twycross, "'Transvestism,'" pp. 123–80, as well as Peter Happé et al., "Thoughts and 'Transvestism' by Divers Hands," *Medieval English Theatre* 5 (1983): 110–22.

19. Lumiansky and Mills, *Chester Mystery Cycle: Essays,* pp. 171, 227–28, 282 (Early Banns, before 1540). The date of the play's suppression is not certain; it may have been as late as 1561–72 according to Clopper, "History and Development." There has been surprisingly little commentary on whether the wives themselves performed as well as produced the play. See the brief discussion by John Marshall, "Modern Productions of Medieval English Plays," in *The Cambridge Companion to Medieval English Theatre,* ed. Richard Beadle (Cambridge: Cambridge University Press, 1994), pp. 309–10 and the experiment in all-male casting of a contemporary performance by Twycross, "'Transvestism.'"

20. MS Harley 2104, f. 4r (about 1500) joins tapsters and hostlers in a guild list that also includes "The Wyfus of the Town: 'Assumcion Beate Marie.'" Lumiansky and Mills, *Chester Mystery Cycle: Essays,* pp. 258–59. By around 1550 the "Cokes, Tapsters, and Hostlers, and Inkeepers" were listed as producing the Harrowing of Hell, the last play on the second day of the three-day cycle (ibid., p. 260). The Early Banns (ca. 1521–32) indicate that the Harrowing was put on by Cooks and Hostlers; the late Banns mention the Cooks only (ibid., p. 172–3).

21. Lawrence M. Clopper, ed., *Records of Early English Drama: Chester* (Toronto: University of Toronto Press, 1979), p. 65.

22. Clopper, *REED: Chester,* pp. 77, 85. In 1576–77 the same group received fifteen pence "of our sister hancocke for the please" (p. 118).

23. Alice Clark, *The Working Life of Women in the Seventeenth Century* (1919; rpt. London: Routledge, 1982), p. 155. See, more generally, Maryanne Kowaleski and Judith Bennett, "Crafts, Gilds, and Women in the Middle Ages: Fifty Years After Marian K. Dale," *Signs* 14, no. 21 (1989): 474–501. P. J. P. Goldberg, "Women's Work, Women's Role, in the Late-Medieval North," in *Profit, Piety, and the Professions in Later Medieval England,* ed. Michael Hicks (Gloucester: Alan Sutton, 1990), pp. 34–50, notes that the 1379 poll tax in the West Riding of Yorkshire indicates a number of women smiths (p. 47), so they were not unique to Chester.

24. Clopper, *REED: Chester,* p. 83. Additional sums were spent for haggis from "Rammesdalees wyffe" by that group that year. Other records (Painters,

Glaziers, Embroiderers, and Stationers, 1571–72) indicate "dooses wyffe" was paid for haggis and for "lethes & leuarse" (pp. 92, 93).

25. *Ibid.*, p. 85.

26. *Ibid.*, p. 108.

27. Lumiansky and Mills, *Chester Mystery Cycle: Essays*, pp. 183–84, 219–20.

28. Judith Bennett, "The Village Ale-Wife: Women and Brewing in Four-teenth-Century England, in *Women and Work in Pre-Industrial England*, ed. Barbara Hanawalt (Bloomington: Indiana University Press, 1986), pp. 20–38; *Ale, Beer, and Brewsters in England: Women's Work in a Changing World, 1300–1600* (New York: Oxford University Press, 1996). See also Goldberg, "Women's Work," pp. 41–42.

29. Rupert Morris, *Chester in the Plantagenet and Tudor Reigns* (Chester, ca. 1895), p. 330. Thomas Hughes, "On the Inns and Taverns of Chester, Past and Present, Part I," *Chester Archaeological Society Journal* 2 (1856): 91–110, quotes the accounts of the Company of Innkeepers, Victuallers, and Cooks for 1583 as having "Received of the Alewyffes in the City at Midsummer, towards our wache" six shillings and fourpence (p. 95). The Midsummer watch included a pageant related to the Harrowing Play, involving a woman with cups and the devil.

30. Rossell Hope Robbins, "John Crophill's Ale-Pots," *Review of English Studies* 20 (1960), 182–89, prints and discusses a late fifteenth-century drink-ing poem related to gossips' songs by John Crophill that "describes an actual occurrence, involving an actual occasion, place, and characters" (p. 189). Rich-ard Leighton Greene, ed., *A Selection of English Carols* (Oxford: Clarendon Press, 1962), pp. 148–53, no. 86, prints the "Good gossips' song." Skelton's poem is edited by John Scattergood, *The Complete English Poems of John Skelton* (New Haven, Conn.: Yale University Press, 1983). "Eleanor Rummynge" is thought to refer to an "Alianora Romyng" documented in Leatherhead, Surrey, in 1525 as "a 'common tippellar of ale'" and who "was fined 2d for selling ale 'at exces-sive price by small measure'" (Scattergood, p. 450, citing J. Harvery, *TLS* October 26, 1946, 521). Edward Wilson, "Local Habitations and Names in MS Rawlinson C 813 in the Bodleian Library, Oxford," *Review of English Studies*, n.s. 41, no. 161 (1990): 12–44, prints a mid-sixteenth-century poem "presented as by a woman to a woman" in the genre of good gossips and ale-wife poems (pp. 23–24).

31. Greene, *Selection*, p. 246:

Some such piece as this was doubtless the model for 'The Good Gossipes songe' in the Chester Play of the Deluge. . . . This is the more probable as the MS. containing the widely variant version, B.M. MS. Cotton Titus A. xxvi, is connected with Mobberly, Cheshire, not far from Chester. Stanza 15 of this version contains a local allusion, not identified:

Gadyr the scote, and lette us wend,
And lette us goo home by Lurcas Ende.

One may conjecture a temporary placename of 'Lucas End' from the dwell-ing in Watergate Street of Henry Lucas, 'hopper', who in 1542 was among the sixteen important tenants summoned to stand the special Christmas watch. Watergate Street was one of the places where disreputable ale-rooms were to be found in cellars.

32. Morris, *Chester*, pp. 381–82.

33. Peter Herman, "Leaky Ladies and Droopy Dames: The Grotesque Real-ism of Skelton's *The Tunnynge Of Elynour Rummynge*," in *Rethinking the Henrician*

Era: Essays on Early Tudor Texts and Contexts, ed. Peter Herman (Urbana and Chicago: University of Illinois Press, 1994), pp. 145–67, suggests that Eleanor and her customers are "vessels . . . for the festive values of transgression, contestation, and inversion."

34. Charles Phythian-Adams, *Desolation of a City: Coventry and the Urban Crisis of the Late Middle Ages* (Cambridge: Cambridge University Press, 1979); Wiltenburg, *Disorderly Women*, pp. 71–95.

35. See John Cordy Jeafreson, "The Manuscripts of the Corporation of the City of Chester," *Historical Manuscripts Commission: Appendix to the Eighth Report* (London: HMSO, 1908), pp. 355a–403b, at 362b–63b.

36. Peter Stallybrass, "Patriarchal Territories: The Body Enclosed," in *Rewriting the Renaissance: The Discourses of Sexual Difference in Early Modern Europe*, ed. Margaret Ferguson, Maureen Quilligan, and Nancy Vickers (Chicago: University of Chicago Press, 1986), pp. 125–26, notes that from sumptuary legislation of 1533 through proclamations of 1574, England tightened regulations on dress as a way of sharpening class distinctions. If it was not until 1574 that women's dress was regulated by national proclamation, then Chester took the lead on a local level of regulating the details of women's apparel.

37. Adrian Wilson, "The Ceremony of Childbirth and Its Interpretation," in *Women as Mothers in Preindustrial England: Essays in Memory of Dorothy McLaren*, ed. Valerie Fildes (London: Routledge, 1990), pp. 68–107. Quotation on p. 88.

38. Ibid., p. 86.

39. Morris, *Chester*, pp. 424–26. Theodore Leinwand, "Spongy Plebs, Mighty Lords, and the Dynamics of the Alehouse," *Journal of Medieval and Renaissance Studies* 19, no. 2 (1989), 159–84, examines the alehouse of a slightly later period as a site, like the theater, where hierarchies were secured, adjusted, or threatened.

40. Morris, *Chester*, p. 425.

41. C. M. Iles, "Early Stages of English Public House Regulation," *Economic Journal* 13 (1903), p. 256. Walter King, "Regulation of Alehouses in Stuart Lancashire: An Example of Discretionary Administration of the Law," *Transactions of the Historic Society of Lancashire and Cheshire* 129 (1979): 31–46, traces the uneven prosecution of alehouse offenses.

42. To be sure, Noah's wife and the alewives were stock figures in medieval art and legend—see, for example, M. D. Anderson, *Drama and Imagery in English Medieval Churches* (Cambridge: Cambridge University Press, 1963), pp. 107–8, 121–22, 154; Patricia Anne Anderson, "Gossips, Ale-Wives, Midwives, and Witches," Ph.D. diss., SUNY-Buffalo, 1992)—but that does not prevent the Chester dramatists from crafting them to local needs.

43. Recent arguments for localized interpretations of the drama include Gail McMurray Gibson, *The Theater of Devotion: East Anglian Drama and Society in the Late Middle Ages* (Chicago: University of Chicago Press, 1989) and Leah Marcus, *Puzzling Shakespeare: Local Reading and Its Discontents* (Berkeley: University of California Press, 1988). To these can be added Miri Rubin, *Corpus Christi: The Eucharist in Late Medieval Culture* (Cambridge: Cambridge University Press, 1991), who calls for an "ethnography of practices" for the study of late medieval religion. This ethnography would be sensitive to the discursive construction of rituals and practices "within a nexus of power relations" and to the ability of religious practice to both construct and question hierarchies. An ethnography of practices would "in critical practice capture and differentiate the meanings of uses within the range of possibilities, to make sense of action within the sphere of possibilities, rather than to ascribe preordained meanings to them. To one working with such an approach a practical joke of the past is not a neutral record of an event, but one which must be seen from

the victim's point of view, and which challenges us to ask why we do not share in the mirth" (p. 3). As Rubin notes, such an approach calls for interpretations that are "local and personal."

44. Morris, *Chester*, pp. 427–31; Judith Bennett, "Misogyny, Popular Culture, and Women's Work," *History Workshop Journal* 31 (1992): 166–88.

45. Lumiansky and Mills, *Chester Mystery Cycle: Essays*, pp. 237, 249.

46. The "pleasures" of marriage and feasting held forth in the scene may also be read both as compensatory for real losses and as ideological inversions of the norm against which the unruly and insubordinate alewives (cf. Bennett, "Misogyny") have transgressed.

47. K. P. Wilson, "The Port of Chester in the Fifteenth Century," *Transactions of the Historic Society of Lancashire and Cheshire* 117 (1965): 1–15.

48. Kowaleski and Bennett, "Crafts."

49. Morris, *Chester*, pp. 243–44.

50. Judith Bennett, "Medieval Women, Modern Women: Across the Great Divide," in *Culture and History 1350–1600: Essays on English Communities, Identities and Writing*, ed. David Aers (Detroit, Mich.: Wayne State University Press, 1992), pp. 147–75.

51. See Wiltenburg, *Disorderly Women*, pp. 97–139, 183–207, for the notion that violence against women is comic when it reasserts normative power relations.

52. Lumiansky and Mills, *Chester Mystery Cycle*, vol. 2, p. 39, after Matthew 24.38–39.

53. V. A. Kolve, *The Play Called Corpus Christi* (Stanford, Calif.: Stanford University Press, 1966).

54. Sutherland, "'Not or I see more neede,'" recognizes similar complexities in the scene. John Elliott, "Medieval Acting," in Briscoe and Coldewey, ed., *Contexts*, pp. 238–51, emphasizes medieval audiences' strong affective identifications with dramatic characters.

3

Women's Networks and
the Female Vagrant

A Hard Case

. . . .

JODI MIKALACHKI

WRITING ABOUT FEMALE vagrants and women's networks might be described as an exercise in futility. The very term "female vagrant" evokes Wordsworth's solitary wanderer, and perhaps the equally lonely career of Tess Durbeyfield, her descendant in the Victorian novel. The reflex of historicization, that is, looking to the research of early modern social and cultural historians to help us "get behind" Enlightenment and nineteenth-century constructions of gender and other social categories, initially offers no better hope for discussion of networks of female vagrants. Quantitative research on migrancy (including vagrancy) in early modern England informs us that networking among vagrants of either sex was a literary myth developed in the popular and wholly fictional genre of the rogue pamphlet. Furthermore, these statistical surveys suggest that women did not constitute an important part of the vagrant population; the surveys' interpretive conclusions understandably concentrate on the dominant statistical profile of the single, young adult male laborer or servant, within fifty miles of his parish of origin, and travelling alone.[1] Neither does the proscribed vision of a vagrant antisociety in the rogue pamphlets provide any framework for imagining women's networks, depicting women largely in alliances with men.[2] Even a recent feminist revision emphasizes the marginality of the female vagrant, comparing her to that great early-modern icon of the exceptional woman, Elizabeth I (Amussen, 1994).

Given this discouraging initial plunge into the field, why then attempt this topic? In a collection about women's networks and alliances in early modern England, this is surely the "hard case," both methodologically and experientially. Methodologically, it is hard because all the available materials seem to be ruled out as anachronistic, fictional, or insufficient to derive a full statistical profile. Experientially, it is hard because the destitution of female vagrants—their existence outside the household- or parish-based social structures of the period—made it particularly difficult for them to develop networks. Both early modern female vagrants and their would-be students in the late twentieth century thus have a hard case to make for women's networks.

It is precisely this methodological impasse, however, that moves me to take on this hard case. For I am increasingly concerned about what I termed the reflex to historicization, that appeal to the historiography of early modern England now almost axiomatic in readings of that period's texts. Writing out of my own demonstrable complicity in this reflex, I hope to point to some of the dangers of unproblematized borrowings from social and cultural history. If I were to read the social histories of vagrancy uncritically, for instance, I would be forced to give up my current topic in the face of "historical evidence" that female vagrants were not statistically important, that little can be known about those who do figure in extant records, and that in any event they did not create or participate in networks with other female vagrants. And yet extant records can and do yield information about female vagrants, and an admittedly small proportion of this material points to possible networks, both "real" and imagined. In this essay, I explore the possibility that one female vagrant, who described her interaction with similar women in jail, may also have participated imaginatively in the promulgation of a fictional vagrant antisociety by producing the kind of festive story associated with vagrants in popular literature. The interpretive difficulties of this exploration form part of my subject. Its interpretive possibilities are to my knowledge unique in studies of early modern literature; that is, the opportunity to examine how a destitute and probably illiterate woman of the lowest social order responded to popular literary stereotypes of her life.

The social historians' argument about vagrancy rests on an absolute distinction between archival and literary sources; that is, between the profile of the solitary and destitute (male) vagrant that emerges from quantitative studies of court records, and the fabulously carefree yet highly organized antisociety of rogues described so lavishly in popular pamphlets. This absolute distinction between the archival and the literary is no longer tenable (Davis, 1988), and the task of exploring what we might make of the new interpretive possibilities of reading literary and archival sources together seems ideally suited to work on under-documented relationships among women (Bennett, 1992a). In the case at hand, a rigid hierarchy of evidence is particularly dubious. One of the earliest and most influential rogue pamphlets was written by a Justice of the Peace who claimed to have interviewed hundreds of vagrants to gather his evidence (Harman).[3] Conversely, the longest and most detailed deposition I have found from a female vagrant, recorded in the case book of another Justice of the Peace, rings with all the festive misrule of literary vagabondage, including citations of the fabled canting language of rogues, catalogued and translated in byzantine detail in the popular pamphlets. Authorial questions of intention, veracity, and participation in cultural stereotyping are thus complicated in all the evidence about female vagrancy, and this is at least partly an effect of the complicated sexual and power relations between the female subject and the male author who invents, records, or represents her in writing.

The analytical challenges of these materials foreground the question of networks or alliances in a methodological sense. For the paucity of archival material and the inherently fragmentary nature of the information it gives about women's lives in fact necessitates comparisons—a kind of "analytical networking" between the scattered records of many vagrant women. Indeed, the extreme marginality of female vagrants, their small numbers, and their exclusion from the normal networks of household and parish highlight the constructed nature of all networks. An interpretive network that considers archival and literary materials as relics of the same society gives us the opportunity to examine in one instance how a vagrant woman's own sense of broader networks of female advice and example may have been constructed, and what her imaginative role in that process may have been. The difficulties of evaluating her depositions, testimony given in a judicial context shaped by the unrecorded questions of her examiner and under conditions of criminal liability, exemplify the doubly "hard case" of (re)constructing networks of female vagrants.

Alice Balstone, the woman whose extant records I shall consider in this regard, was vagrant in and around Dorchester (Hardy country, as it happens) in the 1620s. Her records initially show her in conflict with other women, who inform on her for the petty thefts that precipitate and characterize her disorderly career as a vagrant.[4] Two later depositions, however, one rescinding a paternity accusation made on the advice of two other women in jail, and another describing two occasions of holiday revelry in an alehouse, suggest appeals to broader networks of female vagrancy. Before evaluating these, let me briefly situate Balstone historically in early seventeenth-century Dorchester, then imaginatively in a network of contemporary literary stereotypes, the recent sociohistorical speculation that perpetuates their misogyny, and a composite profile of female vagrant experience that challenges the misogynist portrait.

Given Balstone's designation as "singlewoman" in 1620, when she had been in service until her dismissal for theft, she was probably in her late teens to mid-twenties, suggesting a birth date somewhere in the 1590s or very early 1600s.[5] David Underdown has noted a "baby boom" born after 1600 in Dorchester, whose numbers could not be supported by the household system of order. They grew into a generation of unruly youth, falling into poverty and disorder, and provoking the disciplinary zeal of magistrates and reformers. The early seventeenth century, when Balstone would have been a child or adolescent, was marked by depression and the failure of systems of relief in Dorchester and English towns generally. The 1620s, when she lost her position and fell into vagrancy, were particularly difficult in the Dorchester area, which suffered from both a cloth depression and bad harvests. Begging and vagrancy were strictly punished, the need to distinguish between the deserving and the undeserving poor grew more urgent, and women living outside the patriarchal household embodied a greater threat to the social order even as they became increasingly dependent on illicit activities (Underdown, 1992, pp. 61–89).[6]

Balstone thus fell into masterlessness and vagrancy during a decade that allowed little possibility of recuperation from either. Her later depositions indicate that she left Martinstown, her parish of birth and service,[7] frequenting Dorset fairs and alehouses, and probably making Dorchester itself her base. In June 1629, she figures as the deceased mother of another bastard child in an order enforcing child support on the reputed father, a resident of Burleston (DQSM 1/1, 196).[8] This brief chronicle of destitution stands in stark contrast to speculation about vagrant women in recent social history, where literary stereotypes otherwise dismissed as fictional resurface in casual remarks on the lives of female vagrants. Peter Clark, noting the erosion of kinship and family ties by migration, suggests that "feminine emancipation" may have been "one of the most startling manifestations of this development" (Clark, 1972, p. 153). He refers to a group of two women and ten children, the youngest born on the road and only six weeks old when the group was arrested and sent back from Kent to Worcestershire, as a "Band . . . led by two Amazons" (p. 144). Paul Slack echoes this terminology in describing another "Amazon" who feigned sickness in order to compel charity (Slack, 1974, p. 364).[9] Despite their condemnation of contemporary rogue pamphlets as sources for early modern vagrancy, these historians fall into precisely that form of stereotyping when they turn from the dominant male statistical profile to speculate on female vagrants. Even as they ignore the anxiety about female rogues in the pamphlets, implying that females were unimportant because they were statistically unimportant, they reinscribe the unexamined misogyny of the pamphlets in their speculations on isolated cases.

The stereotype of the female vagrant this work perpetuates is one of willful departure from the patriarchal household in favor of an aggressive self-sufficiency. Within the fabulously licentious world of the fictional vagrant antisociety, the primary expressions of freedom are sexual and linguistic, and women feature prominently in both regards. Thomas

Harman, one of the earliest and most influential rogue pamphleteers, likens the female vagrant to a cow "that goeth to bull every moon, with what bull she careth not." He distinguishes the women's ranks in vagrant society in terms of sexual experience and desirability, producing a long and detailed classification of these female orders as an important subsection of his canting dictionary (p. 94–108). Harman's categories were widely imitated, as was his general account of the sexual appetite and availability of female vagrants. The author of *O per se O* presents this "liberty of wenching" as the chief reason for the numbers of male vagrants, "for if you note them well in their marching, not a tatterdemalion walks his round, be he young, be he old, but he hath his mort, or his doxy, at his heels (his woman, or his whore)" (Judges, p. 367).[10] The repentant narrator of Robert Greene's "Conversion of an English Courtezan" similarly attributes her descent from respectability into a series of sexual liaisons with rogues to her undisciplined girlhood. Noting that "overkind fathers make unruly daughters," Greene's courtesan laments that her parents "cockered me up in my wantonness" when they should have "bent the wand while it had been green" (Judges, p. 227). This feminine wantonness, in all its senses of undisciplined, willful, and licentious, does not simply enhance the celebration of freedom in this literature. It functions as a constitutive trope of vagrancy in general, as though the female, in her natural state of wantonness, were the type of all vagrants, inclined by nature to a life without discipline, and only to be controlled by the imposition of patriarchal authority.[11]

This portrait of the female vagrant as the embodiment of misrule is consistent with the perceived threat to the social order from unruly women in this period.[12] And like the delinquency of other women disciplined for scolding, adultery, or living out of service, the wantonness of female vagrants also took on the trappings of a malignant social illness infecting the whole commonwealth. The pamphlets suggest an overwhelming flood of female vagrants that defies tabulation and beggars description.[13] A contest between a male and female vagrant as to which is "most prejudicial to the commonwealth" is won handily by the latter when she claims, "You men-thieves touch the body and wealth; but we ruin the soul" (Judges, pp. 223, 225). If the general concern about vagrancy in the pamphlet literature can be identified as one of the earliest symptoms of the criminalization of the poor, where law enforcement becomes not so much the detection of particular offences as "the disciplining of a type of person" (Sharpe, 1982, pp. 194–95), then the female vagrant would seem to be a type of person particularly requiring discipline.

And yet willful opposition to the patriarchal order hardly appears in the court records of female vagrants in early modern England. Indeed, the most salient general point about women's experience in this regard is that their initial move into vagrancy was almost never voluntary.[14] Local authorities, anxious to be rid of destitute resident women, would offer to respite punishment when such women committed the petty crimes attendant on their destitution if they would promise to leave the parish. A surprising number of women who accepted this offer did not in fact depart. They reappear in records of the same municipalities as having been whipped, caged, or confined in connection with later offences.[15] If these women were willful, it was in their dogged refusal to be driven into vagrancy, rather than in any wanton desire to escape patriarchal structures.

Others, however, were driven from their households and parishes. Their miserable existence as vagrants explains why so many were willing to endure repeated punishment at home. Once on the road, women lost even the marginal support of being put on work in a house of correction. Instead, they were moved from parish to parish by officials anxious to avoid swelling their poor rate.[16] Once expelled from household and parish, women were virtually barred from reentry into social and economic networks, falling victim to prosecution for living out of service when they attempted to support themselves by casual work.[17] Although examples like those cited by Peter Clark suggest that women did occasionally join together on the road, the case of the Widow Cragge cautions us not to make too much of alliances between women arrested in groups. She was taken in Norwich in August 1631 and August 1632, on both occasions in a group of women, yet with no overlap between the two groups. The other women were also titled widow, suggesting they may have been older women, perhaps congregating out of a mutual need for protection. The alliances they formed do not seem to have been lasting ones (NCM, vol. 1, pp. 188, 237).

Alice Balstone's fragmentary biography gives flesh to this composite profile of the female vagrant derived from court records. The wily and sexually voracious female of the pamphlet literature gives way before a woman whose sexual activity and possible attempts at theft brought her nothing but illegitimate children, criminal charges, the loss of her position, and an early death. In addition, Balstone's case shows how easily women slipped through the growing cracks of the social order in the early seventeenth century. One misstep was all that stood between employment in one patriarchal household and expulsion from the legitimate social order. Balstone's case history serves as a catalogue of the female vagrant's existence once she moved outside that order, including crimes in and around her parish of birth and service, possible prostitution, bastard children, and shifting paternity accusations involving her master and others. Yet Balstone's records also include two distinct pieces of exceptional material. The first of these is a recorded (and later rescinded) paternity accusation of her master. Although maidservants were notoriously vulnerable to sexual exploitation by masters in this period, magisterial paternity accusations are surprisingly rare in the Dorset records.[18] Balstone's accusation of her master thus represents the violation of a local norm that protected male employers and heads of households. The second exceptional record in Balstone's case history is a deposition in which she quotes thieves' cant in the course of describing holiday revelry at an alehouse. In the following analysis, I explore the possibility that both pieces of exceptional testimony emerged from Balstone's participation in some kind of female community, whether the face-to-face community of other women in jail, or the imagined community of canting female vagrants in the rogue literature.

Let me begin with the magisterial paternity accusation. If Balstone violated a local norm in making this accusation, she also confirmed a broadly based element of female vagrant experience. Expulsion on suspicion of pregnancy was how many maidservants entered vagrancy in early modern England, despite the legal responsibility of masters for any child conceived by a woman in their service. Indeed, because of this legal responsibility, masters with intimate knowledge of the potential of such a pregnancy were particularly anxious to dismiss maidservants before a pregnancy was even suspected.[19] The case of Merable Bartram indicates the complexity of master–servant relations in this regard. When she was taken destitute of habitation and lodging in Norwich in 1633, she claimed to have left the service of Ambrose Crane with mutual consent. At some point, however, she must have accused Crane of impregnating her, because two days later she confessed to having falsely accused her master, "but saith she had deserved for yt." When she next deposed, a month later, she explained that she never was with child (NCM, vol. 2, pp. 90, 123, 126, 149, 214). In cases where paternity of illegitimate children born to maidservants has been tabulated, roughly 20 percent were fathered by masters. Masters employed both threats and bribery to persuade women to name other men.[20] Bartram's cryptic insistence that "she had deserved for yt," suggests she may well have had sexual relations with her master. It is possible that he then turned her out of doors in fear of being charged with a bastard child. It is also possible that she may have attempted to manipulate him with the threat of a paternity accusation. Whatever the initial maneuvers, it was she who moved into chronic vagrancy and stints in Bridewell.

Like Bartram, Balstone made her magisterial paternity accusation in response to having been expelled from her household of service. And as in Bartram's case, Balstone's accusation made no difference to her case. Both women became vagrant as a result of their expulsion, and neither maintained her initial paternity accusation. Indeed, in both cases, the paternity accusation survives only in the official record of its withdrawal. The futility of such accusations, whether well-founded or spurious, may suggest why so few maidservants made them. Balstone's account of how she came to make her magisterial paternity accusation (recorded on January 6, 1621, in Sir Francis Ashley's case book) has all the complexity of Bartram's. Where Bartram's account concerns herself and her master only, however, Balstone's invokes members of a women's community that includes a fellow prisoner and the prison midwife:

[T]he same day that she was delivered out of prison the last Assizes, Long Robin commonly so called but his name is Robert Braine who was then delivered also out of gaol sent for her to the widow Pear's house in Dorchester, and being come thither he begged drink of her which she sent for, and when they had drunk it, they met by appointment at Wolvington's house at Frome, where he had knowledge of her body in the Turf house, and that the child wherewith she now goeth was then begotten, and that no other person had knowledge of her body; yet she doth acknowledge that when she was lately supposed to fall in travail with child she was then counselled by the widow Sacer a prisoner to charge her last master Alered Paty therewith, whereupon the midwife coming unto her, and being informed by the widow Sacer that it was Paty's child, she refused to give this Examinant any help unless she would affirm her said master to be the father of the child, whereupon she said if it be my master's it is my master's, wherein she saith that she did wrongfully accuse him for he never at any time had knowledge of her body or made offer thereof. (50)

Balstone certainly furnished enough detail to support her altered paternity accusation, from sites like the widow Pear's house in Dorchester, Wolvington's and "the Turf house" at Frome, to persons like the prison midwife, the widow Sacer, and "Long Robin" himself. Her account of the bullying by the widow Sacer and the prison midwife (who was required to obtain the father's name before assisting with the delivery) provides a plausible explanation for her cited accusation of her former master. The ambiguity of that citation, "if it be my master's it is my master's," recalls Merable Bartram's equally cryptic assertion that "she had deserved for yt," and similarly invokes the complexities of master–servant relations. Indeed, "Long Robin" sounds suspiciously like the soldiers and other transients named by maidservants whose masters threatened or paid them to accuse someone else. Balstone claims that he fathered "the child wherewith she now goeth" on the day they were both "delivered out of prison the last Assizes." Given that at the time of her current deposition "she was lately supposed to fall in travail with child" in prison, she must have been very near delivery when she gave this deposition in January of 1621. Assuming a gestation period of forty to forty-two weeks, the child would have been conceived somewhere in mid- to late March; that is, around the time she committed the theft in her master's household and was examined for it on March 19. On that date, her master was bound over to give evidence against her at the next Assizes. If these Assizes were held within two weeks of this date, and if they were indeed the "last Assizes" to be held before Balstone's deposition on January 6, then she and Long Robin might plausibly have conceived the child as she describes.[21]

It is also, possible, however, that she conceived her child in mid-March, perhaps while still in her master's household. In her deposition of March 19, she recounts having returned most of the stolen money to her mistress when confronted by the latter, having already spent the balance on "victuals, and other necessaries"(Ashley, 45). If she had engaged (with or without her consent) in sexual relations with her master, she may have decided to take 25s, perhaps feeling, like Merable Bartram, that "she had deserved for yt."[22] The bullying of the widow Sacer and the prison midwife might actually have wrung from her a confession she had been persuaded or threatened into withholding. Conversely, the coercive cast she gives to this interaction may have been for the benefit of her examiner as she withdrew the magisterial accusation in favor of Long Robin. As with Bartram, the only clear element of this complex record is that Balstone lost her position and became a vagrant.

Balstone's account of how her magisterial paternity accusation came to be made, however, does provide a rare glimpse of an exchange of information, advice, and perhaps extracommunal norms between three women in jail. In turn, the social history of bastardy in early modern England, as well as the frequency with which illicit pregnancy precipitated a woman's move into vagrancy, provide a context in which to examine Balstone's rescinded paternity accusation. Nevertheless, the complexities of the record in this case—an account of how three women between them produced an accusation that is only recorded in the context of rescinding it—trouble any easy reliance on the very statistical backdrop that opens the record to broader analysis. Whatever the relations among these three women, the network they formed (like the distinct groups in which the Widow Cragge was arrested) was not lasting. When confronted with the judicial authority of Ashley, and perhaps the social and economic power of Balstone's former master, the women's network was judged to have delivered a fiction, while Balstone's colorful tale of Assizes-week celebration with Long Robin was acknowledged in court as the legitimate story.

The interpretive difficulties regarding Balstone's magisterial paternity accusation also inform the other exceptional element in her case, that is, the citation of "thieves' cant"—the supposed canting language of the vagrant underworld—in her last deposition. In both cases, the exceptional material in the local context invokes common elements of a more broadly based portrait of female vagrancy. In the case of the paternity accusation, that portrait is drawn from the life experience of other female vagrants, available to us in the fragmentary biographies from court documents and conveyed informally in the period by women like the Widow Sacer. In the case of thieves' cant, the portrait is drawn from the popular stereotypes of the rogue literature. Both represent instances in which Balstone demonstrated stronger ties to other female vagrants, historical or fictional, than to the community on whose margins she lived after losing her position.

Let us now turn to the questions of how and whether the contemporary literary stereotype of the female vagrant shaped Balstone's understanding of her condition, and how she may have interacted with that stereotype. Her last deposition of September 6, 1624, describing the nocturnal rendezvous and activities of a seeming network of vagrants, bears more resemblance to the legendary antisociety of the rogue pamphlets than to anything discernible in other court records. In that deposition, Balstone quotes several examples of thieves' cant. On Christmas, Christopher Ford cursed, "A poxe confound the Rum Cove of the next kin for he did wronge," to which the Keeper responded, "Yea and the Devil Glimmer him for he is a foresworne knave." On the night of New Year's Day, the Keeper addressed one of the Tinkers, asking, "where is your Mort, 'was she never Cloid since she was heere last.' to which he answered with an oath, noe, unles she bee now, and now I thinke she is, she would not else have missed mee heere this night."

These canting terms are commonly found throughout the rogue pamphlets.[23] Along with this linguistic transgression, Balstone also conveys the social and sexual freedom that informs the popular literary stereotype of vagrant society. Men are attended by women who are their sweethearts or Morts, not their wives. The group sustains its holiday revelry on stolen chickens, rabbits, pork, and beef. Mysterious "gents," one of them attired in "a green sattin doublett cutt and buttoned, and a scarfe about his neck, but noe sword hanginge in it," knock on the window two hours before day and are treated to more stolen meats. When the Tinkers complain of neglect after the arrival of this august company, one of the gents throws beer in their faces, precipitating a general brawl. The popular vision of vagrancy as a permanent manifestation of misrule emerges from Balstone's description of these holiday gatherings.

Balstone's deposition is recorded in the case book of Sir Francis Ashley, a Justice of the Peace and Recorder of Dorchester, which he kept between the years 1614 and 1635. By the time she gave it, she had been vagrant in the vicinity of Dorchester for four years, and may well have been called to depose simply because she moved among the disreputable figures of the neighborhood. Indeed, the keeper of the Boytherstonewood alehouse searched for her as far as Maiden Newton in anticipation that she might be examined, earnestly persuading her "that she would not discover to any their last meetinge at his howse nor who was there at the tyme nor what was then donne, for (sayd he) if you doe I am undon And she promised she would not, and more she sayeth not." Ashley seems to have been sufficiently intrigued by what Balstone did say to record it at length, yet he did not bind her over to give evidence at the Assizes. This may have been because her evidence was inconclusive for what he wanted to prove, or because he handed the matter over to another jurisdiction. It is also possible that he simply found her lively account more imaginative than accurate.

Given that Ashley took no further action on this deposition, why is it recorded at such length, including such careful citations of thieves' cant? Balstone's deposition takes up a full page in a case book that regularly dispatches three to five examinations on a single page. Moreover, the physical record is strikingly regular, very much bearing the appearance of a fair copy in comparison to other pages, where one or all depositions are frequently crossed out, bracketed, and embellished with marginal notes. Most noticeable of all are the actual citations of thieves' cant, set off by extra space and initial capitals, and in one case, quotation marks. These citations are the more remarkable in that indirect discourse is the norm for reported speech elsewhere in the case book. One is reminded of Thomas Harman's sixty-six-page treatise on the habits and language of vagrants. Harman was also a Justice of the Peace and claimed to have written his "Caveat" as a handbook for other Justices to prosecute vagrants. We know that he drew substantially on an earlier pamphlet to develop his own treatise. Was Ashley perhaps drawing on Harman and other pamphleteers as he made his own judicial record? Or did he respond with such interest to Balstone's inconclusive deposition because she drew on material and stereotypes familiar to him?

I began this essay by invoking social historians' rejection of Harman and other pamphlets as documentary evidence for a vagrant underworld. Yet here in Ashley's case book, almost seventy years after the first publication of Harman, a female vagrant testifies to the use of thieves' cant and the general licentiousness of the fictional vagrant underworld. I know of three other references to thieves' cant in archival sources, all of them involving female vagrants.[24] These female examinants do not themselves speak in cant, but merely quote others doing so. Like the vagrants interviewed by Harman, they provide information on the language and practices of a supposed vagrant subculture. And like Alice Balstone, they are all women. Four is a small sample on which to base anything, but there does seem to be a quality of appeasement, if not titillation, in these offerings of vagrant women to inquisitive justices. Indeed, Harman seems to have demanded especially from women the linguistic transgression he associated with vagrants. He delights in producing sexual double entendres from their statements of economic crisis and inquires into the names and number of sexual partners of his principal informant. This information he deems necessary "before I would grope her mind" (pp. 100, 105–7). Whatever else Harman may have done in his "Caveat," I think he left us in that phrase the best description of the prurient juridical fascination with the female vagrant.

Sir Francis Ashley's long and detailed entry on the festivities in Boytherstonewood may not be entirely innocent of such considerations. Did this later Justice share Harman's voyeuristic fascination with the vagrant underworld, perhaps asking leading questions or in other ways distorting the testimony of his female informant? And if we accept this possibility, can we regard Harman's "Caveat" as entirely fictional, especially given his professional and geographical opportunities to interview vagrants? Brought together in this way, Ashley's case book and Harman's "Caveat," representatives of archival and literary documents, respectively, testify to the difficulties of evaluating evidence for the construction and experience of female vagrants in this period. Can we learn anything more from Ashley's record of Balstone's deposition than from Harman's reported conversations with doxies and morts?

Let us posit that Alice Balstone did describe the events at the alehouse more or less as recorded in Ashley's case book, including citations of thieves' cant. Why might she have done so? She ends by reporting her promise not to "undo" the alehouse keeper, "and more she sayeth not," concludes the record. Given Ashley's inaction on the case, she does seem to have withheld whatever information he was after. She nevertheless gives names or descriptions for at least seven people and recounts various kinds of disorderly and criminal behavior, from the illicit pairing of several couples (including herself and Richard Hodges), to brawling, poaching, and possible preparations for robbery. If this was not the information Ashley was looking for, however, if no incident or person in either of these detailed scenes was worth pursuing, is it possible that Balstone invented or improved her account? Did this woman, vulnerable at all times to prosecution under the vagrancy laws, seek to appease the Justice with an elaborate account of festive misrule in the vagrant subculture, complete with tinkers, gents, and thieves' cant?

One wonders how many of Harman's subjects invented accounts to fit his stereotype of the vagrant subculture. Fictional accounts of this world were in fact available much earlier than his immediate source. Harman himself believed that thieves' cant was developed in the 1530s, and literary references go back at least as far as Luther's *Liber Vagatorum*, written around 1509, which lists more than 200 canting terms (Beier, p. 125).[25] Such material was widely available by Balstone's time in the broadside ballads and chapbooks carried by pedlars throughout England. The women interviewed by Harman in the 1560s stand at the beginning of this great explosion in popular literature and its readership, when Harman's influential work itself had yet to be published. Their minds had to be groped, and their words reinterpreted, to produce the titillating narrative he sought. Seventy years later, however, when Sir Francis Ashley made his long and detailed record of Alice Balstone's deposition, the fiction of a sexually and linguistically wanton antisociety of vagrants was widespread. Balstone might have encountered it in printed, dramatic, or musical form, either in Dorchester itself or in the surrounding fairs and alehouses she frequented.[26]

Joy Wiltenburg has pointed to the distinction between the paying public who bought cheap print and the nonpaying crowd of listeners who also consumed it. She notes a greater number of humble workers and possibly women in the latter group "who might enjoy the performance without expecting to hear their distinctive views represented" (1992a, p. 39). Balstone's long deposition to Ashley offers an opportunity to examine how someone in the latter group might respond to this literature, and to the ways it failed to represent her distinctive views and experience. If the women in Harman's tract have their words appropriated and transformed into the stereotype of the vagrant underworld he was so influential in propagating, Alice Balstone had the opportunity to take that stereotype and use it for her own purposes, either to deflect interest from a crime she had promised not to reveal or to appease a Justice who required information of criminal behavior.

Balstone's lively story of festive misrule does seem to have freed her from the dilemma of having to testify again. What is remarkable about it, especially in light of the general emphasis on female sexual experience in the vagrancy pamphlets, is that it includes very little of the stereotypical sexuality of female vagrants. There are general references to the female vagrant's function of sexual availability, as in the noted absence of the Tinker's Mort, Christopher Ford's accompaniment by his sweetheart, and Balstone's own arrival in the company of Richard Hodges. For the most part, however, Balstone invokes the activities of male vagrants: their thievery, the rivalry between different "kins," their brawling, and their canting language.

To the extent that her story was a fabrication, and the inclusion of so much thieves' cant suggests that it was at least partly fictional, Alice Balstone seems to have made certain editorial choices regarding her representation of a vagrant subculture. She virtually excluded the female vagrant from her sexually prominent place in this world of vagrant misrule. In doing so, she wrote herself out of the popular fiction of the vagrant subculture. The available details of her own life indicate that she enjoyed none of the freedom and powers of sexual manipulation ascribed to female vagrants in this literature. Her "glimmering glance" did not save her from prosecution for theft, and her sexual relations with the men of the area led only to the birth of at least two illegitimate children, and perhaps her early death. Her own construction as criminal and transgressive was not something that Balstone could alter in these earlier encounters with the law. In her deposition of 1624, however, she did take a hand in the construction of the female vagrant. By concentrating on the speech and actions of male rogues, Alice Balstone tacitly wrote the female vagrant out of the popular fiction of vagrant life.

I would like to end by suggesting what this omission might mean in terms of Balstone's participation in an imagined network of female vagrants. On the one hand, in deleting the female from the fictional world of the vagrant subculture, she seems to have dissociated her own life from the popular fiction of the female vagrant. The voracious sexual appetites and corresponding wiliness of her fictional counterparts bore no relation to the deprivation and punishment that made up her own life. On the other hand, her deposition is not wholly at odds with the fictional portrait. Despite its omission of transgressive sexual behavior, it does testify to that other form of deviance in the pamphlet literature: linguistic inventiveness. For language, in all its unruliness, is the medium in which Balstone both allies herself with an imagined community of female vagrants and simultaneously resists its misogynist construction. The rogue pamphlet constructed female vagrants in ways consistent with the misogyny of a threatened social order and conducive to their oppression within it. But it also suggested the power of linguistic invention in the shaping of a society at least nominally at odds with patriarchal structures. In her own fictional or edited version of such a society, Balstone was able to challenge the assumptions of the order that claimed to protect and to provide for women. For in writing the female out of the fictional portrait of vagrant society, Alice Balstone tacitly asserted that this fantasy of freedom bore no relation to the lives of abused and abandoned women.

NOTES

I am grateful to Susan Amussen, Judith Bennett, William Carroll, Patricia Crawford, Anne Ferry, Thomas M. Greene, Cynthia Herrup, Sara Mendelson, David Underdown, and members of the Women in Early Modern Europe Seminar, Harvard Center for Literary and Cultural Studies, for reading and commenting on earlier versions of my work on these materials.

1. See especially Peter Clark and Paul Slack, eds., *Crisis and Order in English Towns, 1500–1700* (London: Routledge & Kegan Paul, 1972 and 1974), and A. L. Beier, Joel Samaha, "Gleanings from Local Criminal Court Records," *The Journal of Social History* 8 (1975): 61–79, also dismisses the vagrant antisociety as a myth.

2. For discussions of the rogue pamphlets, Frank Chandler, *The Literature of Roguery* (Boston: Houghton Mifflin, 1907); Frank Aydelotte, *Elizabethan Rogues and Vagabonds* (Oxford: Clarendon, 1913); A. V. Judges, ed., *The Elizabethan Underworld* (London: Routledge, 1930); and their Victorian forerunner, C. J. Ribton-Turner, *A History of Vagrants and Vagrancy and Beggars and Begging* (Montclair, N.J.: Patterson Smith, 1972), chaps. 4–6. Judges showed most caution in dealing with rogue pamphlets, of which he published a selection. He emphasized the severity and often rigorous enforcement of statutory punishments for vagrancy, which included whipping, stocking, branding, and earboring. Two works from the early 1970s that continue to read the rogue pamphlets as evidence of vagrant networks in early modern England are Gamini Salgado, ed., *Cony-Catchers and Bawdy Baskets* (Harmondsworth: Penguin, 1972) and John F. Pound, *Poverty and Vagrancy in Tudor England* (London: Longman, 1971). None of these works addresses gender in the pamphlets.

3. Thomas Harman was a county magistrate in Kent who presented his "Caveat or Warning for Common Cursitors, Vulgarly called Vagabonds," as the result of interviews with hundreds of vagrants who passed by his residence at Crayford (reprinted in Judges, *Elizabethan Underworld*, pp. 60–118). He was largely indebted to a literary source, however, John Awdeley's "The Fraternity of Vagabonds," first published five years earlier in 1561 (reprinted in Judges, pp. 51–60). Harman's "Caveat" was nevertheless the more influential of the two works, and provided most of the information for the depiction of vagrants in later pamphlets (Judges, pp. 494–96).

4. Her master's wife first accused Balstone of the household theft that brings her name into the court records even as it thrusts her outside the patriarchal household and into vagrancy. In Balstone's next recorded encounter with the law, another woman (the wife of the man from whom she bought supper at a local fair) identifies Balstone as the probable thief when two men sleeping overnight in the same place discover they have been robbed. The depositions re-

garding these episodes are recorded in the manuscript case book of Sir Francis Ashley, 45–45v; 47v–48, 49v. This case book has been published, with some calendaring (Dorset Record Society, 1981). I draw on a microfilm of the original for Balstone's records. I am grateful to David Underdown for bringing these records to my attention and for lending me his microfilm of the manuscript.

5. Young people generally entered service outside their household of birth in their early to midteens, and the average age of marriage for non-elite women in early modern England fluctuated between 24 and 26, tending toward the higher end during difficult economic times, when fewer unpropertied people could afford to marry; Keith Wrightson, *English Society, 1580–1680* (New Brunswick, N.J.: Rutgers University Press, 1982), pp. 42, 68, 146.

6. Women were particularly vulnerable to godly attempts at reform in Dorchester. Although opposed to alehouses generally, Dorchester magistrates were exceptionally intolerant of widow alewives. Similarly, they found masterlessness particularly threatening in women, where it was often accompanied by other kinds of unruliness.

7. There are no extant baptismal records for Martinstown before 1653. The earliest Balstone records for Martinstown are two wills, dated 1572 and 1589, made by William and Robert Balstone. Both men were probably dead before Alice Balstone was born, suggesting a middle generation between hers and theirs. The place of residence for both men is listed as Winterborne St. Martin, another name for Martinstown. I refer to Martinstown throughout. The wills themselves have not survived. For records of the wills, see the *Calendar of Dorset Wills*, ed. George S. Fry (London: Fry, 1911), p. 7.

8. I am grateful to Susan Amussen for alerting me to this reference to Balstone's death. The timing and circumstances of Balstone's expulsion from her master's household to some extent explain why she fell into chronic vagrancy, petty crime, and an early death. It is worth noting, however, that Morgan Balstone, a probable male relation of her own generation who was also engaged in disorderly activities around the time Alice's unlawful career began, was not expelled from Martinstown. Rather, he seems to have survived the difficult early decades of the century there, and to have regained social and economic security for himself and his descendants, who eventually assumed the title of gentleman (Ashley, *Case Book*, p. 50; Edward A. Fry, ed., *Dorset Protestation Returns*, p. 157; DRO AD/DT/I1686/115; DRO LH 17; DRO LH 18). Balstones continued to be recorded in Martinstown as late as the 1801 census, where an Alicia Balston was listed as the head of a family.

9. The case that elicits Clark's speculation about feminine emancipation is that of three vagrant women taken in Dover in 1635. All three were living off the slender trade in small wares conducted by one of them, who had buried a child at Lydd a few days before; Clark, "The Migrant in Kentish Towns, 1580–1640," in Clark and Slack, eds., *Crisis and Order*, p. 153. G. R. Quaife, *Wanton Wenches and Wayward Wives* (New Brunswick, N.J.: Rutgers University Press, 1979) also tends to adopt the tone of the rogue pamphlets.

10. Dekker's "The Bellman of London," which ran to four editions in 1608, also reproduces Harman's female taxonomy (reprinted in Judges, *Elizabethan Underworld*, pp. 308–9).

11. The *Oxford English Dictionary* (1989) derives "wanton" from the Middle English "wantowen" or undisciplined, and surveys a range of early modern meanings from frivolity and unrestrained merriment to unruliness, lewdness, and unlawfulness. The term was applied to unmanageable animals and willful children. Its meaning of lewd or unchaste was applied only to women in early use; by the 1590s, it had begun to be used of men also in that sense.

12. See especially Susan Amussen, "Gender, Family, and the Social Order, 1560–1725," in *Order and Disorder in Early Modern England*, ed. Anthony

Fletcher and John Stevenson (Cambridge: Cambridge University Press, 1985); Amussen, *An Ordered Society* (Oxford: Basil Blackwell, 1988), pp. 42–49, 182–89; Linda Fitz, "'What Says the Married Woman?'" *Mosaic* 13 (1980): 1–22; Underdown 1985b and 1985, pp. 34–40.

13. Harman estimates at least two females to every male vagrant. He ends his pamphlet with a list of 215 male vagrants by name, but despairs of providing a similar catalogue of female vagrants, for "the number of them is great, and would ask a large volume" (in Judges, *Elizabethan Underworld*, pp. 78, 110–13). Robert Copland's "The Highway to the Spital-house" (1535/36; reprinted in Judges, pp. 1–25), one of the earliest English rogue pamphlets, also testifies to the uncountable abundance of female vagrants: "Of all sorts that be spoken of afore, / I warrant women enow in store, / That we are weary of them. Every day / They come so thick that they stop the way" (p. 24).

14. In the following summary, I draw on records for Norwich, Southampton, and Dorchester. As urban centers with established provision for the poor, these towns were attractive destinations for vagrants. This very concern to provide for their own poor, however, caused the towns to be especially sensitive to the presence of vagrants, who threatened to nullify their efforts to resolve the issue of poverty in their own communities. For Norwich in this period, see John T. Evans, *Seventeenth-Century Norwich* (Oxford: Clarendon, 1979); John F. Pound, "An Elizabethan Census of the Poor," *University of Birmingham Historical Journal* 8 (1962): 135–61; and Pound, *Poverty and Vagrancy*. For Southampton, see Colin Platt, *Medieval Southhampton* (London: Routledge & Kegan Paul, 1973), pp. 197–215, John Silvester Davies, *A History of Southampton* (Southampton: Gilbert & Co., 1883), pp. 248–92, 293–309, and T. B. James, *Southampton Sources 1086–1900* (Southampton: University of Southampton Press, 1983), pp. xiii–xxxvii, 18–50. For Dorchester, see David Underdown, *Fire from Heaven* (New Haven, Conn.: Yale University Press, 1992). The Dorset records, which are unpublished, are identified by shelf number in the Dorset Record Office (DRO).

15. Judith Bradinge appeared in Southampton on various charges of sexual misconduct, ranging from prostitution to sexual slander to pregnancy out of wedlock. On her second offense, her sentence of public whipping was respited on her promise to depart the town. She nevertheless continued to appear and was sentenced to whipping and the cage on successive occasions (ABS, vol. 1, p. 76; vol. 2, pp. 11–2, 24, 29, 68). The Norwich Court of Mayoralty was more successful in driving Jane Sellars from the city, although she too endured repeated punishment at the post for lewdness and ill rule before finally quitting Norwich for Yarmouth (vol. 1, pp. 77, 110, 112, 188, 200). Two Norwich women promised repeatedly to go as far as Holland, receiving (and in one case destroying) passes to that effect as they continued to be punished for petty crimes and disorderly behavior. For Dorothy Clarke, see ABS, vol. 1, pp. 100, 163, and vol. 2, p. 25; for the four-year saga of Joane Weetinge, see vol. 1, pp. 78, 87, 90, 111, 142, 152, 169; and vol. 2, pp. 23, 143, 149, 166, 176.

16. Joane Guy was sent back and forth between her parishes of employment and birth after the death of her master. She did charwork and was finally ordered whipped as a vagrant in her late master's parish and sent back to her parish of birth to be set on work at the latter's charge (Dorset Quarter Sessions Order Book [DSQM] 1/1, 195v–196). Ursula Hobson, taken vagrant in Norwich in 1631, had been in five separate parishes in as many weeks, none of them her place of birth (Minutes of the Norwich Court of Mayoralty [NCM] vol. 1, pp. 112, 192; vol. 2, p. 219).

17. David Underdown has pointed to the concern in Southampton about charwomen, or "young women and maidens which keep themselves out of service and work for themselves in divers men's houses," or who "take chambers and so live by themselves masterless" (1987, pp. 36–37). For individual cases

in Southampton, see ABS, vol. 1, p. 98; vol. 2, p. 3; vol. 3, pp. 11, 67; and Southampton Court Leet Records [SCLR] vol. 3, p. 511. Norwich brought numerous women before the Court of Mayoralty in the 1630s, including fifteen separate cases on August 25, 1635 alone (NCM vol. 2, pp. 171–72). For cases in and around Dorchester see DQSM 1/1, 12, 52, 88, 175 and 224.

18. Underdown, *Fire from Heaven*, leaves open the question of whether Dorchester masters were more scrupulous, or better able to avoid warranted accusation (pp. 83–84).

19. Masters were required by law to support any child conceived by an unmarried woman in their service if paternity could not be determined; Gordon Schochet, "Patriarchalism, Politics, and Mass Attitudes in Stuart England," *Historical Journal* 12 (1969): 415–17. In Dorset, Elizabeth Hitchcock was sent back and forth between her parishes of birth and service, supplied with official passes declaring her vagrant in both, once she became pregnant and left her master's household (DQSM 1/1, 18v). The Southampton Assembly made repeated efforts to enforce child support on John Manfield for a child born to an unmarried maidservant and an apprentice, both in his service. Manfield had dismissed Alice Fludd, the mother, after learning of her pregnancy, and although he agreed in court to take her back into service, she was found one month later in an almshouse, whence she was taken to Manfield's house by local authorities who again required him to receive her and provide for her (ABS, vol. 1, pp. 90, 96, 99).

20. Keith Wrightson, "The Nadir of English Illegitimacy in the Seventeenth Century," in *Bastardy and Its Comparative History*, ed. Peter Laslett, Karla Oosterveen, and Richard M. Smith (Cambridge, Mass.: Harvard University Press, 1980), has tabulated social relations between parents of illegitimate children in Lancashire and Essex, finding at least 14 percent of the Lancashire fathers, and 23 percent in Essex, to be in a magisterial position vis-à-vis the mothers. In Lancashire, 23 percent of conceptions involved members of the same household, and in Essex, 48 percent (pp. 187–88). J. A. Sharpe, *Crime in Seventeenth-Century England* (Cambridge: Cambridge University Press, 1983), corroborates the social superiority of the Essex fathers. He cites two cases of women offered £5 to accuse other men of paternity, and includes the story of a Colchester master reported to have told a fourteen-year-old servant girl with whom he had had sexual relations that she should accuse a soldier if she got pregnant (pp. 59–60). For similar attempts by fathers of bastards to induce mothers to name someone else, see Amussen, *An Ordered Society*, pp. 111–12.

21. Assizes were held twice yearly in seventeenth-century Dorchester, on varying dates in March and July (David Underdown, personal communication). In 1620, Balstone was twice committed to prison against the next Assizes, on March 19 and September 27 (Ashley, *Case Book*, 45v, 48). If Assizes were held after March 19 that year, then there would be two possible occasions when she was "delivered out of prison the last Assizes." The adjective "last" suggests the July Assizes. Even if these were held at the beginning of the month, however, she would have been at the most six months pregnant on January 6, making it unlikely that she was "lately supposed to fall in travail with child," and suggesting the spring Assizes. If these were held after March 19 in 1620, she and Long Robin would have been delivered out of prison in late March or very early April.

22. Balstone's account of how she came across the money is rather odd. She claims that while she was sweeping the previous Thursday she did "there espy upon a chest in the same room, a certain box standing open, into which this examinant casting her eye, perceived that there was therein to the quantity of £3." This was a considerable amount of money to leave lying in the open. In the context of describing several substantial bribes from men anxious to avoid

paternity charges, Amussen notes that the mandated yearly wages for a maid-servant over the age of twenty was 30s. plus 10s. for livery in 1613 (*An Ordered Society*, p. 112).

23. "Rum Cove" is one of the higher orders of male vagrants in the pamphlet literature, designating a man who has authority over a particular group or "Kin ." "Glimmer" is the canting word for fire, as in the "glimmering glance" or smoldering gaze of the female vagrant as she seduces and defrauds her victims. "Mort" is the generic term for an adult female vagrant in the pamphlets. To "cloy" means to steal or to obstruct, and in the passive form "cloyed" can mean to be intruded upon by other thieves claiming a share, or possibly to be whipped, as in the phrase "cly the jerk" (Judges, *Elizabethan Underworld*, pp. 522–32).

24. William Hunt, *The Puritan Moment* (Cambridge, Mass.: Harvard University Press, 1983), describes several references to vagrant networks in Essex court records, including an account of two female vagrants examined in 1580 who had been overheard speaking "Pedlar's French" (pp. 49–54). Beier, *Masterless Men*, notes a Dorset woman who used canting terms in a deposition of 1613, and gives a general assessment of the relation of the pamphlet literature to the historical experience of vagrants (pp. 123–26). The *Dorset Quarter Sessions Order Book* (DQSM) contains records of vagrant women who exemplified other stereotypes from the rogue pamphlets, including the bearing of false messages or documents. These women were punished to the full extent of the law, including whipping and branding with the letter R to mark them as wandering or dangerous rogues. Their engagement in the stereotypical practices of female rogues in the pamphlets seems to have marked them as particularly dangerous and deserving of immediate and severe punishment. See especially the cases of Frances Medcoth (DQSM, 22); Julian Chipley (159); and Christiana Saunders, Dorothea Bickness, and Mari Masye (209).

25. Copland's macaronic "Highway to the Spital-House" includes a passage of thieves' cant (called "babbling French" by the speaker) among its other citations of Latin, Dutch/Flemish, and "Franglais" (Judges, *Elizabethan Underworld*, p. 24). References to and citations of thieves' cant are standard throughout English rogue pamphlets, many of which contain canting dictionaries or lengthy translations; for example, the "Canters' Dictionary" of 129 words and phrases in [Samuel Rid ?] (in Judges, pp. 407–9), and "The Canting Song," followed by its "Englished" version, in the 1612 "O per se O" (Judges, pp. 381–82).

26. For accounts of popular print, its availability, and its audience in England in the seventeenth century, see especially Margaret Spufford, *Small Books and Pleasant Histories* (Cambridge: Cambridge University Press, 1981), pp. 9–14, Tessa Watt, *Cheap Print and Popular Piety* (Cambridge: Cambridge University Press, 1991), pp. 257–95, 288–97, and Joyce Wiltenburg, in *Disorderly Women and Female Power in the Street Literature of Early Modern England and Germany*, ed. Joyce Wiltenburg (Charlottesville: University of Virginia Press, 1992), pp. 27–44.

4

"No Good Thing Ever Comes Out of It"

Male Expectation and Female Alliance in Dekker and Webster's Westward Ho

· · · · · · · · · · · · · · · · · · · ·

SIMON MORGAN-RUSSELL

TO REMARK THAT THE transaction of adultery requires at least two will-ing participants might seem to make an obvious point; it is perhaps less obvious to point out that the adulterous liaison itself requires a locus for its transaction. In many examples of early seventeenth-century lit-erary culture, the market town of Brentford in Middlesex is depicted as a point of rendezvous for actors in adulterous affairs—as an iniquitous getaway, a location for a "dirty weekend." Although several economic, political, and topographical factors may have contributed to the town's mythical status, the representation of sexual escape from London to Brentford usually assumes that the trips are taken to the mutual plea-sure of both participants in the adulterous liaison. In Thomas Dekker and John Webster's *Westward Ho* (1604), however, an alliance of citi-zen wives critiques this assumption by exploiting the freedom granted by Brentford's separation from the City of London's jurisdiction and governance. Even though the text seems initially to indulge the geogra-phy of male, homosocially inscribed pleasure—the men seem at least partially motivated by their mutual participation in the myth of the Brentford trip—the female characters refuse to fulfill male fantasy and expectation and form alliances to disappoint them. In this essay I ex-plore the male-authored topos of Brentford in the first few decades of the seventeenth century and examine its particular disruption by women in the fifth act of Dekker and Webster's play. However, contextualizing the powerful and effective strategy of resistance that the alliance represents within this morally conventional, male-authored text need not deprive the alliance of its disruptive potential.

1. The "Flesh Exchange" in London and Brentford

Westward Ho, like many of its city comedy contemporaries, is preoccupied with the pursuit of largely illicit sexual exchange: an aged Earl lustfully, but ineffectively, courts Mistress Justiniano, merchant-citizens frequent brothels, and gallants chase citizen wives who themselves seek paramours. The text dramatizes the interaction of three merchant-citizens, Honeysuckle, Tenterhook, and Wafer, with their wives and would-be cuckolders; the intrigue is managed principally by the jealous merchant Justiniano, who, believing his own wife to be false, is determined to prove that all married women are similarly unfaithful. Like many city comedies that consider the "merchant-citizen," the play also characterizes these sexual relationships as economic transactions—particularly, in this play, as transactions that take place in a competitive and congested market. Contained within the restrictive environment of London's city wall, the "inner" or "closed" market of sexual exchange in *Westward Ho*—dramatized in the play as the Rhenish Wine House in Stilliards and Mistress Birdlime's urban brothel—is so crowded that participants risk encountering each others' fleshly transactions in their circulation of sexual activity. The "flesh exchange" managed by Mistress Birdlime within-the-walls is represented in the play as a distinctly congested market: by her scorn for the "Sinfulnesse of any suburbes in Christendom" and her reputation for her "up-rizers and downe-lyers within the Citty" (V.iv.251–52), she distinguishes herself as an urban, rather than a suburban, brothel-keeper, with enough tricks, claims Justiniano, "to keepe a vaulting house under the Lawes nose" (257–58) by allowing cunning women, physicians, or attorneys to take chambers in her house because "all these are good Clokes for the raine" (261–62).[1] The range of her business activities implicates almost all of the play's *dramatis personæ* and some figures besides: she operates as the go-between for the lascivious Earl and Mistress Justiniano (II.ii), for Mistress Tenterhook and Monopoly (II.ii.205–8), and as the owner of the brothel that caters to the merchants Tenterhook, Wafer, Honeysuckle, and a host of other named characters in the play (IV.i). The best demonstration of the extent to which sexual exchange is congested in the play occurs in the brothel (IV.i), when Tenterhook surprises Birdlime's whore, Luce, and, blindfolding her, demands to be identified. Luce produces a significant list of possibilities, including Tenterhook's fellow merchants and jealous husbands (Honeysuckle and Wafer), the gallants pursuing the merchants' wives (Lynstock, Whirlpool, and Sir Gosling), the keeper of the Brentford tavern encountered in the last act of the play (Dogbolt), Mistress Birdlime herself, and several other characters who never appear, such as "Maister *Counterpane* the Lawier," Master Freeze-Leather, and even a real London citizen: "*George* the drawer at the Miter."

The range of sexual circulation in *Westward Ho*, however, extends beyond Birdlime's brothel to include the other women in the play. It is productive to consider this circulation as an economic process in a text that revolves around merchants and mercantile affairs and that describes sexual activity in terms of the market.[2] In his discussion of "Money, or the Circulation of Commodities," Marx comments that the process of circulation: "unlike the direct exchange of products, does not disappear from view once the use-values have changed places and changed hands. The money does not vanish when it finally drops out of the series of metamorphoses undergone by a commodity. It always leaves behind a precipitate at a point in the arena of circulation vacated by the commodities" (Marx, p. 208).

In *Westward Ho*, the precipitate left by the circulation of commodities is incriminating because it reveals the characters' participation in the "flesh exchange." In particular, the passage of Mistress Tenterhook's diamonds demonstrates this exchange. In III.iv, Mistress Tenterhook uses the stones as security for Monopoly's release from his arrest by Sergeant Ambush, to purchase his presence for the trip to Brentford. She instructs Ambush, who is holding Monopoly at Tenterhook's charge, to "not come in my husbandes sight in the meane time" (III.iv.37). Ambush is, however, exposed by Justiniano and made to reveal the security in Birdlime's brothel: the two diamonds that Tenterhook recognizes instantly as those belonging to his wife. The prostitute Luce takes the diamonds from Tenterhook, maintaining that she will keep them as security for the "silk gowne, and six els of Cambricke" (IV.i.215–16) promised in payment for her services. Tenterhook is not content with this exchange, but is advised by his fellow merchants to "respect your credit." Luce retains the stones, but Mistress Birdlime believes that "the getting of these two Diamondes maie chaunce to save the Gentlewomens credit" (228–29): she arrives at Brentford to present the diamonds as an indication of Tenterhook's presence at the brothel even as he confronts his wife about her liaison with Monopoly. The eventual return of the diamonds to their point of origin, which through their circulation have incriminated several characters in extramarital sexual activity, emphasizes the distinct limitations of the "closed" market and its containment within a circumscribed "City" system of exchange.

In this respect, at least, London's "flesh exchange" had much in common with other urban markets, fraught with competition and monopoly. *Westward Ho*, however, establishes an alternative market for sexual transaction in the retreat to Brentford, a town located at the confluence of the Thames and the Brent ten miles west of St. Paul's and the City and an essential stage in the trade routes to and from southwest England. A map of the Hundred of Isleworth prepared by Moses Glover in 1635 shows the town of Brentford occupying a position at the edge of the paper, consisting of a single street punctuated with a few landmarks such as inns, wharves, and its market, and terminating as the buildings of Old Brentford emerge from the page (fig. 4-1).[3] As Roy Canham points out in *2000 Years of Brentford*, London's expansion as a mercantile center had a concomitant effect on the settlements surrounding the City, so that "it was the capital's consumption of food . . . which so rapidly changed the structure of their economy" (Canham, p. 6).[4] Canham proposes that the development of the market in New Brentford—its importance indicated by Norden's renaming of New Brentford as "Market Brentford" in his 1593 description of the county of Middlesex—"reflected the growing pressure of the capital's food requirements" and offered "A means for the seller of avoiding the congested markets of London, and for the London buyer of sidestepping the keen competition of the London market . . . [and] an opportunity of escaping the regulations laid down to govern trade by city authorities." The same characteristics that contributed to and derived from Brentford's status as a thriving market town also determined its function as a locus of illicit sexual activity. As many editors of early seventeenth-century texts point out, Brentford's representation on the stage suggests that it was apparently inviting as a place of sexual liaison; the frequency of its mention in this context testifies to the town's reputation in the popular literature of the period.

What distinguishes "sinfull Brainford" (Middleton and Dekker, IV.ii.187) from the "sixepenny Sinfulnesse the suburbes" (*Westward Ho*, V.iv.250) is the type of illicit sexual activity performed there. Instead of suburban prostitution, Brentford provided a location for the extramarital assignation, a conveniently situated place for London citizens to "be merry a night or two" in secure, fair lodgings, and to pose as married couples when "God wot they are neither man nor wife, nor perhaps of any acquaintance before the match made in some bawdy taverne" (Greene, 1964, p. 271). The town was close to the City and easily accessible to London citizens by land or by water, and it provided an abundance of inns—more, in fact, than elsewhere in the parish. Seventeenth-century texts are replete with references to "sinfull Brainford." In Middleton and Dekker's *The Roaring Girl*, Mistress Openwork is told by Goshawk that her husband "this very morning went in a boate with a tilt over it, to the three pidgions at *Brainford*, and his punke with him under his tilt" (IV.ii.23–25). She also remarks that Goshawk is keen to make "that voyage" with her—"this water-spaniell dives after no ducke but me, his hope is having mee at *Braineford* to make mee cry quack" (31–33). Dekker's *Pennywise, Pound Foolish* describes the movements of "two unchast lovers" who are "sometime whorried to Playhouses" by coach, and "sometime to *Brainford*, to lye there," the town represented in this text, along with Barnet, Blackwall, and Bloomsbury, as one of the "bawdy *Bees*

FIGURE 4-1   Section of Moses Glover's map of the Hundred of Isleworth (1635) showing Brentford. Map is on display at Syon House, Brentford, Middlesex. (Reproduced
here by kind permission of his Grace the Duke of Northumberland.)

lying neere and about *London*," and Massinger's Luke Frugal reflects on
the "raptures of being hurried in a coach / To Brentford, Staines or
Barnet" (Massinger, II.i.106–8). Historical figures also contribute to
Brentford's popular reputation: Jonson's Epigram 129, "To Mime," which
Herford and Simpson declare "[a]nother fling at Inigo Jones" (Jonson,
1925–52, vol. 11, p. 28), claims "That there's no iourney set, or thought
upon, / To *Braynford, Hackney, Bow*, but thou mak'st one" (Jonson, 1925–
52, vol. 7, p. 81), and Laurence Hutton remarks that "[a] favorite suburban resort of Jonson was the Three Pigeons . . . of Brentford" (Hutton,
p. 177), though he gives no source for this information.[5]

One explanation for the function of Brentford as a place of extramarital
assignation is the opportunity that the town offers for "sidestepping"
the congestion of sexual circulation in London because it presented a
market outside the City's saturated economy of flesh. The function of
the town as a flesh exchange is confirmed in several texts by the discussion of the sexual activity performed there in terms of the town's market.
Mistress Openwork, for example, confronts the rumors of her husband's

attempts to "catch fresh *Salmon* at *Brainford*" (Middleton and Dekker, IV.ii.75) in terms of economic exchange:

> MIST. OPEN. Is't Market day at *Braineford*, and your ware not sent up yet?
>
> MAIST. OPEN. What market day? what ware?
>
> MIST. OPEN. A py with three pidgions in't, 'tis drawne and staies Your cutting up.
>
> (125–28)

Mistress Openwork is referring to Brentford's most notorious inn, the Three Pigeons, commodified in her accusation as a freshly baked pie, awaiting Openwork's penetrative ministrations. And *Westward Ho*'s Tenterhook, presuming that he has been cuckolded in Brentford, expresses his grief not in terms of sexual infidelity but as economic failure: "Wee are abuzd," he laments, "Wee are bought and sold in *Brainford Market*" (V.iv.14).

Brentford's status, however, can be explained in broader cultural terms. Theodore Leinwand sees the movement of the drama in *Westward Ho* from London to Brentford in terms of a "sexual–social topography," so that "citizens sleep with their wives and their whores in the City, but citizen wives sleep with their lovers in the country" (Leinwand, 1986, p. 47). "The cry 'westward ho!' inaugurates a departure from the City," claims Leinwand, signaling "release from civic ordinance and the ward's close watch over the morality of city inhabitants." Brentford offers the gallant an ideal opportunity for an adulterous rendezvous, because in leaving the City "[h]e retreats to a non-*bürgerlich* world that threatens the citizen's freedom—a 'freedom' that is overdetermined, at once economic, political, and religious," while the location of "the inn at Brainford reminds the merchant-citizen that his base of power is both circumscribed and vulnerable." Although Leinwand discusses *Westward Ho*'s citizen wives at greater length later in his book, he neglects to position them in the "sexual–social topography" described here, and he overlooks their potential to participate in the disruption of the popular expectation of the trip to Brentford.

The assumptions that surround proposed trips to Brentford and the Three Pigeons in a number of dramatic texts suggest also that the sexual activity performed there was consensual and that the escape from London was enjoyed equally by both participants. It is important to note, however, that the fantasy of this escape from urban scrutiny is largely male-authored. Invariably, visits to Brentford are engineered by male characters and treated by women with a range of reactions varying from complicity to contentment to outright refusal. It is Subtle in *The Alchemist* who proposes to Dol that they escape "[t]o *Brainford*, westward, if thou saist the word. . . . wee'll tickle it at the *pigeons*" (Jonson, 1925–52, vol. 5, V.iv.77, 89), and her ambivalent response to his suggestion is

nothing more than "Content; I am weary of him" (79), so that the trip to
Brentford is accepted partly as a means of evading their third partner,
Face. Moll Cutpurse in *The Roaring Girl* responds very differently. Moll
is not amenable to Laxton's suggestion "to sup at *Brainford*" (Middleton
and Dekker, II.i.271), and she thrashes him so badly at their moment of
rendezvous that he calls a "pox athe three pigions, I would the coach
were here now to carry mee to the Chirurgions" (III.i.128–30). While
male-authored representations of Brentford ostensibly offer women an
opportunity for "what cheere you will," the inevitable masculine interpretation of this "cheere" is to "but bee merry and lye together" (II.i.252).
The distance between a less restrictive interpretation of "cheere" and
its much more specific male counterpart is nowhere more directly articulated than in *The Roaring Girl*. Having met Laxton at the appointed
place and time for the proposed trip to the Three Pigeons, Moll refuses
the scenario Laxton has imagined. She might, according to Laxton, be
"admirably suited for the three pigions at *Brainford*" (III.i.49), but she
accuses him of being an individual "That thinkes each woman thy fond
flexable whore, / If she but cast a liberall eye upon thee" (68–71). Moll
continues to interrogate the male assumption that a merry woman is a
sexually accessible one, the supposition that she is available, "Cause
youl'e say / I'me given to sport, I'me often mery, jest, / Had mirth no
kindred in the world but lust?" (99–101). As Kathleen McLuskie remarks
in *Dekker and Heywood: Professional Dramatists*, the distinction in this
speech between mirth and lust "denotes the possibility of separating
social from sexual pleasure, of allowing women the same freedom to
partake of the witty pleasures of the town without the imputation of
licentiousness" (McLuskie, p. 138).

I would like to argue, however, that while the movement westward
from the City offers the gallants an escape from the restrictions of the
merchant husband's "*bürgerlich* world" (as Leinwand claims), it also
affords the citizen wives a similar release from civic—and marital—governance. Rob Shields discussed the development of Brighton as a "dirty
weekend" resort in the 1920s and 1930s. Shields considers the town's
"liminal status . . . *vis-à-vis* the more closely governed realms of the
nation—the productive industrial areas, the 'serious' world of London
and the Parliament, or the 'innocent' arcadian spaces of the agricultural
counties" (Shields, p. 74), a liminality that courts a "derivative form of
Rabelaisian carnival" revealed in the staging of transgressive pleasures
and carnivalesque violence. I would like to suggest that Brentford functions as a similarly liminal space in the seventeenth century: the same
characteristics that determine its availability for construction as a male
fantasy for retreat—its "openness" as a site of flesh exchange, its status
as an unauthorized space removed physically from systems of City governance—also allows the women in the play the possibility of revolt.
Although many texts in this period evoke the myth of Brentford and

assume that its liminal position supports popular male fantasy, *Westward Ho*'s staging of the trip down the Thames effectively disrupts this myth by revealing other "freedoms" that the liminal retreat affords—that male expectation of desire can be destroyed by the rebellion offered by an alliance of women.

2. "A Py with Three Pidgions in't"

Of all the texts in which an adulterous escape to Brentford is proposed, only *Westward Ho* dramatizes the movement west from the City and the assignation's subsequent events. As in other texts, the rendezvous outside the City's limits is suggested by male characters—Sir Gosling Glowworm, Linstock, and Captain Whirlpool—who offer the excursion as a means of avoiding the close confines of sexual exchange in London. In order to convince their paramours of the necessity of this precaution, the three gallants rely on the aid of Justiniano, who assures them that he can "make three Conies bolt at a clap into your pursenets" (*Westward Ho*, II.iii.35). Justiniano's "clap" is the false warning of the approach of husbands as the women and the gallants are carousing in Stilliards. In response to the panic this threat of exposure engenders in the women, Linstock suggests a ride out of town "to mine host *Dogbolts* at *Brainford*." Linstock's description of Dogbolt's facilities clearly communicates to the women Brentford's appeal as a place of assignation: "there you are out of eyes, out of eares, private roomes, sweet Lynnen, winking attendance, and what cheere you will" (73–75). The town's allure lies in the safeguards against the intrusion of a cuckolded husband and the privacy afforded by the selective blindness and deafness of the "attendance." In their discussion of the travel arrangements and points of rendezvous, Justiniano and Sir Gosling again emphasize the privacy of chosen locations: "thats private," they claim of the Greyhound in Blackfriars, and they propose to "take Boate at Bridewell Dock most privately" (II.iii.104 and 108) for their river journey westward. Brentford is represented, then, as a safe, secure, and convenient haven for illicit sexual liaison, a haven constructed for the women in the text by male characters as a means of establishing a location for the gratification of their own desires.

It is worth considering *Westward Ho*'s Brentford excursion in terms of the dynamics of adultery formulated in recent critical and theoretical discussion of the subject. The alliance of women represented in the dramatic text results from the male homosocial relationships implicit in the structure of the adulterous liaison. Despite the great pains taken by the gallants to transport their supposed mistresses to Brentford, the women have an entirely different idea about the outcome of the trip. Having arrived at Dogbolt's tavern, the gallants retire to take tobacco and Mistress Tenterhook inquires of her companions, "What string may wee three thinke that these gallants harp uppon, by bringing us to this sinfull towne of *Brainford*?" (V.i.46–48). Monopoly and his company's intentions seem quite clear since "they brag one to another, that this night theile row westward in our husbands whirries" and an awareness of the gallants' ulterior motives prompts the women to take evasive maneuvers. Mistress Tenterhook advises them: "wenches lets bee wise, and make Rookes of them that I warrant are now setting pursenets to conycatch us" (54–58). The terms in which the adulterous act is characterized by Mistress Tenterhook—that the gallants hope to "row westward in our husbands whirries"—describes an interesting relationship between the gallants and their rivals, the citizen husbands, emphasizing the connection between the cuckold and the cuckolder. Adulterous transaction has seen significant theoretical interest in recent years, though in many discussions of the adulterous liaison the relationship between the male participants is elided and the focus of investigation is directed toward the relationship between man and wife. Coppélia Kahn, for example, describes the transaction as an articulation of "man's vulnerability to woman":

> Only a *husband* can be cuckolded; a man whose mistress betrays him doesn't qualify for the title. An unfaithful husband confers no such galling label on his wife; it is the fate of men alone. A man is dishonored, his masculine identity is weakened, and he acquires an indelible stigma when he is cuckolded. But he can regain a measure of dignity by branding his wife a whore. (Kahn, 1991, p. 251)

Kahn's description of the cuckolded husband's "stigma" coincides with the concern between the male characters in V.iv, when Tenterhook suggests raising the "towne in an insurrection" (*Westward Ho*, V.iv.23). But Justiniano advises otherwise: "if you trompet a broad and preach at the markct crosse, your wives shame, tis your owne shame" (80–81), recommending instead that the wronged husbands stand in private judgement over their wives, so that upon opening shop "you may aske any man what he lacks with your cap off, and none shall perceive whether the brim wrings you" (99–100). Although Justiniano's counsel seeks to conceal the shame inevitably accrued by the cuckolded husband, his solution still locates the dynamic of the adulterous act within the relationship of husband and wife.

In her discussion of Lévi-Strauss's *The Elementary Structures of Kinship*, however, Gayle Rubin describes the "commodification" of women and its role in transactions between men in kinship systems in terms that are more relevant to the dynamics of cuckoldry described by Mistress Tenterhook:

> If it is women who are being transacted, then it is the men who give and take them who are linked, the woman being a conduit of a relationship rather than a partner to it. . . . And it is the partners, not the presents,

upon whom reciprocal exchange confers its quasi-mystical power of social linkage. The relations of such a system are such that women are in no position to realize the benefits of their own circulation. (Rubin, 1975, p. 174)

The exchange of the commodified woman between men in Rubin's formulation concurs with Eve Kosofsky Sedgwick's analysis of cuckoldry in *Between Men: English Literature and Male Homosocial Desire*. Sedgwick's study modifies René Girard's description of the "calculus of power that was structured by the relation of rivalry between the two active members of an erotic triangle" (Sedgwick, 1985, p. 21), a model that represents the "bonds of 'rivalry' between males 'over' a woman" (p. 23), or, for our purposes, the relationship in *Westward Ho* of the gallant to the citizen resulting from the pursuit of the citizen's wife. Sedgwick discusses the dynamics of cuckoldry in William Wycherley's *The Country Wife*: "'To Cuckold,'" she claims, "is by definition a sexual act, performed on a man, by another man" (p. 49) and it "differs additionally from more directly sexual male homosocial bonds in that it requires a woman" (p. 50). Sedgwick further describes the bond of cuckoldry as: "*necessarily* hierarchical in structure, with an 'active' participant who is clearly in the ascendancy over the 'passive' one. Most characteristically, the difference of power occurs in the form of a difference of knowledge: the cuckold is not even supposed to know that he is in such a relationship."

The same machinery of homosociality is present in Dekker and Webster's text, so that heterosexual relations function as a "strategy of homosocial desire" (Sedgwick, 1985, p. 49) in the text. There are strong homosocial bonds between the men in the two groups—the gallants take tobacco together, "brag one to another" about their sexual exploits, and, once Monopoly has been thwarted by Mistress Tenterhook's feigned illness, they unite against the "common enimy" (*Westward Ho*, V.i.240) of woman. As Mistress Tenterhook predicts, to foil one of the gallants is to foil them all; Monopoly is adamant that "Since we must swim, lets leape into one flood, / Weele either be all naught, or els all good" (262–63). Similarly, the citizen husbands are united in their supposed mutual cuckolding, a bond that becomes most explicit as they locate their wives in Brentford with Tenterhook's fraternal pronouncement of "brother *Honny-suckle*, and brother *Wafer*" (V.iv.5–6). The husbands are also connected by their brothel bonhomie in IV.i, a relationship that extends to a larger male population that includes their gallant rivals. Moreover, there is also a recognition of the shift in the "power of knowledge" between cuckold and cuckolder: as a result of Justiniano's revelation of the gallants' plans, Tenterhook, Wafer, and Honeysuckle hope to relinquish the cuckold's passivity for the more active role as "pittifull fathers" standing over the "poore mouse-trapt-guilty-gentlemen" (V.iv.88–89) they have caught at Brentford. Ultimately, because the accusations of adultery are not applicable, the two groups of men in *Westward Ho* are easily reconciled by Justiniano, who persuades the citizens that "your Wives are chast, these Gentlemen civill, all is but a merriment, all but a May-game" (V.iv.277–78). Any opprobrium is displaced onto Mistress Birdlime the bawd, and what remains is nothing more than "harmelesse meryment" (308).

To consider the group of women in *Westward Ho* as either a mediating factor in the homosocial relations within and between the two groups of men—or, in terms of Rubin's argument, a commodity that is the "conduit" of a relationship between men—elides the representation of a powerfully determined female homosociality that develops among Clare Tenterhook, Judith Honeysuckle, and Mabel Wafer, and the more extended world of female citizenry mentioned, if not directly observed, in the text. According to Rubin, the system in which women circulate as commodities does not allow them "to realize the benefits of their own circulation" (Rubin, 1975, p. 174). *Westward Ho* seems, at first, to reproduce this sexual economy by presenting its audience with the familiar myth of the Brentford liaison and the attendant expectation of adulterous transaction. As Monopoly's name suggests, the expected outcome of the rendezvous is the passage of the woman-as-commodity from husband to gallant, so that the gallant "has the monopoly" on the transacted commodity. But this system of sexual exchange is disrupted by the citizen wives who refuse to circulate as commodities and instead assert a different economy in which they participate as the transac*tors* rather than the transac*ted*.

In *Man's World, Woman's Place*, Elizabeth Janeway suggests that "locked out of the larger community of a man's world, women . . . develop profoundly ambiguous feelings about any sort of community they may set up for themselves. . . . [c]attiness and disloyalty are expected" (Janeway, p. 111). Monopoly's view of women's interaction echoes Janeway's statement; when asked by Mistress Honeysuckle "[D]o you think we can fall out?," Monopoly replies: "In troth beauties . . . that there was no inheritance in the amity of Princes, so think I of Women, too often interviewes amongst women, as amongst Princes, breeds envy oft to others fortune" (*Westward Ho* I.ii.76–79). Monopoly, of course, is proved to be mistaken later in the play, because it is the strength of the women's alliance that successfully disrupts his expectation of sexual gratification. Evidence of a network of women's communities can be found in *Westward Ho* as early as act I, scene ii, however, when Mistress Honeysuckle and Mistress Wafer "are come to acquaint [Mistress Tenterhook] with an excellent secret: we two learn to write" (I.ii.120–21). The women in the text see writing as a means of attaining agency, even if that agency is achieved through the arrangements of the writing master. The female writing community, like the male homosocial brothel roster, extends beyond the *dramatis personæ* to include other "Wives, Maides, and Daughters" (II.i.64) and, by name, "Mistress *Flapdragon* (the Brewers wife)" (107).

In the final act of *Westward Ho*, the disruptive potential of female homosocial alliances is pitted explicitly against the male-scripted expectation of an adulterous Brentford liaison. Wise to the intentions of Monopoly and his companions, the women decide to show them that "Cittizens wives have wit enough to out strip twenty such guls" (V.i.159–60). "It were better," suggests Clare Tenterhook, "We should laugh at theis popin-Jayes, then live in feare of their prating tongues: tho we lye all night out of the Citty, they shall not find country wenches of us" (168–70). Clare's perception of Brentford as a "fooles Paradise" rather than a cuckolder's heaven becomes a female-authored construction of Brentford that offers an interesting contrast to its male-authored counterpart. While the successful adventures of the gallants would enable them to "brag one to another," the successful disruption of this male expectation by the women is described as currency in the development of female homosociality: "The Jest shal be a stock to maintain us and our pewfellows in laughing at christnings, cryings out, and upsittings this twelve month" (171–73).

While this sisterhood is not revealed onstage in *Westward Ho*, a representation of the type of female homosociality demonstrated at women's events such as "christnings" occurs in III.ii of Middleton's *A Chaste Maid in Cheapside*, in which a group of gossips and puritan sisters gather around the bed of Mistress Allwit. The women at the christening are presented as monstrous, consuming—in Allwit's opinion at least—vast amounts of wine and "comfits," talking, making the room hot with their "thick bums," and, Allwit suspects, emptying their bladders on the floor as he lurks suspiciously at the social event's margins.[6] The women's jest in *Westward Ho* is expected to operate in much the same way as the gallants' *post facto* bragging and the husbands' longed-for discovery of their wives' adultery with Justiniano's description of "the glory that it will be for you three to kisse your wives like forgetfull husbands, to exhort and forgive the young men like pittifull fathers" (*Westward Ho*, V.iv.94–96). The laughter generated at the gulling of both husbands and gallants is to be shared amongst the participants of female-centered activities and the network of women's communities that invade the otherwise male-centered text. A hint of this is displayed in the spirits of the women who, safe from the unwanted intentions of the gallants, "hugg one another a bed and lie laughing till we tickle againe to remember how wee sent you a Bat-fowling" (V.iv.126–28). Of the three groups within the text, the women come out on top. Because no adultery has taken place the husbands have not been "wrung under the withers" (17), but they also lose their opportunity to stand as judges over their "shamed" wives and the "mouse-trapt-guilty-gentlemen" (88–9). Similarly, the gallants find themselves with very little to brag about, so much so that Monopoly loses faith in the myth of Brentford: "I'me accurst to spend mony in this Towne of iniquity: theres no good thing ever comes out of it" (V.i.213–14). The women, on the other hand, get to be "merry" but not "mad"

(160), and succeed in evading the "pursenets" of all their would-be coneycatchers—husbands, gallants, and the ever-suspicious Justiniano alike.

Although *Westward Ho* is the only play that stages the trip west along the river to Brentford, the suspicion that surrounds female alliance outside City jurisdiction sends ripples of insecurity through other texts. In an anonymous text published in 1620, *Westward for Smelts*, a group of rowdy fishwives led by the Fishwife of Brentford tell a sequence of tales to pass the time during their trip home. The Fishwife of Brentford's tale, discovered at its conclusion to be autobiographical, recounts how a young wife successfully cuckolds her husband with the aid of her friend Mother Jone. Mother Jone—the Fishwife herself—stands in for the wife while she is seeing her lover, and in the dark takes a knife cut on the nose from the spiteful husband. Consequently, when he confronts his wife the next morning and sees that she does not bear any wound, he takes this is as a sign that "the heavens will not suffer the innocent to suffer harme" (Anon., p. 18) and is sufficently contrite. Thus, concludes the Fishwife of Brentford, "had she [the wife] more libertie than before, and the old woman had gold for her wound, which wound was so well cured (I thanke God!) that you can scarce see it on my nose!" The scene of this adultery is Windsor, and the connection of Brentford and Windsor with successful female alliance against men also occurs in Shakespeare's *The Merry Wives of Windsor*, when, as part of their plan to delude the suspicious Master Ford and the amorous Sir John, Mistress Ford and Mistress Page disguise Falstaff as Gillian of Brentford, a popular folk figure of the sixteenth-century. Although the editor of the Percy Society's edition of *Westward for Smelts* notes mention by Malone that the tale told by the Fishwife of Brentford is the source for Shakespeare's setting of *The Merry Wives of Windsor*, he remarks that "[t]here seems to be no real grounds for such a conjecture" (Anon., note p. 10). It is worth reflecting, however, that the Windsor–Brentford connection in these texts may be indicative of the anxiety generated by the "release from civic ordinance and the ward's close watch over the morality of city inhabitants" (Leinwand, p. 47) that these spaces outside of London offer women.

If Dekker and Webster's Brentford turns out to be less iniquitous than its popular reputation promises, it is the alliance of the citizen wives against male expectation that makes it so. In act II, scene i, Justiniano poses the question of women's infidelity: "Do all tread on the heele? Have all the art / To hood-winke wise men thus? And (like those builders / Of *Babels* Tower) to speake unknowne tongues, / Of all (save by their husbands) understood" (228–31). In *Westward Ho*, the answer would seem to be affirmative: the play is a cautionary tale that preys on every suspicious husband's fears and every prospective gallant's insecurities because it shows that women—in groups—have the ability to hoodwink men to their own advantage. It is difficult to claim that the female alliances articulated by *Westward Ho* are designed by its male authors to privilege the strength and success of women's collective effort. The wit taught by "Your Cittizens wife" is "to receive all and pay all: to awe their Husbands, to check their Husbands, to controule their husbands" (I.i.31–32) and to use their independence to cuckold husbands or to jilt lovers at their own choosing, but the play's conclusion sees the citizen wives return to London—and to marriage. Do they, like the young wife in the Fishwife of Brentford's tale, have "more libertie than before?" The articulation of female homosociality as a threat to male-dominated institutions necessarily credits it with some agency, and in spite of its representation as a warning for the London citizen husband, the women's alliance in *Westward Ho* expresses a powerful and successful alternative to the male homosociality in the text, a strength that is disruptive of male expectation within the play and, ultimately, of the extratextual— and male-authored—reputation of "sinfull Brainford."

NOTES

I would like to acknowledge the help and encouragement of David Hawkes, Karen Robertson, Barbara Traister, and Paul Winters during the writing of this essay. The financial support of Lehigh University's English Department helped with its genesis, and a research release granted by the English Department at Bowling Green State University furthered its revisions.

1. Citations from *The Dramatic Works of Thomas Dekker*, edited by Fredson Bowers (New York: Cambridge University Press, 1955), vol. 2. Mistress Birdlime's denial of her affiliations with the suburbs is not the only indication of her keeping a house in the City. The "Hot-house in Gunpowder Ally (neere crouched Fryers)" (I.i.8–9) that she cites as a cover for her activities might be entirely fictitious, but her brothel is clearly on the north side of the Thames: when she makes her way from her house to Brentford in IV.i she must go "downe to Queene-hive" to be carried to "Lambeth *Marsh*" (234–36), crossing from the north bank to the south.

2. It is also worth considering the implication of the text itself in a system of theatrical economy. In a much-quoted passage from *The Gull's Hornbook*, Dekker remarks that "[t]he theatre is your Poet's Royal Exchange upon which their Muses—that are now turned to merchants—meeting, barter away that light commodity of words." Also see "The Poet's Royal Exchange: Patronage and Commerce in Early Modern England," *Yearbook of English Studies* 21 (1991): 53–62. Kathleen McLuskie, *Dekker and Heywood: Professional Dramatists* (New York, St. Martin's, 1994), discusses the relationship of drama to the marketplace.

3. According to Glover's map, New Brentford, "together With Y^e Oulde is Extended one Mille, in one Streete onely." Brentford Market is easy to locate on the map. The Three Pigeons is almost immediately above the Market, marked here as "Y^e Doves," the name by which it was also known at this time. Other inns labelled are the George, the Lion, and the Boar's Head. Seventeenth-century spellings of Brentford vary considerably, most commonly on some variation of "Brainford."

4. John Chartres's "Food Consumption and Internal Trade" examines London's function as consumer and its "consequent impact on agrarian change, market structure, and the transport system" (Beier, 1985, p. 170). He notes that, for the traffic of grain into London, "for much of the period before 1640 over-

land and river supply routes predominated" (p. 178), routes that included Brentford.

5. Charles Hindley, *Tavern Anecdotes and Sayings* (London: Chatto and Windus, 1875), remarks that Brentford's notable tavern, the Three Pigeons, "appears at one time to have been the resort of low people, sharpers, &c." (p. 375), and remembers that John Lowin, "the original Falstaff, then grown old," was at one time its landlord.

6. Thomas Middleton, *A Chaste Maid in Cheapside*, ed. Bryan Loughrey and Neil Taylor (London: Penguin, 1988). For an interesting discussion of the incontinence staged in this scene of *A Chaste Maid in Cheapside*, and its connection with the uncontrollable nature of women, see Gail Kern Paster's *The Body Embarrassed: Drama and the Disciplines of Shame in Early Modern England* (Ithaca, N.Y.: Cornell University Press, 1993), chap. 1, especially pp. 52–63.

PART II

Alliances in the Household

5

"A P[ar]cell of Murdereing Bitches"

Female Relationships in an
Eighteenth-Century Slaveholding Household

. . . .

KATHLEEN M. BROWN

IT WAS A SULTRY AUGUST MORNING IN 1714 at the Tayloe plantation in Lancaster County, Virginia. Betty Mazey, a hired white woman, was spinning in the lodging chamber of the main house. Mary, an enslaved woman of African descent, was beginning her daily chores of cooking, fetching water, gardening, and laundering. In addition to these two women, an Indian[1] servant woman worked in and around the buildings of the main house, sharing with Mary the responsibility for the most strenuous and least desirable household tasks. Madam Anne Tayloe, widow and mistress of this household of female laborers, had left the main house for the plantation "office," one of several small buildings clustered nearby that gave the plantation the appearance of a manorial village. Normally, such an office might have been the site of the plantation's bookkeeping, where a diligent owner attempted to balance the credit for tobacco shipped to London with expenditures for clothing, tools, supplies for slaves, and wages. At adjacent offices, or "dependencies," as they were also known, African, Indian, and white laborers performed the hot, unpleasant labor of cooking, laundry, and craftswork that allowed the plantation to function.

On this particular morning, however, as Betty Mazey subsequently reported to the Lancaster County court, the work of Tayloe's servants and slaves was disrupted when the enslaved woman Mary entered the

87

lodging chamber where Mazey was spinning. Mary insisted that Mazey come upstairs to see their mistress. With great reluctance, Mazey recalled, she followed Mary up the stairs and over to the window that overlooked the plantation office. There the two women could see Anne Tayloe, framed by the office window, holding what appeared to be a chamber pot with an infant stuffed inside it.[2]

"By the persuasion of the Indian and negroe woman," Mazey subsequently testified, she decided to investigate further. She walked over to the office where Anne Tayloe stood, looking "very badly." Mazey asked Tayloe, "Madam[,] whats the matter with yo?" According to Mazey, Tayloe replied, "What should be the matter with me," and attempted a smile. "Madam yo know that best yor selfe," remarked Mazey, to which Tayloe responded, "Aye God help me Betty soe I do."

Tayloe then requested that Mazey bring her a hoe. "I went and fetched her one and gave it to her sideways," Mazey later reported to the Lancaster justices of the peace. "She s[ai]d Betty come here I cant tell which." Unwilling to be drawn into Madam Tayloe's project with the hoe, Mazey claimed to have ignored her mistress's request: "I took noe notice of her but sett down the hoe and went to spinning againe."

About half an hour later, Tayloe returned to the house. Urged by Mary to see for herself where Tayloe had been digging, Mazey followed the enslaved woman over to a section of ground that appeared to be "broke up." Mazey later saw a blood-stained chamber pot in the kitchen, which she believed to be the one Tayloe had been holding earlier. The most damning evidence against Tayloe, however, came from Mary, who reported seeing the chickens scratching at an object in the yard. It was a "peice of a child," according to Betty Mazey, a leg, which Mary promptly buried, showing the white woman where she had done so.

The scandal that erupted around Madam Anne Tayloe's alleged act of infanticide in 1714 provides an instructive, if disturbing, illustration of the complex politics of female relationships in early eighteenth-century Virginia. To male investigators, Tayloe's household of female laborers appeared suspiciously autonomous and intimate. After hearing rumors of Tayloe's wrongdoing, one man declared the women to be a "p[ar]cell of murdereing bitches," a statement that reflected his belief that the members of the household were in league in killing Tayloe's unwanted child. But as testimony at the county court hearing suggests, the women of the Tayloe household were less a collectivity than a mosaic of different interests, whose interactions were infused with a delicate domestic politics. Male assumptions that shared domestic routines, gossip, and a common knowledge of the female body were sufficient conditions for female collaboration were a misreading, revealing more about men's own fears of unsupervised women than about the existence of female community in the Tayloe household.

The Tayloe case also offers a unique opportunity to examine the politics of female gossip in the eighteenth century. Even as they lived,

worked, and socialized among men, women constituted their own critical communities through gossip and visiting. Women's sense of who they
were usually depended upon whom they defined as their female peers
and what those friends, neighbors, and kin said about them. While their
men gathered at militia musters, white women gave meaning to their own
relationships in the semiprivate, socially truncated domestic contexts
of tea table and porch, dressing room, bedside, and kitchen hearth. Relationships forged through whispered information and shared judge-
ments—the juridical side of female gossip—often spilled over into the
heterosocial public of church and festival. Rooted in domestic sociabil-
ity, this female subculture infiltrated women's interactions in more public
settings. In its juridical and community-defining roles, gossip was perhaps the closest thing to a female public.[3]

Gossip's creation of imagined female communities, its mustering of
women through speech, and its function as a testing ground for female
identity and character all bore parallels to the competitive culture of the
militia muster. Yet, ultimately, whereas male success involved vaunting
male identity publicly—celebrating it as an entity distinct from domestic relationships—survival in the female world of gossip required a sub-
mergence of female identity through marriage and the scrupulous avoid-
ance of publicity. Gossip in eighteenth-century Virginia was not the
foundation of an oppositional or independent female culture; rather, it
usually functioned to regulate women's conduct in ways that preserved
publicly constituted social hierarchies.[4]

Gossip's elite victims, moreover, were far more likely to be female than
male by the eighteenth century. Elite men's immoral conduct may still
have been the subject of talk after 1700, but it was less likely to provoke the legal action or community furor it had during the seventeenth
century. In contrast, the fear of scandalous "publicity" compelled elite
women to behave in accordance with the formal laws and common sense
of patriarchy. Female self-perceptions and interactions with other women
thus remained infused with patriarchal values.

The regulatory and conservative functions of gossip, however, were
occasionally offset by the porous boundaries of the female communities it
created. The diffuse and potentially unpredictable ways through which
gossip produced knowledge—including the deliberate spread of rumor, the
embellishment of twice-told tales, and the appropriation of information
through eavesdropping—enabled even women formally excluded from elite
white social circles to participate in it. This ability of enslaved and nonelite
white women to gain access to communities of gossip gave it a potentially
subversive power. The words of slaves, white domestics, and other ordinary women could sustain or destroy the reputation of elite mistresses and
neighbors. This leveling potential of gossip might have created a serious
problem for eighteenth-century class and race hierarchies had not the growing rift between male and female publics marginalized the political import
of all female speech, no matter what the race or class of the speaker.

As the Tayloe case illustrates, however, the existence of a female
public realm did not necessarily mean the existence of an oppositional
female culture. Gossip circulated not only among women, but among men
as well. The spread of such gossip to men became the vehicle by which
information about Tayloe reached the male public, where Tayloe became
subject to the logic of the county courtroom. The politics of female gossip was, therefore, permeated by the potential to expose women to the
scrutiny of the male public. Nor did the female public necessarily indicate the existence of a collective female identity that transcended race
and class divisions. Although gossip did contain a democratizing tendency—any woman could become the victim of rumor—it was also one
means by which women reproduced differences among women, revealing their separate interests even if they occasionally subverted racial and
class hierarchies.

IN 1705, NINE YEARS before justices listened to the evidence concerning Madam Tayloe's alleged infanticide, Virginia formally codified the
collection of laws that defined the condition of the colony's African
slaves; many of these laws had been produced in a piecemeal fashion
during the preceding sixty-five years. One declared "negroes, mulattoes,
and Indian servants, and others, not christian," to be "persons incapable
in law, to be witnesses in any cases whatsoever." This statute effectively
made Betty Mazey, the only white woman in residence on the Tayloe
plantation other than Madam Tayloe and her daughter, a relatively important figure in both the actual events of August 10 and in the subsequent courtroom rendition of those events in the months to come.[5]

A second law, passed in 1710, had an equal impact on events and
subsequent court narratives. Following a call by the Governor's Council
for a law to prevent the murder of illegitimate children, the Virginia
Assembly adopted a century-old English statute to punish infanticide.
The law specified that any free woman caught concealing the death of
her bastard child would be executed for murder whether or not the
murder could actually be proved. White women who could not provide
proof of an illegitimate child's stillbirth, in other words, were automati-
cally judged guilty of infanticide. This statute reflected several historical conditions in the colony. Virginia had a long history of high bastardy
rates among white female servants, rates that surpassed those in both
Old England and New England. In addition, new concerns over interra-
cial unions that could potentially undermine the racial foundations of
slavery and freedom heightened legislative vigilance over the sexual
activity of white women. Servant women like Betty Mazey were probably the population legislators had in mind when they adopted the infanticide law. But wealthy widows such as Madam Tayloe technically
fell under the purview of the law, compelling local officials to use the

intrusive tools of sexual regulation on elite women whose alliances with powerful men ordinarily protected them from such legal scrutiny.[6]

It is impossible to know with certainty whether knowledge of these laws excluding black testimony and defining infanticide informed the decisions made by Tayloe's female domestics on August 10 or only retrospectively influenced the testimony of witnesses, leading to the creation of narratives that neatly addressed the specifications of the law. One also wonders whether Betty Mazey exaggerated the passivity of her own conduct to avoid her mistress's censure, implicitly laying responsibility for bringing the infanticide to light on the enslaved woman Mary. Although it is important to keep both of these possibilities in mind when interpreting Mazey's courtroom testimony, her description of the events of August 10 rings true in certain details. Mary's initiative and Mazey's relatively passive role in the discovery of Tayloe's alleged infanticide was in keeping with their places in the Tayloe household division of labor, as well as with what is known more generally about patterns of female labor in eighteenth-century Virginia. Mazey's attribution of initiative to Mary, moreover, suggests that the enslaved woman was well versed in the law prohibiting black testimony, a degree of legal savvy that appears to have been common among enslaved Virginians and free people of color throughout the late seventeenth and early eighteenth centuries.[7]

When the justices assembled in September to investigate charges of bastardy and infanticide against Madam Anne Tayloe, Betty Mazey supplied crucial information about the day's events. Yet she had only reluctantly been drawn into those events. If Mary and the Indian woman had not alerted her to the strange goings-on in the household, Mazey would have had little information for the court. Although forbidden by law to testify, the two domestics had made Mazey's testimony possible, and indeed, had acted as catalysts for the subsequent legal inquiry. Legally distanced from the investigatory method of the courtroom, Mary and the Indian woman were crucial to the process of collecting evidence and making sure it reached the eyes and ears of Betty Mazey, the only woman, other than Tayloe's daughter, eligible to serve as a witness against Tayloe in court.

TAYLOE'S CASE CAME to the Lancaster County court for a preliminary hearing on September 9, 1714, one month after the alleged infanticide took place. Representing the county's most prominent families, the six justices of the court pressed Mazey for details about Tayloe's physical condition. Mazey appeared reluctant, however, to divulge information of such an intimate nature:

> JUSTICES: did you see in Madam Anne Tayloe's Bed or Linnen a signe of a lying in woman since the 10th of August?

MAZEY: upon one sheet I see signes[.]

JUSTICES: Did you ever know that ever made Mad[a]m Anne Tayloe ever took any thing to make her miscarry[?]

MAZEY: Noe[.]

Hoping she would shed some light on Tayloe's claim to have menstruated during the summer of her alleged pregnancy, the justices attempted to extract still more confidential information from Mazey. Their line of questioning suggests that they believed the servant women of the Tayloe house to be intimately acquainted with their mistress's body. Mazey, however, answered their questions with terse, careful answers, avoiding words like "courses," "terms," or even "blood" to refer to menstruation in front of the male justices:

JUSTICES: How long have yo lived with Mad[a]m Anne Tayloe[?]

MAZEY: About a yeare[.]

JUSTICES: Were you used to wash her Linnin or make her Bed?

MAZEY: Yes sometimes.

JUSTICES: When you were used to make her Bed have yo niver tooke notice of any signes as of a woman not with child[?]

MAZEY: It is not soe often that I did. I never minded.

JUSTICES: Was yo there when Madam Elizabeth Churchill was over there last[?]

MAZEY: Yes[.]

JUSTICES: How long ago was that[?]

MAZEY: I dont know that, It was some time in the summer [.]

JUSTICES: was Mad[a]m Anne Tayloe then in such condicon as women that commonly are not with child[?]

MAZEY: I can't tell indeed [.]

JUSTICES: In what condicon did yo conceive yo Mis to be in when yo spoke to her and said Mad[a]m looke upon yor Pettycoat[?]

MAZEY: To be as she should be[,] as other women used to be[.]

JUSTICES: That question requires further explanation[.] what doe yo mean by being as she should be[;] as women with child or not with child?

MAZEY: Not with child.

Madam Tayloe interrogated only one witness in her own defense, a neighbor named Mrs. Dare who seems to have been a midwife or healer. Tayloe asked "Mrs. Dare, when yo were with mee, when my head and face was sweated[,] Mrs. Payne tels me you told her yo see some thing about mee that was not fitt to be seen." Showing little hesitation about speaking frankly in front of the male justices, perhaps as a result of her experience with such matters, Dare answered, "Yes, I did, I see her with her monthly courses upon her att that time and I covered her with the

Bed clothes." Tayloe apparently believed that if enough witnesses cast doubt upon the notion that she was pregnant during the summer, the justices would have only Mazey's cautious, often secondhand testimony. As Mazey herself put it, "I see her have something like a child, but I can't be positive—it was a child by reason I did not touch it."

The evidence the justices sought about Tayloe's body was enmeshed in an extensive network of female gossip. Mazey, Dare, and two other witnesses mentioned several women who had played key roles in passing information to others. Mazey reported hearing of Tayloe's pregnancy from "people up and down." Tayloe's own witness, Mrs. Dare, became involved in the case because her gossip about Tayloe got back to its source. Dare told her friend Mrs. Payne that she had seen evidence of Tayloe menstruating. When news of Mrs. Dare's observation filtered back to Tayloe through Payne ("Mrs. Payne tels me you told her . . ."), Tayloe decided to call Dare to the witness stand.

Female gossip networks also served as the vehicle by which men were drawn into the case, with Tayloe's Afro-Virginian and Indian servants playing a central role in disseminating information across gender lines. Mary and the Indian woman not only intervened in the events of August 10, urging Betty Mazey to witness the child in the chamber pot and the broken ground, but they also spread word of Tayloe's transgression beyond the plantation to the surrounding neighborhood. James Burn, a white man who had lived at the Tayloe plantation since 1710, claimed to have learned of Tayloe's pregnancy from "neighbors." But he heard details of the child in the chamber pot from one of Tayloe's domestics, probably Betty Mazey. When news of the infant's burial and unearthed leg reached neighbors, Burn learned from Mr. John Pinkard's wife that "it was buried behind the house of office [privy] between two stones or under two stones."

News had traveled so swiftly on August 10 that James Burn had already heard about an infant being killed when he arrived at the plantation that evening. When the justices asked him how he had learned of the day's events, he reported "I heard it talked of by the Indian children something about a child, and I had a mistrust that it was Mad[a]m Anne Tayloes." One can almost imagine Burn riding towards the Tayloe plantation when forced to slow down by the clamor of Indian children circulating the scandalous tale they had heard from their mothers, perhaps even from Tayloe's Indian domestic herself.

Another Tayloe employee, Samuel Steele, learned of the dead child from Mazey and Mary because he happened to be working at the plantation on August 10. Steele reported that he "heard Betty Mazey and the negroe woman Mary call that there was such a thing as a child seen." The same women "told mee that they thought it was from Mad[a]m Anne Tayloes" body. Steele also learned from Betty Mazey that she "had carried a hoe" to Tayloe "to burie the child." Of the infant, he heard "the negroe woman Mary and Betty Mazey say the poultry had scratched it up once or twice."

Steele heard one other significant comment on the evening of August 10 that no other witness reported. Infuriated by what the Indian children had told him, James Burn clattered on toward the Tayloe house, where he confronted Mazey, the slave Mary, Tayloe's daughter, and perhaps even Tayloe herself. Lashing out at the women verbally, Burn called them "a p[ar]cell of murdereing bitches," declaring that he "had a mind to have them all hanged." Like the justices who so thoroughly interrogated Mazey and who were so certain that she could reveal deep secrets about her mistress's physical condition, Burn assumed that all the women in the Tayloe household had collaborated in the child's death. Upon hearing the news of a dead infant, he had immediately "mistrust[ed]," or suspected, that the child must be Tayloe's, perhaps because of his own illicit relationship with the widow. He also believed that Tayloe had taken something to terminate the pregnancy and related to the justices a suspicious conversation he had with Tayloe's daughter about a "ugly stinking" weed that would allegedly "wash the freckles of[f] her face." When Burn arranged to see Samuel Steele the next day at the horse races at Bailey's track, however, he had thought the better of his outburst. He urged Steele "not to say anything of the disturbance between him and the s[ai]d family the night."

Burn's dramatic ride, his angry confrontation with the servants, and his subsequent recantation to Steele illuminate the distance between male and female public cultures as well as their uneasy connection. The female public constituted by gossip met the male public at the moment when Burns confronted Betty Mazey, Mary, and the Indian servant at the Tayloe plantation with rumors of Tayloe's misdeed. In retrospect, Burn regretted his passionate denunciation of the women. When he and Steele met again, this time in the public forum of the local racetrack, Burn tried to minimize the significance of his outburst. He urged Steele to think of the context for his exclamation as domestic and private—a "disturbance between him and the s[ai]d family"—and implied that such words carried less weight than those uttered publicly among men. Hoping that the male bond evoked by his retraction at the racetrack would trump Steele's spectator– participant status in the female speech community at the Tayloe plantation, Burn cast the public realm of female gossip as an essentially private and lesser world, distinct from the public world of men.

Although Burn and the justices approached the female-dominated Tayloe household as if its occupants commonly shared in a secret female culture based on their knowledge of menstruation, abortion, birth, and infanticide, the relationships among the women were far more complicated. Class, race, and the household division of labor separated the four women who lived in such intimacy in the Tayloe plantation house, shaping their knowledge and concerns differently. While Betty Mazey spun, reluctant to learn more intimate details about her mistress, Mary and the Indian woman watched Tayloe closely. Despite being unable to testify in court, they intervened aggressively in the unfolding events, situating Betty Mazey to witness Tayloe's behavior. The two servants' social distance from their mistress and their assumption that the distance between the two white women might be more easily brooked was revealed in the way they chose to respond to Tayloe's behavior. Rather than approaching Tayloe themselves to ask her about the child in the chamber pot, they designated Mazey to speak with her, compelling her to serve as a go-between for the wealthy mistress and her domestics. As the court testimony suggests, Tayloe's African and Indian servants were observant, well versed in the networks of white people who employed and regulated them, and not averse to disapproving of their mistress's conduct in semipublic ways.

Tayloe's status, the reticence of Betty Mazey, and the reliance upon hearsay evidence from Mary and the Indian woman may ultimately have saved Tayloe from conviction. Although she spent some time in jail after the September inquest, a year later she was at liberty; at that time Joseph Tayloe (probably her son or stepson) presented her, along with James Burn, to the county court for living incontinently. Burn's "mistrust" that the dead infant was Tayloe's seems, indeed, to have sprung from his firsthand knowledge of Tayloe's—and his own—sexual misconduct, a union that violated status boundaries as well as the laws governing sexual behavior. When he accused the women of the household of being "a p[ar]cell of murdereing bitches," he appears to have spoken as an angry father-to-be who resented what he believed to be the female household's collaborative effort to kill his child.[8]

Unfortunately, we cannot discern Mary's motives from the records with any degree of certainty. Was she hoping that news of the wrongful death of an infant would ultimately disrupt Madam Tayloe's household, making it possible for her to work elsewhere? Was her exposure of her mistress's misdeeds a way of voicing her disapproval of Tayloe's dalliance with Burn, a man whose inferior status and fortune might diminish the status of the household of which she was a part? Was spreading the news of the dead child her means of enforcing the rules of a patriarchal society and thereby getting revenge against a domineering mistress? Or might her behavior be more accurately read as a protest against the destruction of a child, a maternalist rather than paternalist reaction that crossed racial boundaries? Lacking additional evidence, we cannot answer these questions with confidence. What is certain, however, is that Mary, Betty Mazey, and the Indian woman were divided by their place in both the Tayloe household and in colonial society at large; only with considerable effort did they bridge their differences to expose the wrongdoing of their mistress.

ALTHOUGH ELITE WOMEN IN Virginia enjoyed advantages of education and material comfort over their poorer and enslaved counterparts, they too were vulnerable to the growing institutionalization of patriarchal power in the eighteenth-century. Significantly, Anne Tayloe initially confronted patriarchy not in the persons of men, but in the gossip of women. As a result of the publicizing function of gossip, Tayloe's neighbors soon heard word of her misdeeds. She subsequently suffered the humiliation of the Lancaster justices' inquiry into the details of her menstruation, a legal intrusion that was at odds with her class privilege but in keeping with the colony's long history of regulating the sexual behavior of white women.

James Burn's outburst against the "p[ar]cell of murdereing bitches" was, in this context, a telling misreading of the women of the Tayloe plantation, the domestic politics of their household, and the means by which Tayloe's alleged infanticide became publicly known. Although they may have appeared to Burn to share a common interest in killing the child and hiding evidence of its death, the women of the Tayloe household seem to have had very different motives. Implicitly, if not explicitly, they supported the values of patriarchal law, collecting evidence and channeling it to individuals who could testify. They did so not as a collectivity, however, but as individuals whose interests in the activities of their mistress had been molded by their place in the household economy and their access to the legal system. Years of personal contact with Madam Tayloe, remembered, reimagined, and reinterpreted in whispered conversations among household members and neighbors, undoubtedly also shaped the motives of Mazey, Mary, and the Indian woman. Yet we can only speculate about these motives and the politics of the gossip in which they were embedded. Like James Burn, we are outsiders to this world, compelled to imagine its contours from court records that failed to acknowledge its existence or consider the significance of its internal politics.

NOTES

Portions of this essay first appeared in *Good Wives, Nasty Wenches, and Anxious Patriarchs: Gender, Race, and Power in Colonial Virginia* (Chapel Hill, 1996) and are reprinted here, in altered form, with the permission of University of North Carolina Press.

1. Throughout this essay, the term "Indian" refers to peoples resident in Virginia before the arrival of Europeans as well as the decendents of these indigenous populations.

2. This case involving Anne Tayloe's alleged bastardy and infanticide can be found in *Lancaster Orders 6*, September 9, 1714, pp. 68–76, Virginia State Library and Archives, Richmond, Virginia. For more information on the Tayloe family, see "Virginia State Papers: Resignation of John Tayloe from the Council," *Virginia Magazine of History and Biography* 17 (July 1909), 369–70. Tayloe likely was the wife of Joseph Tayloe, former clerk of the Lancaster Court, and the mother or stepmother of Joseph Tayloe Junior. By 1714 she was a widow.

3. My use of the term "female public" to describe the publicity and community resulting from gossip draws upon the following: Jurgen Habermas, *The Structural Transformation of the Public Sphere: An Inquiry into a Category of Bour-*

geois Society (Cambridge, Mass.: MIT Press, 1989); Nancy Fraser, "Rethinking the Public Sphere: A Contribution to the Critique of Actually Existing Democracy" in *Habermas and the Public Sphere*, ed. Craig Calhoun (Cambridge, Mass.: MIT Press, 1992), pp. 109–42; Arlette Farge, *Fragile Lives: Violence, Power and Solidarity in Eighteenth-Century Paris* (Cambridge, Mass.: Harvard University Press, 1993), pp. 13, 14, 20, 35. I am also indebted to Bonnie Smith for suggesting this term and Belinda Davis for helping me to define it. For a fuller discussion of this female mode of public life in Virginia, and for the history of gender and race in the colony, see Kathleen M. Brown, *Good Wives, Nasty Wenches, and Anxious Patriarchs: Gender, Race, and Power in Colonial Virginia* (Chapel Hill: University of North Carolina Press, 1996), chap. 9.

4. As such, the female public of eighteenth-century Virginia was considerably less autonomous and less capable of challenging the values of male public culture than Nancy Fraser's "subaltern counterpublic;" see Fraser, "Rethinking the Public Sphere," p. 123.

5. William Waller Hening, ed., *The Statutes at Large* (Richmond, Va.: S. Shepherd, 1809–23), October 23, 1705, III, pp. 238, 250, 298; see also ibid., April 1691, II, pp. 86–88; April 27, 1699, III, p. 172.

6. Ibid., October 25, 1710, III, p. 516. See also Lois Green Carr and Lorena S. Walsh, "The Planter's Wife: The Experience of White Women in Seventeenth-Century Maryland," *William and Mary Quarterly*, 3d ser., 25 (October 1977): 542–71; Brown, *Good Wives, Nasty Wenches*.

7. See, for example, Carole Shammas, "Black Women's Work and the Evolution of Plantation Society in Virginia," *Labor History* 26 (Winter 1985): 5–28; Lorena Walsh, "The Experiences and Status of Women in the Chesapeake, 1750–1775," in *The Web of Southern Social Relations: Women, Family, and Education*, ed. Walter J. Fraser et al. (Athens, Ga.: University of Georgia Press, 1985), pp. 1–18; Brown, *Good Wives, Nasty Wenches*.

8. *Lancaster Orders 6*, October 13, 1715, November 9, 1715, p. 114. James Burn was subsequently brought before the county court for riding through town on horseback, waving a sword, and allowing "a great concourse of Negroes to assemble at his plantacon." See ibid., p. 114, November 14, 1716, p. 162.

6

The Appropriation of Pleasure
in *The Magnetic Lady*

HELEN OSTOVICH

WHAT IS TRUE PLEASURE, and who is allowed to have it? Or rather, who is allowed to have *her*? In *The Magnetic Lady*, Ben Jonson reduces these questions to matters of gender and class, allegorizing pleasure as two nubile fourteen-year-old girls, one the heiress Placentia, the other her foster-sister and waiting-woman Pleasance. Both names suggest delights ranging from sweet amiability to sexual gratification, although neither girl offers much beyond her own ignorance in the way of personality. But then Jonson does not offer them as anything other than figures of male fantasy, to be contemplated and competed for in the presence of other men, ratifying and ranking male victories or losses. The girls are conventional objects of desire, tokens of economic and social exchange, female bodies whose reproductive powers men appropriate as vehicles for transmitting and securing property. These blanket binaries inhibit more complicated characterizations that might otherwise mitigate the satirical context. But they do allow Jonson to establish the rightness of this system of feminine "nature" in the service of masculine "culture" by showing what happens when a household of women reappropriates maternity and motherhood in the course of their own pursuit of independent pleasure or profit.

The very idea of women taking control of their own sexuality and procreativity threatens the dominant male order with illegitimate heirs that might topple the established rule. Although *The Magnetic Lady* develops the most explicit matriarchal takeover bid in all of Jonson's work, the most compelling image of that horror appears in Jonson's unfinished last play, *The Sad Shepherd*. There, the witch Maudlin describes the process by which her newly dead mother transmitted magic power to her through an embroidered belt. In relating this story to her own daughter, Maudlin implies that the matriarchal line will perpetuate itself through similar acts of female generation. The belt itself is both a sign and a product of sexual sovereignty:

> A Gypsan lady, and a right beldame,
> Wrought it by moonshine for me, and starlight,
> Upo' your grannam's grave, that very night
> We earthed her in the shades, when our dame Hecate
> Made it her gang-night over the kirkyard,
> With all the barkand parish-tikes set at her,
> While I sat whirland of my brazen spindle.
> At every twisted thrid my rock let fly
> Unto the sewster, who did sit me nigh,
> Under the town turnpike, which ran each spell
> She stitched in the work, and knit it well.
>
> (II.iii.39–49)

Independent female power emerges as malevolently unnatural, associated with howling dogs, eerie nights, and ghastly mortality. Hecate—originally goddess of women and nurturer of children, though by Jonson's day identified solely with witchcraft—presides over the graveyard scene with uncanny moonlight. The graveyard itself is "Under the town turnpike" at a crossroads, traditionally the site of hauntings. Perhaps as a sign of her alliance with mysterious female power and magical transformation, Hecate was often depicted as three bodies: Selene, the moon-driver linked with menstruation and pregnancy; Artemis, patroness of untamed nature, fertility, and childbirth; and an Erinys or Fury, an avenging underworld spirit bent on punishing men. The symbols carried by these figures—a torch, a serpent, a phallus, and a key[1]—signify attributes of masculine authority which Hecate appropriates for her own dark purposes (figure 6-1). The triple Hecate is a concept that Jonson links with the Three Fates, who spin, wind, and finally cut the thread of human life. The most remarkable and shocking evidence of maleficent witchcraft in *The Sad Shepherd* resides here in the phallic exercise of spindle and ejaculatory thread. This activity suggests the mimicry of male sexuality by women who not only exclude men but also usurp male privilege simply by redefining the spinster's tools, tokens of a woman's place.

A similar redefinition dominates *The Magnetic Lady*, where a governess, a nurse, and a midwife model themselves on the triple Hecate. Birthing, childcare, and other "smock-secrets" become powerful weapons in the hands of a cabal of middle-aged women who reinterpret female

FIGURE 6-1 Triple Hecate, or Diana triforme, bronze, Museo dei Conservatori, Rome, Italy. The triple figure holds five symbols, reading from left to right: a phallus, a torch, a serpent, and a lock (the buckle in one hand and the strap in the other). (Courtesy of Alinari/Art Resource, N.Y.)

sexual pleasure and fecundity for the biological and financial perpetua-
tion of the matriarchal line. Their engagement in these activities violates
orthodox expectations for their gender. Like the emasculating women
of *The Masque of Queens*, the hermaphroditic Ladies Collegiate of *Epicoene*,
and the chorus of ignorant she-critics in *The Staple of News*, they invite
conflicting responses from the (male) audience, who perceive a confed-
eracy of women bent on achieving power as both "threatening and lu-
dicrous" reversers of patriarchal control (Maurer, p. 247).

In *The Magnetic Lady*, the threat of the world turned upside down is
compounded by the implications of witchcraft in the inverted household hierarchy: servants rule their employer while scolding and brawling amongst themselves (Underdown, 1985b, pp. 118–19). The hero Compass describes members of Lady Loadstone's household as contentious,
"so diametrall / One to another, and so much oppos'd" (I.i.7–8) that they
cannot make it through half the day without quarrelling. In an age of
"anxious insistence on absolute sex difference," men were expected to
be sturdy and robust, and women to be soft, delicately tender, and sub-
missive (Parker, p. 61). Maleness implied autonomous thinking, clear
decisionmaking, and direct action, whereas femaleness signified its opposite: emotionality, dependence, indecisiveness, requiring control by
a male. Women's pursuit of their own pleasure or independence defied
the biblical notion of the "passive and obedient feminine role, legislated
by men as punishment for Eve's transgression," and certainly the "emerging English woman" of the early seventeenth century was discovering
ways of asserting her own equitable rights both in public and in private
(Millard, p. 144). But Jonson takes pains to demonstrate that traditional
gender binaries benefit society. Women who cannot conform undermine
the existing social structures, as Jonson makes clear in his depiction of
the effete males connected with the household. Although Lady Loadstone herself is first described as "a brave, bountifull Housekeeper, and
a vertuous Widow" (induction, 106–7), her femininity catches her in a
bind of contradictory gender roles. Despite her authority as head of a
household, she cannot exercise her power efficiently. She needs to find
a suitable husband for her niece Placentia, but cannot rely on her own
judgment. With the exception of Compass, the companion of her late
husband, Lady Loadstone's male advisers are vulgar, duplicitous, and
exploitative. Doctor Rut and Parson Palate, as their names imply, pass
judgments based on physical sensation. Her brother, Sir Moth Interest,
Placentia's financial trustee, only wants to retain control of his niece's
fortune whether the girl marries or not. Lady Loadstone is confused by
the competing versions of manliness among Placentia's suitors: Practice,
the lawyer whose real desire is for public office and who in any case
prefers the other girl, Pleasance; Sir Diaphanous Silkworm, the effemi-
nate courtier; and Bias, the money-grubbing underling who, for instant
cash in hand, would sell out Placentia's rights to her uncle. In fact, when
a *real* man, Captain Ironside, disrupts Placentia's birthday party by

throwing Sir Diaphanous's wine in his face and drawing his weapon in disgust at this "halfe man . . . perfum'd braggart" (III.ii.4–5), Lady Loadstone is so unnerved by the display of potent masculinity that she retires to her room in a near-suicidal swoon. There she remains virtually until the end of act IV, fueling prejudices against female authority by abdicating responsibility in the crises that assail her house.

This view of women, I hasten to say, does not square with the evidence of women's domestic power as wives and widows in the seventeenth century,[2] nor does it square with Jonson's depictions in other plays where the women develop fuller characters outside the satiric or ironic outline demanded by the plot. Although Lady Pecunia in *The Staple of News* is as empty and malleable a cipher as either of the two girls in *The Magnetic Lady*, Grace Welborne in *Bartholomew Fair* has sense and dignity. But then Grace refuses to become the kind of woman who supercedes a man's role as a head of household: she will not marry Cokes because she cannot respect him, even though she might gain control of his estate, "gouerne him, and enioy a friend, beside" (IV.iii.15; Jonson, 1925–52, vol. 6). Mistress Fitzdottrel of *The Devil Is an Ass* has endured matrimony to a fool; rather than demean herself by taking a lover, however, she prefers to take the other half of the political alternative that Grace rejects: to seize control of the estate which her husband has almost squandered away, and thus "govern him" as well. Perhaps the most fully developed woman of sense in Jonson is Prue in *The New Inn*, but the failure of that play on stage might have prompted a return to the more popular and demeaning views expressed in *The Magnetic Lady*.

The real power in Lady Loadstone's household is Polish, her female adviser and "sometime governing Gossip" (I.iii.41). Polish is the *hic mulier* or man–woman who determines to wrest her share of authority from a system that denies women the enjoyment of an "authoritative self" (Greene and Kahn, 1985a, p. 21). She has engineered the long-term plot that exploits female control of birthing and childcare and thereby subverts male control of marriageable virgins: fourteen years before, she had switched her own infant with the orphaned heiress, planning to profit eventually from the Steel family fortune. In devising this plan, Polish recognized the value of women as tokens of male pleasure, sexual and economic: "[Women] have no significant power or influence within a system which is controlled by men and works to their benefit. Men, not women, have the power to determine the value of women in the exchange and the meanings associated with them" (Greene and Kahn, 1985a, p. 7). That is, in a phallocentric culture, men appropriate female reproductive power and use it to affirm patriarchal law: the father names and possesses the child, and the woman is merely the "conduit of a relationship rather than a partner to it" (Krueger, p. 23). In her bid to appropriate pleasure for herself, Polish usurps the male appropriative function by assigning herself the right to name the child and place a value on her. But her construction of values is exposed as a lie by Compass, the superior male assigner of meaning, in a manipulative game that counters Polish's game and restores patriarchal law. The contest between Compass and Polish pits fertility, the sign of a woman's strength, against chastity, the male control of that strength (Parker, p. 59). Polish is outdone in this battle because the rules in place, despite her rearrangement of the details, are still male rules, and she cannot finally defeat the male construction of female duality and duplicity represented by her own daughter, false Pleasure, and corroborated by her foster-daughter, true Pleasure.

The true condition of Placentia, the false pleasure, is what really shapes each act of the play. And her true condition, not recognized until the end of act III, is that she is pregnant. In act I, Dr. Rut attributes her physical weakness and odd cravings to "greene sickness," the affliction of post-pubescent virgins with strong biological urges. Hence, the birthday-party assembly of suitors and the pressing need to fix a wedding-day. In act II, Dr. Rut decides her bloated abdomen is a *"Tympanites"*: "A wind bombe's in her belly, must be unbrac'd, / And with a Faucet, or a Peg, let out, / And she'll doe well: get her a husband" (II.iii.20–22). Pushed by Polish's desire for a titled alliance as well as by Placentia's apparently involuntary desire for a man, Lady Loadstone chooses Sir Diaphanous as the husband-to-be. Both Polish and Placentia seem to prefer him on the basis of his showy appearance and his influence at court. Placentia thinks "The Courtiers is the neater calling" (II.i.14), and Polish rhapsodizes: "O fine Courtier! / O blessed man! the bravery prick't out, / To make my dainty charge, a Vi-countesse! / And my good Lady, her Aunt, Countesse at large!" (II.iii.70–73).

At this point Jonson is playing on the conventional "saint or slut" duality in characterizing the two girls. The obscenity of Polish's description is very close to the surface: the courtier seems sexually well furnished ("prick't out"), or at least fashionably well equipped enough to turn a girl into a "Vi-countesse"—punning on "vice" and "cunt"—with the help of her "aunt," the common euphemism for "bawd." This same joke is repeated in a subsequent conversation between Placentia and Sir Diaphanous:

> PLACENTIA. And will you make me a Vi-countesse too? For,
> How doe they make a Countesse? in a Chaire?
> Or 'pon a bed?
> DIAPHANOUS. Both wayes, sweet bird, Ile shew you. (II.v.76–78).

While Sir Diaphanous teases Placentia with sexual jokes, Compass warns Pleasance directly against sexual involvement with his rival for her love, the lawyer Practice. Curiously enough, Compass's language is just as heavily—perhaps even more crudely—loaded with explicit sexual puns: "But keepe your right to your selfe, and not acquaint / A common Lawyer with your case. If hee / Once find the gap; a thousand will leape after" (II.vii.9–11). The assumption here is that an unsupervised virgin, once

initiated sexually, will devour all males in her path. Compass's unmer-
ited reprimand emphasizes the value placed on a bride's chastity. "Acquaint," "case," and "gap" all refer to the female pudenda, and "common" suggests engaging in brothel (or "leaping-house") traffic, in which
whores were called "common customers." Whereas Placentia's reception
of such language is ambivalent, Pleasance seems genuinely confused by
it: "This Riddle shewes / A little like a Love-trick, o' one face, / If I could
understand it. I will studie it" (II.vii.12–14).

The other parallel to this concern with illicit sexuality is Sir Moth
Interest's unnatural breeding of Placentia's money, which keeps com-
pounding and expanding, very like Placentia's abdomen. Sir Moth defends his usury as an imitation of human generation: "this present world
being nothing, / But the dispersed issue of the first one" (II.vi.58–9). The
equation between monetary increase and sexual generation, in which a
child is the interest on his father's investment, emphasizes the role of
women as bonds cementing the exchange of persons and property in
marriage (Shell, 1982, pp. 48–51). In a market-based society that views
women as valuable goods, the irresponsible woman who gives herself to
a lover without marriage transgresses patriarchally imposed norms designed to benefit her male guardians with additional property and family (Newman, 1991, pp. 133, 143). In act III, the violence at the dinner
table frightens Placentia into labor, and her value as a bride plummets.
Her labor ironically resolves the quarrel between Ironside and Sir Diaphanous, since the captain's attack on the unworthy suitor has provided
the evidence that saves Sir Diaphanous from an unworthy bride and
someone else's bastard. Like Sir Moth's illicitly generated funds, the girl
has proved to be "Of light gold. / . . . And crack't within the Ring"
(III.vii.19–20) and the child, a "slip" or counterfeit coin (III.vii.26, 27).
The male reaction to this news is to "laugh, and geere at all" (III.vii.10).

Jonson's jeering attitude toward the women in this play has been clear
all along. The critical framework of the play establishes the crucial goal
of subordinating female figures to male control. The printed play suggests an unusually respectful emphasis on women and their place by list-
ing the six female roles first in the *dramatis personae*, but this apparent
female priority over the male roles is an illusion soon dispelled. The induction and the choruses between the acts are arguments among men
clearly aimed at the privileged male audience. Here, as in most of the
play proper, women are either absent or silent. Of the two on-stage spectators, Damplay has been characterized as the unruly audience, unable
to discern true art from false and, like the women of the Loadstone household, twisting the evidence to suit his own pleasure. It is significant that
he is the only member of the chorus to object to what he calls "a pittifull
poore shift o' your Poet, *Boy*, to make his prime woman with child, and
fall in labour, just to compose a quarrell" (III.chorus.1–3). But Damplay's
attempted defense of women simply labels him unobservant and mistaken, as Jonson's theatrical spokesman, the Boy-apprentice, contemp-

tuously points out. Damplay's petulant reply, "I care not for marking the *Play*: Ile damne it" (III.chorus.19), stamps him as temperamentally feminine, illogical "Even to license, and absurdity" (III.chorus.26), in the Boy's words. The rational male audience is expected to discount Damplay's opinions.

From the male audience's point of view, Placentia embodies soulless, mindless fecundity, outside the meaning conferred by patriarchal control. Conception itself, according to medical theory since Galen, is a sign of female sexual pleasure, usually moderated within marriage; conception outside marriage suggests the excessive pleasure assumed to run rampant in whores and other bastard-bearers.[3] Placentia's belly, unsanctioned by holy matrimony, proclaims her fallen status; the shifting of her shape, like the shifting of her identity, announces her transgression of the laws of church and state. Act IV thus focuses on the delivery of the child and the concurrent travail of the gang of women—Polish, the nurse Keep, and the midwife Mother Chair—to protect Placentia and themselves from the consequences. They plan to deny the birth and convince Lady Loadstone that her niece has merely suffered "a fit o' the Mother" (IV.vii.29), that is, hysteria. The midwife is the chief organizer of this scheme: she has sent the baby to a wet nurse, prepared an herbal remedy that will get the new mother up and about, ordered the bed linen bleached, and calmed the frantic recriminations between Polish and Nurse Keep: "Come, come, be friends: and keepe these women-matters, / Smock-secrets to our selves" (IV.vii.40–41). Such secrecy among women, especially over childbirth, raises threats of false attribution of paternity, substitution of children, and infanticide, all skeletal fears Jonson rattles in the last two acts of the play. The fact that Placentia's baby is a boy increases the seriousness of such threats. Women's exclusive control of childbirth implies, as Adrienne Rich puts it, "a potentially dangerous or hostile act, a conspiracy, a subversion" of legitimate male rights (cited in Parker, p. 55). Further, the assumption that any midwife is a witch makes Mother Chair—that "Mother of Matrons" (IV.vii.18), "mighty Mother of Dames" (V.ii.21)—fit in neatly with the demonized motherhood articulated in Polish's and Keep's hysterical denunciations of each other as "witch," "Gipsey," "Hag," and "She-man-Divell" (IV.iv). Their innately female inability to control their emotions and their tongues is the loud and explicit means by which Compass learns their "horrid secret" (V.iv.31).

The motif of childbirth in act IV thus has issue on many levels: the true heiress, Pleasance, now drops into Compass's hands along with a valuable court appointment he has been expecting and even the delivery of a blank marriage license. Compass marries the girl and buys the support of the lawyer Practice with the reversion to the court office. Together they will prove Pleasance's right to the Steel fortune. Significantly, the focus on reproduction and who controls it has shifted: the female-controlled physical act has deviated into male-controlled economic and legal fact. The two mutually exclusive domains have their origins in gender and class, though both sides make the same claim to Lady Loadstone of having proof of her niece's purity. The crude wisewoman, Mother Chair, relies on natural magic to transform the evidence of childbirth into a statement of innocence; Polish hails her as a miracle worker in effecting Placentia's restoration to Lady Loadstone's good graces:

> CHAIR.   See, who's here? she'has beene with my Lady;
> Who kist her, all to kist her, twice or thrice.
>
> NEEDLE.   And call'd her Neice againe, and *view'd her Linnen*.
>
> POLISH.   You ha' done a Miracle, Mother *Chaire*.
>
> (V.ii.12–15)

But the gentleman-scholar Compass has his own magic that nullifies this miracle when he promises Lady Loadstone knowledge that will "render . . . / Your Neice a Virgin, and unvitiated" (IV.viii.53–54). The superior insights of males educated in the classical arts and sciences have from the beginning of the play quashed women's learning. Captain Ironside and Compass are Oxford graduates in philosophy and mathematics; even the Boy in the critical framework has studied Terence at Westminster (as had Jonson himself). In Polish's attempt to praise the religious learning of Placentia's putative mother, "witty Mrs. *Steele*" (I.v.31), she merely garbles references and exposes herself as laughably ignorant. Even Polish's name reflects only superficial worldly refinements in fashion and flattery, not the manly acquisition of hard knowledge. In traditional moral terms, the World, or Worldliness (Polish), and the Flesh (Mother Chair— *la chaire* is flesh in French, but her name also suggests the reproduction of the flesh in the birthing-chair), leagued in a devilish compact, are not proof against superior Wisdom. When these two modes of knowing conflict, the results are predictable. Nurse Keep is frightened by Compass's uncanny perspicacity: "I told it? no, he knowes it, and much more, / As he's a cunning man" (V.ix.16–17). Although Polish tries to dismiss him as "a cunning foole," she is finally unable to prevent his superior cunning from overriding her version of the true niece and heiress.

Act V completes the degradation of motherhood by demanding the name of the father. This exigency is both a routine call for responsible paternity and an amusingly Lacanian declaration of patriarchal law, which represses the mother in order to reassure itself about its masculine unity and identity (Furman, p. 73). At first, Polish attempts to protect her "world of secrets" by incarcerating the newly married Pleasance in an outhouse for kitchen trash—ideologically, another misplacing of daughter and birthright in the drama of switched identities. Pleasance is the only outsider-witness to the birth of Placentia's child and the only obstacle to Placentia's future security, even though Pleasance has no idea yet of the value of what she knows: "I know nothing / But what is told me; nor can I discover / Any thing" (V.ii.7–9). But after Pleasance is released from her imprisonment, she begins to learn about Polish's "Pretending to be Mother" (V.ix.3), and about Placentia's pretending *not* to be mother. When none of the gang of women will admit the truth of Pleasance's birth, Pleasance uses her knowledge of the other birth to expose the matriarchal plot. The charge is infanticide, metaphorical in Pleasance's case—in the sense that the life that should have been hers was "killed"—but feared literal in the case of Placentia's infant:

> COMPASS. Bring forth your Child, or I appeale you of murder,
> You, and this Gossip here, and Mother *Chaire.*
> CHAIR. The Gentleman's falne mad!
> > *Pleasance steps out.*
> PLEASANCE.   No, Mrs. Mid-wife.
> I saw the Child, and you did give it me,
> And put it i' my armes, by this ill token,
> You wish'd me such another; and it cry'd.
> PRACTICE. The Law is plaine; if it were heard to cry,
> And you produce it not, hee may indict
> All that conceale't, of Felony, and Murder.
>
> > > > (V.x.68–76)

Pleasance's complicity with patriarchal power is what finally defeats Polish's conspiracy of women. Although Pleasance's act may seem to glorify feminine virtue, in fact she simply celebrates her subjugation in marriage and the domestic sphere delegated to wives. Her victory ironically completes the suppression of her self begun by Polish fourteen years before: Pleasance colludes in the appropriation of her own birthright in order to enhance the male authority to which she willingly submits. Here, more cogently than at any other point in the play, Jonson shatters the illusion of female power by co-opting a woman to strike the final blow.

Although the false Placentia remains silent, her mother Polish confesses and names Needle, Lady Loadstone's steward and tailor. Jonson has constructed a double gibe here at women's judgment. The first jeer is at women's work, needlework. The needle had, by 1630, become a signifier of sexual difference: women embroidered to promote the feminine virtues of chastity, humility, and obedience—recall Maudlin's embroidered belt as the deliberate inversion of those feminine virtues— and "Few men would risk jeopardising their sexual identity by claiming a right to the needle" (Parker, p. 81). As a *woman*'s tailor, moreover, Needle is already trivialized and his sexual exploits reduced to a small prick. The second jeer targets women's perspicacity. In *Discoveries*, Jonson mocked certain bad poets as frivolous jinglers:

> Others there are, that have no composition at all; but a kind of tuning, and rhyming fall, in what they write. It runs and slides, and only makes a sound. Women's poets, they are called; as you have women's tailors.
> > They write a verse, as smooth, as soft, as cream;
> > In which there is no torrent, nor scarce stream.
>
> > > > (880–86)

Jonson sees these inadequate versifiers—would-be poets—as merely mimicking and thus undermining the privileged position of true poets, in the same way that unruly women—would-be men—ape and sabotage male behavior in their attempts to disrupt patriarchal control. This clown-ish repetition by inferiors temporarily displaces the worthy originals by challenging, even ridiculing, the assumption that the established author-ity is supreme, genuine, and inimitable.

The embroidery references are thus pertinent to the play in establish-ing the difference between true art and false, true judgment and false, and hence true pleasure and false. In the induction of *The Magnetic Lady*, Jonson tells us: "A good *Play*, is like a skeene of silke: which, if you take by the right end, you may wind off, at pleasure . . . how you will: But if you light on the wrong end, you will pull all into a knot, or elfe-locke; which nothing but the sheers, or a candle will undoe, or separate" (in-duction, 136–41). In the chorus that ends act IV, Damplay complains that the poet has "almost pucker'd, and pull'd into that knot" the whole thread of his argument. But as act V demonstrates, the male poet has controlled his material, and as Compass says: "I ha' the right thred now, and I will keepe it" (V.x.81). It is the household of women who have puckered the thread and pulled all into a knot that must now be cut out. By implication, women who refuse to devote themselves to women's work end up unfitted for any role. Although Polish defends her strata-gems as her "right" and "power" as a mother, Compass denies her gen-der identity: "Out, Hag. / Thou that hast put all nature off, and woman" (V.ix.5–6). When she claims, "Love to my Child, and lucre of the por-tion / Provok'd me" (V.x.86–87), she claims no more than what moti-vated any of the men to compete for either girl's hand, but the fact of her gender displaces her argument. Although Polish had managed to get Placentia married to Bias with a settlement of £10,000, Jonson ironically straightens Bias out, patriarchally speaking. Bias repudiates the bargain, refusing to "take a wife, / To pick out Mounsieur *Needles* basting threds" (V.x.115–6).

Sir Moth Interest is also snagged in the threads of his own making. His wayward lust for money, aroused in act V to feverish intensity, con-tinues to parallel Placentia's misguided sexuality, with Needle as the misleader who causes both their falls. Needle wants to reconcile the dif-ferences that have arisen among Lady Loadstone, Sir Moth, and Dr. Rut as a result of Placentia's misdiagnosed pregnancy. Needle pretends to suffer from walking and talking in his sleep so that Rut may demonstrate his medical competence by curing the tailor. Needle's condition is thought to be prophetic: "Hee'll tell us wonders" (V.v.1), Dr. Rut prom-ises. The "wonders" concern messages from the ghost of a city alderman's widow, who, for love of Sir Moth, had supposedly buried £300,000 in the garden, and dropped another £600,000 down the well. The planting of the money in the muck both parodies natural propagation and sullies it: Interest tries to harvest the coins by pulling "these five peices [*sic*] /

Vp, in a fingers bredth one of another" but "The durt sticks on 'hem still" (V.vii.62–64), thus emblematizing Compass's already expressed opinion that Sir Moth's "thoughts" are "Baser then money" (IV.iii.51–52). Interest's decision to go down the well for the larger sum of money burlesques, even more broadly, the merging of voracious sexual and economic appetites, and their material issue in "the possession of a fortune . . . newly drop't him" (V.x.4–5). As Interest remarks, in a testament to his own prowess: "There never did accrew / So great a gift to man, and from a Lady, / I never saw but once" (V.vii.83–85).

When Interest climbs into the bucket to enter the well, the chain breaks, and he falls ignominiously into the water, a nightmare of the greedy man swallowed by the object of his consuming desire, the libidinous man engulfed by the monstrously feminized "conduit" of his lusts. Needle delivers the old man from the well in a mock rebirth that echoes the earlier childbirth, with its comment on the result of precipitate and insatiable passion. The fact that Interest was seduced into this fall by the thought of a woman he met at "Merchants-Taylors-hall, at dinner, / In *Thred-needle* street" (V.vii.86–87) links his illicit hungers to the other needlework allusions in the play. He admits finally that he trapped himself in "nets of cous'nage" spun out of his own avarice: "each thred is growne a noose: / A very mesh" (V.x.109–11). Compass, however, holds on tight to "the right thred," his bride Pleasance and her £16,000 portion, with interest, even though he coerced the parson into marrying them unlawfully in noncanonical hours.

Why, you may ask, does Compass win Pleasance, the true Pleasure? Metaphorically, pleasure is the true pole to which the compass needle points when it enters a lodestone's magnetic field. The compass needle, according to William Barlow's *Magneticall Aduertisements* (1616) is "the most admirable and vsefull instrument of the whole world" and its substance "ought to be pure steele, and not iron. For most assuredly steele will take at the least tenne times more vertue then iron can doe, but especially if it hath his right temper" (pp. 66–67). (Jonson cites Barlow as a popular source of magnetic knowledge at I.iv.5.) A compass's circular shape (figure 6.2) makes it "most fit to be vsed for the obseruation of the variation alone" (Barlow, p. 69), that is, for surveying a whole plot accurately without the directional points marked on a compass card. In Compass, then, Jonson creates a character whose status over the course of the play is already allegorically confirmed. Captain Ironside is another predictable winner in the magnetic context; Barlow explains that a lodestone should be capped and set in an iron mold in order to protect its power. Although Needle certainly obeyed the first principle of magnetic motion, mutual attraction, or *coition* (in fact, obeyed it too literally) Barlow's experiments with the "common sowing needle," a lodestone, and a thread indicate that these just prove attraction and repulsion without the compass-needle's versatility and responsiveness (Barlow, pp. 21–28). Needle is essentially outclassed.

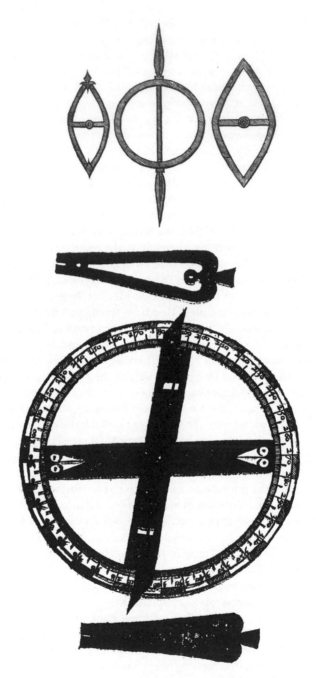

FIGURE 6-2 *Magneticall Advertisements*. (Top) Compass-needles. Barlow prefers the middle model, which is effective without a compass-card. (By permission of the Folger Shakespeare Library). (Bottom) Compass card with Barlow's design for a more exact needle. (By permission of the Folger Shakespeare Library.)

Polish is, of course, discredited by her gender and her class from effective participation in the magnetic metaphor, even though she is more than once called a "fly," a term for the compass card (figure 6-2). Barlow points out that, if the combined weight of the compass needle and the fly presses too heavily on the pin connecting them to the lodestone, then the motion of the fly will be dull and uncertain, and hence the fly itself will be unreliable as an analytical tool (Barlow, p. 71). Polish's behavior indicates that she cannot compete effectively under pressure: she can act as a guide in plotting only some, but not all, of the angles. Other meanings of "fly" elaborate on her inadequacy as a surveying instrument. As a parasite, "with her buz, / Shee blowes on every thing, in every place!" (V.vii.1–2), and as a demonic incarnation, she is "good at malice; good at mischiefe; all / That can perplexe, or trouble a busines, throughly" (V.vi.11–12). Discretion, not simply direction, in seeking true pleasure is what divides the deserving from the undeserving. Pleasure merely draws men into competition—whether to enjoy legal rights or social privileges, to arouse scholarly wit or soldierly valor, or to delight in material possession or physical sensation. Just as the lodestone identifies metals with natural magnetic force, so pleasure itself becomes the testing ground that separates men of true mettle from false. The victor is the one who is best able to contain and control pleasure's magnetic pull until he measures its purely objective value.

What is true of the design of the inner play is also true of Jonson's construction of the entire play. The magnetic device Jonson has in mind is the mariner's compass, a navigational tool which consists of a box, a compass card, and a magnetized needle turning freely on a pivot. In simple terms, the analogy works as follows. The frame-play is the box of a mariner's compass. It contains the compass card or inner play, which measures the diverse desires of Lady Loadstone's household by displaying various directional goals. Compass, as the poet's mouthpiece in the inner play, is the true guide to social and economic pleasure, just as the Boy in the frame-play is the playwright's mouthpiece and true guide to theatrical pleasure. In plotting the course of the inner play, Jonson shows the household of women guided back to patriarchal rule by Compass's discovery of the true heiress and exposure of the false heiress. In the frame, the Boy guides the audience to the discovery of Jonson's art: Probee is the man of probity, guided by and eventually espousing Jonson's idea of true comedy; Damplay is exposed as inadequate and unruly, because he will not accept the poet's judgment as superior to his own. The mariner's compass, then, promises— to those who view it correctly—the satisfaction of correctly reached destinations. Jonson's play promises the same pleasure. Hope of pleasure draws the spectators to the theater, just as it draws the suitors to Lady Loadstone's house. And the theater, like the two girls, offers the occasion to test the powers of discrimination, an option reserved for male participants.

Although their bodies are magnetic, Placentia and Pleasance themselves are entirely passive, giving no readily interpretable signs of their actual desires or responses. Placentia never utters a word during her labor and childbirth—a remarkable feat of endurance that few women could emulate. Pleasance reveals none of her feelings about Polish, Lady Loadstone, or the rights she has been denied through changing places with Placentia. Even when Compass asks her to trust and obey him without question, she simply replies, "With you the world ore" (IV.v.17). She makes no outcry at their furtive wedding ceremony nor at her later imprisonment by Polish. Marguerite Waller traces a similar pattern of female absence in Thomas Wyatt's sonnets: the women in the text vanish, only registering as fetishes that allow for the emergence of a dominant male who can remove obstacles and appropriate what he desires (Waller, p. 177). Structurally, Jonson's text embeds crises of female purity within an overarching plot of male competition. The true heiress justifies the wit of her victorious suitor with her virtues of devotion, chastity, and subservience, and retrieves what she has lost simply by waiting.[4] Her value, her honor as a female, is measured by what she lacks: sexuality and volition (Fisher, 1989, p. 76). Since the false heiress cannot provide the same empty unsexualized body, she cannot serve as a pretext for, or enhancer of, male social exchange. Richard Brathwaite shares this conclusion when he advises: "Now (gentlewomen) . . . if you prefer honor before pleasure or what else is dear or tender, your fame will find wings to fly with. This will gain you deserving suitors. Portion may woo a worldling, proportion a youthful wanton, but it is virtue that wins the heart of discretion" (p. 250).

Pleasure, whether true or false, is not a woman's prerogative in *The Magnetic Lady*. What strikes a female audience of Jonson's play most insistently is the complete nullification of a woman's point of view. Although pregnancy and childbirth have been the chief physical correlatives of the struggle to emerge victoriously on the social and economic scene, the infant itself never appears on stage. For the playwright and his male audience, the metaphors presumably make the point by dismissing female power as merely physical and thus contemptibly comical; for women in the audience, especially those who have given birth, the baby *is* the point. Nevertheless, the play ultimately shrugs off mother and child. Placentia's fate rests entirely at the discretion of the patriarchy that condemns her as worthless. Coupled with Needle, who can neither provide for her nor marry her, she awaits the verdict of Captain Ironside, Lady Loadstone's new husband. The childless widow and the virginal child are appropriated by the strongest and wiliest males, who aggrandize themselves by putting "the magic stamp of men's meaning" (Jones, 1985, p. 99) on their women's passivity and silence. The mothers are disempowered and cast down, if not out. In the patriarchal victory that ends the play, their final place is simply not important.

NOTES

1. As in the triple Hecate in Margarete Bieber, *Ancient Copies: Contributions to the History of Greek and Roman Art* (New York: New York University Press, 1977), plate 71, "Decorative Symmetry on Roman Hekateia," fig. 431 and 432. I am grateful to my daughter Ellis Ostovich for locating these telling representations for me. For another view of women, witchcraft, and the appropriation of the phallus, see Cotton, especially pp. 321–22.

2. See Margaret J. M. Ezell, *The Patriarch's Wife: Literary Evidence and the History of the Family* (Chapel Hill and London: University of North Carolina Press, 1987), chap. 1 and 2. Ezell points out that widows usually arranged their daughters' marriages and also often acted as executors of the estates (p. 18); in fact, the women of both families of prospective in-laws, supported by friends of the family, did most of the factfinding and decisionmaking in arranging matches throughout the seventeenth century (pp. 21–22). In chap. 2, she argues that women in private were very powerful; although patriarchalism seemed rigid in public institutions, in *domestic* life, it was challenged, argued, and undermined by both men and women. Women's legal power was also being asserted in increasingly large numbers of suits brought by women in consistory courts or in chancery; on the issue of the wife's separate estate and on trusts, see Maria Cioni, *Women and Law in Elizabethan England with Particular Reference to the Court of Chancery* (New York: Garland, 1985), chap. 4; and Amy Louise Erickson, *Women and Property in Early Modern England* (London and New York: Routledge, 1993), on how inheritance affects unmarried women and widows (parts II and IV).

3. For the historical view of paternity suits and other effects of illegitimate births, including the incidence of abortion and infanticide, see Susan Amussen, *An Ordered Society: Gender and Class in Early Modern England* (London: Basil Blackwell, 1988), chap. 4, especially pp. 111–18. For popular views of conception, see Angus McLaren, *Reproductive Rituals: The Perception of Fertility in England from the Sixteenth Century to the Nineteenth Century* (London: Methuen, 1984), chap. 1, especially p. 16. For other theatrical treatments of culpable sexuality and conception, see Coppélia Kahn, "Whores and Wives in Jacobean Drama," in *In Another Country: Feminist Perspectives on Renaissance Drama*, ed. Dorothea Kehler and Susan Baker (Metuchen, N.J.: Scarecrow Press, 1991), especially pp. 248–53.

4. I have reapplied Krueger's argument concerning the structure of medieval French "wager" romances, "Double Jeopardy," in *Seeking the Woman in Late Medieval and Renaissance Writings*, ed. Sheila Fisher and Janet E. Halley (Knoxville: University of Tennessee Press, 1989), pp. 26–30.

7

Female Alliance and the
Construction of Homoeroticism
in *As You Like It* and *Twelfth Night*

. . . .

JESSICA TVORDI

IN THE DRAMATIC LITERATURE staged during the early modern period
in England, female characters frequently form primary alliances with
other women—alliances characterized by friendship, familial duty, socioeconomic dependence, service, the rejection of heterosexuality, and,
in some cases, homoerotic desire. Although these alliances are often central to the plays that depict them, they are frequently dissolved in order
to bring about heterosexual pairings, that work to limit female autonomy
both socially and sexually. Rarely is there an effort by these female characters to resist this heterosexual imperative and acknowledge a space that
privileges female alliances outside its purview. The alliances formed by
Celia and Rosalind in *As You Like It* and Maria and Olivia in *Twelfth Night*
are representative of this resistance. Characterized by a combination of
female loyalty and socioeconomic dependence, the participants in these
relationships support one another in the face of male challenges to female authority, and they rely upon one another to secure their positions
within social and economic hierarchies. Whereas Rosalind and Olivia turn
away from the security of the female alliance toward relationships with
men, Celia and Maria oppose Rosalind's and Olivia's interests in heterosexual involvements, revealing that they are thoroughly invested in their
friendships and are willing to take extreme measures to maintain them.
Their motivation for such resistance is tied both to the socioeconomic

importance of these friendships and to the intense emotional and, as I will argue throughout this chapter, erotic attachment to the other woman, an attachment most obvious in the case of Celia. Although these female alliances are problematized by the fact that *As You Like It* and *Twelfth Night* seem to mark them as invalid through the plays' inevitable movement toward marriage, Celia and Maria challenge and refigure the plays' heterosexual imperatives.

While female alliances are featured in a number of early modern literary texts, with the exception of the work of Valerie Traub, Harriette Andreadis, and Katherine Park, studies of homoeroticism have been largely limited to male homosocial institutions in early modern England. Male same-sex acts have more frequently found their way into early modern juridical literature, and the tradition of male homoeroticism, especially its representation on the early modern transvestite stage, has long been recognized by literary scholars. Like male homoerotic desire, female homoerotic desire is an area worthy of study because it enables us to see the complexities of desire within a fairly rigid sex-gender system that frequently forces heterosexual alliances upon both men and women. Female homoeroticism, however, remains less accessible than male homoeroticism because it was seldom articulated in print. Many early scholarly discussions of gender and sexuality in early modern literature began with a reexamination of the function of the transvestite figure and addressed the possibility of how that figure might illuminate studies of female homoeroticism.[1] The female transvestite's activities, however, tend to highlight the potential for male characters—*As You Like It*'s Orlando and *Twelfth Night*'s Orsino, for example—to cross erotic boundaries through their interactions with the transvestite figure rather than to illuminate discussions of the representation of female sexuality. Female transvestite figures in Shakespeare's plays are primarily interested in heterosexual relationships, and their engagement in activities that are limiting both for themselves and for other women often works to dissolve the female homosocial or homoerotic alliance.[2]

A number of scholars have begun to look beyond the transvestite figure in their analysis of female homoerotic desire in the early modern period. Valerie Traub (1994) has suggested that the erotic verbal displays of a number of Shakespeare's most "feminine" heroines, including Celia, rival those of his plays' heterosexual couples. This language of desire is an important key to uncovering the erotic aspects of female alliances; even more important, however, are the negotiations that such characters engage in both inside and outside the female alliance. For Traub, the difficulty of teasing out female homoeroticism is due in part to the fact that the "palpable 'femininity' of these characters blinds us . . . to the eroticism evident in their language of desire" (p. 80). Traub asserts that "the 'femme' woman . . . challenged neither gender roles nor reproductive imperative" (p. 79) and it is on this point that my discussion of female homoerotic desire departs from hers. Although the behavior of

Celia and Maria is deceptively "feminine" in comparison with the "masculine" performances of the transvestite figure, each represented woman directly challenges masculinist constructs of feminine subjectivity by transgressing accepted boundaries of gender, sexuality, and power, both in their interactions with Rosalind and Olivia and with other characters.

When considering how heterosexuality regulates women's erotic practice, it is relatively easy for many feminists to accept that power struggles exist between men and women who form socioerotic alliances. There is a tendency, however, among some lesbian feminist scholars to ignore power differences exercised within female alliances; or, if such struggles are acknowledged, they are characterized as demonstrations of culturally learned behavior that is essentially patriarchal in nature.[3] If we desentimentalize female homoerotic alliances—if we recognize that Celia's behavior toward Rosalind is manipulative and combative, and that Maria's attempts to interfere in the romantic affairs of Olivia reflect her desire to retain her importance within Olivia's household—then the erotic and political dynamics of such relationships reemerge. Because the only institution in which early modern women consistently exercised authority was within the home, focusing on household governance reveals that a woman's negotiation of power within the domestic power structure was similar to a man's negotiation of power in the public sphere. If the regulation of power and sexuality constituted the central issues of the early modern household, the various struggles that such regulation invited necessarily affected homosocial and homoerotic relationships among women.

The alliances of Celia and Rosalind and Maria and Olivia differ significantly in respect to class: the alliance of Rosalind and Celia is drawn from a model of same-sex friendship, stressing their similarities and their shared experiences as women of the same class; the alliance of Olivia and Maria is based upon a model of same-sex service. Celia and Rosalind are first cousins and thus members of the same class, although their social status in relation to one another changes during the play. Maria and Olivia are a gentlewoman and a countess, and although Maria manages to elevate her class status through her marriage to Sir Toby Belch, her position is still fixed beneath that of Olivia. The alliances of Celia and Rosalind and Maria and Olivia also differ significantly with respect to the degree of homoerotic expression: while Celia continually voices her love for Rosalind, Maria shows her complete devotion to her mistress through actions, not words. Although the absence of female homoerotic discourse in *Twelfth Night* suggests that Celia's and Maria's shared experiences do not include same-sex love, the relationship in *Twelfth Night* is full of silences that become meaningful if we use *As You Like It* to map what occurs before *Twelfth Night* begins or what is presented as occurring offstage. The friendship of Celia and Rosalind suggests ways to read the domestic alliance of Maria and Olivia, an alliance heretofore unexamined for its homoerotic potential in a notably queered play. *As You Like It*'s investment in heterosexuality jeopardizes the female homoerotic alliance of Celia and Rosalind, while *Twelfth Night*'s relative uninterest in promoting heterosexual norms enables a more positive treatment of the female homosocial alliance of Maria and Olivia, opening up a space for female homoeroticism.

Many scholars have recognized the importance of Rosalind's and Celia's friendship in *As You Like It*, but few have considered Celia's erotic agency within this alliance.[4] Although Rosalind's appropriation of male power through her masculine disguise as Ganymede appears transgressive, Celia's verbal displays of her love for Rosalind and her attempts to coerce Rosalind into a homoerotic alliance are more so. Throughout the course of the play, Celia demonstrates no interest in heterosexual relationships and speaks frequently of her love for Rosalind. Rosalind is virtually silent about her love for Celia, and she eventually abandons that alliance to pursue a relationship with Orlando. Yet Celia is far from silent and compliant. Royal Shakespeare Company actors Fiona Shaw and Juliet Stevenson note that "it is clearly Celia . . . who leads and drives the [opening] scenes" of *As You Like It*, noting "that the rhythms of her language are very indicative of a confident, even assertive, young woman" (Shaw and Stevenson, p. 59). Indeed in pursuing her alliance with Rosalind, Celia materializes not only as confident and assertive, but also as a character who aggressively, and sometimes ruthlessly, woos the object of her desire and who persistently resists the play's movement away from the ideal of the female homoerotic alliance.

Celia's and Rosalind's alliance is presented in the tradition of same-sex friendship similar to the girlhood friendships of Hermia and Helena in *A Midsummer Night's Dream* and Emilia and Flavina in *The Two Noble Kinsmen*. While these alliances are characterized as friendships, they are described with language that is emotionally and erotically charged. Helena, for example, describes herself and Hermia as being "Like to a double cherry, seeming parted, / But yet a union in partition, / Two lovely berries moulded on one stem" (III.ii.209–11). Emilia's description of her alliance with Flavina provides an equally erotic rendering of the oneness she and her friend experienced: "The flow'r that I would pluck / And put between my breasts (O then but beginning / To swell about the blossom), she would long / Till she had such another, and commit it / To the like innocent cradle, where phoenix-like / They died in perfume" (I.iii.66–71).[5] Celia makes a declaration similar to those of Helena and Emilia that reveals the intensity of her attachment to Rosalind: "We still have slept together, / Rose at an instant, learn'd, play'd, eat together, / And whereso'er we went, like Juno's swans, / Still we went coupled and inseparable" (I.iii.69–72).[6]

Celia initially depicts her alliance with Rosalind as intensely loyal, loving, and completely reciprocal. By employing the image of "Juno's swans . . . coupled and inseparable" to describe her relationship with Rosalind, Celia suggests that, like swans who have mated for life, she and Rosalind are united in a permanent alliance. If we read Celia's statement carefully, the possibility emerges that she views her alliance with Rosalind as not only close, but physical, not only as a pairing, but as a permanent, lifelong attachment. Moreover, Celia's description of this relationship is reinforced by two other characters in the play: Charles, who remarks that "never two ladies loved as they do" (I.i.112), and Le Beau, who similarly notes that their "loves are dearer than the natural bonds of sisters" (I.iii.265–66). While both statements are ambiguous, each suggests that Celia's and Rosalind's love for one another surpasses the accepted boundaries of communion between women.

In spite of these representations of the female alliance as firmly reciprocal, there is little evidence during the course of the play to support such claims. Le Beau states that Rosalind is "here detained by her usurping uncle / To keep his daughter company" (I.ii.264–65), and his further discussion of Duke Frederick's anger over the peoples' sympathy for Rosalind's plight (267–73) suggests that if Rosalind is kept under Duke Frederick's surveillance she can pose no threat to his rule. If Rosalind is embroiled in a silent power struggle with her uncle, she is also enacting a similar struggle with Celia, who impersonates her father's authority in order to control Rosalind. While Celia attempts to maintain this female alliance, Rosalind proves a lukewarm participant. When Rosalind replies to Celia's questions concerning Rosalind's lack of mirth, Rosalind reveals that she is an unwilling subject to her uncle's rule and her cousin's love: "Unless you could teach me to forget a banished father, you must not learn me how to remember any extraordinary pleasure" (I.ii.3–6). If Rosalind is going to forget the physical loss of her father and "remember any extraordinary pleasure," she must also forget the loss of privileges that she enjoyed as the daughter of the rightful duke and as the heir to his kingdom. Although Rosalind mourns the emotional loss of her father, she also acknowledges her preoccupation with the political aspect of her dilemma when she eventually complies with Celia's wishes: "I will forget the condition of my estate, to rejoice in yours" (14–15). Through Rosalind's display of longing for Duke Senior, Celia is quick to observe that their love for one another is unequal: "thou lov'st me not with the full weight that I love thee" (7–8). Rosalind's preoccupation with the loss of her father and the implications of that loss suggest that the weight of Rosalind's love for Celia has changed since Rosalind was demoted at court. These hierarchical differences reveal that this alliance is not reciprocal; it is strained and, as a result, in a perpetual state of negotiation.

Celia's various actions throughout the play suggest a desperate effort to recover the relationship that she herself is guilty of mythologizing. In an attempt to restore her alliance with Rosalind, Celia exercises her authority as her father's heir in two ways: first, Celia uses subtle forms of manipulation that represent both women as equal, thus veiling her own power; and second, she directly challenges Rosalind's authority by displaying her power openly. Whether denying the difference of power or bringing attention to it, Celia's goal is to use her political power to negotiate the gap between her own desires and those of Rosalind. As a result, Celia's political and erotic motives become permanently entangled. For example, when Celia suggests to Rosalind that the present and past power differences in their relationship are inconsequential—when Celia promises Rosalind that she will "render thee again in affection" (19) what Duke Frederick has taken away from her—she offers to restore Rosalind's power in exchange for Rosalind's love. Celia takes this manipulation a step further by elucidating her love for Rosalind through her lack of interest in romantic involvements with men—an uninterest that Celia attempts to make Rosalind adopt. When Rosalind asks Celia, "what think you of falling in love?" (24), Celia responds with some cautionary advice about the dangers of falling in love with a man: "Marry I prithee do, to make sport withal. But love no man in good earnest, nor no further in sport neither, than with safety of a pure blush thou mayst in honour come off again" (25–28). Celia's willingness to discuss heterosexual love is conditional: it is a subject for sport, not serious contemplation. Although Celia appears to be offering Rosalind friendly advice, she is conveying a veiled directive. If Rosalind sports no further than "the safety of a pure blush," she will maintain her virginity, her place within the realm of the female homoerotic, and her subservient position to Celia.

While Rosalind continues to deny this female alliance, Celia continues to stress the importance of their relationship. When Celia's more subtle forms of erotic negotiation fail to draw Rosalind away from her heterosexual desires, Celia resorts to more overt displays of power. Rosalind's first meeting with Orlando—which provides a real, rather than a hypothetical, male sexual threat to Celia's desires—forces Celia to display her power directly. After Orlando has been banished by Duke Frederick, Celia again asks Rosalind to explain her misery. When Rosalind reveals that she no longer thinks of her father, but of her "child's father" (I.iii.11), Celia mocks Rosalind, calling her affection for Orlando "burs . . . thrown upon thee in holiday foolery" (13–14) and orders her to "hem them away" (18). Throughout this scene, Celia expresses her contempt for Rosalind's interest in heterosexual love: Celia demands that Rosalind "wrestle with [her] affections" (20) and questions the possibility of Rosalind's falling so quickly "into so strong a liking" (25) of Orlando. Agnes Latham, the editor of the Arden edition of *As You Like It*, suggests that Celia, in using the word "liking," "can't quite bring herself to say love" (p. 24, n. 25); however, the *OED* lists "pleasure," "fleshly liking," and "one's beloved," among possible meanings of "liking," suggesting that Celia is entirely conscious of the sexual desires and emotional feelings that Rosalind harbors for Orlando.

Rosalind's dazzling display of masculine agency in the Forest of Arden tends to obscure Celia's own self-determining speech and actions, both at court and in exile. At court, Celia clearly articulates her desires, while Rosalind remains silent until prodded. While Rosalind quietly pleads her case before Duke Frederick, Celia directly challenges the authority of her father. When they both face exile, it is Celia who contrives their escape as Rosalind stands by seemingly helpless. Rosalind's suggestion that she dress herself as a man to aid their escape is the first moment of agency that the play allows her, and it is at this point that the configuration of power in their relationship shifts. Rosalind seizes the opportunity to reconstruct herself, casting off the image of one who is silent and power-less by assuming a male persona that enables her to take charge of her own desires. These disguises are initially liberating for Celia because they allow her to hold onto the hope of reclaiming their alliance outside the confines of her father's court. What Celia fails to realize is that her alli-ance with Rosalind depends entirely upon their remaining within the court, where Celia still exercises some power over Rosalind. Once in exile, Rosalind, dressed in male attire and posing as Celia's brother, will no longer be under her control. However much their escape appears to be a joint venture, Rosalind is now in charge. Rosalind is no tyrant, but her crossing over into another gender forces Celia into a performance of female subservience that she has not consciously sought; moreover, it enables Rosalind to extricate herself from an unwanted and unequal alliance.

Throughout her stay in the Forest of Arden, Celia alternates between compliance and resistance: her silence during Rosalind's manipulations of others is in keeping with her subservient gender role as Ganymede's sister Aliena, but her verbal defiance when she is alone with Rosalind recalls the power she exerted at court. In the presence of Orlando, Celia reluctantly complies with Rosalind's demand that she play the role of preacher at the mock wedding of Rosalind and Orlando. After Orlando exits, however, Celia retaliates in a violent verbal display that seems to anticipate a physical attack. Celia directly admonishes Rosalind for ag-gressively pursuing her heterosexual interests by confronting the issue of Rosalind's sexuality: "You have simply misused our sex in your love-prate. We must have your doublet and hose plucked over your head, and show the world what the bird hath done to her own nest" (IV.i.191–94). As Celia threatens to remove Rosalind's male clothing, she threat-ens to expose Rosalind's private parts—both her "head" and her "nest," which are slang for the female genitalia.[7] By aggressively pursuing Orlando, Rosalind has violated "her own nest," metaphorically relin-quishing her virginity; however, because Celia sees herself and Rosalind as one (I.iii.93), Celia implies that Rosalind has violated her as well.

When Rosalind defends her affection for Orlando as having "an un-known bottom" like the Bay of Portugal (197–8), Celia points out that Rosalind's love is actually "bottomless, that as fast as you pour affection in, it runs out" (199–200). Celia quickly transforms Rosalind's metaphor for the vastness of her love for Orlando into another reference to Rosalind's private parts. Peter F. Mullany has associated Celia's use of "bottomless" with the popular Renaissance joke about the bottomless vagina. Mullany's illustration of Spenser's use of this joke in *The Faerie Queene* represents the vagina as a foul pit; moreover, his discussion of the Bay of Portugal in relation to Shakespeare's Sonnet 137—"the bay where all men ride"— suggests unlicensed sexuality (Mullany, 1973, pp. 51–53). Within the context of this scene, Celia's use of "bottomless" suggests not only that Rosalind is fickle, but is sexually accessible, which seems to be confirmed by Rosalind's own admission that she plans "to sigh till he [Orlando] come" (207).[8] Through Rosalind's language of sexual anticipation, Celia recognizes that Rosalind can easily exchange one love object for another, that Orlando has earned her own place in Rosalind's heart, and that he will soon enjoy the access to Rosalind's body that Celia desires.

After Rosalind's final rejection of Celia, the play effectively silences Celia, who temporarily disappears from the text. During her absence we discover that she is engaged to Orlando's brother, Oliver, a surprising admission in light of her devotion to Rosalind. It is also surprising that *As You Like It*, a play that seems so preoccupied with the intricacies of courtship, should fail to display the erotic negotiations of Celia and Oliver. In much the same way that Celia's and Rosalind's relationship was first revealed by Charles and Le Beau, Oliver and Rosalind reveal the details of Celia's and Oliver's courtship. Rosalind describes them as being "in the very wrath of love" (V.ii.39) and concludes, "Clubs cannot part them" (40)—a phrase that could just as easily have been applied to Celia and Rosalind by Charles or Le Beau. Although these scenes of courtship are not worked out before a skeptical audience, the play itself challenges the validity of the impending nuptials between Celia and Oliver. While Rosalind sees no reason to question Celia's sudden interest in a heterosexual relationship, Orlando, Celia's former rival, does. Upon discovering his brother's engagement, Orlando asks Oliver, "Is't possible . . . That but seeing, you should love her? And loving woo? And wooing, *she should grant*?" (V.ii.1–4; emphasis mine). Orlando is the only character to question Celia's acceptance of Oliver's proposal, and his questions provide a cue for the audience to ask why Celia has consented to this arrangement, which seems the antithesis of everything she has sought throughout the play. Rather than offer Celia's verbal compliance to heterosexual norms, which might acknowledge Oliver as a satisfactory substitute for Rosalind, the play offers Celia's silent compliance to the inevitability of marriage. As a result, *As You Like It* fails to contain the idea of a female homoerotic space that Celia has envisioned.

The service alliance of Maria and Olivia has much in common with the same-sex friendship of Celia and Rosalind in *As You Like It*.[9] Maria supports Olivia in the face of male challenges to her authority, revealing that she is thoroughly invested in this alliance. After the female transvestite figure threatens the female alliance, Maria works to challenge that figure's authority with respect to heterosexual love, much in the same way that Celia challenges the masculinist imperatives of the cross-dressed Rosalind. In *Twelfth Night*, however, the evidence for a homoerotic alliance between Maria and Olivia is scarce: if Maria loves Olivia in the same way that Celia loves Rosalind, she does not reveal her feelings on stage. Although the absence of a female homoerotic discourse based on same-sex friendship in *Twelfth Night* suggests that Celia's and Maria's shared experiences do not include same-sex love, the homoerotic possibilities of same-sex service are a central theme in the play. It is also important to point out that *Twelfth Night* provides a more open framework for the possibilities of homoerotic activity than *As You Like It*. *As You Like It* is primarily concerned with recovering male bonds, which is achieved through the reconciliation of the two sets of brothers and complemented by the marriages of Celia and Rosalind, which join the play's two prominent families.[10] *Twelfth Night*, on the other hand, is preoccupied with the erotic fulfillment of its characters, whether heterosexual or homoerotic, and each of the play's erotically transgressive pairings, to borrow a phrase from Lisa Jardine, are "eroticized relationship[s] of 'service'" (Jardine, p. 33). If the relationship between Maria and Olivia is read within the context of a world that reveals a duke expressing an intense and sometimes erotic attachment to a female character whom he has accepted into his household as a male page, a countess falling in love with an unwanted suitor's cross-dressed servant, and two men enjoying an alliance that is both homoerotic and service oriented,[11] the female alliance of service takes on a different meaning. In fact, in a play in which so many service alliances cross boundaries of sexuality, it would be unusual if the alliance of Maria and Olivia did not have an erotic component.

The alliance between Olivia and Maria is primarily one of social and political convenience. Maria derives her authority from her connection to Olivia, making her efforts to preserve Olivia's autonomy a form of self-preservation. Similarly, Olivia employs Maria's services to keep order in her household and to help fight off her unwanted male suitors. The alliance of Maria and Olivia marks their mutual interest in enjoying their female sovereignty, which they secure by creating a fortress against unwanted male attention and intervention. Olivia is clearly Maria's mistress, yet *Twelfth Night* depicts two women who jointly run a household in which all male characters are figured as subordinate to them. Although none of *Twelfth Night*'s female characters reveal the near obsessive homoerotic desires of Celia, they all demonstrate an interest in securing a female alliance as a means of friendship, pleasure, and security. For example, Viola's first impulse after being shipwrecked and separated from her brother is not to cross-dress and offer herself in service to Orsino, but to forge an alliance with Olivia similar to the one enjoyed by Maria: "O that I serv'd that lady, / And might not be deliver'd to the world" (I.ii.41–42).[12] Viola's anxiety about being out in the world reminds readers that securing female authority within private spaces is central to the success of the female alliance.

Maria's service has earned her an authoritative position within Olivia's home, and, unlike Celia, she uses her power to work in conjunction with Olivia to secure their household. When Valentine returns from an unsuccessful suit on Orsino's behalf, it is clear that Maria is central to Orsino's negotiations: "So please my lord, I might not be admitted, / But from her handmaid do return this answer" (I.i.24–25). Maria is the conveyer of Olivia's refusal and, although she does not make this decision for Olivia, she frequently speaks and acts on Olivia's behalf throughout the play.[13] Maria appropriates Olivia's authoritative position when she acts as Olivia's proxy, frequently regulating male discourse in Olivia's absence; in particular, she deflects the conversation from the topic of Olivia's mourning and her refusal to marry to the transgressions of the male members of Olivia's household. Maria's first appearance reveals her unwillingness to speak of any suit when Sir Toby asks, "What a plague means my niece to take the death of her brother thus?" (I.iii.1–2), which prevents both the suit of Orsino and Sir Toby's own suit on behalf of his friend, Sir Andrew Aguecheek. Rather than directly defend Olivia's decision not to marry, Maria turns the conversation to Sir Toby's transgressions, eventually moving the conversation back to Sir Andrew to voice Olivia's final refusal of the suit: "I heard my lady talk of . . . a foolish knight that you brought in one night here to be her wooer" (14–17). Through the presence of Maria, the play announces Olivia's rejection of her male suitors and the secure position of the female alliance within the play.

Just as Olivia employs Maria to strengthen her authority,[14] Sir Toby and Sir Andrew attempt to use Maria's influence to help them to negotiate with Olivia. While Orsino attempts to woo Olivia with the help of his male servants, Sir Toby recognizes the importance of Maria in his own negotiations on behalf of Sir Andrew. Sir Andrew understands that Maria is a potentially useful figure to him because she is Olivia's chambermaid: "Good Mistress Accost, I desire better acquaintance" (I.iii.51–52). By getting acquainted with Maria, Sir Andrew hopes to take advantage of her alliance with Olivia. If Sir Andrew can gain Maria's favor, he will be able to gain access to her mistress and pursue his suit without the interference of Sir Toby. Maria, however, has little interest in their advances, either for herself or for Olivia. As they discuss the possible meanings of "accost" in relation to her person—which Sir Toby clarifies as "front her, board her, woo her, assail her" (55–56)—Maria attempts to extricate herself from a situation that implies a direct sexual threat to both her and Olivia. Sir Toby and Sir Andrew prevent her from leaving and continue their jests, asking her if she is "full of them [jests]" (76). Maria's reply, "Ay, sir, I have them at my fingers' ends: marry, now I let go your hand, I am barren" (77–78), reveals that she is disgusted by the behavior of these men. This slight, recognized by both men, marks her departure and, as Maria seems to stand in for her mistress, Sir Andrew recognizes that his pursuit of Olivia has also suffered a detour: "your niece will not be seen, or if she be, it's four to one she'll none of me" (102–4).

Although Olivia and Maria seem to be working together to achieve the same goal—to secure their female authority, subdue male dissenters, and discourage male suitors—Olivia's decision to admit Viola/Cesario into her household places them, temporarily, at cross purposes. Olivia's and Maria's ritualistic preparation for Cesario's appearance implies that the outcome of his interview has already been determined. Olivia is attended by Maria, and, before Cesario enters, Olivia requests her veil and demands that Maria "throw it o'er my face" (I.v.167). This act marks Olivia's determination to turn away yet another of Orsino's servants unsatisfied and Maria's determination to assist her mistress in this scheme. When Cesario is admitted, however, Maria's authority is seriously undermined. Like Orsino, Sir Toby, and Sir Andrew, Cesario is willing to challenge the validity of Olivia's mourning; unlike these other "men," Cesario is also willing to question directly the power that Olivia has invested in Maria. When Olivia reprimands Cesario for his sauciness, Maria offers to turn him out: "Will you hoist sail, sir? Here lies your way" (204). Cesario, unwilling to acknowledge Maria's authority, demotes Maria from the position of handmaid to that of household drudge: "No, good swabber, I am to hull here a little longer" (205–6). Cesario's personal appeal, along with his refusal either to leave or pursue his suit in the presence of others, leads Olivia to dismiss Maria and her other attendants and to remove her veil. At the very moment that Olivia and Maria first stand together resolved to turn away Orsino's latest messenger—the only display of their joint powers and desires witnessed by the audience—Olivia essentially dissolves her alliance with Maria in favor of the possibility of one with Viola, another man's servant.

While Rosalind's mock marriage to Orlando results in Celia's silence, Olivia's sudden interest in Cesario spurs Maria to action. Through Maria's involvement in the humiliation of Malvolio, which Karen Robertson calls "a deliberate and energetic construction" of revenge (Robertson, p. 116), Maria's energies are redirected in a scheme that helps her to restore her authority within Olivia's household in two ways: first, it transforms the hostile sexual attacks of Sir Toby, Sir Andrew, and Feste on Olivia and Maria into political attacks directed toward another transgressor, Malvolio; and second, it allows Maria to humiliate Malvolio, the one member of Olivia's household who most resents Maria's authority. There is, however, a second revenge plot in *Twelfth Night*, one that enables Maria to challenge the heterosexual intervention of the transvestite figure and to vent her anger at her mistress—and it is at this point that Maria's activities may have some bearing on her feelings for Olivia. When Sir Toby encourages Sir Andrew to take his own revenge on Cesario for usurping what Sir Andrew sees as his own place as Olivia's suitor, Maria joins with them in an attempt to remove Cesario from Olivia's household. After Sir Andrew reads his written challenge to Cesario for Sir Toby's approval and resolves to "give't him" (III.iv.173), Maria reveals that Cesario is in the house: "You may have very fit occasion for't: he is now in some commerce with my lady, and will by and by depart" (174–76). Maria is protecting her own and Olivia's interests: she knows that Sir Andrew has no chance with Olivia, but recognizes that Cesario may be a threat to her own desires. By temporarily jeopardizing Cesario's well-being, Maria is able to exact her own revenge on Olivia who, although exhibiting a great deal of sexual agency in choosing to woo Cesario, appears to have turned her back on female homosociality.

In addition to the alliances of Orsino and Viola/Cesario and Olivia and Viola/Cesario, *Twelfth Night* depicts another relationship that denotes dependency, service, and desire: Antonio's alliance with Sebastian, which provides yet another lens through which to view the alliance of Maria and Olivia. It is significant that the scene in which Olivia appears to dismiss one servant, Maria, in favor of another, Viola/Cesario, is followed by the first appearance of Antonio and Sebastian, who offer a display of male homoerotic desire that Stephen Orgel reads as "overtly homosexual" (Orgel, 1989, p. 27). The temporary breakdown of Maria's and Olivia's alliance is highlighted by the intensity of Antonio's interest in Sebastian, which is not only similar in intensity to Celia's unrequited passion for Rosalind but also provides a textual occasion for a consideration of Olivia's and Maria's social and sexual interests in homoerotic terms. Like Maria's and Olivia's alliance, Antonio's and Sebastian's relationship is one of mutual dependency: Antonio serves Sebastian, and Sebastian, in turn, is indebted to Antonio. Antonio takes in and provides for the shipwrecked Sebastian, and eventually assists him in his quest to seek out Orsino, who is Antonio's enemy. Antonio's love for Sebastian compels him to risk his life in Illyria rather than part from Sebastian: "But come what may, I do adore thee so, / That danger shall seem sport" (II.i.46–47). Although it may appear that Antonio has more invested in this relationship than Sebastian, and that perhaps Sebastian is merely dependent upon his friend for his purse, when they are reunited at the play's end Sebastian's emotional attachment to Antonio far outweighs any obligations to his friend for his economic support and seems to rival his love for Olivia: "Antonio! Oh my dear Antonio, / How have the hours rack'd and tortur'd me, / Since I have lost thee!" (V.i.216–18).

Within the context of household rule, Maria and Olivia are mimicking the homoerotics of male same-sex service typified by Antonio's relationship with Sebastian and Viola/Cesario's relationship with Orsino.[15] The text makes it clear that Maria attaches great importance to her position as Olivia's servant. The frequency with which Maria refers to Olivia as "my lady" reminds the other characters and the audience of Maria's

subordinate position as Olivia's handmaid. Yet it also provides an opportunity for Maria verbally to lay claim to Olivia, to acknowledge both
her pleasure in serving her and the power that such a position wields.
Olivia, on the other hand, clearly takes great pleasure in ruling. While
Olivia's household may appear unruly, none of her subordinates are
completely successful in their attempts to force her to marry. Olivia has
announced that she will mourn the deaths of her father and brother for
seven years; she has also sworn to Sir Toby that "she'll not match above
her degree, neither in estate, years, nor wit" (I.iii.106–7), suggesting the
possibility of her making any match at all rather slim. Her seven-year
plan is clever in that it gives her ample time to master her skills as a
mistress, and may, as she ages, take her out of the marriage market altogether. More significant, it will also allow her to continue to share both
her authority and her bed exclusively with Maria, who would indeed
seem to be the perfect "match," because she is not above her mistress in
degree or estate. While Maria's and Olivia's interdependency does not
directly reveal itself to be homoerotic in the same way that Antonio's
and Sebastian's does, the attacks on Olivia's and Maria's joint authority
and heterosexual indifference reveal a male revolt against a female attachment that is dangerous in terms of its political and, quite possibly,
erotic implications.

   Although *Twelfth Night* eventually requires the marriages of Maria
and Olivia, these nuptials do not mark the dissolution of Maria's and
Olivia's alliance; instead, these marriages strengthen the bond between
them. After Olivia discovers that Maria had a hand in Malvolio's humiliation, she fully expects Maria to account for her actions and appoints
Malvolio his own "plaintiff and . . . judge" (V.i.353). When Fabian claims
that Maria wrote the letter at Sir Toby's urging and reveals that Sir Toby
has married Maria to compensate for his crime, Olivia, who seems to take
some pleasure in their abuse of Malvolio, speaks no more of Maria's
punishment. Ultimately, Maria's marriage to Sir Toby elevates her class
status and secures for her a more equal social position in relation to
Olivia,[16] making Maria's punishment less pressing than that of a servant.
Olivia's good-natured attitude toward the transgressions of Sir Toby and
Maria brings attention to the fact that she and Maria have essentially
solved their problems: by making convenient marriages, they fulfill
cultural expectations of womanhood without relinquishing their authority or their friendship.[17]

   The activities of Celia and Maria in their attempts to maintain their
respective relationships with Rosalind and Olivia are strikingly similar,
but the ways in which each play ultimately comments upon female alliances are surprisingly different. *As You Like It* defeats a nonmutual alliance that is specifically homoerotic, while *Twelfth Night* preserves a
mutual alliance that is erotically ambiguous. The differences in the outcome of each alliance rely in part on the nature of that alliance—whether
it is homoerotic or homosocial—and how each character's feelings are

displayed, but also on the extent to which each play is invested in heterosexuality. The extent of *As You Like It*'s and *Twelfth Night*'s treatment of homoeroticism depends largely upon each plays' ideological
demands in terms of heterosexuality. That is, if a play is particularly
concerned with asserting the authority of heterosexual alliances, that
play's treatment of female homoeroticism will be more explicit and the
containment of the female homoerotic alliance more severe. Celia's verbal displays of her love for Rosalind challenge the validity of heterosexuality in the play and force a conclusion in which Celia's female homoerotic
desire seems to disappear. If the alliance of Maria and Olivia is homoerotic,
it poses no threat to the heterosexual order as long as it is hidden. Whatever the nature of this alliance, it is protected through the women's silence and ultimately secured through their marriages to men who are
ineffectual and show more interest in male homosocial and homoerotic
bonds than they do in heterosexual love.

Regardless of whether *Twelfth Night*'s characters continue to transgress erotic boundaries, *Twelfth Night* privileges female autonomy and
female homosociality in a way that *As You Like It* does not. While *As
You Like It* ends with the recuperation of male bonds through marriage,
Twelfth Night ends with the anticipation of Orsino's and Viola's marriage, which will officially admit Viola into the female homosocial space
created by Maria and Olivia. When Olivia discovers in the play's final
scene that Cesario, the original object of her desire, is actually a woman,
she expresses joy over the possibilities of their future alliance, exclaim-
ing, "A sister! You are she" (V.i.325). Olivia welcomes a sororal alliance
with Viola, and Viola, in turn, will be able to fulfill her initial impulse to
form an alliance with Olivia. While the ending of *Twelfth Night* implies
the potential for homoerotic fulfillment, it stresses unlimited possibilities
for female homosociality in an intimate circle of female characters. Ultimately, *Twelfth Night* imagines a world in which marriage is necessary
but continues to privilege both female authority and female alliances.

NOTES

1. Although Valerie Traub has pointed out that "the desires circulating
through the Phebe/Rosalind/Ganymede exchange, [and] the Olivia/Viola/Cesario
interaction, represent woman's desire for woman," the strength of her analysis
lies in her discussion of the role the female transvestite figure plays in seduc-
ing male characters; *Desire and Anxiety: Circulations of Sexuality in Shakespearean
Drama* (New York: Routledge, 1992), p. 108. However, Traub has also criticized
this "dependence on the transvestite heroine as the privileged stage representative of early modern female desire" because it "tempts us to depend upon the
changeability of dress as the originating instance of homoeroticism"; "The
(In)Significance of Lesbian Desire in Early Modern England," in *Queering the
Renaissance*, ed. Jonathan Goldberg (Durham, N.C.: Duke University Press,
1994), p. 70.
2. For example, in her discussion of Shakespeare's transvestite heroines,
Marjorie Garber argues that "[t]heirs was a recuperative pattern: however out-

spoken they were, however much they challenged authority . . . they did not mitigate, but rather confirmed, the remanding of women back to their proper places at the end of the play"; *Vested Interests: Cross-dressing and Cultural Anxiety* (New York: Routledge, 1992), p. 72. Similarly, in her discussion of *Twelfth Night*, Jean Howard, *The Stage and Social Struggle in Early Modern England* (New York: Routledge, 1994), p. 112, observes that "the political threat of female insurgency enters the text not through Viola . . . but through Olivia, a figure whose sexual and economic independence is ironically reined in *by means of* the crossdressed Viola."

3. The problem of discussing power within female alliances is best illustrated by the ongoing debate between two groups of lesbians: anti-sadism/masochism (S/M) lesbian–feminists and lesbian sex radicals. The first group, in general, is anti-S/M, denounces butch–femme relationships, and considers any form of female heterosexual activity an act of coercion; the second group advocates S/M activity, butch–femme relationships, lesbian dildo use, and is interested in deregulating a variety of non-normative sexual practices. As Margaret Hunt, "Report of a Conference on Feminism, Sexuality, and Power: The Elect Clash with the Perverse," in *Coming to Power: Writings and Graphics on Lesbian S/M*, ed. by the Members of Samois, 3rd ed. (Boston: Alyson Publications, 1987), has pointed out, however unsavory the S/M advocates may seem, the anti-S/M position's attempts to define and limit female sexuality is dangerously reductive, serving only a small minority of the feminist and lesbian population. For example, while consent is the central issue for S/M practitioners, anti-S/M advocates question "whether 'real' consent is even possible in a patriarchal society" (p. 87). For a helpful examination of this debate on both sides of the Atlantic, see Emma Healy, *Lesbian Sex Wars* (London: Virago, 1996).

4. For discussions of the homoerotic nature of Celia's and Rosalind's alliance, see Valerie Traub, "The (In)Significance of Lesbian Desire," pp. 70–72; and Gilchrist Keel, "'Like Juno's Swans': Rosalind and Celia in *As You Like It*," *Conference of College Teachers of English Studies* 56 (September 1991): 5–11. The most extensive study of Celia's and Rosalind's relationship is Fiona Shaw's and Juliet Stevenson's discussion of these roles, which they took on in the 1985 Royal Shakespeare Company's production of *As You Like It* . Although they do not discuss the homoerotic nature of this alliance, Shaw and Stevenson trace several important shifts in Celia's and Rosalind's relationship that complement my own argument. See Shaw and Stevenson, "Celia and Rosalind in *As You Like It*," *Players 2: Further Essays in Shakespearean Performance by Players with the Royal Shakespeare Company*, ed. Russell Jackson and Robert Smallwood (Cambridge: Cambridge University Press, 1988), pp. 55–71. I am grateful to Karen Robertson for suggesting this article to me. The majority of the discussions of women in *As You Like It*, however, tend to focus on the issues of gender and sexuality through the examination of the activities of Rosalind. See Clara Claiborne Park, "As We Like It: How a Girl Can Be Smart and Still Popular," in *The Woman's Part: Feminist Criticism of Shakespeare*, ed. Carolyn Ruth Swift Lenz, Gayle Greene, and Carol Thomas Neely (Chicago: University of Illinois Press, 1980), pp. 100–16; Catherine Belsey, "Disrupting Sexual Difference: Meaning and Gender in the Comedies," in *Alternative Shakespeares*, ed. John Drakakis (New York: Methuen, 1985), pp. 166–90; Phyllis Rackin, "Androgyny, Mimesis, and the Marriage of the Boy Heroine on the English Renaissance Stage," *PMLA* 102 (January 1987): 29–41; and Elaine Hobby, "'My affection hath an unknown bottom': Homosexuality and the Teaching of *As You Like It*," in *Shakespeare and the Changing Curriculum*, ed. Lesley Aers and Nigel Wheale (London: Routledge, 1992), pp. 125–42.

5. See *A Midsummer Night's Dream* (pp. 217–49) and *The Two Noble Kinsmen* (pp. 1639–81), in *The Riverside Shakespeare*, ed. G. Blakemore Evans (Boston: Houghton Mifflin, 1974).

6. William Shakespeare, *As You Like It*, ed. Agnes Latham (London: Methuen, The Arden Shakespeare, 1975).

7. Eric Partridge cites both "bird's nest" and "head" as slang for the female genitalia in *Romeo and Juliet*, although he does not acknowledge this particular usage of these terms in *As You Like It*. See Partridge, *Shakespeare's Bawdy* (New York: Dutton, 1969), p. 66.

8. For a discussion of the heterosexual implications of Rosalind's language, see Robert H. Hay, "Addenda to Shakespeare's Bawdy: *As You Like It*, IV.i. 201–208," *American Notes & Queries* 13, no. 4 (December 1974): 51–53.

9. Very little criticism on *Twelfth Night* addresses the importance of Maria's function within the text or the significance of her relationship with Olivia. Many of the discussions of Maria tend to assume that she consciously schemes to marry Sir Toby from the play's beginning due to a romantic as well as a social interest. See Kenneth Muir, *Shakespeare's Comic Sequence* (New York: Barnes & Noble, 1979), p. 96; and Richard A. Levin, *Love and Society in Shakespearean Comedy: A Study of Dramatic Form and Content* (Toronto: Associated University Presses, 1985), pp. 118, 130, 151. For discussions of Maria's marriage that highlight the issue of social mobility rather than romantic love, see Cristina Malcolmson, "'What You Will': Social Mobility and Gender in *Twelfth Night*," in *The Matter of Difference: Materialist Feminist Criticism of Shakespeare*, ed. Valerie Wayne (Ithaca, N.Y.: Cornell University Press, 1991), pp. 29–57; and Karin S. Godin, "'Slander in an Allow'd Fool': *Twelfth Night*'s Crisis of the Aristocracy," *Studies in English Literature* 33, no. 2 (Spring 1993): 309–25. Both Laurie E. Osborne and Karen Robertson acknowledge the significance of Maria's relationship to Olivia and Maria's agency in executing the revenge plot. See Laurie E. Osborne, "Letters, Lovers, Lacan: Or Malvolio's Not-So-Purloined Letter," *Assays* 5 (1989): 63–89; and Karen Robertson, "A Revenging Feminine Hand in *Twelfth Night*," in *Reading and Writing in Shakespeare*, ed. David Bergeron (Newark: University of Delaware Press, 1996), pp. 116–30. My reading of Maria throughout this article is indebted to Robertson's discussion.

10. See Joel Fineman, "Fratricide and Cuckoldry: Shakespeare's Doubles," in *Representing Shakespeare: New Psychoanalytic Forms*, ed. Murray M. Schwartz and Coppélia Kahn (Baltimore: Johns Hopkins University Press, 1980), p. 75; and Louis Adrian Montrose, "'The Place of a Brother' in *As You Like It*: Social Process and Comic Form," *Shakespeare Quarterly* 32 (1981): 28–54.

11. For discussions of Orsino's and Olivia's relationships with Cesario/Viola, see Jean Howard, *The Stage and Social Struggle*, p. 114; Lisa Jardine, "Twins and Travesties: Gender, Dependency, and Sexual Availability in *Twelfth Night*," in *Erotic Politics: Desire on the Renaissance Stage*, ed. Susan Zimmerman (New York: Routledge, 1992), pp. 32–33; Valerie Traub, *Desire and Anxiety*, pp. 130–35. For discussions of the homoerotics of Antonio's and Sebastian's relationship, see Joseph Pequigney, "The Two Antonios and Same-Sex Love in *Twelfth Night* and *The Merchant of Venice*," *English Literary Renaissance* 22 (1992): 202–10; Stephen Orgel, "Nobody's Perfect: Or Why Did The English Stage Take Boys for Women?" *South Atlantic Quarterly* 88 (1989): 7–29; Stephen Greenblatt, *Shakespearean Negotiations: The Circulation of Social Energy in Renaissance England* (Berkeley: University of California Press, 1988), p. 91; and Janet Adelman, "Male Bonding in Shakespeare's Comedies," in *Shakespeare's "Rough Magic": Renaissance Essays in Honor of C. L. Barber*, ed. Peter Erikson and Coppélia Kahn (Newark: University of Delaware Press, 1985), pp. 73–103.

12. William Shakespeare, *Twelfth Night*, eds. J. M. Lothian and T. W. Craik, The Arden Shakespeare (London: Methuen, 1975).

13. Laurie E. Osborne points out that Olivia also stands in for Maria when she inadvertently duplicates the language of Maria's letter in her discussion with Cesario in V.i. See Osborne, "Letters, Lovers, Lacan," p. 70.

14. Elizabeth Brown has examined how the presence of Cleopatra's hand-maids, Iras and Charmian, supports Cleopatra's efforts to create a particular image of herself, both in life and in death, and how the "construction of her domestic staff . . . exposes the extent of Cleopatra's isolation from the world outside her palace" ("'Companion me with my mistress': Cleopatra, Elizabeth I, and Their Waiting Women," also in this volume). Similarly, Maria's presence as Olivia's companion supports Olivia in her efforts to construct herself as hetero-sexually unavailable and isolated from the concerns of Illyria.

15. For a helpful discussion of the homoerotics of male service alliances in seventeenth-century comedy, see Mario DiGangi, "Asses and Wits: The Homo-erotics of Mastery in Satiric Comedy," *English Literary Renaissance* 25 (Spring 1995): 179–208.

16. See Cristina Malcolmson, "'What You Will,'" p. 34.

17. Lisa Jardine, "Twins and Travesties," pp. 27–38, argues that at the play's end the female characters are subordinate to their husbands. As Jardine her-self suggests, however, Olivia's "eroticized relationship of 'service' with Cesario is the most socially and sexually transgressive" (p. 33) in the play, and it is this relationship of service, with Sebastian serving Olivia, that forms the core of their marriage.

8

"Companion Me with My Mistress"

Cleopatra, Elizabeth I, and Their Waiting Women

. . . .

ELIZABETH A. BROWN

THE COURT OF ELIZABETH I provides a useful model for the staged ver sion of Cleopatra's court in Shakespeare's *Antony and Cleopatra* (Jankowski, 1989, 1992; Morris; Rinehart). Comparisons of Elizabeth and Shakespeare's Cleopatra tend to focus on how these queens managed display and spectacle as a component of their political power.[1] However, the differences in the ways they structured their courts, specifically their attendant women, are also striking. This investigation of the complex correspondences between the courts of these two queens focuses on the alliance between the monarch and her waiting women. Although historians have often discounted the role of Elizabeth's female courtiers and critics have largely ignored the waiting women in Shakespeare's play, an examination of the presence or absence of an extensive network of family members, courtiers, advisors, and servants who provide support for and validation of power reveals a surprising strength of Elizabeth's use of her Privy Chamber and a corresponding weakness in Cleopatra's use of her household as a strategy of power.

The complex workings of Elizabeth's Privy Chamber have seldom come under serious scrutiny.[2] Early in her reign she apparently forbade her women to participate in politics, and historians have cited this prohibition at face value without much further examination. Yet, in addition to the expected tasks of personal care and companionship, her gentlewomen had two politically significant functions: first, the queen used them to extend and amplify her physical presence; second, they had an important role in the critical management of access. The formation of a staff that could accomplish these functions was no accidental or trivial matter, and its success depended largely on Elizabeth's skillful use of her kinship connections. The absence of such connections in Shakespeare's construction of Cleopatra's court has, as we shall see, significant consequences for her political success.

Elizabeth's Privy Chamber consisted of a semiprofessional corps of women with sixteen paid and six or more unpaid positions. These women were a constant presence in the queen's life. Most had duties associated with her care, including supervising her linens, wardrobe, and jewels, assisting with dressing and personal hygiene, serving food, and nursing her during illness—duties that gave them close contact with her backstage persona. Others, like the changing corps of young maids-of-honor, provided companionship and entertainment such as dancing or playing cards. As a group, the attendant women also added to the "prestigious show on ceremonial occasions" (Wright, p. 151), accompanying the queen on progress, for example, or forming part of her escort to chapel. At the same time, the Privy Chamber formed a barrier around the queen that, as Susan Frye argues, "guarded access to the body she had situated at the center of the integrated networks of decision making and representation" (1993, p. 104).

The Privy Chamber staff was a surprisingly stable group with a very low rate of turnover. In forty-four years, only twenty-eight women held the sixteen paid positions (Wright, pp. 157–8). Some, like Blanche Parry and Mary Radcliffe, never married and served for almost the entire reign. Most of the others, like Lady Katherine Carey Knollys and Katherine Carey Howard, later Countess of Nottingham, came from two or three generations of the queen's Boleyn cousins from the Howard, Carey, and Knollys families. Although many were married or otherwise related to important men of the court,[3] the considerable influence of an attendant like Lady Knollys depended at least as much on her own close association with the queen as on her husband's position at court. The women of the Privy Chamber thus participated in an elaborate network of influence and political interconnection based primarily on kinship relations.

Although Pam Wright's description of Elizabeth's attendants is useful for its focus on this often overlooked aspect of the queen's reign, her argument that the Privy Chamber was largely apolitical underestimates the political importance of personal relationships in Elizabeth's court and assumes the existence of a private sphere apart from politics. For a ruling queen, however, the public and private cannot be separated. The details of Elizabeth's life, including the events and personnel within her Privy Chamber, had a political significance and, no matter how "privy," were never really *private*. The Privy Chamber women had almost constant access to the center of power and held considerable power themselves because of their potential ability to influence the queen. As Sharon Kettering argues in her discussion of French noblewomen and patronage, "the actual power of noblewomen can be hard to evaluate because it was hidden behind institutional powerlessness." Women might lack recognized positions of authority and might even be officially sanctioned from exercising authority, but their power nevertheless could manifest itself indirectly "through personal relationships by women" (Kettering, p. 818). We know that Elizabeth's Privy Chamber exercised this power of personal relationships because other courtiers acknowledged it. Courtiers continually curried favor with or sought support from the Privy Chamber women, and staff members used their positions close to the queen to protect and promote the interests or careers of their friends and relations.

One courtier who used the queen's attendants in this way was Sir Robert Sidney, whose relationship with the court is chronicled in his agent Rowland Whyte's letters covering more than five years of pursuing Sidney's interests at court.[4] In his continuing suits to the queen for leave from his military post abroad or for promotion, Sidney, who was related to the Dudley family on his mother's side, frequently relied on the help of two aunts, Catherine Dudley Hastings, Countess of Huntingdon, and Anne Russell Dudley, Countess of Warwick, both of whom were prominent among the Privy Chamber women. Sidney expected these relations to look out for his interests at court, and they likewise expected to be employed to pass on his gifts and letters to the queen or to advise when specific requests might best be heard. Lady Huntingdon, in particular, was an extremely influential friend. Whyte wrote of her that "she governes the Queen, many hours together very private" (*HMC Penshurst*, vol. 2, p. 472). He reports that she brought Sidney's suits to the queen's attention and offered advice about their timeliness; she was also willing to confer with others at court, including Sidney's enemies, about his interests: "[Lady Huntingdon] is resolute not to deliver your letter to the Queen till there be cawse, and that she will talke with [Lord Cobham] and lay breach of faith and promes to his charge: and yf need be she will thoroughly deale with the Queen about yt" (vol. 2, p. 412). Whyte believed that the queen's concern for Lady Huntingdon's grief over her husband's death in December 1595 prompted Elizabeth, in the face of opposition from other court factions, to grant Sidney a much-coveted leave to return to England to comfort his aunt and deal with her business affairs:

> My Lady has your leave safely in her cabinet, so you may boldly come over. You need to make haste, it is not possible Lady Huntingdon should continue long, so weak she is. Lord Borough's friends mightily storm that he hath no leave. If my lady Huntingdon's desire to see you had not moved the Queen, you had not come over in haste. (vol. 2, p. 204)

Whyte's letters to Robert Sidney also reveal that if the queen sometimes granted suits that her women brought to her attention, she also used the Privy Chamber staff to keep courtiers hanging on indefinitely in hopes of preferment or return to favor, often reading their letters or receiving their gifts but giving no definite answers in return. Whyte's petitions on behalf of Robert Sidney must often have been received as follows: "Your leave was by my Lady Huntingdon moved, which the Queen has not granted nor denied" (vol. 2, p. 410). Clearly, Elizabeth saw her Privy Chamber as a crucial part of her exercise of power. Although she expected them to remain loyal to her and to promote her goals, she nevertheless allowed those in favor to play a role with very real, if unofficial, political consequences. That she was able to use the Privy Chamber women simultaneously as an extension of her body for public display and as a way to reinforce her remoteness and inaccessibility reveals her understanding of the complex management of power.

Queen Elizabeth apparently formed close attachments to some of her women, especially the most senior. In fact, she came to the throne with some important connections to attendants already in place. On her accession, she appointed to the Privy Chamber Katherine Ashley and Blanche Parry, women who had already been with her for most of her life and who remained in her service until their deaths. Evidence of Elizabeth's affection for at least some of her women appears in the nicknames she gave them and in her often kind and intimate letters (Bassnett, pp. 9–10; Luke, p. 399). On at least two occasions Elizabeth insisted that she be the one to break the news of a loved one's death. When Mary Radcliffe's brother was killed in Ireland, Whyte reports that the information "by the Queen's command is kept from her, who is determined to break yt unto her herself" (*HMC Penshurst*, vol. 2, pp. 383–84). Earlier, she kept the news of the Earl of Huntingdon's death from his wife until she herself could break the news; her subsequent visit to Lady Huntingdon, Whyte reported, "much comforted her" (vol. 2, pp. 202–4).

A further measure of Elizabeth's attachment to the closest of her ladies appears in the reports of her reaction to their deaths. For example, in 1568 the queen was said to be "much concerned at the death of Lady Knollys" (*HMC Salisbury*, vol. 1, p. 400). And when Mary Radcliffe died shortly after her brother in 1599, she was buried "as a nobleman's daughter by the Queen's command" (*HMC Penshurst*, vol. 2, p. 417). Not surprisingly, the deaths of those close to her affected Elizabeth more as she approached the end of her own life; the death of her cousin Lady Nottingham, who had served her for nearly their entire adult lives, reportedly hastened the queen's death only a few weeks later (Strickland, p. 772). It is difficult for outsiders (especially 400 years later) to assess the nature and closeness of any relationship, and Elizabeth's friendships, if that is the term for them, are complicated by the inequality of rank. Doubtless neither party had any confusion about who was mistress; yet the evidence suggests that daily interaction, a lengthy shared history, and the exchange of confidences, especially in long-standing associations, may move a relationship beyond the institutional roles of mistress and attendant.

Some of the waiting women clearly offered Elizabeth this sort of companionship, but their complex kinship connections provided the additional benefit of extending her presence beyond the palace, a benefit notably absent in the organization of Cleopatra's household. Even those of Elizabeth's women who remained single were not isolated from the outside world; those who married, often more than once, had ties to numerous people who were affected by their connections to the queen and who, furthermore, expected to benefit from the kinship or social connection to a Privy Chamber gentlewoman. As Barbara A. Hanawalt has shown in her study of Lady Honor Lisle's network of family connections, noblewomen were able to "procure a share of the power through kinship, gifts, patronage, and such weapons as gossip and humiliation" (1988, p. 188). Although Lady Lisle was active during the reign of Henry VIII, twenty-five years before Elizabeth came to the throne, her extensive connections to her children, stepchildren, godchildren, and foster-children as well as servants, family retainers, and her husband's associates, resembled those of many noblewomen in Elizabeth's time. Indeed, the indirect evidence of Barbara Sidney's activities (implied by her husband's letters to her while he was posted abroad) show a similar interest in acquiring suitable godparents for their children, sending gifts to friends and relatives, nurturing important connections at court, and generally making use of this network to further their own interests. As Hanawalt emphasizes, such networks required constant maintenance through letter writing and gift giving. A Privy Chamber gentlewoman was thus able to provide her relations and friends the advantage of her access to the queen and to important courtiers with obvious consequences for their social and political positions.

The epitaphs of some of Elizabeth's Privy Chamber women suggest a similar attention to maintaining elaborate kinship networks and illustrate the reciprocal importance of these ties outside the Privy Chamber both to the waiting women and to the queen. The monument of Lady Dorothy Stafford in St. Margaret's Church, Westminster, for instance, constructs her first as wife, second as daughter and granddaughter with connections to pre-Tudor royalty, and third, as an important waiting woman to the queen:

> Heer lyeth ye Lady Dorothee Stafford, wife & widdowe to Sr William Stafford Knight, Davghter to Henreye Lo: Staforde, ye only sonne of Edward ye last Dvke of Bvckingham, her mother was Vrsvla Davgher to ye Covnesse of Salisburye, ye only daughter to George Duke of Clarence, brother to King Edward ye 4. She continued a true Weddoe [sic] from ye age of [ ]7 till her death. She served Q: Elizabeth 40 Yeares lying in her bedchamber, esteemed of her, loved of all doing good all she covlde to every body never hurted any, a continual [?] rembra[n]cer of the poore

as she lived a religious life, in great reputation of honor & virtue in ye world so she ended in continual fervent meditation [3 or more words illegible] wch instant (as all her life) so after her d[—] to ye poore, died aged of 7[?]8 yeers, ye 22 of September 160[o?]. In whose remembrance Sr Edward Stafford her sonne hath caused ys memorial of her to be in the same forme [?] & place as she her self long since requyred them.[5]

This epitaph, presumably an expression of the way she herself wished to be remembered, links Lady Stafford's long service and physical proximity to the queen with her role as a benefactress. Blanche Parry's epitaph similarly calls attention to her long attendance on the queen and also makes clear that even a single woman who devoted nearly her entire life to Elizabeth's service had numerous connections and responsibilities to the world outside the court:

Here vnder is intombed Blanche Parrye, davghter of Henry Parrye of New covrte wthin the county of Heref. Esqvier, chiefe gentlewom of Queene Elizabethes most honorable privie chamber & keper of her maties Ivells [jewels], whom she faithfvllie served from her highnes birth, beneficiale to her kinsfolke and countryemen, charitable to the poore insomovche that she gave to the poore of Bacton and Newton in Herefordshire seaven score bvshells of wheate & rye yerelie forever wth divers somes of money to Westmynsteer and other places for good vses, she died a maide in the eithtie two yeres of her age the twelfe of Febrvarye, 1589.[6]

Elizabeth's waiting women thus functioned in a variety of ways that benefited both the queen and the complex networks of family and associates extending from them.

Shakespeare greatly expands the little that Plutarch says about Cleopatra's women, Charmian and Iras, and although his representation of Cleopatra's court is simpler and more exclusively feminine, the women of the Egyptian court have functions similar in most respects to those of Elizabeth's attendants. Like Elizabeth's Privy Chamber women, Cleopatra's female attendants provide care and companionship. She also makes effective political use of them in ceremonious display and to control access to her person and even her reputation after death. The notable difference is the absence in the staged court of the complex kinship networks that are precisely what made Elizabeth's women most politically useful. As staged, Cleopatra's women have no family ties and no obligations to anyone apart from her, and this contrast to the elaborate network of Elizabeth's court exposes the extent of Cleopatra's political isolation.

The brief glimpses that we have of the Egyptian waiting women are suggestive of longterm working relationships among women who must live and work together. To the extent that they are engaged in a common enterprise—the service and glorification of Cleopatra—they clearly are allied to her and to each other. Although it is clear that Shakespeare represents Charmian and Iras not as slaves (as is sometimes assumed) but as aristocratic gentlewomen, they do not have powerful friends and families who might deflect some of their attention or loyalty from the queen or outside connections who might find their relationship to Cleopatra useful and give them a stake in her survival. With one exception, the play offers no evidence that they have goals or desires separate from hers. If they sometimes attempt to influence or manage their mistress, they do so not to achieve their own or others' goals, but to further hers.

Early in the play, Cleopatra's women help to establish the opulent atmosphere of the Egyptian court and the magnificence of its queen. But this function does not explain why Shakespeare has so greatly expanded the characters of Charmian and Iras as they appear in Plutarch's account. Clearly the exotic Egyptian queen, as opposed to a Roman matron however highly connected, must have conspicuous and splendid attendants. But in a play that is already diverse and lengthy, it is less clear why these attendants should have speaking parts and even one scene in which their mistress scarcely appears. Charmian and Iras have lines in nine scenes and appear as part of Cleopatra's entourage in several more. Although they presumably accompany Cleopatra in the opening scene, the first time we meet them directly (I.ii) is also the only time they appear without Cleopatra and so the only time that we see them focused on something other than their mistress. Away from Cleopatra, Charmian, Iras, and the other members of the household do not, as we might expect, talk about Cleopatra; they do not, in other words, *gossip* about her in the way that Antony's followers, from the opening lines, maliciously dissect and condemn him. Instead, this scene is as close as Charmian and Iras come to having private lives.

Their conversation is not completely private since the women are not alone together. Enobarbus and the lower servants seem to be setting up a banquet, and perhaps the discussion takes place while the characters are at work on this task. The talk is familiar and intimate. With the soothsayer, Alexas, Mardian, and Enobarbus, Cleopatra's women discuss their futures, the possibility of husbands and children, and about how they will age. The women usurp the soothsayer's role by offering fortunes more outlandish than his and while the humorous sexual innuendo of the conversation celebrates the subversive power of women over men, it also represents their recognition that they have deferred conventional kinship alliances. Only the women hear fortunes from the soothsayer. Alexas, though summoned to have his palm read, receives instead Charmian's mock prayer for his future: "O let him marry a woman that cannot go, sweet Isis, I beseech thee, and let her die too, and give him a worse, and let worse follow worse till the worst of all follow him laughing to his grave fiftyfold a cuckold."[7] Here, a succession of dead women and a female deity are imagined working together against men.

As might be expected among young, single women consulting a soothsayer, much of the talk is about marriage. Charmian imagines that she will "be married to three kings in a forenoon and widow them all. Let me have a child at fifty, to whom Herod of Jewry may do homage. Find me to marry me with Octavius Caesar, and companion me with my mistress" (I.ii.25–29). Part of her attitude here is a good-natured skepticism about soothsaying, so that Octavius is the most unlikely possibility she can think of for a husband. Similarly, the idea of Octavius married to an Egyptian lady-in-waiting diminishes him in somewhat the same way that Cleopatra's epithets ("scarce-bearded Caesar") make him seem smaller and younger (Jankowski, 1992, p. 157). On another level, she duplicates Cleopatra's pattern of taking powerful Roman men as lovers, and by imagining herself married not to Antony, her mistress's lover, but to that lover's chief rival, she inverts their roles. Even when cloaked in teasing and idle talk, imagining Cleopatra as *her* companion suggests competition with her mistress. And her assumption, that as the wife of Octavius she would outrank Cleopatra, is almost a prediction of Octavius's victory. In addition to this momentary display of competitive triumph, the exchange with the soothsayer has a darker side. Despite her easy jokes about numerous illegitimate children and dead or cuckolded husbands, Charmian wishes to marry and have children; but we know, as she does not, that her wish will be sacrificed to the greater demands of her position as Cleopatra's lady-in-waiting. The little that the soothsayer does tell her—"You shall outlive the lady whom you serve" (I.ii.30)—has for the audience a resonance of which she is unaware. This scene is almost the only time Charmian and Iras express motives and desires that deviate even slightly from those of the queen. Even so, they do not appear to resent their positions or their mistress; indeed, the soothsayer's words, "You shall be more beloving than beloved" (I.ii.22), reiterate the women's fundamental loyalty to Cleopatra. Cleopatra's attendants, unlike their Roman counterparts, do not complain about her or about Antony. Nowhere in the play do we see Charmian and Iras overtly disloyal to or critical of Cleopatra. The longevity of their association also gives the women the freedom to advise or to manage her excesses, but they do not gossip about her; nor do we see them conferring with each other or with the male courtiers about how to deal with her.

Cleopatra's women are, like many of Elizabeth's, conspicuously devoted to their mistress. Their long service has given them a familiarity and a shared past, even if the history that they share is primarily Cleopatra's. As many a courtier has sworn with less validity, their lives belong entirely to her, and in the end they literally will have no life beyond that of the woman they serve. At the same time, what we learn of them in act I, scene ii, makes their willingness to die with Cleopatra a generous and poignant act. They have, after all, lives with ambitions and desires to give for her. In this sense, her women humanize Cleopatra by showing her to be someone who can inspire devotion of a different sort than the fascination she engenders in men.

If Cleopatra uses her women for her own ends, they also sometimes manage her for those same ends when necessary. For instance, in the two messenger scenes (II.v and III.iii), Charmian and Iras attempt to soothe Cleopatra's anger at the news of Antony's marriage to Octavia and to protect the messenger. Charmian comes close to reprimanding the queen: "Good madam, keep yourself within yourself, / The man is innocent" (II.v.75–76). At the second encounter with the messenger, the women have coached him in how to reply to questions about Octavia so that he answers satisfactorily and even earns something like an apology: "Thou must not take my former sharpness ill" (III.iii.38). Placated by the messenger's careful answers and by the supporting chorus her women provide, Cleopatra decides that she need not seriously fear Octavia as a rival.

The waiting women's support for and validation of Cleopatra's positions figure prominently during Cleopatra's leisure moments. After Antony has gone, we see Cleopatra and her women passing "this great gap of time / My Anthony is away" (I.v.5–6). Significantly, during Antony's absence, Cleopatra's court is feminized, apolitical, and, because it is populated almost exclusively by women and eunuchs, apparently celibate. Despite her reputation among the Romans, Cleopatra does not consort with other men while Antony is away. Nor does she appear to engage in political activity; rather, she and her women gossip, drink, play games, write letters, speculate about Antony's activities, and wait for him to return. This scene comes closest to the sort of exchange that we expect among women long intimate and familiar with each other. The main subject of conversation is, of course, Cleopatra and, specifically, her past relationships. From the Egyptian point of view, Antony is only the latest in a line of Roman men who have been enamored of Cleopatra and to whom she has allied herself. Charmian at least has apparently served the queen long enough to remember when Cleopatra's Roman lovers were Julius Caesar and Pompey. She seems even to be teasing Cleopatra about her past:

CLEOPATRA.   . . . Did I, Charmian,
                              Ever love Caesar so?

CHARMIAN.   O that brave Caesar!

CLEOPATRA.   Be choked with such another emphasis!
                      Say 'the brave Antony.'

CHARMIAN.   The valiant Caesar!

CLEOPATRA.   By Isis, I will give thee bloody teeth
                      If thou with Caesar paragon again
                      My man of men.

CHARMIAN.   By your most gracious pardon,
                      I sing but after you.

CLEOPATRA.   My salad days,
                      When I was green in judgment, cold in blood,
                      To say as I said then.
                                                      (I.v.66–75)

In a similar "waiting for Antony" scene (II.v), Cleopatra and her women tell stories about the queen and her lover. Charmian recalls the time Cleopatra had a salted fish placed on Antony's fishing line as a joke, and Cleopatra remembers the subsequent events:

> That time—O times!—
> I laughed him out of patience; and that night
> I laughed him into patience; and next morn,
> Ere the ninth hour I drunk him to his bed;
> Then put my tires and mantles on him, whilst
> I wore his sword Philippan.
>
> (II.v.18–23)

Plutarch condemns these episodes as Antony's "follies and boyish extravagances" (Plutarch, p. 257). Shakespeare, however, places them not in the critical mouths of the Romans where he found them but in the more indulgent context of women's gossip where they seem less pejorative, and where Cleopatra, even on the level of grammar, is the agent of all the action and Antony her passive object. Charmian functions in these scenes as a keeper and interpreter of Cleopatra's memories, insisting on the validity of the past before Antony's time in Egypt.

In addition to performing the usual duties of waiting women, Cleopatra's women contribute importantly to her public image of magnificence. The sheer numbers of people who accompany her everywhere add to her substance. The contrast to the sober, silent, and unadorned Octavia is clear. In her four scenes, Octavia appears "with her train" only once (in act III, scene vi, when she returns to Rome without Antony), and it is precisely the "unaugmented greeting" and the lack of "populous troops" that so irritate Octavius about her "market-maid" arrival. Cleopatra's train, by contrast, is a prop, indeed an ornament, to her magnificence and a crucial part of the spectacles that she stages. In this respect, her female attendants are less agents of her power than extenders and amplifiers of her presence in space. In Enobarbus's description of Cleopatra on the Cydnus, for example, they appear as part of the display along with the "pretty dimpled boys": "Her gentlewomen, like the Nereides, / So many mermaids, tended her i'th' eyes, / And made her bends adornings" (II.ii.207–20). As a political message, the barge spectacle suggests something beyond a memorable vision intended to show her wealth and power. It is also, as Lucy Hughes-Hallet argues, "a piece of erotic display" (pp. 77–78) through which Cleopatra intends to seduce Antony and cement their political alliance with a personal and sexual one. By attracting all spectators to herself, she outmaneuvers the Roman attempt to absorb her. Antony loses face and the initiative because, although his power is "enthron'd i'th' marketplace," his display is overshadowed by Cleopatra's and ignored by the populace.

Beyond their politically important decorative presence in Cleopatra's spectacles and their supporting roles in the internal plays designed to control and manipulate Antony, the attendant women do not participate in political matters. They are completely absent, for instance, from the scene in which Cleopatra consults with Enobarbus on military matters (III.vii). Nor does Shakespeare pick up Plutarch's statement that Octavius declared war not on Antony nor even on Cleopatra but on her servants "who are chiefly responsible for directing her affairs" (Plutarch, p. 236). In the play, Cleopatra alone directs her political activity. The attendants do, however, initiate one act with political consequences in the aftermath of Actium (III.xii). As Antony grieves over his shame in fleeing the battle and instructs his followers to make their peace with Caesar, Cleopatra enters supported and led by Charmian and Iras. This configuration is a new one, because the women usually follow the queen. They are accompanied by Antony's personal attendant Eros, an indication of the extent to which the households of Antony and Cleopatra have coalesced. Unlike the political and military advisors, these attendants are able to overlook the political shame of the defeat and to effect a reconciliation. With her usual resources failing and facing certain defeat, Cleopatra begins to depend on her women in new ways, allowing them to lead her and to instigate her actions. From this point on, Charmian and Iras take a more active part in the outcome of the action. For example, it is Charmian's idea to retreat to the monument and send a false report to Antony of Cleopatra's death (IV.xiii). Earlier (I.iii), Cleopatra rejects Charmian's advice regarding Antony, but this time she agrees.

The retreat to the monument further exposes the weakness of a household structure that enforces the queen's isolation from the outside world and her subsequent dependence on a domestic staff similarly cut off from everything but herself. This isolation and retreat has often been noted in discussions of the spatial movements of the play as Cleopatra's once vast world shrinks to the stone monument where she and her women will die. But from the point of view of the separation between Cleopatra's court and the outside world, the monument scene comes into focus as an emblem of her privy chamber's isolation from alliances of politics and kinship such as Elizabeth enjoyed, alliances that contributed to that queen's relative stability. Cleopatra has no waiting women deeply connected to the outside world, and consequently she is vulnerable.

In the final scenes, Charmian and Iras serve as witnesses first to Antony's death and then to Cleopatra's. As her only companions in the monument, the women perform the usual tasks of comfort and support in addition to helping draw the heavy burden of Antony's dying body inside. As Antony dies, Cleopatra seems to need her women as witnesses both to her sorrow and to his greatness: "O see, my women, / The crown o'th' earth doth melt" (IV.xv.62–63). But their part in her story is to be even more important. As Cleopatra recovers from her swoon and resolves to die, she clearly includes the women in her plan:

> Our lamp is spent, it's out! Good sirs, take heart:
> We'll bury him; and then, what's brave, what's noble,
> Let's do't after the high Roman fashion,
> And make death proud to take us. Come, away.
> This case of that huge spirit now is cold.
> Ah, women, women! Come; we have no friend
> But resolution and the briefest end.
>
> (IV.xv.85–91)

Charmian and Iras are essential as the stage managers of the suicide scene and assist in arranging and managing this final spectacle. Shakespeare shows us much of the backstage routine of this spectacle, the assembling of the players, the gathering of costumes and props, and even the preparation of the internal audience:

> Show me, my women, like a queen: go fetch
> My best attires. I am again for Cydnus,
> To meet Mark Antony. Sirrah Iras, go.
> Now, noble Charmian, we'll dispatch indeed,
> And when thou has done this chare, I'll give thee leave
> To play till doomsday.—Bring our crown and all.
>
> (V.ii.227–32)

Cleopatra intends her suicide to be a political maneuver which will spoil Octavius's intention to display her in triumph in Rome, reassert her status as queen, and ensure her place in history. Throughout the play and in all her dealings with others, Cleopatra has fused the political and personal dimensions. Now at the end of her life, as she takes on the "high Roman fashion," she confers political import on the personal gesture of her suicide with its vision of herself and Antony restored to greatness beyond life. Both waiting women die, apparently willingly, with their mistress. Charmian remains behind only long enough to adjust Cleopatra's crown and close her eyes to perfect the spectacle before she too applies an asp and dies.

As Shakespeare represents them, both waiting women seem equally important as intimates of Cleopatra and as agents and expressions of her will. Although Plutarch says that Iras was Cleopatra's hairdresser, Shakespeare does not specify this presumably lower status position for her. In addition, when the soothsayer tells them, "Your fortunes are alike" (I.ii.51), he makes no distinction between them. Nevertheless, Charmian seems to outrank her colleague. For one thing, she has more lines. Furthermore, Charmian seems to have an easier relationship with Cleopatra; she can refuse to play billiards (II.v.4), tease the queen, correct, and even scold her. In stage-managing the suicide, she has the more important job of making an outside contact to arrange for the asps. She also survives long enough to make the formal presentation of Cleopatra to the Romans. And yet, in the final scene, Iras declares that she will put out her eyes before seeing Cleopatra and herself paraded in Rome, thus identifying herself with the queen's humiliation. Iras dies first, and Cleopatra echoes the earlier unspoken competition between herself and her women when she suggests that, as the first to meet Antony, Iras is both an example for Cleopatra and a potential rival for Antony's affections (V.ii.299–302).

The loyalty of her women confers on Cleopatra the dignity she achieves at the end of the play. She and her women have established a connection with each other that Antony, for all his famous ability to inspire devotion in followers, fails to achieve. Unlike Cleopatra, Antony seems, by the end, to expect that his followers will defame or betray him or inadvertently show him up. Cleopatra, however, is at all times utterly confident of the companionship, loyalty, and devotion of her women. As an alliance, however, Cleopatra's relationship with her women is necessarily unequal not only because she is the queen and they are her attendants, but also because her interests and hers alone must be of primary importance to all parties. From the vantage point of the twentieth century, we may wonder what characters like Charmian and Iras or women like Elizabeth's attendants have to gain from an alliance that focuses almost entirely on the central member and that seems to require so much self-effacement from the supporting players. One answer, of course, is that they had no choice. Did Lady Mary Sidney, who nursed Elizabeth through smallpox only to be disfigured when she contracted the disease, resent a duty that required such sacrifice? Did ladies-in-waiting who were forbidden to marry or imprisoned when they married without the queen's permission resent her and their enforced submission? Although their surviving letters about Elizabeth cannot necessarily be taken at face value, it seems that surprisingly often they did not.[8] The expressions of reverence and devotion in many of these letters often go beyond ritualistic formalities or cynical and mercenary attempts to acquire or regain favor. Royal service was both a means of promoting one's financial and political self-interest and a source of honor to one's family and to oneself. It also put the female courtier near the center of important events and people. In other words, attendants can benefit from the alliance in more than material ways. Charmian and Iras's willingness to die with their queen similarly implies a close identification with her interests and perhaps also an awareness that their connection with royalty and great events gives them an immortality of their own.

Nevertheless, this exclusive identification with the monarch does not make a court politically successful. Charmian's and Iras's relationship to their mistress reveals a fundamental weakness of the Egyptian regime. Unlike Elizabeth's women, they are not members of influential families with important connections besides the queen. Nor do they grant or deny access to her, pass on favors for courtiers, or discuss political affairs with her or others. Likewise, she does not use them individually to communicate with the outside world. In other words, as staged, Cleopatra's attendants do not engage in court intrigue. In this sense, Cleopatra's court, for all its voluptuousness and exoticism, seems politically unsophisticated. While she has Antony and while they are successful in their military challenge to Rome, Cleopatra's strategy works well for her. But in defeat, the simple and univocal nature of her court, lacking a complex network of familial and political alliances, leaves her vulnerable. As the final spectacle of her suicide shows, she still has enormous resources to shape the interpretation of her life and death, but the absence of a network of kinship bonds reaching beyond herself and her women politically cripples Cleopatra and becomes a fundamental liability in her exercise of power. With Antony gone, no one fights for her—because the only ones who might have a vital interest in her survival are those who are so closely identified with her that they die with her.

Shakespeare's staging of the household of this queen who was in many ways evocative of and analogous to Elizabeth reveals how important the household structure of a monarch, especially that of a queen, can be. As the epitaphs of Dorothy Stafford and Blanche Parry show, the connection between the monarch and her women moves in two directions, not only conferring on the women status and influence at the center of power, but also connecting the queen to a vast network of her subjects. Elizabeth's shrewd use of these complex alliances with and among her women, in her constant need to juggle the conflicting demands and suits of courtiers, was an important component of her power.

That Shakespeare stages Cleopatra without such alliances comments on their importance in Elizabeth's court, and the play's version of an isolated and unconnected Egyptian queen offers an analysis of the causes of Cleopatra's downfall and of Elizabeth's success. At the same time, the absence of complex kinship networks in the representation of the court of a ruling queen suggests also that Shakespeare's audience, like many historians of Elizabeth, may prefer to see female power stripped of its connections to the social world. In this way, politically powerful women like Elizabeth or Cleopatra can be seen as exceptional and isolated cases, rather than as the most prominent examples of women who knew very well how to make best use of the power available to them.

NOTES

I am grateful to Susan Frye and Karen Robertson for their extensive assistance with this essay, to the participants at the 1992 SAA Seminar on Women's Alliances, and to my colleagues at the University of Rio Grande for reading and listening to earlier versions of this material.

   1. Given the date of *Antony and Cleopatra*, we might expect Anne of Denmark's court to be at least as important as Elizabeth's as a model for Cleopatra's court. Like Cleopatra and Elizabeth, Anne understood the use of spectacle as a political strategy. Barbara Lewalski, *Writing Women in Jacobean England* (Cambridge, Mass.: Harvard University Press, 1993), argues that Anne used court masques as "a vehicle for self-affirmation and for subversive intervention in Jacobean politics" (p. 15). She shows how the early masques evoke Queen Elizabeth as a source of power. I suggest that Shakespeare similarly evokes the pre-

vious queen. Unlike Anne, who set up her court as a rival or oppositional center of power, both Elizabeth and Cleopatra were queens ruling in their own right and were more concerned with suppressing sources of internal opposition. Shakespeare's representation of Cleopatra's court thus seems closer to the relatively univocal nature of Elizabeth's than to the internally factious and tripartite Jacobean court.

2. Many treatments of Elizabeth I deal with her waiting women only cursorily or not at all. Among those who do consider the women of the Privy Chamber are Susan Bassnett, Susan Frye, Christopher Haigh, Christopher Hibbert, Lisa Hopkins, Mary M. Luke, Anne Somerset, David Starkey, Agnes Strickland, Roy Strong, Neville Williams, Violet Wilson, and Pam Wright.

3. Husbands of Privy Chamber women included two Lord Admirals (Edward Lord Clinton and the Earl of Nottingham) and Vice-Chamberlain Sir Francis Knollys. Similarly, Lady Knollys's brother and nephew were successively Lord Chamberlains, and Leicester's sisters, Lady Mary Dudley Sidney and Lady Huntingdon, were also prominent in the Privy Chamber.

4. I am grateful to Susan Frye for directing me to this material.

5. Susan Frye provided the text of this epitaph and that of Blanche Parry and descriptions of their locations. Dorothy Stafford's epitaph, located to the north of the west portal, is accompanied by a plaster effigy of a woman dressed in black with covered head and wearing a ruff, kneeling before a lectern. All ampersands and abbreviations appear in the original; "y" replaces the letter thorn; the original carvings are in block capital letters. Bracketed material is unreadable and words followed by question marks are only partly legible.

6. Blanche Parry's tomb, to the left of the west portal, shows a plaster figure kneeling and facing the lectern. Another monument to Parry located in St. Faith's Church, Bacton, also commemorates her closeness to the queen in figures of the two women kneeling together; David Starkey, ed., *Rivals in Power: Lives and Letters of the Great Tudor Dynasties* (London: Macmillan, 1990), p. 207.

7. William Shakespeare, *Antony and Cleopatra*, ed. Maynard Mack (Baltimore: Penguin, 1960), I.ii.59–64. All quotations from the play are from this edition and are noted in the text.

8. Lady Mary Sidney, for example, seemed to bear Elizabeth no grudge twelve years after recovering from the smallpox she contracted while nursing the queen. In a letter to her husband's agent, she added a postscript "begging him to inquire of Mistress Edmonds and Mistress Skudamore of the Privy Chamber, of her Majesty's health" Historical Manuscripts Commission, *Report on the Manuscripts of Lord De L'Isle* and Dudley Preserved at Penshurst Place, vol. 2 (London: HMSO, 1888–1905), p. 21, a request whose circumstances make it unlikely to be intended solely for flattering effect. Also of interest is the avenue of communication she chooses: women of the Privy Chamber.

PART III

Materializing Communities

9

Tracing Women's Connections from a Letter by Elizabeth Ralegh

. . . .

KAREN ROBERTSON

ASSEMBLING EVIDENCE OF WOMEN'S alliances presents a challenge because historical records tend to privilege male experiences as performed within the major institutional structures of a society. Evidence that women engaged in collective rather than singular activity remains frustratingly elusive; while men's connections in early modern England were often marked by formal legal instruments such as indenture or guild membership, women's groupings were often more informal and less frequently documented.[1] Letters by and about women are a resource that can provide suggestions of women's connections, even though women's letters in the sixteenth and early seventeenth centuries tend to have somewhat restricted purposes and are often written to men, usually those with greater power in the patronage network. This essay considers one tantalizing example of collective activity by women: a list of women's names added as an endorsement to the back of a letter written by Elizabeth Throckmorton, Lady Ralegh, soon after her husband's conviction for treason. At first glance, the list of names seems arbitrary and difficult to identify, the titles and surnames uncontextualized by place or institutional rank. Identifying the names, in itself a difficult task, provides suggestive evidence that this list marks an informal alliance of women based in a kinship network. When the names are examined within the context of Elizabeth Ralegh's life,[2] the evidence suggests that she called on those women in her circle of kin who had themselves recently been engaged in struggles with the legal system, particularly around issues of inheritance and widowhood.

The names are an unusual addition to a very common kind of letter that appears in the Elizabethan and Jacobean Hatfield papers and the Calendar of State papers: a letter of supplication written by an aristocratic woman in her attempts to salvage some property from the economic disaster that has ensued from her husband's imprisonment or death. These letters were usually addressed to William or Robert Cecil, because the Cecils' positions as secretaries to the monarchs placed them at the apex of distribution and adjudication of leases of Crown lands. A woman's letter, by registering her web of social connections and affirming her social place, formed an element in her self-defense against economic catastrophe. In inviting its recipient to remedy an injury, a letter of complaint implies an ideal structure of hierarchical and economic relations. Despite the appropriate formulations of submission,[3] the supplication enfolds a demand.

Elizabeth Ralegh's letter is one of several that she wrote in her attempts to stave off the disaster that ensued on Sir Walter Ralegh's conviction for treason. Sir Walter's fall after the death of Queen Elizabeth I was precipitous, and he was tried and convicted of treason in November 1603. Although sentenced to death, he was granted a stay of execution and was held in the Tower, eventually for thirteen years.[4] During the first years of his imprisonment he and his wife wrote and appealed for economic protection, particularly of the estate of Sherborne granted to him by Elizabeth in 1599.[5] Although the estate, like all property of a convicted traitor, was forfeit to the king, Ralegh believed it was protected from seizure because he had conveyed the estate to his eldest son Walter in 1602. On July 30, 1604, Lady Ralegh received letters patent which seemed to confirm her possession, a confirmation that was rescinded several years later when the Court of Exchequer decided that the deed of transfer was void because of a clerical error.[6] Despite a personal appeal by Lady Ralegh to the king, he granted the estate to his favorite, Robert Carr.[7] Ralegh remained in prison until 1616, when he was granted permission to lead an expedition to Guiana. On that disastrous trip, he failed to find gold and provoked a Spanish attack in which his eldest son, Walter, died. Returning to England, he was executed on October 29, 1618 under the old treason sentence.[8]

Elizabeth Ralegh was a redoubtable woman who never remarried but lived on as a widow until 1647 (figure 9-1). She had survived the early death of her father, Sir Nicholas Throckmorton, when she was six, and had become a lady-in-waiting to Elizabeth I in 1584, a year before the death of her stepfather, Adrian Stokes. After her secret marriage to Sir Walter and her hidden pregnancy in 1591, she and her husband were imprisoned by Elizabeth I.[9] Sir Walter was received again at court, but Elizabeth I never allowed the wife of her favorite to return. Despite Eliza-

FIGURE 9-1 Elizabeth Throckmorton, Lady Ralegh. (Courtesy of the National Gallery of Ireland.)

beth I's implacable hostility, Elizabeth Ralegh continued to seek read-mission, a tenacity that also marks her behavior at the time of Ralegh's imprisonment for treason.

The letter, endorsed by a group of women's names, was written around the time of her pregnancy with her son Carew, when Ralegh's life had been spared, although he had not been pardoned. In July 1604, Sherborne had been placed in trust for Lady Ralegh and her son (Edwards, vol. 1, p. 468), but that favor was threatened by the Lord Admiral, Charles Howard, Earl of Nottingham, who had been granted Ralegh's patent for wine licenses and claimed not only the current and future profits, but also the arrears (Edwards, vol. 1, p. 459). Lady Ralegh petitioned Robert Cecil, specifically to prevent the seizure of property by the Lord Admiral and for protection of herself and her children. She wrote:

> As it hath plesed your Lordshept hetherto to be our only cumfort in our lamentabell misfortuns, so I most humbly beseich your Lordshept, both in cumpassion and justes, to speke one word to me Lord Admirall not to take from us by strong hand that which his Magesti hath geven us for our relife.
>
> I might have hoped that me Lord Admirall—if wee might hope for anithing from any leving man—would rather have geveng us sumthing back agayne of his great porcion. His Lordshepe hath six thowsand pound, and three thowsand pound a yeare, by my husban's falle. And, since hit pleseth God that his Lordship shall build uppon our ruines, which wee never suspected, yet the porcion is great and I trust sufficient, out of onn poour gentelman's fortun to take all that remaines, and not to louke backe before his Magisti's grant, and take from us the debts past, wich your Lordshept knoos ware stayed from us, by a proclmation, befor my husban was suspected of ani offence.
>
> If me Lord's grant do beare them, and his conscience warrant hime, wee must yeild willingly to Gode's will and the King's. But if me Lord Admirall have no onn word, in his grant, for them, then what neither the Keng, lawe, nor conscience, have geven from us, I treust his Lordship will espare us willingly.
>
> God knous that our debts ar above three thoussand pound, and the bread and foode taken from me and my children will never augment my Lorde's table, though hit famish us. If your Lordshept, without his Lordship's ofens, can in charitie parswade his Lordshept to relinquish ether all, or but half, of that wich bclongs not unto him, wee shall be more and more bound to your Lordshept. (Edwards, vol. 2, p. 408–9)

The back of the letter was endorsed with the names of Lady Ralegh and eighteen other women. Given married women's limited access to formal structures of power, they used letters of complaint to announce their need and to mobilize protection.[10] They often used a rhetoric of equity in their letters to affirm an ideal structure of hierarchical and economic relations violated in practice and to invite restitution.[11] Their equity claims could be bolstered by support from powerful connections, most immediately their kin. The most readily available source of power for the majority of women lay in their capacity to form the next generation of kinship through marriage and reproduction. While such capacities are the most conservative and traditional locus of agency for women, it is important that we acknowledge women's negotiation of the powers available to them. The commonplace that the Tudor Court was thickly intermarried[12] tends to obscure the significance for women of that process and the importance they attached to the kin links that they forged. Clearly two partners are biologically necessary for reproduction, but the cultural attribution of reproduction to women also implies responsibility for the formation and preservation of the next generation. Such responsibilities are conceded in Sir Walter's moving letter to his wife on the eve of his execution in 1603, in which he urges his wife to remarry after his death and designates his namesake Walter "thy child": "To witness that thou didst love me once, take care that thou marry not to please sense, but to avoid poverty, and to preserve thy child" (Edwards, vol. 2, p. 384). Women's comprehension of the central social power granted them is often displayed in their violation of normative prohibitions against women's public voice. Deathbed instructions, wills, and mother's legacies are locations from which women assert and mark their connections with one another and the significant generational alliances they have formed, primarily (though not exclusively) with kin. Exceptional women entered print culture by asserting this central responsibility.[13]

Despite their limited participation in formal institutional groupings as women, women did affirm their support for one another, particularly over common threats to economic survival. When basic economic rights were at issue, women could draw on connections with other women, usually women of the same class. In this period, there are a number of examples of the king, husbands, and male relatives attempting to disinherit women. Though their legal position was often weak, aristocratic women did attempt to resist such moves. The most well-known example is the struggle of Anne Clifford to inherit her father's land[14]; in this essay, I discuss the suit of a Neville daughter against the inheritance by her male cousin of the baronetcy of Abergavenny. Letters such as the one sent by Elizabeth Ralegh demonstrate women's active and cooperative opposition to the legal operations of primogeniture and inheritance. The women who endorsed Elizabeth Ralegh's plea seem to be responding to perceived parallels between her economic vulnerability and their own, as I will show.

Sir Walter Ralegh's conviction in 1603 precipitated his wife into the dilemmas shared by the wives of traitors, in particular the economic consequences ensuing from the forfeiture of a traitor's property. The common signal of such disasters is a ripple of letters directed to a Cecil seeking favor in the distribution of such property.[15] Also expected is a letter from the wife or widow of the traitor seeking some protection or alleviation from economic disaster; Lady Ralegh did send such a letter. An uncommon feature of Sir Walter's conviction was the delay in execution, which placed him in an unusual legal limbo in which he found himself convicted but neither pardoned nor executed. The long imprisonment during which Ralegh was held in the Tower also shifted the balance between husband and wife. Where earlier Lady Ralegh had stayed at home in Sherborne or at her brother's estate in Surrey while Sir Walter traveled to court and sailed to Guiana, now she moved between Sherborne, London, and the Tower, in an ongoing attempt to change the family's fortunes.

Immediately after the trial, Sir Walter saw himself as isolated and abandoned. He wrote to his wife in 1603, "To what frind to direct thee I knowe not, for all mine have left mee in the true tyme of triall" (Edwards, vol. 2, p. 285). "Friend" in this context signals not only mutual benevolence but also the complex links of patronage, kinship, and favor that marked the interdependencies of the Tudor gentry and aristocracy.[16] Whatever her husband's despair, Elizabeth Throckmorton was resolute in her efforts to protect the property, the inheritance of her son, Walter, and the life of her husband, using the tools of petition and manipulation of the patronage system.

Elizabeth Ralegh had learned to turn to kin early in her life; her father died in 1571, when his daughter was young, probably only six.[17] The following year her mother, Anne Carew, loaned her daughter's portion of £500 to the Earl of Huntington, the repayment of which Elizabeth Throckmorton continued to seek throughout her life (Rowse, p. 57).[18] The mother's financial problems were resolved by her remarriage in 1572 to Adrian Stokes, the widower of the Duchess of Suffolk. Despite her poverty and her father's early death, Elizabeth, assisted by her brother Arthur, used her father's rank and connection to Queen Catherine Parr to garner a position as maid-in-waiting to Queen Elizabeth I. She was sworn into service to the queen on November 8, 1584 (Rowse, p. 104). Her stepfather died in 1585 and left her hangings and a bedstead from the Duchess's chamber. Her mother's death two years later removed one potential source of support during the disaster of her pregnancy, her secret marriage to Sir Walter in 1591, and the queen's subsequent anger. During the decade of her banishment from Elizabeth's court, Elizabeth Ralegh never gave up her attempts to be readmitted. It is intriguing that, in this earlier trouble, she turned to another woman for help. In an unsympathetic letter, Henry Howard describes her efforts to use the medium of a female ally, Lady Shrewsbury: "The league is very strong between Sir Walter Ralegh and my Lady Shrewsbury and Sir Walter Ralegh's wife. Much hath been offered on all sides to bring her into the Privy Chamber to her old place, because she is a most dangerous woman, and full of her father's inventions" (Rowse, p. 231). In a letter to Cecil, Howard describes her as an angry Proserpina: "His wife, as furious as Proserpina with failinge of that restitution in Court which flatterie had moved her to expecte, bendes her whole witts and industrie to the disturbance of all motions, by councell and encouragement, that may disturbe the possibilitie of others' hopes, sinc her owne cannot be securid" (Edwards, vol. 2, p. 439). A more sympathetic view of her bantering vivacity appears in Ralegh's postscript to a letter to Lord Cobham in 1602: "Bess remembers herself to your Lordship, with a challendg [sic] that shee never hard from yow" (Edwards, vol. 2, p. 255).

The disaster of Ralegh's treason conviction did not deter her energy, despite the economic catastrophe, a chaos Ralegh described to Cecil: "My tenants refuse to pay my wife her rent. . . . Alas! all goes to ruin of that littell which remayneth. My woods ar cutt down; my grounds wast; my stock—which made up my rent—sold. And except sume end be had, by your good favor to the Kinge, I perishe every way" (Edwards, vol. 2, p. 293). Yet poverty did not diminish his wife's state. Her visits to her husband in the Tower caused comment about the presence of her coach (Edwards, vol. 1, p. 490). She finally moved into the Tower with her husband, and a second son, Carew, was born and baptized in the Chapel of St. Peter and St. Paul on February 15, 1605.[19]

Elizabeth Ralegh concentrated her efforts on the protection of the estate of Sherborne, leased to Ralegh by Elizabeth I in 1592 and granted in perpetuity in 1599. The estate, like all property of a convicted traitor, was forfeit to the king, and it attracted suitors at the time of Ralegh's conviction. Robert Cecil, at the intersection of a series of letters seeking the estate at Sherborne, writes to one suitor, "There hath not been so few as a dozen suitors for it" in October 1603 (Edwards, vol. 2, p. 467). Lady Ralegh, too, wrote to Cecil a series of petitioning letters seeking to stay confiscation of the estate, in the common currency of submission and plea. Ralegh wrote to Cecil in 1605, "My wife tolde mee that your Lordship had pleased to move his Majestie for Sherburne, and that his Majestie was graciously disposed toward the releife of her and her poore children" (Edwards, vol. 2, p. 319). She not only spoke and wrote directly to Cecil himself, but she also sought assistance from powerful court figures. Cecil, declining a petition from one suitor for Ralegh's property, blames Elizabeth Throckmorton for his inability to satisfy the seeker. "[B]ut without the wife of Sir Walter hath made such means by some of good reckoning about the King as she shall hope to obtain a gift of all his goods, besides that all his chattels will hardly pay the depts."[20] The comment uses the very agency of Lady Ralegh to deflect any anger at disappointment from himself to a more vulnerable target, a woman acting effectively in disaster. Some of her temperament comes clear in this description by Sir Walter himself who, despite imprisonment, did not find himself immune from blame by his wife. He complained to Cecil in 1605, "Shee hath alreddy brought her eldest sonne in one hand and her sucking child in another, crijng out of her and their destruction; charging mee with unnaturall negligence, and that having provided for myne own life I am without sense and compassion of theirs" (Edwards, vol. 2, p. 318).[21]

In her 1604 letter to Robert Cecil, already quoted here, her appeals to compassion, justice, pity, and charity enclose an account of economic debt and unjust profit. The list of nineteen women's names on the back of the letter[22] is an endorsement that presents a series of small puzzles. When Robert Cecil received letters addressed to him in either his public or private capacity, he or his secretary annotated the letter by noting sender, subject matter, and from time to time other pertinent details. When a letter was signed by several people, their names appear in the endorsement; for example, one sent to the Privy Council by three Vice Admirals was endorsed: "Vice-Adiralls Lord Thomas Howard, Lord Mountjoye, Sir Walter Raleigh, to the lords" (Edwards, vol. 2, p. 190). The holograph in Elizabeth Ralegh's hand is without a date, although the document has been dated and annotated with Lady Ralegh's name in a hand that has not been securely identified.[23] The date of 1604 is complicated by Lady Ralegh's reference in the letter to her "children," since she did not give birth to her second son, Carew, until February of the following year. It is unclear whether the date is inaccurate, or whether she wrote during her pregnancy in 1604 and used the plural "children" in anticipation of the birth to bolster her plea. The list of women's names was added in the hand of Captain Thomas Brett, who later worked for Cecil's heir as Receiver-General in 1612.[24] The women listed in the endorsement to Lady Ralegh's letter have not signed it, but are aligned in some way with her. The date and circumstances of Brett's annotation of the letter remain uncertain. It may be that he was filing past papers for the Second Earl of Salisbury and added the endorsements at the time of his employment in 1612. Or he himself might have been the bearer of the letter in 1604, presenting it to Robert Cecil with the list of those supporting Lady Ralegh. Another Brett was involved with the property transactions of 1604; in July of that year, Sir Alexander Brett became trustee of Sherborne for Lady Ralegh and her son (Edwards, vol. 1, p. 468). These mysteries have received no attention from the editor of the letters, nor has the puzzle of the names received comment. A cursory inspection of the names from the perspective of Sir Walter Ralegh reveals only a group of women connected to Ralegh through his military and familial networks. Lady St. Leger was the daughter-in-law of Ralegh's old friend Warham St. Leger; her husband accompanied Ralegh on his last disastrous trip to Guiana in 1617. Lady Herbert could refer to the Countess of Pembroke, a kinswoman of Ralegh, who persistently supported him and urged her son to do so as well.[25] Lady Pawlett probably refers to the widow of Sir Antony Paulett who preceded Ralegh as Governor of Jersey. Lady Bronker's husband, Sir Henry Brounker, not only was President of Munster but had custody of Arabella Stuart in 1603.

While such identifications are quite simple to make from the perspective of a notable male figure, when the connecting thread in this list is traced from Elizabeth Throckmorton, the claim that this list records a set of Lady Ralegh's kin links is much more difficult to establish. Even though the bilateral kinship system of England privileges both maternal and paternal kin, recognition of the kin links of women is difficult because their marks on the record are not only less frequent but are often ambiguous. A central difficulty of tracing women's kinship ties is the disappearance of the names of female relatives because of name changes at marriage. Amy Louise Erickson reiterates Mary Prior's observation that the process of "tracing women [cuts] across the grain of the historical record. Mothers' names are not always recorded in parish baptismal registers; the most common social phenomena, such as women exchanging their family name upon marriage—every marriage—create enormous obstacles for the historian. Even for historians not specifically tracing women, kin by marriage are difficult to identify" (Erickson, p. 18).[26] Further, even when women's natal family connections are recognized and the siblings are identified, contemporary Northern European notions of kinship involve too restricted a field. Joel T. Rosenthal urges that attention be paid along "a horizontal plane, towards the more flexible bonds and relationships between siblings, cousins, and the other cognatic and agnatic kin who often lived, worked, schemed, and fought together" (1990, p. 103), yet the task of uncovering cognates, particularly female cousins, is extremely difficult because of the transmutation of women's names at marriage. Family records and genealogies of the peerage trace the male line and pay little attention to the sisters who disappear into other families. It is easy to confuse women because female cousins often share the same Christian name, names drawn from a limited store with repetitions of Anne, Catherine, Mary, and Elizabeth. Using *Burke's Peerage*, the *Dictionary of National Biography* (DNB), the *Calendar of State Papers*, Kathy Lynn Emerson's useful volume *Wives and Daughters: The Women of Sixteenth Century England*, as well as collections of letters particularly those recorded by the Historical Manuscripts Commission, I have identified one-half of the women who appear on the list.[27] Despite their rank and connection to major figures at court, the women's names remain at the very verge of historical recoverability.

When analyzed from the perspective of Lady Ralegh, a network of female allies of Elizabeth Throckmorton herself appears. From the perspective of cousinage traced through the families of Elizabeth Throckmorton's parents, nine of the eighteen names on this list can be identified as her cousins, several through her mother's family. "Cousin" is the term used for those affines linked through shared grandparents, though the more distant reaches of the family tree could be acknowledged or not.[28] The claim of kinship was a more flexible category than simply consanguinity. Cousinage was determined not only by direct blood ties but also by linkages through second marriages and step-families.[29] The crucial significance of second marriages can be illustrated by the Throckmorton connection to the Tudors. Nicholas Throckmorton's mother was Katherine, "daughter of Sir Nicholas, lord Vaux of Harrowden . . . and widow of Sir William Parr, K. G. She was thus aunt by marriage to Queen Catherine Parr, and Sir Nicholas claimed the queen as his first cousin" (*DNB*, vol. 19, p. 810). Queen Catherine acknowledged the link, and her cousin joined her household soon after her marriage to Henry VIII. Elizabeth Throckmorton's royal connection established her as far superior in standing to Sir Walter, who came from a family of minor West Country gentry. A less exalted example is Richard Carew's dedication of his *Survey of Cornwall* to his "kinsman" Ralegh.[30]

While the reasons for the women's endorsement of the letter must remain speculative, the clusters of women from four family groupings—Carew, Neville, Hastings, and Norris—are kin of Elizabeth Throckmorton who had themselves recently been involved in contentions over inheritance. Elizabeth Ralegh seems to have summoned support in her time of need from groups of women who recognized in her dilemma difficulties that they themselves had suffered.

The first group of connections are those most closely linked to her by blood and affection—her brother's wife, Lady Throckmorton, and her mother's kin—and thus those most closely affected economically by her sudden poverty. Her brother, Sir Arthur Throckmorton, had been knighted in 1603, although the couple lived retired from court, according to her brother's diary.[31] Through her mother, Anne Carew, Elizabeth Throckmorton was connected to the Killigrews,[32] who in turn were cousins of the Cornwallis family (*Cornwallis Correspondence*, p. 29). Mrs. Killigrew and Lady Cornwallis then can be seen as family connections of Elizabeth Ralegh's mother.

Primary evidence of Lady Ralegh's turning toward her mother's family is the decision to name her second son Carew. He was christened at St. Peter ad Vincula in the Tower on February 15, 1605.[33] While parish records do not indicate the name of the godparents selected for the christening, the name Carew is also the name of her uncle, Sir Francis Carew, and is the name taken by her younger brother Nicholas when he was adopted as his uncle's heir. The adoption is one signal of her uncle's continuing connection and bond with the young orphans of his sister's family.[34] Early evidence of the connection is Elizabeth Throckmorton's baptism at Beddington, her uncle's property, in 1585, as well as the frequent mentions of the estate in her brother's diary. Elizabeth Ralegh actually intended to bury her husband in the family vault in Beddington after his execution in 1618 (Edwards, vol. 2, p. 413). The name Carew might also signal a turning toward Ralegh's connections since it was the name of Ralegh's older brother, and it may also refer to Sir George Carew, a friend of Ralegh who remained loyal throughout the long years of Ralegh's imprisonment and pleaded with James I for Ralegh's life in 1618.[35]

The second group of women were members of the Neville family who had recently been engaged in a long and contentious inheritance suit over the Barony of Bergavenny. When the direct male line of the baronetage ended with the death of Henry Neville, 4th Baron of Bergavenny, in 1586, the title was claimed by his male cousin Edward, who died before he was summoned to Parliament in 1589. Mary Neville, Lady Fane, daughter of the 6th Lord of Bergavenny, disputed the system of male primogeniture and tried to prevent the inheritance of Edward's son; the case was not settled until 1604 when the title was granted to the male heir.[36] Mary's stepmother, Lady Sydley, was the second wife of Edward Neville, 6th Lord Bergavenny.[37] The Bergavenny case was intimately familiar to the Throckmorton family because Mary Neville Fane's cousin, Catherine, had married Clement Throckmorton. Catherine Neville, Elizabeth Ralegh's aunt on her father's side, is the linch pin connecting the Throckmortons and the Nevilles and linking four of the women on the list. Mrs. Goring, also named Mary Neville, is her sister.[38] Lady Oxenbridge is Catherine Neville's granddaughter.[39] Lady Fane's cousin, Ursula,[40] had married into the St. Leger family and was mother-in-law to the Lady St. Leger whose name appears on the list. Mary Neville Fane's first cousin once removed,[41] Sir Henry Neville, had married Anne Killigrew, thus forming a link with the Mrs. Killigrew named on the list.[42] Although the name of Catherine Neville, the closest Neville kin to Elizabeth Throckmorton, does not appear on the list (unless she had been granted an honorific title[43]), three of her cousins do appear.

The final cluster of three names forms a web connecting the Norris and Hastings families, a set of women made significantly aware of a widow's economic difficulties after the death of Bridget Kingsmill's husband, Thomas Norris, in Ireland. Bridget Kingsmill had sought Lady Ralegh's assistance in the economic troubles following her husband's death. She wrote to Lady Ralegh in 1600, enclosing a draft of a letter to Cecil and hoped: "I trust if Sir Walter Ralegh will take the pains to polish them, he shall also prevail in the subscribing" (*CSP Domestic Elizabeth 1588–1601*, p. 447). She wrote to the couple, detailing the circumstances of her property:

> Nevertheless I had had no consideration, not so much as to enjoy the little remnant left me, which is my house and land, the building whereof cost my husband five thousand pounds, besides the "Ordinance" and other defensible furniture, to the value of a thousand pounds: all which the garrisons there placed make use of, as also of the wood, hay, cattle and pastures, not sparing to spoil, as is incident to such people. . . . (*HMC Cecil*, vol. 10, p. 447)

Bridget Kingsmill's stepmother was Elizabeth Hastings. Lady Hastings had been prevented from becoming a countess by the death of her husband, the heir of the 4th earl of Huntingdon, and she then wed Justice Kingsmill.[44] Bridget Kingsmill Norris's sister-in-law was Catherine Norris, sister of Thomas Norris and the widow of Sir Antony Paulet. Lady Pawlett's name thus appears in the endorsement, not simply a representative of her husband, but as a "sister" to another woman on the list. The Huntingdon family was a Throckmorton connection; this is perhaps why Anne Carew had loaned her daughter's portion of £500 to the Earl of Huntingdon. The Hastings family may have felt some obligation to Elizabeth Ralegh, since the portion was never repaid, despite Elizabeth Ralegh's pressing for repayment throughout her life.

The cluster of women's names, not immediately identifiable as connected, mark a network of family ties formed through women's connections. Marriage alliances at the royal level have begun to be recognized as the material of diplomacy in the sixteenth century.[45] The list of women's names on the back of Lady Ralegh's letter gives access to a web of connection that today would barely be perceptible without the letter. It suggests that women were aware of and could turn to kinship alliances constructed through the female line.

Women's function as linkage or connection is acknowledged overtly by male writers, although the connections so formed did not necessarily guarantee that affines would demonstrate loyalty to their new kin. The transformative failure of one such connection surfaces in the Ralegh treason trial. George Brooke, one of the conspirators tried at the same time as Ralegh, had been closely linked to Robert Cecil through Cecil's marriage to Brooke's sister, Elizabeth (who had, however, died some years earlier). Brooke, in writing to Cecil after his conviction, calls on that connection in terms that attempt to mobilize a line of love from husband to wife to brother. He invokes the memory of his sister as an agent who forms a connection between the two men, "by the memory of her whom Cecil yet loves" (November 18, 1603, *CSP Domestic James I 1603–1610*, p. 54). The transformation of Cecil and Brooke into brothers is a potential connection that failed to transform an affine into an agnate. In George Brooke's case, female agency beyond the grave did not save the "brother" of the female line from execution.

If this list records women who supported Elizabeth Ralegh in her quest to save some property from the wreckage, it raises the question of how and why such links operate. The dense intermarriages of the prominent families of Tudor England mean that many such connections could be traced, and the names on the letter certainly do not record all of Elizabeth Ralegh's kin. Half of the names on the list are of women who had recent experience with problems of inheritance and the vulnerability of women before the law. As the wives or widows of soldiers, a number of these women might have recognized parallels with or vulnerability similar to Elizabeth Ralegh. Certainly women did offer other women support in property struggles.[46] Finally, the issue of affective ties arises. Friendship is a term under profound scrutiny at the moment, particularly with the development of queer theory and the reevaluation of homosocial and homoerotic bonds in the period.[47] If these women did try to support Elizabeth Throckmorton as she protested the distribution of her husband's property, kin linkage through cousinage overlaps with the category of friend.[48] They stand by their kinswoman, who finds herself friended, unlike her friendless husband.

NOTES

I would like to acknowledge the help of my research assistant, Damien Keane, whose thorough work uncovered the Kingsmill-Norris connection. I would also like to thank James Brain, Miriam Cohen, Susan Frye, Elizabeth Robertson, and Paul Russell for their invaluable assistance on this essay.

1. See Mary Wack's essay in this volume on the exclusion of Chester women from guilds.

2. In this paper I call her Elizabeth Ralegh because that was the signature she used immediately after her secret marriage to Ralegh; A. L. Rowse, *Ralegh and the Throckmortons* (London: Macmillan, 1962), p. 164.

3. Submission was an important aspect of such letters. For example, in 1562 when Lady Margaret Douglas, Countess of Lennox, and her husband were imprisoned in the Tower for their part in the marriage of their son to Mary Queen of Scots, the countess was instructed by William Cecil that the queen "desire[d] that her husband's submission should come from himself, and not by her teaching." The queen found his subsequent letter "a very slight amends" (*CSP Domestic Elizabeth 1547–1580*, p. 204).

4. He was released from the Tower on January 30, 1616; Edward Edwards, *The Life of Sir Walter Raleigh*, vol. 1 (London: Macmillan, 1868), p. 563.

5. He was granted a lease in 1592 and the property in perpetuity in 1599.

6. The deed was missing a crucial phrase "shall and will from henceforth stand and be there seised," which meant that the deed had never been properly activated, the son had not been put in possession, and thus the estate was forfeit to the king; Robert Lacey, *Sir Walter Raleigh* (New York: Atheneum, 1974), p. 317.

7. Lady Ralegh requested an audience with the king; when that was refused, she went to Hampton Court and fell on her knees before him. The story of her petition in 1608 was well known, although the king's reply, "He mun have it for Car" may be apocryphal; William Oldys, *Life of Sir Walter Raleigh* (London, 1740), p. 360.

8. Elizabeth Throckmorton's resistance continued after Ralegh's execution in 1618. Lady Ralegh had to petition to protect his books from seizure by Sir Thomas Wilson. See her letter to Lady Carew asking for assistance in November (?) 1618 (Edwards, *Life*, vol. 2, p. 414). In 1621 a bill of restitution of her son, Carew Ralegh, was passed in the House of Lords, but went no further. Sponsored by the Earl of Pembroke in 1623, Carew Ralegh presented himself to the king, who found him too like the ghost of his father, and the son withdrew to travel on the continent. In 1624, a bill of restitution was presented again and passed by Parliament, but the king refused to sign it, although in 1624 a provisional settlement for Carew's future was arrived at with a pension of £400 per year; his father's goods and chattels were granted in trust for the family. The bill was presented again in 1626, but it did not finally pass with royal assent until 1628.

9. The course of the story of the birth and baptism of their first child, Damerai, can be followed in Rowse's summary of Arthur Throckmorton's journal. Essex was one godfather, Arthur the other. Anna Throckmorton, Arthur's wife, was godmother. Damerai died; a second son, Walter, was born in 1593. A third son, Carew, was born in 1605.

10. See Lynn Magnusson, "The Elizabethan Woman as Suitor: Epistolary Rhetoric and Shakespearean Intertexts," First Plenary Session, Rocky Mountain Medieval and Renaissance Association Conference, Banff, Alberta, May 15, 1997, for analysis of the exigencies and performances of women's letters.

11. Amy Louise Erickson, *Women and Property in Early Modern England* (New York: Routledge, 1995), observes that scholarly attention to common law

with its severe limitation of women's rights tends to obscure the importance of equity courts (p. 5).

12. "Almost all its members came from established Tudor Court families, and the web of intermarriage and family connection was extremely tight: they were practically all each others' cousins in the most literal sense"; Simon Adams, "Eliza Enthroned? The Elizabethan Court and Its Politics," in *The Reign of Elizabeth I*, ed. Christopher Haigh (London: Macmillan, 1984), p. 69.

13. See Wendy Wall, "Dancing in a Net: The Problems of Female Authorship," in *The Imprint of Gender: Authorship and Publication in the English Renaissance*, Wendy Wall (Ithaca, N.Y.: Cornell University Press, 1993), on the mother's legacy and women's negotiations of authorship.

14. In that struggle Clifford was supported not only by her mother, but also by Queen Anne; *The Diary of Lady Anne Clifford*, ed. Vita Sackville-West (London: Westminster Press, 1923), p. 48, entry for January 1617.

15. The fall of a prominent man can be traced in the Hatfield papers and the Calendar of State Papers by the letters seeking distribution of his property. Robert Cecil said that he had had at least twelve requests for Ralegh's property (Edwards, *Life*, vol. 1, p. 467).

16. Barbara Harris observes that "marriage and kinship formed the basis of the patron/client relations at the center of early Tudor politics" (p. 260). Adams, "Eliza Enthroned?," p. 70, points out Sir Walter's singularity as dependent solely on Elizabeth's favor and suggests that his lack of a powerful familial base as well as his manner provoked much enmity.

17. She was baptized on April 16, 1565, at Beddington (Rowse, *Ralegh*, p. 57).

18. See her letter to Robert Cecil in 1594–95 (Edwards, *Life*, vol. 2, p. 399).

19. Personal correspondence, Terry Radley, Sexton of the Chapel Royal of St. Peter ad Vincula, October 2, 1994.

20. Letter to Sir James Elphinstone, 16 Oct. 1603, *HMC Cecil*, vol. 15, p. 259.

21. Sir Walter had conveyed the property to his son Walter in 1602. On July 30, 1604, Lady Ralegh received letters patent which seemed to confirm her possession of Sherborne, but the confirmation did not withstand the king's desire to reward Robert Carr. In 1607 the Court of Exchequer requested Sir Walter to show proper title. After judicial deliberation, the transfer of the property was voided because of a clerical error (see note 6), and thus the estate was forfeit to the king, who granted it to Robert Carr (Lacey, *Raleigh*, p. 317).

22. "Lady Rawlegh. Lady Saltingstone. Lady Woodroofe. Lady Bronker. Lady Pawlett. Lady St. Leger. Mrs. Killegrew. Lady Kingsmell. Lady Cornwallis. Lady Oxenbridg. Lady Throgmorton. Lady Walssh. Lady Sydley. Lady Herbert. Mrs. Blanch. Lady Martin (?). Lady Cheek. Lady Trafford. Mrs. Goring" (Edwards, *Life*, vol. 2, p. 409).

23. The hand is identified by Edwards as that of Robert Cecil, though Robin Harcourt Williams, Librarian at Hatfield House, is not certain that the identification is correct (personal communication, June 5, 1997).

24. I am grateful to Robin Harcourt Williams for his assistance in the identification of Brett's hand. This may be the Mr. Brett introduced to Cecil by Elizabeth Ralegh in 1595 when she sought his support for a suit by Brett against Sir Ralph Horsey (Edwards, *Life*, vol. 2, p. 400).

25. The Herbert family's support of Ralegh was loyal, and Philip Herbert sponsored Carew Ralegh at court in 1623.

26. Feminist epistemology has developed arguments about situated knowledge. See Gunew's introduction to *Feminist Knowledge: Critique and Construct* (London: Routledge, 1990), pp. 13–35.

27. I would like to thank Carole Levin and Donald Foster for their generous suggestions at the outset of this project.

28. David Cressy, "Kinship in Early Modern England," *Past and Present* 113 (1986): 38–69, explains the operations of the system as one "of interdependence and mutual obligation which, however dormant or latent for much of the time, could be activated by relatives when needed. Participants understood the system in terms of possibilities, resources, and obligations" (p. 47).

29. "Cognate" describes all kin related by blood. "Agnates" are blood relations through the father's line, a category significant in patrilineal societies. "Affines" are relations formed through marriage. The system of cousinage in Tudor England draws on all these possibilities. I am grateful to Bonnie Urciuoli and James Brain for their assistance with these categories. The terms "cognate" and "agnate" are terms from Roman law.

30. He signs himself, "Your Lordship's poor kinsman, Richard Carew of Antonie." The kinship was through Anne Carew, Elizabeth Ralegh's mother. Both Richard Carew and Anne were descended from Sir Nicholas Carew of Haccombe; F. E. Halliday, ed. *The Survey of Cornwall* (London: Andrew Melrose, 1953) p. 77.

31. Throckmorton's diary has an unfortunate gap between 1596 and 1609. The volumes are extant between 1578 and 1595 and then between 1609 and 1613 (Rowse, *Ralegh*).

32. William Killigrew, groom of the chamber to Elizabeth I, received a bequest in Sir Nicholas Throckmorton's will, "my best coat and cloak that he will choose" (Rowse, *Ralegh*, p. 56).

33. "Carew Rawley was Baptized ye 15th February the sonne of Sir Walter Rawley kt." Private correspondence from Terry Radley, Sexton of the Chapel Royal of St. Peter ad Vincula, October 2, 1994.

34. Family loyalties have long roots. Following Wyatt's rebellion in 1554, Sir Nicholas Throckmorton was imprisoned in the Tower along with his wife's cousin, Sir Gawen Carew, while Sir Peter Carew managed to escape on a ship provided by Walter Ralegh, Sir Walter's father (Rowse, *Ralegh*, p. 21).

35. George Carew, Baron Carew of Clopton and Earl of Totnes. "In 1618 he pleaded with James I on behalf of Sir Walter Raleigh with whom he had lived for more than thirty years on terms of great intimacy, and Lady Carew, his wife, proved a kind friend to Ralegh's family after the execution" (*DNB*, vol. 3, p. 961). Sir George was knighted in 1585. In 1599–1600 he became President of Munster, succeeded by Lord Brounker. F. E. Halliday, *Survey*, points out that "collateral branches of the families of Raleigh, Edgcumbe, and Carew (both of Devon and Cornwall) intermarried, which probably accounts for Sir Walter's elder brother being called Carew Raleigh" (p. 77).

36. Cecil's investigation of the pedigree, during the winter of 1588, after the Armada, engages with the question of female inheritance. The material includes "lists of noblemen now living that had their baronies by inheritance from women; also of noblemen, being barons, that have their baronies and their titles by their ancestresses," *CSP Domestic Elizabeth 1588–1601*, February 1589, p. 581). Her petition in 1598 claims the title through her mother, Elizabeth Beauchamp (*CSP Domestic Elizabeth 1598–1601*, p. 122). The title passed to Edward Neville, grandson of George the 4th baron, although Mary Neville, Lady Fane, was granted a consolation, the barony of Le Despencer (*Burke's Peerage*, p. 13).

37. Mary Neville's stepmother Elizabeth, the second wife of her father, married Sir William Sedley after the death of her first husband. Though the spelling is different, I suspect that this is the Lady Sydley whose name appears on the list. John Chamberlain *The Letters of John Chamberlain*, ed. Norman Egbert McClure (Philadelphia: American Philosophical Society, 1939), comments on "Sir William Sidley of Kent that married the Lady Abergavenny" (vol. 1, p. 415). Elizabeth, Lady Sedley, born Darell, then Neville, then Sedley (index).

38. Mary Neville, George Goring's wife, remained a simple Mrs. Goring until her husband's knighthood in 1608. Sir Henry Goring married into the Kingsmill family.

39. She married Daniel Oxenbridge.

40. Ursula St. Leger and Sir Richard Grenville's wife were heroines of a siege at Carrigaline, Cork, in Ireland in 1569.

41. Cousinage is determined through descent from a shared grandparent, or a more remote ancestor. First cousins are descended by an equal number of steps from shared grandparents. Children of first cousins are second cousins to one another.

42. In 1561, *CSP Domestic* records "A remembrance for Mr. Henry Killigrew to move secretary on behalf of his cousin . . . Killigrew" (p. 513).

43. Clement Throckmorton was not knighted. Catherine was "daughter of Sir Edward Neville, second son of George Neville, third baron Bergavenny" *DNB*, vol. 19, p. 809.

44. Sir George Kingsmill, Judge of Common Pleas, died in 1606. Chamberlain, *Letters*, reports that Kingsmill treated his widow well: "And hath dealt kindly with his Lady Hastings leaving her all his moveables (some few legacies reserved) and all his lands and leases during her life" (vol. 1, p. 226). McClure traces her marriages: Sarah Harington, to Francis Lord Hastings, heir of the 4th Earl of Huntingdon, to Kingsmill, to LaZouche (Chamberlain, *Letters*, index).

45. Benjamin G. Kohl, "Diplomatic Dreams: Carrara Marriage Alliances in the Trecento," presented at the Annual Meeting of the Renaissance Society of America, Vancouver, B.C., 6 April 1997.

46. Anne Clifford's mobilization of support through the maternal line for inheritance of her father's property and her advice from Queen Anne is well known. Aemilia Lanyer's dedicatory poems to *Salve Deus Rex Judeorum* construct a female alliance. Martha Howell, "Fixing Moveables: Gifts by Testament in Late Medieval Douai," *Past and Present* 43 (1996): 3, analyzes the way in which women's wills document female alliance.

47. Indeed, at times Renaissance queer theory seems to institute male homosocial bonds as the central axis of connection in the period.

48. For contemporary anthropological analysis of the way that kinship is used to double friendship, see Sarah Uhl, "Forbidden Friends: Cultural Veils of Female Friendship in Andalusia," *American Ethnologist*, 18, no. 1 (1991): 90–105.

10

Sewing Connections

Elizabeth Tudor, Mary Stuart, Elizabeth Talbot, and Seventeenth-Century Anonymous Needleworkers

. . . .

SUSAN FRYE

MATERIAL OBJECTS ARE PROVIDING new means to recover the alliances of early modern women. Women's domestic needlework, for example, reveals political and imaginative interconnections among women as they worked within but also sought to expand the prevalent social and symbolic economies of sixteenth- and seventeenth-century England. For highly visible, highly placed women like Elizabeth Tudor, Mary Queen of Scots, and Elizabeth Talbot, Countess of Shrewsbury ("Bess of Hardwick") in the sixteenth century, and for thousands of largely anonymous women of the merchant and gentry classes in the seventeenth century who painstakingly imitated the possessions of the wealthy, needlework provided the means to perpetuate, use, and even cautiously restructure the cultural category of "woman" from within a community of women.

Women responded to the unchanging injunction to perform domestic needlework[1] by evolving a subculture within which patterns and pictures articulated their lives. These patterns—such as the busy bee of the community worker or the strawberry of generation—and pictures— often of Diana and Actaeon, Lucrece, Judith, and Esther—formed visual expressions of narratives offering alternatives to the passivity, privacy, and silence that needlework was supposed to enforce. In the sixteenth century, only exceptional women like Mary Queen of Scots and Elizabeth Talbot, Countess of Shrewsbury, had access to volumes containing prints and could pay professional embroiderers and artists to draw on cloth the pictures that they wished to embroider. By the seventeenth century, the women who had access to a print shop and money for thread could browse among a variety of prints and have a desired picture drawn on cloth. These needleworkers did not confront their society's equation of needlework with chaste labor so much as they accepted it and made it their own. They took seriously the masculinist association of the needle with the tongue, but instead of letting the needle silence them, they used it as their instrument of communication in the tradition of the silenced Philomel. For Englishwomen, as Jane Burns writes of the fictive women of the Old French romance *Philomela*, "female knowledge, skills, and talents . . . feed into an elaborate economy of women's collective work grounded in sight, hearing, and touch as alternatives to speech" (Burns, p. 117).[2] Women created their own patterns, shared patterns with other women, and chose the subjects of their own needlework pictures and worked them in company with kinswomen, mistresses, and dependents. A few women in the sixteenth century, as well as many more women whom we know of in the seventeenth century, used needlework to explore alternative narratives of the feminine as political, authoritative, active, and expressive, although invariably chaste and productive. Indeed, needlework became a dynamic discourse through which its practitioners simultaneously obeyed and defied the injunction to passive silence. Needles became pens as well as minute, multiply stabbing swords, as women worked patterns and narratives into their lives that conveyed their sense of themselves in the world.

Women's alliances can be seen through needlework because early modern English women sewed them to be seen. This essay considers the many politicized forms of female alliance made visible in needlework, and the ways in which women continued to rework the injunction to silence by taking action through textiles. Part 1 considers how, as a young, illegitimate, and disempowered member of the royal family, Elizabeth Tudor used gifts of needlework-covered translations to "sew" herself the family she would need in order eventually to ascend the throne. Similarly, as discussed in part 2, Mary Queen of Scots, the disempowered royal prisoner, and her jailer, Elizabeth Talbot, sewed works that expressed their political alliances and conflicts. For a time, these two women sewed alongside one another in pursuit of different ambitions ending in the same goal: the English throne. While Mary pursued a needlework identification with her French past as well as her claim to the Scottish and English thrones, Talbot pursued an imagined identification with a number of powerful mythic female figures, especially Penelope and Lucrece. In the final two sections of this essay, I consider the shift from sixteenth-century needleworkers whose names we know to the seventeenth-century needleworkers who left behind largely anonymous samplers, needlework boxes, bed testers, mirrors, writing desks, and pictures. While aristocratic women used needlework to accomplish political relationships that would further their personal and dynastic ambitions, the anonymous women's needlework pictures testify to a collective search for historical connection with figures like Judith, Jael, and Esther. However such figures may have been bounded by their own patriarchal societies, they still represent activity and political action in marked contrast to the values of passivity and silence supposedly enforced through domestic textile production.

1. Elizabeth Tudor and Katherine Parr

As an eleven- and twelve-year-old, the future Elizabeth I—at that time styled the bastard Lady Elizabeth—sought to demonstrate her accomplishments as an educated young woman to her father, Henry VIII, and to her educated stepmother, Katherine Parr, by presenting them with New Year's gifts of matched sets of needlework-covered calligraphic manuscripts in 1544 and 1545. Despite their display of her abilities in needlework and in writing two different italic hands, these gifts also demonstrated her intellectual and religious relationships to the court. The three extant volumes in fact contain ambitious translations: in 1544, for her stepmother, Elizabeth translated a section of Calvin's *Institutes*, and for her father, she translated Katherine Parr's prayers into Italian, Latin, and French. In 1545, again for Parr, she translated Marguerite de Navarre's Protestant text *Glass of the Sinfull Soul*; John Bales published the translation on the Continent in 1548[3]—Elizabeth's first publication.

New Year's gifts at the Tudor court carried immense significance, and Elizabeth's were no exception. The gift one gave a personage at court was a painstakingly considered form of self-representation. Gifts given at the New Year were duly noted in lists executed in ornate calligraphy. Ideally, the gift must be "valuable" in some way. By "valuable" I mean that the gift must register and enshrine the values of the giver and the receiver. As Joel Rosenthal points out in the context of aristocratic philanthropy, the gift stands for "the continuing nature of the ties between giver and recipient" (Rosenthal, 1972, p. 10) by making a statement about their shared relation to larger groups and networks. The point of the gift was to create a bond through what the gift said about the power of the recipient and the submission of the giver. The ideal court gift articulated the giver's self-perceived place within the "reciprocal expectations"[4] of the court and thus made a statement about the discrimination, merit, and position of the giver in terms of the social hierarchy.

To her father, Elizabeth's gifts demonstrated her proper upbringing as the daughter of one of the best-educated humanist princes in Europe, and thus her suitability for her position as third in line to his throne. This demonstration was particularly suitable in 1544, the year in which she and Mary were restored to the succession, an event that Mary marked by commissioning a portrait of herself (Hearn, p. 47). Elizabeth's seeking of her father's approval and attention seems not to have been wholly successful, however. Her father's complete approval depended on the one factor over which she had no control—her female sex—and was thus reserved for her brother Edward.

To her stepmother, Katherine Parr, Elizabeth's gifts demonstrated her commitment to an already existing alliance that offered her more intellectual and emotional nurturance than her dynastic ties to her father. Through her gifts to Parr, the Lady Elizabeth articulated her attachment to a woman who had helped to reconnect her father with his children, a woman who took a vital interest in Elizabeth's education and who was, as Elizabeth's gift to her father demonstrated, herself an author in the acceptably pious vein of the 1530s and 1540s.[5] In the absence of her father's interest, Elizabeth reached out to Parr through the association of the discourses of protestant humanism and emblematically ciphered needlework. Translating Marguerite de Navarre for Katherine Parr meant asserting their bond through religion, female kinship, and authorship. As she wrote in her "Epistle Dedicatory," the work came from her "humble daughter," who "knowing the affectionate will and fervent zeal which your highness hath toward all godly learning as also my duty toward you . . . hath moved so small a portion as God hath lent me to prove what I could do." In other words, this is a gift that "proves" what the twelve-year-old Elizabeth can do.

Elizabeth's gifts to Parr bring together the memories and activities of six different women: Elizabeth herself, Marguerite de Navarre, Katherine Parr, Anne Boleyn, and even Lady Margaret Beaufort, who was Henry VII's mother and thus Elizabeth's great-grandmother. In his recent edition of *The Glass of the Sinfull Soul*, Marc Shell points out that Marguerite de Navarre very likely had presented Elizabeth's mother, Anne Boleyn, with a copy of her protestant work when they renewed their association in 1534–5 (Shell, 1993, p. 3).[6] Moreover, Elizabeth's choice of the title, *The Glass of the Sinfull Soul*, echoes the choice that her great-grandmother made when Beaufort translated a work from the French titled *The Mirror of Gold for the Sinful Soul*. Thus Elizabeth's gift brings herself into association with these women through a composite self-display of needlework, calligraphy, and translation.[7]

Although curiously little of Elizabeth's early correspondence survives, it seems that the Parr–Elizabeth alliance served not only to educate and support Elizabeth but also to hinder and even endanger her. After Henry VIII's death, Elizabeth stayed with Parr at Chelsea and Hatfield, where she became increasingly familiar with the Lord High Admiral, Thomas Seymour, younger brother of Edward VI's regent Edward Seymour, the Lord Protector and Earl of Somerset. Because Thomas Seymour married Parr four scant months after the death of Henry VIII in June (or as early as May) 1547, Elizabeth was caught up in the Lord Protector's anger at the match and was probably denied the court because of her association with Parr. After Parr's death in childbirth later that year, Elizabeth's association with Thomas Seymour landed her in the middle of an investigation of their supposed relationship. Eventually, Seymour was executed in part for treasonously plotting to marry an heir to the throne. Nevertheless, it was at Parr's and Seymour's establishment that Elizabeth met young William Cecil, who became manager of her estates and revenues and eventually the figure whose careful management of her government resulted in so much of its success. In the case of Parr, Elizabeth's needlework-covered translations articulated a relationship that caused trouble for Elizabeth but on balance worked to her advantage.

Elizabeth's needlework-covered translations were only the beginning of her lifelong work as an author. She went on to translate Petrarch, Horace, Seneca, and, in her sixties, Boethius's *Consolation of Philosophy*,[8] leaving behind her needlework with her disempowered youth. Like the left panel of Anne Clifford's remarkable triptych at Appleby Castle that depicts her youthful education by juxtaposing an intricate piece of needlework, her lute, and her books with her young figure, the young Elizabeth used her needlework gifts to prove her proper education as "woman" and female intellect. No one mentions Elizabeth doing any kind of needlework once she was queen. Even John Taylor, author of the popular patternbook, *The Praise of the Needle* (1631), who offers his consumers a vision of their connection to English queens through needlework, is hard pressed to say anything specific about Elizabeth's needlework. The embroidered accomplishments of Mary Tudor and Catherine of Aragon may be on view at the Tower, Taylor explains, but he is forced to substitute the story of Elizabeth's imprisonment under her sister Mary for a discussion of her needleworks' whereabouts (Taylor, Sig. A3). Once Elizabeth succeeded to the throne, she not only continued translating authors of significance to her life, she also crossed into the public male realms of poetry and speech writing that were denied most women. In leaving behind her needlework for other, more public forms of expression, Elizabeth was in part signaling her departure from the strict construction of the feminine she had been so anxious to project when young and on the margins of power.

2. Mary Queen of Scots and Elizabeth, Countess of Shrewsbury

A very different and more conflicted alliance developed between Mary Queen of Scots and Elizabeth, Countess of Shrewsbury, from 1570 to 1584, when Queen Elizabeth designated George Talbot, Earl of Shrewsbury, as Mary's warden.[9] These two women came from very different backgrounds and had such conflicting dynastic ambitions that it could not have been easy for them to be thrown together for fourteen years. True, they did not always inhabit the same house as they moved among

Chatsworth, the lodge at Buxton, Sheffield Castle, Sheffield Manor, Wingfield, and Tutbury. Nevertheless, during their early years together Talbot was willing to learn as much as possible about needlework from the Queen of Scots, and the two collaborated extensively to produce emblematic pieces meant to express and realize their differing ambitions.

Mary Stuart, daughter of Marie de Guise, had been raised at the French court in expectation of her marriage to the dauphin who, as it turned out, survived only a few months as Henri II. For Mary Stuart, as for Elizabeth Tudor and Anne Clifford, needlework had formed part of a comprehensive humanist education. Throughout her life, it fashioned the visually emblematic counterpoint to her authorship of letters and poetry. After choosing to return to Scotland in 1561 following her husband's death, Mary employed two professional embroiderers, Ninian Miller and Pierre Oudry, the latter also a portrait painter, to help produce and maintain the textiles so necessary for Scotland's cold and ill-furnished palaces (Swain, 1986, p. 19).

After Mary's escape to England in 1569, the majority of her needlework asserts her identity as former queen of France, as present queen of Scotland, and as heir in waiting to the English throne. Indeed many of the several dozen extant cushions and individual octagon-shaped pictures in tentstitch that she produced during her imprisonment constitute ciphers of her political identity and consequent ambition. The spider octagon, in which a rather malevolent spider patiently waits in the web surrounded by little spider attendants, recalls Robert the Bruce's lesson in waiting for one's moment, and in so doing suggests that Mary can outwait Elizabeth. The dolphin octagon plays on the English pronunciation of "dauphin" as a reminder of her connections to the powerful de Guise family and her French marriage. A cushion now at Oxburgh Hall is a second version of a rectangular piece that played a more immediate political role when Mary gave it to the Duke of Norfolk during their illicit courtship. The design, of a hand clipping off a barren vine so that the fruitful vine may flourish, surmounted by the same cipher as Mary's signet ring (Swain, 1973, p. 94), bears the motto, "Virescit Vulnere Virtus"—"Virtue flourishes by wounding." The message, that the barren stalk of Elizabeth should be cut away so that the fruitful branch of Mary might flourish, made the cushion admissible evidence at Norfolk's trial in the course of which he was found guilty of treason and bound over for execution (Swain, 1973, p. 75).[10]

Thus the majority of Mary Queen of Scots's needlework constructed a different message from her pleas contained in the letters, poems, gifts of needlework, and oral communications sent to Queen Elizabeth pleading for a personal audience as a prelude to release. Despite her outpouring of requests, Mary refused to enter into the various possibilities extended to her, like that of the proposed marriage to Robert Dudley, whether out of suspicion or because such plans interfered with her perception of the regal identity conveyed in her surviving textile production. Mary

Stuart's needlework conveys the strong sense of her own dynastic identity that made continued conflict with Queen Elizabeth inevitable. Yet for all her needlework's attempts to exclude and cut off Elizabeth, her work still relies on her kinship to Elizabeth in order to construct her own imaged identities. Elizabeth is necessarily present in all of Mary's work, because Elizabeth is the power to be outwaited, the curtailer of her liberty, the vine to be cut off if Mary is to flourish.

Mary's companion and jailer, Elizabeth Talbot, Countess of Shrewsbury, derived from a very different background than her prisoner. She was born Elizabeth Hardwick, the daughter of a family of impoverished gentry in Derbyshire. Three marriages in ascending order of social importance and a stint as Elizabeth's lady-in-waiting led to her wealthy, well-born, and contentious last husband, George Talbot, Earl of Shrewsbury. Because of her dedication to her own and her family's social mobility, Elizabeth, Countess of Shrewsbury, was just as committed to her own dynastic ambitions as her impressive prisoner was to hers. Talbot's needlework not only expressed but also in some sense helped her to achieve those ambitions.

Elizabeth Talbot's remodeling and building of country houses embodied her intense commitment to financial and dynastic management. If the buildings were impressively designed and situated, then their interiors must be made equally impressive with tapestries, plasterwork, carpets, and portraiture, together with worked cushions, bed hangings, and wall coverings. In fact, if Talbot's first ambition was to build and remodel her stately homes, many of which became her responsibility on her marriage to George Talbot, her second ambition was to furnish them as inexpensively as possible, though always in a manner befitting her rank and the buildings' grandeur. Mary Queen of Scots came into the Talbots' custody early in their marriage, at a time when Elizabeth Talbot had need of her expertise in furnishing her great houses. Mary's influence is visible in the methods and execution of the large needlework projects necessary for Chatsworth, Old Hardwick, and, after the earl's death, Talbot's masterpiece, New Hardwick Hall.

Covering a great deal of grand but empty space was of paramount importance to Elizabeth Talbot, so that she had no time for much intricate needlework. Likewise, Mary seems to have been more caught up in the design than in elaborate stitches. As a result, their work was produced in coarse tentstitch, a stitch that Mary learned as a girl at the French court (Swain, 1973, p. 30) that allows for maximum coverage of space in a minimum of time. The dozens of octagons that the two produced together—Mary working her initials into those that were her own—were probably designed to be appliquéd onto large pieces of material to form bed or wall hangings, as most of them were early in the seventeenth century (Nevinson, p. 194). Mary's octagons may have been intended as gifts to supporters like the unfortunate Norfolk, but they also served as the means to furnish her apartments with highly personal emblems of her royal identity that no one in England would have been willing or able to supply. The effect of these large needlework pictures designed to be hung together is far from the subtle, intimate effect of young Elizabeth Tudor's bookcovers. The needlework of Mary Queen of Scots and Elizabeth, Countess of Shrewsbury, rather creates the effect of large gestures and the louder voice used to address a crowd. Both the subjects and execution of Mary's and Elizabeth's needlework from this period suggest an imagined, possibly public, audience for these visualized identities writ large.

Initially the ambitions of Mary Queen of Scots and Elizabeth, Countess of Shrewsbury, gave them reasons to work together, to spend months choosing patterns from Mary's herbals and other books of prints,[11] and to fashion these pictures into their trademark octagons and other pieces. The two of them had many reasons to cooperate—Mary took Elizabeth Pierrepont, Elizabeth Talbot's granddaughter, into her retinue from the age of four (Durant, p. 98) as a mark of favor, and Talbot knew throughout Mary's imprisonment that her captive might readily become her queen. But eventually the two women found themselves in conflict.

Women's alliances through needlework may vary as widely as the time, place, and subject of the needlework. Alliances, moreover, can form the basis of conflict and competition, as in the case of the Scots queen and the wealthy countess. The first split between Mary Queen of Scots and Elizabeth Talbot came when Talbot arranged the ambitious marriage between her daughter and Henry Stuart, Lord Darnley's younger brother. Their union produced Arbella Stuart in 1575, a personage with an immediate claim to the English throne that rivaled Mary's and that of her son, James. Although Queen Elizabeth was displeased by this match and its subsequent offspring, the Shrewsburys continued as wardens of Mary Queen of Scots—an expression of Elizabeth's continued confidence in them (Steen, 1994, p. 14) despite the dynastic move that the marriage represented. As bad feelings grew between Stuart and Talbot, Mary tried to drive a wedge between the queen and the countess by spreading rumors of treasonous activity on the part of both the countess and the earl. The rumors became especially vicious after 1583, when Elizabeth and George Talbot finally decided to live permanently apart and the earl moved to take over his wife's rents and revenues. At this time, Mary spread rumors in letters to her sympathizers about the countess's activities against the queen. She also charged that the countess was responsible for starting the rumors that she and the earl were romantically and politically involved with one another (Durant, pp. 119–20; 129–34).

In the end, the queen and privy council acted on the countess's behalf, restoring her revenues to her and relieving her and her husband of the care of Mary Queen of Scots. While she supported her former lady-in-waiting, Queen Elizabeth was careful not to promote her granddaughter Arbella too much. The crown seized Arbella's English lands and revenues when she was two years old, as James VI had earlier seized her

Scottish title and inheritance (Steen, 1994, pp. 14–16). Arbella's lack of funds guaranteed her dependence on her queen's and her grandmother's generosity. As the queen no doubt hoped, this dependence necessarily limited the scope of Arbella's operations. Thus Queen Elizabeth was an ever-present factor in Elizabeth Talbot's political life, just as she was in Mary Stuart's. The three formed a triangle of shifting alliance and misalliance for fourteen years.

Meanwhile, Elizabeth Talbot continued building her houses and creating needlework patterns and pictures—activities that materially expressed her connection not only to her family present and future, but also her identification with strong mythic female figures. The source of Elizabeth Talbot's impulse to complete large needlework pieces was dynastic, and she seems to have owed much to Mary Queen of Scots's experience with equipping the Scottish castles. Like her, Talbot hired professional embroiderers, including the "Webb the imbroderer" paid "18s 4d a quarter" according to the accounts of 1598 (Girouard, p. 24). In so doing, she was following Mary Stuart's French practice of including professional embroiderers in her household; they not only drew the necessary patterns on the cloth to be embroidered but also helped to perform much of the needlework together with the mistress, her maids, and the other young people present in her household. Talbot's needlework production was a matter of industry on a large scale. At the same time, because she chose to work particular moments in the narratives of mythic females that she found compelling, the needlework that she oversaw and helped to complete is deeply involved with powerful—if always chaste—female figures like Diana, Penelope, and Lucrece.

The most impressive hangings that greet the visitor in the Great Hall of New Hardwick are those of the commanding figures of Penelope and Lucrece, produced in a manner used at the French court in Mary's time of cutting up and appliquéing designs onto a large background cloth— in this case, the designs were cut from medieval ecclesiastical garments. The High Great Chamber on the third floor is the proud home of tapestries illustrating Ulysses's story, culminating in his return to the faithful Penelope, but they were purchased in 1587 (Girouard, p. 56), at least a decade after Penelope first appeared among Talbot's own needlework hangings. In the 1570s, Talbot, perhaps with the advice of Mary Queen of Scots and certainly with the assistance of professional and amateur embroiderers, produced the homemade, tapestry-sized series of hangings known as the "Virtues," of which a vigorous and resourceful-looking Penelope (figure 10-1) and a muscular-armed Lucrece are the most prominent. The fact that Shrewsbury named two daughters Temperance and Lucrece, two figures in this series, suggests that she connected these mythic narratives with her own life.

Elizabeth Tudor, Mary Stuart, and Elizabeth Talbot each obeyed in her own way the masculinist imperative to perform needlework. In sewing together a family through needlework-covered manuscripts, Eliza-

FIGURE 10-1 Elizabeth Talbot, Countess of Shrewsbury ("Bess of Hardwick"), "Penelope" from the Great Hall of New Hardwick Hall, Derbyshire. Appliqué design cut from medieval ecclesiastical copes on velvet. (By permission of the National Trust.)

beth sought—and received—the two-edged support of Katherine Parr, abandoning such projects when she could publicly cross the line to write poetry and public speeches. Mary Stuart sewed herself into a web of referents to her rank, marital connection, exile, and imprisonment under Elizabeth I. Elizabeth Talbot took up the needle to add to the wealth of her own household and in so doing sewed imagined alliances with Diana, Penelope, and Lucrece that connected her life to their narratives and their narratives to her dynastic ambitions.

3. Seventeenth-Century Women's Alliances

The needlework exchanged and produced among Elizabeth Tudor, Katherine Parr, Mary Stuart, and Elizabeth, Countess of Shrewsbury, displays the shifting political alliances among them as well as the ability of women to use needlework in sewing together familial and imaginary alliances. Needlework is just as important in recovering the domestically politicized alliances of less visible women of the merchant and gentry classes. Seventeenth-century domestic needlework pieces survive in large numbers; they are guarded within families and passed down from older women to the next generation precisely because the equation between needlework and the feminine proved so persistent. Not only can their samplers tell us something about the female connections within their lives, but also the seventeenth century saw the production of large numbers of needlework pictures as women took advantage of the revolution in print culture that made available hundreds of different narratives from which to choose a needlework subject.[12] By the seventeenth century, England was in the midst of a trade boom that led to the proliferation of domestic possessions once only visible in royal palaces. Thus, like Elizabeth Tudor, Mary Stuart, and Elizabeth Talbot, women in the seventeenth century were able to decorate their far smaller homes with sumptuous imitations of the book covers, bench and chair cushions, bed testers, turkey carpets, and wall hangings of the privileged. When they worked textiles involving design, like privileged women, seventeenth-century needleworkers chose subjects that constructed imaginary alliances with female figures from myth and history. I will consider first what kinds and methods of alliances we may recover through samplers; I will then follow with a discussion of the significance of needlework pictures in recovering women's alliances.

Besides signifying women's acceptance of the dominant values of the society, women's textiles like the spot sampler remind us of female networks of exchange and information that might otherwise be invisible to us three to four hundred years later. The sampler was originally a piece of linen with a variety of patterns stitched on it over several years— perhaps over a lifetime.[13] Usually the spot motif sampler functioned as a reminder of how to stitch a particularly difficult motif, or of how to perform the stitches themselves. Women must have learned these stitches from other women—the kinswomen, dependents, mistresses, or friends with whom they daily plied their needlework in what may well have been the most enduring of women's alliances. Lady Mary Margaret Hoby, for example, records in her spare diary entries from the turn of the seventeenth century that she did needlework nearly every day. Hoby frequently records that she "wrought tell :6" (Hoby, p. 65) or that after eating breakfast "I wrought[t] and reed of the bible tell dinner time : after, I wrought, and did my deutie in the house" (p. 86). On the rare occasion when she is more expansive, we find that she was not performing this daily work alone: "I went and wrought with my Maides tell allmost night" (p. 170). Anne Clifford, whose diary tends to be more forthcoming, also assumes the presence of dependents while specifying what was read to the needleworkers—"Montaignes Essays," for example, "the Fairy Queene," or "Ovids Metamorphosis" (Clifford, 1995, pp. 59, 69, 113). But she does make distinct note of needlework begun with her cousin when she finishes "the long cushion of Irish stitch which my Coz.

Cecily Nevil began when she went with me to the Bath" (p. 60). Spot samplers and nearly all needlework are the textile record of a lifetime of such interconnections among women.

In the seventeenth century, samplers—and the needlework boxes, cushions, bed hangings, and pictures that were the girls' next tasks—remain artifacts of the relationship between cousin and cousin, mother and daughter, aunt and niece, grandmother and granddaughter. The pattern books that were common toward the end of the sixteenth century became ubiquitous in the seventeenth century, as male authors like John Taylor cashed in on the tradition of needlework as chaste female industry. Taylor's verse introduction to *The Schoolhouse of the Needle* attempts to pass his book off as participating within the alliances through which women traditionally learned new stitches. After cataloging the various stitches available, "Tent-worke [,] Raisd-worke, Laid worke, Frost-worke, Net-worke" and so on, he suggests that learning patterns from his book is like learning them from one's mistress or mother: "So Maids may (from their Mistresse, or their Mother) / Learne to leave one worke, and to learne another. / For here they may make choyce of which is which, / And skip from worke to worke, from stitch to stitch" (Taylor, Sig. A2v). The appearance of so many patterns in print doubtless contributed to the refashioning of the sampler into the first demonstration of a young girl's proficiency in the basics of needlework. Looking through the hundreds of seventeenth-century samplers in the collections of the Victoria and Albert Museum in London reveals large differences in the level of the girls' expertise that signals difference in age and manual dexterity, but also apparent difference in the degree of willingness to complete the assigned task. There is also a range of threads used for the samplers, suggesting differences in financial status. Those produced in wealthier households—or, perhaps, households with fewer daughters—were completed in shiny silk threads, while the far more common samplers were produced in the duller and cheaper (if colorful) green and red thread available to less wealthy or more thrifty households.[14]

Pattern books made available another form of intergenerational alliance among female members of a family—through the ownership of such books. The pattern books acquired by one generation frequently continued to be used two and even three generations later. This intergenerational ownership of books explains why so few pattern books are extant and why those that remain are so heavily cut up, like those in Britain's National Library of Art. Rozsika Parker has pointed out that Sarah Wilkinson's sampler of 1699 incorporates the stock male and female figures that derive from Richard Shorleyker's *Scholehouse of the Needle*, first published in 1624, seventy-five years before (Parker, figure 51). Other fashions in needlework, like crewel work, and other forms of needlework, like white and raised or stump work, evolved during the seventeenth century. But to a large extent the patterns and narrative pictures can be difficult to date, because for nearly one hundred years, from the 1590s to around 1700, they look very much alike from decade to decade. The very conservatism of this part of the domestic needlework tradition argues a rigid structure of the expectations of feminine accomplishment imposed not only by educational texts and male authors' expectations, but by older generations of women who scrupulously taught succeeding generations the structure of femininity through and within household work. This constant acquisition of skills and patterns across generations and within groups of associated women necessitated women's interconnections through and within the textiles hanging on the beds and walls of fathers, brothers, and husbands.

4. Seventeenth-Century Women's Alliances Through the Biblical Past

We have seen that when Elizabeth Tudor, Mary Stuart, and Elizabeth, Countess of Shrewsbury, performed needlework, they were simultaneously conforming to the prevalent conception of the feminine and using their needlework to screen and advance their political ambitions. Their self-display of simultaneous conformity and nonconformity to society's ideals is similar to the work of less visible seventeenth-century women. For if in the seventeenth century most of the young girls of the merchant and gentry classes and the aristocracy were producing samplers according to a fairly rigid conception of form, when these girls grew older they produced needlework pictures that simultaneously conformed to and challenged wholly masculinist conceptions of domesticity. Thus the final form of women's alliances that I will discuss is the imaginative connection among women through needlework narratives of figures like Judith and Esther.

By the seventeenth century, many more merchants and gentry could aspire to having their domestic space filled with the carefully worked textiles that marked the rooms inhabited by the upper classes. While women in agricultural and working-class households used any spare moment to card, spin, and weave cloth for sale, women in more affluent households laboriously worked textiles that would add substantially to the household wealth. As the research of J. L. Nevinson, Margaret Swain, and Roszika Parker reveals, the domestic embroiderer in the seventeenth century need not, like Elizabeth Talbot and Mary Stuart, employ professional embroiderers, but could go to a print shop to select a print as the pattern for her needlework pictures. At times the design was already printed onto cloth, but often a woman would look through the newly available books for prints and loose engravings. After she selected a subject, she might draw it onto the silk or linen to be embroidered—the cloth itself may well have been bought at the printer's. Later in the century, when raised or "stump" work became popular, consumers could purchase pre-inked patterns and kits that included bits of wooden arm, hands, and face, plus micah for windows, ready to be sewn into the appropriate place in the picture.[15]

When seventeenth-century women overwhelmingly chose certain Biblical narratives to replicate in needlework pictures, like Elizabeth Talbot they were forming an imaginative alliance with courageous female figures. Their figures were located in the Biblical past whose stories articulated action and power while acting in a context that is simultaneously political and personal: Esther appears in state before Ahasueras with her plan to save the Jews from Haman's planned extermination (figure 10-2); Judith holds up Holofernes's head by the hair; Jael pounds a stake through Sisera's skull; Solomon ingeniously determines the real mother of the child before him. The fact that dozens and in some cases hundreds of women selected these prints and thus these narratives suggests a deep engagement with the figures that persistently reappear. As Rozsika Parker points out, "Among those [prints] available from Peter Stent, 'Susannah and the Elders' and 'The Sacrifice of Isaac' were often embroidered, but no embroidery survives of 'Moses Lifting the Serpent'" (Parker, p. 97).

Rozsika Parker's enumeration and analysis of seventeenth-century needlework pictures in *The Subversive Stitch* was pathbreaking; this essay might not have come into existence without it. To her analysis of "the embroidered pictures of biblical scenes" as pictures that allowed women to give a "particular emphasis to the feminine ideal" (Parker, p. 96), I would add that women also used these pictures as an imaginative means to push boundaries of acceptable female behavior to include vigorous, public, political activity. These women used needlework, the supposed instrument of their immobility and silence, to place themselves in narratives that they associated with their own time as well as to connect with other women across time. In doing so in large numbers, these women not only reached back to female figures in the Biblical past, but also across to their own like-minded contemporaries.

What kind of imaginative connection could exist among women through the century's most popular picture, the story of Esther and Ahasueras? Needlework versions of this narrative usually feature the moment in which Esther appears before her husband, Ahasueras, King of Persia, in order to set in motion her successful plea for the lives of the Jewish people. The many women who worked this narrative side-by-side imaginatively reached out to a female figure of undeniable authority from the past. They chose pictures of Old Testament narratives, which formed the root of patriarchal authority in the seventeenth century, and yet were also a rich source for narratives of women bound within patriarchal institutions who manage to achieve concrete results. These pictures of Esther are not fantasies of liberation from all the constraints of female gender roles. Esther is herself caught within legal and narratival systems that seek to deny women public action: She is a married woman who fasts until she is on the point of fainting in order to gain her

FIGURE 10-2 Panel with the story of Esther and Ahasueras, dated 1652. Haman can be seen at upper right hanging from the gallows. (By permission of the Burrell Collection.)

husband's permission to speak. When she thus gains her husband's attention, she invites him to an elaborate banquet where Haman's corruption is exposed, the mass murder of the Jews that he ordered is avoided, and the evil Haman is hanged. To choose the narrative of Esther, then, is to choose a narrative in which a female figure succeeds in public action in spite of the injunction to silence. Esther Sowernam, who may or may not have been a woman, defended women in response to Thomas Swetnam in a pamphlet titled *Esther hath hang'd Haman: or an answere to a lewd Pamphlet, entituled, The Arraignment of Women* (1617). The prominence that Sowernam thus gives to the story of Esther in order to defend women further suggests that Esther is a triumphant figure through whom contemporary women could associate as they sought to counter the more repressive constructions of the feminine within the culture.

The study of the textile artifacts from women's everyday lives reveals the extent to which women reached out to other women in their extended families, in overtly political alliances, and through historical and mythic figures. What the named and unnamed women of this article have in common is their perception of needlework as embodying the female relationships that expressed identity. Elizabeth Tudor, Elizabeth Talbot, and Mary Stuart used needlework to create and disrupt alliances with other women, to represent and display their identities in both imagined and politicized relations. Women in the seventeenth century took advantage of developments in print culture to select, often collectively, favored narratives that made connections to female figures in the past. The study of women's material culture is just beginning to open new ways to think about women's lives and women's subjectivities. Textile work in particular registers women's search for ways to represent the possibility of political female activity within the heart of domestic space.

NOTES

I would like to thank Karen Robertson for her many valuable suggestions regarding this essay.

1. The ideology of needlework is crucial to the study of gender roles in this period. Juan Vives, *A very frutefull and pleasant boke called the Instruction of a Christian Woman . . .* , trans. Rycharde Hurd (London, 1540), insists that a girl should "both lerne her boke" and "handle wolle and flaxe: whiche are two craftes yet lefte of that olde innocent world, both profitable and kepers of temperance (Vives, Sig. Ciii, v) in the belief that this would help her to "holde her tonge demurely" (Vives, Sig. E2v); and John Taylor, *The Praise of the Needle* (London, 1631), admonishes that the needle "Will intreate [women's] peace, inlarge their store, / To use their tongues lesse, and their Needle more" (Taylor, Sig. Av). The standard contemporary work on women's needlework is Roszika Parker, *The Subversive Stitch* (1984; rpt. London: The Women's Press, 1989), to which I am deeply indebted.

2. On the subject of the relations between women's weaving and women's writing and other forms of expression, see Nancy K. Miller, "Arachnologies: The Woman, The Text, and the Critic," in *The Poetics of Gender*, ed. Nancy K. Miller (New York: Columbia University Press, 1986), 270–295; see also Ann Rosalind Jones, "Dematerializations: Textile and Textual Properties in Ovid, Sandys, and Spenser" in *Subject and Object in Renaissance Culture*, ed. Margaret de Grazia, Maureen Quilligan, and Peter Stallybrass (Cambridge: Cambridge University Press, 1996), pp. 189–212.

3. Elizabeth's three calligraphic manuscripts are "The Glass of the Sinful Soul," Bodleian Library, Oxford, Cherry 36, reprinted in Marc Shell, *Elizabeth's Glass* (Lincoln: University of Nebraska Press, 1993), pp. 111–44, followed by a reproduction of the manuscript. This work was first published by John Bale as *A Godly Medytacyon of the Christen Sowle* (Marburg: Dirik van der Straten, 1548). Elizabeth's English translation of John Calvin's *Institution Chrétienne* is MS #R.H. 13/78, Scottish Record Office; and her translations into Latin, French, and Italian, of Katherine Parr's *Prayers, or Meditations*, titled "Precationes sev meditationes" are British Library, MS Royal 7.D.X.MS. Margaret Swain first pointed out that the three extant manuscripts point to a missing fourth manuscript. See Swain, "A New Year's Gift from Princess Elizabeth," *The Connoisseur* (August 1973), pp. 258–266.

4. David Cheal points out that "Interpersonal dependence is everywhere the result of socially constructed ties between human agents," so that "the contents of those ties are defined by the participants' reciprocal expectations. It is these reciprocal expectations between persons that make social interaction possible, both in market exchange and gift exchange" *The Gift Economy* (London: Routledge, 1988),

p. 11. The germinal anthropological work on the meaning of gift-giving, as James Brain pointed out to me, is Marcel Mauss, *The Gift*, trans. W.D. Halls (1950, rpt. New York: W. W. Norton, 1990), who points out the importance of reciprocity, self-interest, and paying attention to the gift itself.

5.   On Katherine Parr's prayers, see Janel Mueller, "Devotion as Difference: Intertextuality in Queen Katherine Parr's *Prayers and Meditations (1545),* in *Huntington Library Quarterly* 53(1990): 171–97; Elaine V. Beilin, *Redeeming Eve: Women Writers of the English Renaissance* (Princeton, N.J.: Princeton University Press, 1987), pp. 72–75; and John N. King, "Patronage and Piety: The Influence of Catherine Parr," in *Silent But for the Word: Tudor Women as Patrons, Translators, and Writers of Religious Works,* ed. Margaret P. Hannay (Kent, Ohio: Kent State University Press, 1985).

6.   But see also Anne Lake Prescott's argument that Elizabeth was working from the Geneva edition of 1539 ("The Pearl of the Valois and Elizabeth I," in *Silent But for the Word,* pp. 66–67). Prescott's discussion of Marguerite's *Miroir* as "a book with a past" and her discussion of the translation itself provide important religious and intellectual context for Elizabeth's endeavors.

7.   Elizabeth may also have been asserting her membership in the group of intellectual women headed by Katherine Parr that John King discusses in "Patronage and Piety." According to King (p. 49), this group included Parr, Anne Seymour, Catherine Brandon, and Mary Fitzroy.

8.   See Elizabeth I, *Englishings of Boethius, De Consolatione Philosophiae, A.D. 1593; Plutarch, De Curiositate, A.D. 1598; and Horace, De Arte Poetica (part), 1598,* ed. Caroline Pemberton (London: EETS, OS 113, 1899) and the more recent editions of Leicester Bradner in *The Poems of Queen Elizabeth I* (Providence, R.I.: Brown University Press, 1964), pp. 13–68.

9.   I have encapsulated the long and complex histories of Mary Queen of Scots and Elizabeth, Countess of Shrewsbury, in the interest of making my argument about their alliance and its relation to Queen Elizabeth. Even the needlework of each is the subject of diverse books and articles. See for example Margaret Swain's enduring *The Needlework of Mary Queen of Scots* (London: Van Nostrand Reinhold, 1973), which is a biography by way of the queen's needlework. On Elizabeth, Countess of Shrewsbury, see David Durant's biography, *Bess of Hardwick: Portrait of an Elizabethan Dynast* (New York: Atheneum, 1978). On her embroidery, see John Nevinson, "An Elizabethan Herbarium: Embroideries by Bess of Hardwick after the Woodcuts of Mattioli," in *The National Trust Yearbook* (London: 1975), pp. 65–69; and Joan Allgrove McDowell's meticulous "The Textiles at Hardwick Hall," in *Hali Magazine,* nos. 39 and 40, 1988. Margaret Ellis has described Elizabeth Talbot's work in detail in "The Hardwick Wall Hangings: An Unusual Collaboration in English Sixteenth-century Embroidery," *Renaissance Studies* 10 (June 1996): 280–300.

10.   My thanks to Joanne Gaudio for exploring this point in a seminar paper.

11.   On the books owned by Mary Queen of Scots and shared with Elizabeth Talbot as the source of their needlework pictures, see Margaret Swain, *Figures on Fabric: Embroidery Design Sources and Their Application* (London: Adam & Charles Black, 1980), pp. 26–37.

12.   Again, I am focusing on the subject of women's needlework in order to recover women's alliances. For overviews of seventeenth-century needlework, see Parker, *Subversive Stitch,* pp. 82–109; Swain, *Figures on Fabric,* pp. 32–33; and Liz Arthur, *Embroidery at the Burrell Collection 1600–1700* (London: John Murray, 1995).

13.   On samplers, see Parker, *Subversive Stitch,* pp. 84–86, 128–39; Jane Toller, *British Samplers: A Concise History* (Chichester, Sussex: Phillimore, 1980); *The Goodhard Samplers. 300 Years of Embroidered Samplers—A Superb Collection, 26 October–30 November 1985* (Swansea: Glynn Vivian Art Gallery, 1985);

and Liz Arthur, *Embroidery at the Burrell Collection 1600–1700* (London: John Murray Publishers Ltd., 1995), 59–62.

14. I am grateful to the Curators of Textiles at the Victoria and Albert Museum for allowing me to examine a large number and variety of sixteenth and seventeenth century domestic textiles. Margaret Swain pointed out to me that the red and green samplers are the most common because red and green thread was least expensive.

15. For this information on stumpwork, or raised work as it is also called (which to a large extent is evident from viewing so many pictures with identically shaped wooden body pieces) and for a general sense of the subject after reading so many of her books and articles, I am indebted to a conversation with Margaret Swain in Edinburgh, August, 1994.

11

"Faire *Eliza's* Chaine"

Two Female Writers' Literary Links to Queen Elizabeth I

. . . .

LISA GIM

THROUGHOUT HER REIGN, Queen Elizabeth I functioned as a gender anomaly by occupying both male and female roles. Yet assessing her effect on the gender structures of the latter half of the sixteenth century is difficult for two reasons: first, because we cannot know the extent to which she fashioned her anomalous position; and second, because she did not intervene to better significantly the situation of women during her lifetime.[1] To seventeenth-century women, however, Elizabeth clearly provided a provocative gender model. Because she had become a symbol of national pride and religious and political achievement, her exercise of public authority could not be simply dismissed. Moreover, her success in embodying a complex set of gender identities suggested that her accomplishments need not be seen merely as those of an exceptional woman. Instead, other women might seek to emulate her education and abilities even though they could not attain her political position. Accordingly, seventeenth-century female authors "rewrote" her not as the exception to her sex but as the paradigm—the woman whom Bathsua Makin termed "the Crown of all" women.

This essay treats two seventeenth-century women's texts about Elizabeth I: Bathsua Makin's *An Essay to Revive the Antient Education of Gentlewomen, in Religion, Manners, Arts and Tongues: with An Answer to the Objections against this Way of Education*, and Diana Primrose's *A*

Chaine of Pearle. Or a Memoriall of the peerles graces, and Heroick Vertues of Queene Elizabeth of Glorious Memory, in which both writers make significant attempts to portray Elizabeth as an important gender model because of her intellectual and social accomplishments. Unlike contemporary men writing panegyrics about the queen, these female authors specifically stress her transgressive behavior. In their advocacy of Elizabeth, both Makin and Primrose point to her as a key link in their conceptualizing a historical chain of female achievement. Their works suggest that Elizabeth had a strong effect on women by inspiring them imaginatively rather than materially.[2] Because studying the "great" figures of history can often obscure the lives of less remarkable people who constitute the larger social forces in history, recent feminist historians have been generally critical of tracing the influence of the "exceptional woman." Natalie Zemon Davis (1976) and Joan Wallach Scott, for example, argue that analysis of the exceptional woman's historical role constitutes a kind of "compensatory" gesture that elides the activities of women in history as a whole. However, the emphasis that seventeenth-century women place on the imaginative influence of Elizabeth—as seen in their literary representations of her—suggests that the notion of the exceptional woman's influence on gender modeling bears further reevaluation.[3] These writers disregard stipulations about her exceptionality as monarch, and ideological attempts to contain Elizabeth's androgynous position, with formulations like the doctrine of "the monarch's two bodies" (Kantorowicz; Axton). Instead, they stress that other women can and should imitate the queen's intellectual qualities and her autonomy. It is this issue of gender that motivates both Makin's and Primrose's arguments.

Bathsua Makin's text more directly presents Elizabeth I as an example for other women to imitate. *An Essay to Revive the Antient Education of Gentlewomen* (1673) advances an extensive argument advocating a return to educational values of the past for women. Citing in detail the example of the educated elite of Tudor England, Queen Elizabeth, the Grey and Cooke women, Lady Mary Sidney, Margaret More Roper, and Lord Burleigh's daughters, Makin uses the learned women of history as the basis for her argument for female education.

The daughter of an educator (Henry Reginald),[4] Makin was a linguist, writer, and teacher, and also the inventor of a shorthand system that she dedicated to Queen Anne.[5] She held the position of tutor to Charles I's daughter, Princess Elizabeth, around 1640 (Teague, 1986, p. 16). After the Civil War, Makin apparently administered her own girls' school (advertised at the back of her *Essay*) at Tottenham High Cross, in which girls were to spend "halfe the time" learning: "works of all sorts, dancing, musick, singing, writing [and] keeping accompts"; and the other half of their schooling "gaining the *Latin* and *French* Tongues; and those that please may learn *Greek* and *Hebrew,* the *Italian* and *Spanish*" (p. 52). Her epistolary association with the Dutch female scholar Anna Maria van

Schurman influenced her thinking on education and is reflected in the praise van Schurman receives in the *Essay*.[6]

In the *Essay*, Makin structures her argument as though it were an answer to a fictitious male "objector" to female education whose imagined letter the author provides and uses as a starting point for her treatise. Since Makin's point is to advocate female education, she seeks to persuade readers of both sexes of its value and feasibility, despite her dedicatory inscription to women as her readership.[7] The work's organization, under headings that document female learning in various disciplines (e.g., "Women have formerly been educated in Arts and Tongues") or in sections that propose specific educational philosophies ("Care ought to be taken by us to Educate Women in Learning"), testifies to this strategy. Her pamphlet is not simply a philosophical treatise on female ability, but rather a pragmatic agenda for a return to a humanist classical education for women—the sort that Queen Elizabeth and other Tudor women had received, and which she herself offers in her girls' school. In this regard, Makin's mention of contemporary female scholars is critical.

Although Elizabeth is not the only contemporary learned figure whom she cites, Makin's representation of the queen is significant for two reasons: Elizabeth is an exemplary model of female educational achievement, and her use of her education validates women's public speech and activity. The author points to Elizabeth repeatedly as an example of female excellence in disciplines such as religion, Latin, and Greek: "How learned She was, the World can testifie. It was usual for her to discourse with Forraign Agents in their own Languages. Mr. *Ascam,* her Tutor, used to say, She read more *Greek* in a day then many of the Doctors of her time did *Latin* in a week" (p. 11). Not only does Makin hail Queen Elizabeth as "the Crown of all" in the context of the illustrious educated women of history whom she describes, but also the monarch serves as active proof of the use of such an education in public life. Makin stresses the relation between education and public agency several times, asserting that "Women have not been meer Talkers (as some frivolous Men would make them) but they have known how to use languages, when they have had them. Many Women have been excellent Oratours" (p. 12). As evidence, she mentions the Latin orations given by the queen at Oxford and Cambridge,[8] "delivered at the Universities by Queen *Elizabeth's* own Mouth . . . ample testimony of her Oratory," and also praises her writings, "Those ingenious Fancies, and pleasant Poems bearing her Name" (p. 20). Makin's purpose in extolling Elizabeth differs markedly from the usual epideictic praise of a virtuous or admirable woman. To Makin, the queen's example proves that contemporary women equipped with knowledge can make valuable contributions to the world: "The memory of Queen *Elisabeth is* yet fresh. By her Learning, she was fitted for Government, and swayed the Sceptre of this Nation with as great honour as any man before her" (p. 28).

Makin insists further that the queen's knowledge and ability made her not merely equal to men but unsurpassed in history, because she fulfilled England's destiny in a way her forebears did not. Using a birth metaphor, the author emphasizes Elizabeth's contribution to the English church in terms of her distinctly female power to create both biologically and intellectually: "Our very reformation of Religion, seems to be begun and carried on by Women. . . . *Henry* the Eighth made a beginning out of State Policy, his Feminine Relations acted out of true Piety; this stuck in the birth till his Daughter Queen Elizabeth carried it to the height it is now at" (p. 29). Makin's metaphor emphasizes the queen's maternal role to the "child" that is the English church, suggesting Elizabeth as either mother who could carry the child ("sowen" by female Protestant martyrs like Anne Askew to whom Makin refers earlier) to be delivered, or as midwife who could deliver the child "stuck in the birth" beyond the point that previous Protestants had taken it.[9]

By citing the gender models of educated and powerful women of past history, especially Queen Elizabeth, Makin is attempting to assert alternative roles for women from those that she sees around her in seventeenth-century society. In the Stuart period, a backlash against female power and intellectualism—manifested in various forms of misogyny, most obviously in the proliferation of the texts of "the woman debate" and in the witchcraft persecutions of 1540–1640 (Amussen, 1988, pp. 181–89; Thomas, 1971)—and an increasing emphasis on the family as the model of hierarchical order was evidenced in social practices (Underdown, 1985a, 1985b) and literature (Henderson and McManus; Woodbridge, 1984). Moreover, with Elizabeth's death, the regal presence of the "exceptional woman ascendant" had vanished; James I replaced Elizabeth's flexible use of androgynous gender metaphors with distinctly paternalistic ones of his own.[10] Undeniably, by the 1660s aristocratic women lost some ground in terms of the social view of female education (Stone, pp. 142–44; Alexander, p. 245). While sixteenth-century noblewomen had frequently been educated in Greek and Latin, James's own daughter Elizabeth was trained only in "female arts" like dancing and music. Social conditions did not particularly improve for women under the rule of Charles I. Although this court did not condone misogyny, Queen Henrietta Maria's fashioning of women as the desirable objects of a court of platonic love meant that passive female virtues were emphasized (Latt, p. 40). Makin's pamphlet on education thus constitutes an emphatic response to such social and intellectual restrictions on her sex.

Makin's goal is to stress the value of female intelligence, a point that she makes repeatedly: "My meaning is, Persons that God hath blessed with the things of this World, that have competent natural Parts, ought to be Educated in Knowledge. . . . Had God intended Women onely as a finer sort of Cattle, he would have not made them reasonable" (pp. 21–23). Her examples of broadly educated Tudor noblewomen were suited especially to her own educational model for women (Barbour, p. v), which she envisions as extending to "the whole *Encyclopedeia* of Learning [which] may be useful in some way or other to them" (p. 24).

Throughout the *Essay*, Makin emphasizes that the women she praises are not merely representations of female virtue to be admired. Rather, she urges that their example be followed actively, intellectually, and verbally:

> I hope Women will make another use of what I have said; instead of claim-
> ing honour from what Women have formerly been, they will labour to
> imitate them in learning those Arts their Sex hath invented, in studying
> those Tongues they have understood, and in practicing those Virtues
> shadowed under their Shapes; the knowledge of Arts and Tongues, the
> exercise of Virtue and Piety, will certainly (let men say what they will)
> make them honourable.[11] (pp. 21–22)

In linking rhetorical practice—"Arts and Tongues"—to the "exercise of Virtue and Piety," Makin draws on the memory of Elizabeth as an orator who authorized her own public speaking with precisely such connections between her virtue and her right to speak publicly. In her "Golden Speech" of 1601, Elizabeth had said,

> Of My selfe I must say this, I neuer was any greedy scraping grasper,
> nor a strict fast-holding Prince, nor yet a waster, My heart was neuer set
> vpon any worldy goods, but onely for my Subjects good. . . . Mr. Speaker,
> I would wish you and the rest to stand vp, for I feare I will yet trouble
> you with longer speech. . . . Since I was Queene yet did I neuer put My
> Pen to any Grant but vpon pretext and semblance made Me, that it was
> for the good and availe of my Subiects generally. . . . The zeale of which
> Affection tending to ease my People, & knit their hearts vnto vs, I em-
> brace with a Princely care farre aboue all earthly treasures. . . . Thus,
> virtue and God that gaue me here to sit, and placed mee ouer you, knowes
> that I neuer respected my selfe, but as your good was consceiued in
> mee. . . . (A3–A3v)

The speech specifically links the queen's right to speak at great length and to wield her pen with authority to her virtuous love for her people and her faith in God. Moreover, Elizabeth presents her virtue and piety not merely as a demonstration of the trust given to her by God and her people, but more importantly as a validation for her honorable deploy-ment of monarchical power. Makin's *Essay* echoes such connections; she argues that virtue and piety are tied to rhetorical study and intellectual exercise, so that women who pursue learning will benefit doubly.

A consideration of Makin's pamphlet in its historical context further illuminates Makin's motivations for praising Elizabeth. The majority of female writers who wrote about Elizabeth were not her contemporaries but were seventeenth-century women, writing long after 1603—in con-trast to their male counterparts, many of whom wrote works praising the queen during her lifetime. Yet the female writers' works differ significantly in terms of context and motivation from even retrospective works about her by seventeenth-century male writers because female authors consistently take her gender as their focus. Male writers' praise was often motivated by politics or religion. For example, a general trend in the 1610s–1630s was to extol the Tudor queen as an oblique means of criticizing the Stuarts (Neale, pp. 14–15; Hill, pp. 41–57). The relaxing of censorship laws on writings about royalty during the 1640s–1660s (Hill, p. 42) and publication of Elizabeth's own writings probably heightened interest in Elizabethan court histories even further.

While these trends may in part explain interest in and knowledge about the queen on the part of women writers, they do not adequately explain why the queen was such an appealing gender image for seventeenth-century women. To a limited extent, some female writers (particularly those writing religious texts) sometimes used praise of Elizabeth to reflect political and religious criticism. But the main body of women's retrospective praise—which turns upon the subject of her gender and appears in writings not only by Makin and Primrose, but also by Esther Sowernam (1617), Anne Bradstreet (1643), and Sarah Jinner (1658) to name a few—was clearly motivated by factors of social change affecting women that caused them to look to strong female models from previous ages.

During the Civil War period, women became more assertive about their demands as many temporarily assumed the leadership roles their husbands had played in homes, manors, and businesses; they also made distinct political contributions including petitions and protests directed to Parliament (Stone; Fraser, 1984). Additionally, publications by female authors increased dramatically from 1640 to 1660 (Crawford, 1985, pp. 211–67; Hobby, 1988). However, these developments did little to change the legal standing of women, and without economic power they were unable to transform their protofeminist stances into social reality (Jordan, 1990, pp. 295–311; Stone, pp. 227–28). As the notion of the woman as a courtly object of love returned in the Restoration (Stone, pp. 225–26), the increased liberties women had earned during the Civil War period were diminished; this provoked strong assertions about their sex's capability from female authors like Bathsua Makin, Aphra Behn, Lady Mary Chudleigh, Mary Astell, and Hannah Wolley. Such cultural shifts had a considerable impact on moving women toward formulating cohesive feminist assertions at the beginning of the eighteenth century.[12] Makin's argument is plainly a part of this social context.

While Makin used the example of Elizabeth in her *Essay* to advance specific arguments about women's worth in the public sphere and to assert the necessity of educating women, Lady Diana Primrose wrote her panegyrics to the queen to portray Elizabeth in particular as the most appropriate intellectual and ethical model for her sex, and to affirm conceptual connections between this powerful female authority and women who might follow her example. In *A Chaine of Pearle. Or a Memoriall of the peerles graces, and Heroick Vertues of Queene Elizabeth of Glorious Memory* (1630), Primrose praises the Tudor monarch's female power by retracing her princely virtues. Primrose's *Chaine*, like Makin's *Essay*, insists on the importance of Elizabeth as a gender model, extolling the queen for her wise exercise of regal and righteous authority and counseling all women to emulate her. Yet Primrose's work focuses on the queen's gender-transgressive qualities and actions even more emphatically than Makin's, praising Elizabeth not only for her knowledge but also for her autonomy. She chooses to omit physical beauty as a category for praise, instead stressing intellectual attributes relating to "science," "prudence," and "fortitude," in addition to the more conventional virtues like religion, temperance, clemency, justice, patience, and bounty that were most commonly attributed to the female ruler. Primrose's poem further revises the gender terms of the traditional encomium, which commonly included a blason of the queen's physical appearance, to accommodate the vantage point of a female poet praising the queen.[13]

Beginning by designating her readership as "All Noble Ladies and Gentle-women," Primrose presents her poem to her female audience as not simply a celebration of Elizabeth that will keep her fame current, but also as a work that will allow her readers to participate in her reflected glory through their reading of it: "You shall erect a Trophie to her Name,/ And crowne your selves with never-fading Fame" (A2). Furthermore, the context of the dedication and induction make clear that her topic is gender. Elizabeth is identified as "Thou English Goddesse, Empresse of our Sexe" (A4v), and Primrose's "induction" establishes that the poem's object is twofold: first, to praise the queen; and second, to encourage other women to emulate Elizabeth as a gender model. Primrose asserts that by recreating Elizabeth's "Chaine" of virtues in this poetic catalogue, she will create not only a "Trophie" to the queen's name, but also will give to other women a gift, for by actively "wearing" this chain—that is, by imitating Elizabeth's intellectual and moral virtues—they, too, can crown themselves with acclaim.

Although almost nothing is known about Diana Primrose's life, the title page of her poem indicates that she is "a Noble Lady." Since so little is known about Primrose's identity, contextualizing her text is more difficult than in Makin's case.[14] Primrose's text predates Makin's and may respond more directly to the general nostalgia in the 1620–1630s for the Elizabethan period. Numerous publications praising Elizabeth's abilities and lauding her "golden reign" were produced throughout the seventeenth century, particularly from the 1620s to the 1680s. For example, Thomas Heywood's play *If You Know Not Me, You Know Nobody* was reprinted in 1630 and published in a prose version in 1631. Possibly even more significant in terms of influencing readers to historicize the Tudor queen was the first English translation (from the Latin) of William Camden's *Historie of the Reign of Queen Elizabeth*, which appeared in two volumes in 1625 and 1630 and which was reprinted several times in succeeding decades. Although it is difficult to assess the impact that Camden's history had, Anne Bradstreet also mentions the work specifically in her 1643 poem to Elizabeth, indicating that other seventeen-century women may have read this history. Furthermore, Elizabeth's "Golden Speech" was reprinted in 1628, two years before Primrose's text was published. Primrose's allusions to events in the queen's reign demonstrate her familiarity with descriptions from these popular texts. Yet, even though the publication of her poem may stem in part from nostalgia for the Tudor golden age,[15] to suggest this motive as the primary one would obscure the explicit, gender-specific connections that Primrose seeks to make between the queen and female capability. Taken in the context of other women's works that imagine and represent women's connections to the monarch, *A Chaine of Pearle* is a significant protofeminist tribute by a female poet to the queen. Texts by women written in the Stuart period that celebrate the queen stand apart from those by male writers with the agenda of political comparison, most notably in the terms of the qualities and accomplishments chosen for praise. While most men commend either Elizabeth's political achievements and thrift (as Camden does in his *Historie of the Reign of Queen Elizabeth*) or her endurance as a stoic woman (as Heywood does in *If You Know Not Me, You Know Nobody*), females praise her intelligence, autonomy, and gender transgressions of the masculine political world, which they present as a model for their sex to follow. Primrose's poem is a case in point.

In *A Chaine of Pearle*, the queen serves as both a historical paragon and the gender paradigm that other women should emulate. The title of *A Chaine of Pearle* functions as a metaphor that simultaneously governs the poem's purpose and reveals its structure. The author uses the term, "Chaine of Pearle," to describe figuratively Elizabeth's ten virtues, each of which is a "pearle." Repeatedly punning on "pearle," she describes the queen's "peerles Graces and Heroick Vertues" (A). Primrose's use of the figure alludes to the pearls Elizabeth characteristically wore as emblematic of her chastity.[16] The chain also describes a metaphorical necklace that Primrose's poem constructs, linking Elizabeth to women readers who will be empowered by "wearing" her pearls—that is, by following the virtues she exemplifies. It also refers to a literal chain of pearls described in the "second Pearle," involving a gift given by the Spanish ambassador Don Taxis that I will discuss later. Primrose's poem insists on the links that connect the queen with contemporary women. Her emphasis stands in marked contrast to the sentiments of male writers who, while praising the queen as an "exceptional" and "masculine" woman, stress that Elizabeth is unique to her sex. James I, for example, had a eulogy engraved on Elizabeth's memorial that calls her learned "beyond her sex." Even though occasionally Primrose may echo the notion that some of the queen's virtues are unsurpassed, she insistently portrays Elizabeth as the model that her sex can and should follow.

In her celebration of the female ruler, Primrose emphasizes Elizabeth's female gender in transgressive contexts throughout the poem; the queen's abilities and actions are repeatedly juxtaposed to men's and her qualities continually exceed and triumph over theirs. This idea marks four of the "Pearles" in particular: those that celebrate Elizabeth's fortitude, science, chastity, and bounty. Although Elizabeth's "seventh Pearle" of fortitude is a conventional virtue of monarchs, Primrose gives it an unusual cast by using Elizabeth's gender-transgressing episodes as instances to prove it. Elizabeth's appearance has an androgynous character when dealing with threats to herself and the state: her wrathful, "braue vndaunted Looke, when *Parry*/ Was fully bent *SHEE* should by him miscarry. . . ." was so powerful that "The Wretch confest, that *Her* Great Majestie / With strange amazement did him terrifie" (C). Primrose's description of Tilbury, at which Elizabeth's valor and regal deportment fired up her army, stresses her traversal of gender roles and the link between the queen and her nation for "[Her] words deliver'd in most Princely sort, / Did animate the Army and report / To all the World her Magnanimity, / Whose haughty Courage nought could terrify" (C).

Primrose uses the word "Prince" rather than "Queen" repeatedly in her poem to identify Elizabeth, underscoring not only her androgyny, but also her supreme power as monarch. This usage echoes Elizabeth's own preference for the term in situations necessitating unquestioned authority. Primrose's "eighth Pearle" similarly devotes a verse to praising Elizabeth's "masculine" properties—her intelligence and education—achievements Primrose denotes as "Science," the foremost "of the Vertues Intellectuall." Primrose's verse specifically focuses on Elizabeth's oratorical power, even more so than Makin's text, presenting this not as mere skill, but as a rare talent that elevates the learned queen to a position of preeminence as a woman ruling and conquering men: "On her Sacred Lips / Angells enthron'd, most Heavenly *Manna* sips. . . . / *SHEE* was able to drowne a World of men, / And drown'd with Sweetnes to reuiue agen" (C2v).

This praise of the queen's literary prowess is significant, because it suggests not just that Primrose values rhetoric, but perceives it as an instrument of power, "able to drowne a World of men" as well. Although a woman's ability to charm men through sweetness is often used as a conventional figure in panegyric verse, Primrose insists that Elizabeth's verbal authority has substance. Her power over men derives not from simple female charm, but instead derives from the science of learning and her intelligence. Developing her argument, Primrose describes Elizabeth's able *ex tempore* Latin excoriation of an insulting Polish ambassador who berated her in a prepared Latin speech in her own court. The sovereign's ability to "imparadise Her *Parliaments*" with "*Oratory-ravishments*" and her proficiency in Greek demonstrated in her addresses at Oxford provide additional proof of her verbal powers: "Her Speeches to our *Academians*, / Well shew'd *SHEE* knew among *Athenians*, / How to deliver such well-tuned Words, / As with such Places punctually accords" (C2v).

The notion of female virginity retained in defiance of men receives emphasis in Primrose's "second Pearle" praising Elizabeth's chastity. In recounting first the queen's retention of her inviolability, Primrose's verse concludes by telling how she inspired a "Lady of the Court" to resist the Spanish Don Taxis's attempted seduction while keeping his intended bribe of "rare Orient Pearle." The celebration of English nationalism resonates in such an anecdote: an Englishwoman's repulsion of a Spanish assault on her chastity was, of course, an echo of Elizabeth's repulsion on a national scale of the Spanish Armada, a metaphor of virginity retained that was employed in many representations of Elizabeth's and England's victory over Spain (Montrose, 1986, p. 315; Frye 1992, p. 108). In her speech at Tilbury, for example, Elizabeth underscored her chastity as an emblem for national inviolability: "[I] think foul scorn that *Parma* or *Spain*, or any Prince of Europe should dare to invade the borders of my Realm, to which rather than any dishonor grow by me I my self will take up arms."[17] Her "invasion" by any "Prince of Europe" was portrayed frequently as tantamount to her rape.

Unlike traditional representations of chastity as merely virginity preserved for a husband's or father's possession, Primrose's "second Pearle" makes the sanctity of the female body relevant to a woman's autonomous identity. When Primrose describes how Elizabeth chooses to remain virgin and unwed, the monarch's chastity becomes not only an assertion of her righteous power over herself and her nation, but also her triumph over all attempts at male domination:

> How many Kings and Princes did aspire,
> To win her Loue? In whom that Vestall Fire
> Still flaming, never would *Shee* condescend
> To *Hymen's* Rihtes, though much *Shee* did commend,
> That braue French *MONSIEVR* who did hope to carry
> The Golden fleece, and faire *ELIZA* marry.
> Yea, Spanish *PHILIP*, Husband to her Sister,
> Was her first Sutor, and the first that mist her:
> And though he promis'd that the *Pope* by Bull
> Should license it, *SHEE* but held it but a Gull
> For how can *Pope* with Gods owne Law dispence? (B2)

By emphasizing that Elizabeth's virtue is "Vestall" and by describing consent to marriage as a "condescension"—a lowering of the queen's will to that of a husband—Primrose presents Elizabeth's refusal to marry as a positive exercise of her unsubjugated female autonomy.

Primrose's recontextualizing chastity thus may be read as a resistant revision of patriarchal conduct books' definitions, in which chastity is seen as a female sexual commodity or moral virtue rather than as a characteristic of female autonomy. Furthermore, Primrose emphasizes Elizabeth's unviolated autonomy as a model for other women to emulate by defining chastity as not just a physical condition of female virtue, but more important as a spiritual and moral condition that all women, not simply virgins, may attain: "For whether it [chastity] be termed Virginall / In Virgins, or in Wiues stil'd Conjugall, / Or Viduall in Widdowes, God respects / All equally, and all alike affects" (B3v). To Primrose, Elizabeth's defiance of men and of foreign kings becomes a "Document" for other women to value chastity by, and a "Noble President" that inspires "that Noble Lady of the Court" to likewise reject the advances of the Spanish Don Taxis.

In the last, "tenth Pearle," in which Primrose describes Elizabeth's "Bounty" (defined as her aid to foreign allies), the queen appears once more as a transgressive gender figure in a powerful image of the woman on top. In its final vision of female power, with Elizabeth triumphing over Philip of Spain, *A Chaine of Pearle* metaphorically presents a woman bringing a man to his knees:

> Provinces and Princes found her Aid
> On all Occasions; which sore dismaid
> Spaines King whose *European* Monarchy
> Could never thriue during her Soverainity;
> So did *Shee* beate him with her Distaffe, so
> By Sea and Land *Shee* did him ouerthrow;
> Yea so that Tyrant on his knees *Shee* brought,
> That of braue England Peace he beg'd, and thought
> Himselfe most happie, that by begging so
> Preserv'd all Spaine from Beggery and Woe.
>   Here all amaz'd my *Muse* sets vp her rest,
>   Adoring *HER* was so Divinely blest. (C3v)

While most such gender inversions portray the dominance of female over male as disorderly, particularly in artistic renderings of the shrewish wife (Stallybrass, 1991, pp. 201–20), by contrast Primrose validates them; the female English ruler beating the male Spanish king with her "distaff" becomes a reaffirmation of the proper order that is specifically right for England. Primrose graphically asserts Elizabeth's female ascendancy over men, which male writers carefully sought to avoid universalizing, as part of a cultural gender order. In her rendition, both women and the nation have triumphed through Elizabeth's sovereignty.

While Bathsua Makin and Diana Primrose acknowledge Queen Elizabeth as exceptional, at the same time they isolate aspects of Elizabeth's education, character, and behavior as a pattern for other women to imitate. Their emphasis points to women writers' recognition of the queen as embodying transgressive gender qualities and offering a viable paradigm to authorize women's intellectual participation in the public realm.[18] Fixing upon her gender in relation to her real and intellectual power, depictions by women writers disregard the patriarchal trope of the queen's "two bodies" (Axton) which sought to portray the queen as an anomaly—sovereign first, woman last—and instead evoke Elizabeth as a proven, historical model of both female authority and authorship. For seventeenth-century women in particular, she serves as an alternative to female passivity, as a figure to "animate" her sex as astrologist Sarah Jinner claims in her preface to *An Almanack or Prognostication for the year of our LORD* 1658:

> When, or what Commonwealth was ever better governed than this by the virtuous Q. Elizabeth? I fear I shall never see the like again, most of your Princes now a dayes are like Dunces in comparison of her: either they have not the wit, or the honesty that she had: Somewhat [sic] is the matter that things do not forge so well! . . . why should we suffer our parts to rust? Let us scowre the rust off, by ingenious endeavouring the attaining [sic] higher accomplishments.[19]

By invoking the name and example of Queen Elizabeth, women writers of this period linked themselves both imaginatively and historically with her.[20] Even though such connections had to have been imagined, they opened a significant ideological space for protofeminism because "imagined" communities can prove as powerful a force as "real" ones, as Benedict Anderson has argued in the context of nationalism (1991). For Anderson, despite the fact that nationalism is largely "*'imagined'* because the members of even the smallest nation will never know most of their fellow-members, meet them, or even hear of them," it remains "one of the most powerful ideological forces conceivable"(p. 6).[21] Analogously, Makin's and Primrose's works demonstrate the power of such imagined connections among a community of educated women. For Bathsua Makin in her *Essay*, the power of such an imagined alliance among intellectual women enabled her not only to hypothesize a communion with a contemporary female readership in her *Essay*, but also helped her to cultivate her real project of a school for women, "Where, by the blessing of God, Gentlewomen may be instructed in the principles of religion; and in all manner of Sober and Vertuous Education" for a rate of "20 *l. per annum*" (p. 42), gaining knowledge that might materially alter female social roles. For Diana Primrose, penning the *Chaine of Pearle* and detailing Elizabeth's accomplishments essentially offered other women, who might "put on" "faire *Eliza's* Chaine" of heroic virtues, an opportunity to forge a conceptual bond with this Tudor queen who had exercised androgynous roles and embodied unequivocal female authority. It is particularly significant that the figure of Elizabeth I—a publicly active and unmarried monarch—opened avenues for women to imagine and state their gender roles differently. The fact that this ruler's actions, speeches, and shifting gender identities resurface in seventeenth-century women's texts reveals the pervasive power of her representation for female authors. Their conceptualization of women's gender roles as flexible and to some extent changeable demonstrates the significance of Queen Elizabeth I's example for imagined female alliances across the boundaries of class and time.

NOTES

1. Elizabeth's agency has been scrutinized by both feminists and new historicists. Joan Kelly Gadol, "Early Feminist Theory and the *Querelle des Femmes*, 1400–1789," in *Women, History and Theory: The Essays* (p. 88) contends that Elizabeth's influence on ideas about her sex was minimal. In the same vein, Allison Heisch, "Queen Elizabeth I: Parlimentary Rhetoric and the Exercise of Power," *Signs* Autumn 1, no. 4 (1975): 31–55; and Heisch, "Queen Elizabeth and the Persistence of Patriarchy, *Feminist Review* 4 (1980): 45–66, concludes that the queen was not only contained by patriarchy but even served it, in employing its codes as "an honorary male." Louis Montrose, "The Elizabethan Subject and the Spenserian Text," in *Literary Theory, Renaissance Texts*, ed. Patricia Parker and David Quint (Baltimore: Johns Hopkins University Press, 1986), pp. 303–40, argues that Elizabeth's power was constructed not only by the queen but also by her court and subjects. Susan Frye, *Elizabeth I: The Competition for Representation* (Oxford: Oxford University Press, 1993), has examined the question of the queen's representation from a more complex viewpoint, noting how it shifted with the contexts and times it served. Carole Levin, *The Heart and Stomach of a King: Elizabeth I and the Politics of Sex and Power* (Philadelphia: University of Pennsylvania Press, 1994), has also examined the queen's use of male and female gender roles.

2. Elizabeth's deployment of androgynous roles could not and did not evoke literal imitation, because no other woman could hold the variety of gender roles that a virgin queen could; neither did her reign change the social conditions of her sex by design. But the queen became a female figure whom other women could invoke when extolling female abilities. Thus, she served as a conceptual gender model if not a literal role model for them.

3. Susan Dwyer Amussen, "Elizabeth I and Alice Balstone: Gender, Class, and the Exceptional Woman in Early Modern England," in *Attending to Women in Early Modern England*, ed. Betty S. Travitsky and Adele F. Seeff (Newark: University of Delaware Press, 1994), pp. 219–40, stresses reevaluating the "exceptional woman" but in a different context from mine. Amussen looks at two "exceptional" early modern women, Elizabeth I and Alice Balstone, examining their atypical experiences in terms of marriage and reputation. Her argument is that, "by looking at the lives of these uncommon women, we can begin to see how the lives of all women and the choices they were free to make have been shaped by patriarchy . . . and . . . were limited by their position in society" (p. 234).

I have treated other representations of Elizabeth by seventeenth-century female authors, in my dissertation, "Representing Regina: Literary Representations of Queen Elizabeth I by Women Writers of the Sixteenth and Seventeenth Century" (Brown University, 1992), presently under revision as a book; and in "'Authorizing Women': The Representation of Queen Elizabeth I by Three Seventeenth-Century Women Writers," in the session, "Authorizing Women," presented at the MLA Convention, Toronto, December 28, 1993.

4. Jean R. Brink, "Bathsua Reginald Makin: 'Most Learned Matron.'" *Huntington Library Quarterly* 54, no. 4 (1991), notes that her father's name may have been spelled variously as Reynolds, Reginollles, or Reginald (pp. 314–15).

5. Makin began her teaching career at the remarkable age of fourteen, published at sixteen, was called a "good Chymist," and was said to have medical skills as well (Virginia Blain, Isobel Grundy, and Patricia Clements, eds. *The Feminist Companion to Literature in English* (New Haven, Conn.: Yale University Press, 1990), pp. 704–5; Brink, 1991, pp. 315–17). Her brother-in-law, John Pell, was also a noted academic. Barbour in her introduction to *An Essay to Revive the Antient Education of Gentlewomen* (1673; Auguston Reprints Society,

1980) lists her birthdate as "circa 1612," (iii) but Brink (and also Blain et al.) give 1600 as her birthdate, noting that she married Richard Makin in 1622. Brink provides the most detailed and precise biography of her. See also Frances Teague, "New Light on Bathsua Makin," *Seventeenth-Century News* 44, nos. 1–2 (1986); and Teague, "Woman of Learning: Bathsua Makin," in *Women Writers of the Seventeenth Century*, ed. Katharina Wilson and Frank M. Warnke (Athens: University of Georgia Press, 1989), pp. 285–94, (Teague has a book forthcoming on Makin.) Makin appears to have been operating her school even into her seventies when her pamphlet was published in 1673 as its enclosed advertisement indicates (p. 42).

6. In fact, Makin's *Essay* was most likely directly influenced by van Schurman's own work praising educated women, *De Ingenii muliebris . . .* (1641), which devoted extensive praise to Elizabeth I. This work was translated into English in 1659 by Clement Barksdale as *The Learned Maid, or Whether a Maid may be a Scholar?* See Pieta van Beek, "'One Tongue is Enough for a Woman': The Correspondence in Greek between Anna Maria von Schurman (1607–1678) and Bathsua Makin (1600–167?)," *Dutch Crossing*, Summer 19, no. 1 (1995), pp. 24–48 for a discussion of the correspondence and connections between the two female scholars. Other discussions of Makin's work in the context of ideas on education in the period include Brink, "Bathsua Makin: Educator and Linguist," in *Female Scholars: A Tradition of Learned Women before 1800*, ed. Jean R. Brink (Montreal: Eden Press Women's Publications, 1980), pp. 86–100; Mitzi Myers, "Domesticating Minerva: Bathsua Makin's 'Curious' Argument for Women's Education," *Studies in Eighteenth Century Culture* 14 (1985): 173–92; Teague, "Woman of Learning"; and James L. Helm, "Bathsua Makin's *An Essay to Revive the Antient Education of Gentlewomen*," in *The Canon of Seventeenth-Century Educational Reform Tracts. Cahiers Elisabethains* 44 (1993): 45–55.

Makin's other surviving texts include a memorial poem, "Upon the much Lamented Death of the Right Honourable, the Learned Lady Langham" (1664), and a collection of poems called *Musa Virginea* with a publication date of 1616. Blain, *Feminist Companion,* and Brink, "Bathsua Reginald Makin," are skeptical that the 1646 Parliamentary plea often attributed to her, *The Malady and Remedy of Vexations and Unjust Arrests and Actions*, was actually authored by Makin.

7. Makin dedicates the *Essay* "to all Ingenious and Vertuous Ladies," and "more especially to her Highness the Lady Mary, eldest daughter to his Royal Highness, the Duke of York" (p. 3).

8. As a part of her progresses to these two universities, the queen gave orations to students and scholars after being entertained there. Elizabeth's Latin orations at Cambridge (1564) and Oxford (1566 and 1592) appear in John Nichols, *The Progresses and Public Processions of Queen Elizabeth I*, 3 vols. (1823, rpt. New York: Burt Franklin, 1966), vol. 1, pp. 175–79; 214–15; and vol. 3, pp. 147–48). While at Oxford in 1566, she also made a short speech of thanks in Greek in response to an oration given by the university's King's Professor in that language. The account is mentioned in Nichols, vol. 1, p. 208, but no transcript is given. The audiences at such gatherings were quite large; her farewell in Latin at Oxford in 1566 may have been heard by as many as 1,800 people (George Rice, introduction to his edition of her speeches, *The Public Speaking of Queen Elizabeth* (New York: Columbia, 1951), p. 45).

9. In either sense, the notion of Elizabeth "carrying out" the church as infant child and nurturing it sustained contemporary notions of Elizabeth's relationship to the church. Despite her virginity, Elizabeth often used maternal metaphors to refer to herself in relation to her people. Because of her virginity, she was frequently portrayed as the nurturing protector to the Protestant church in a manner parallel to the Virgin Mary's relationship to the Catholic church.

Roy Strong, *The Cult of Elizabeth: Elizabethan Portraiture and Pageantry* (Berkeley: University of California Press, 1977), discusses this notion in relation to the celebration of the queen's Accession Day, (pp. 117–28). Makin further stresses that the queen's motives are purer that her forbears' since she acts out of true "piety" rather than out of political "policy."

10. James's attitude toward learned women was perhaps best illustrated in his response upon being presented with a young woman praised for her Latin, Greek, and Hebrew; he said, "But can she spin?"; Carroll Camden, *The Elizabethan Woman* (Mamaroneck, N.Y.: Paul P. Appel, 1975), p. 43.

11. Makin does qualify her program on two counts: (1) she assures male readers that it will not lead to gender disorder, but will motivate both women and men to better themselves (by competition—because men are hierarchically above women); and (2) she argues that not all women are intellectually suited for such study: "I do not mean, that it is necessary to the *esse*, to the *substance*, or to the Salvation of Women, to be thus educated. Those that are mean in the World, have not an opportunity for this Education: Those that are of low Parts, though they have opportunity, cannot reach this; *Ex quovis ligno non fit Minerva"* (p. 22).

12. Elaine Hobby, *Virtue of Necessity: English Women's Writings 1646–1688* (London: Virago Press, 1988), contends that this development forced women not only to retreat from politics, but also made them "of necessity" retreat to a stance that asserted their virtue in their writings (p. 18); Lawrence Stone, *The Family, Sex, and Marriage in England 1500–1800* (New York: Harper & Row, 1979), argues that because of such repression, women moved toward a more strident feminism, which at the end of the seventeenth century became a political factor in the confluence of the eighteenth-century revolutions in America and France (pp. 227–28). In women's writings of this period, we often see both impetuses at work, sometimes in seeming contradiction of the feminist goal that the author strives to attain.

13. Panegyrics to the queen most often proceeded from a male gaze, frequently using Petrarchan language to praise the queen as a beautiful, unattainable, desirable physical female object, even in the context of lauding her actions as England's queen—as evidenced, for example, in Walter Ralegh's poetry, Edmund Spenser's *Faerie Queene* (1596), and James Aske's celebratory poem, *Elizabetha Triumphans* (1588). For significant discussions of the gendered language of praise and women poets, see Ann Rosalind Jones, "Assimilation with a Difference," *Yale French Studies* 62 (1981): 135–53; Jones, "Surprising Fame: Renaissance Gender Ideologies and Women's Lyric," in *The Poetics of Gender*, ed. Nancy K. Miller (New York: Columbia University Press, 1986), pp. 74–95; and *The Currency of Eros: Women's Love Lyric in Europe: 1540–1620* (Bloomington: Indiana Univ. Press, 1990b).

14. In the absence of genealogical records to identify her family background, Germaine Greer, Susan Hastings, Jeslyn Medoff, and Melinda Sansone, *Kissing the Rod: An Anthology of Seventeenth-Century Women's Verse* (New York: Noonday Press, 1988), who include part of Primrose's long poem in their anthology, speculate that Diana Primrose may have been related to Gilbert Primrose, head of the reformed church in France and later chaplain under James I, indicated by the poem's publication date of 1630 (p. 83). Nichols, who prints part of Primrose's poem in *The Progresses and Public Processions of Queen Elizabeth* (vol. 3, p. 640), gives a publication date of 1603—probably in error but clearly seeking to place it along with eulogies of the queen written upon her death.

15. Greer et al., *Kissing the Rod*, suggest that Primrose's motive in writing it was to rebuke Charles I for a lackluster reign: "Diana Primrose's purpose in writing a panegyric on a queen dead twenty-seven years is clearly to criticize Charles I by implication. Elizabeth's ten ornaments . . . may have all been con-

sidered lacking in Charles. By 1630, his imprudence in trusting Buckingham and allying himself with papist interests combined with his lack of concern for Protestant feeling had begun to seriously alienate him from a large proportion of his subjects" (p. 83). This explanation, however, much diminishes Primrose's stated purpose in the poem—to establish the queen as a gender model for emulation. Moreover, there is no decisive evidence to indicate whether Primrose was a member of Charles's, James's, or Elizabeth's court.

16. Greer et al. note that in his *Hesperides* (1648), Robert Herrick possibly alludes to *A Chaine of Pearle* in one of his "To His Booke" poems. Herrick writes, "Say, if there be 'mongst many jems here; / one Deserveless of the name of *Paragon* / Blush not at all for that; since we have set / Some *Pearls* on *Queens* that have been counterfet" (p. 84). While they suggest this may be a cryptic contribution to the "mystery surrounding Primrose's identity," I suggest a different reading here. Herrick may be making a critical allusion to the "first Pearle" Primrose ascribes to Elizabeth, "Religion"—which she describes as the "goodliest pearle which did chiefly gaine a Royall Lustre to all the rest." Religion was obviously a topic of great concern to Herrick. While Primrose praises the queen for gaining the pearl of "true Religion," Herrick, as a Cavalier poet and Anglican parson (who by 1647 would be expelled from his position at Dean's Priory), may well have found the bestowal of that "pearl" undeserved and a subject for comment.

17. Text from Leonel Sharp to the Duke of Buckingham, in *Cabala, Mysteries of State* (1654, p. 260).

18. In fact, in *Esther hath hang'd Haman: Or an answere to a lewd Pamphlet entituled, The Arraignment of Women. With the arraignment of lewd, idle, froward and vnconstant men and hvsbands*, Esther Sowernam calls Elizabeth "a pattern for the best men" as well as for women "to imitate" (1617, A2v-A3v).

19. Jinner (1658), Br. Other of Jinner's almanacs express protofeminist concerns for women as well; Bernard Capp, *English Almanacs: Astrology and the Popular Press* (Ithaca, N.Y.: Cornell University Press, 1979), p. 124.

20. Another such literary example is Lady Mary Wroth's Queen Pamphilia in *The Countesse of Mountgomeries Urania* (1621), who parallels Elizabeth in some of her actions and speeches.

21. Benedict Anderson, *Imagined Communities: Reflections on the Origin and Spread of Nationalism* (London: Verso, 1991), argues further that the power of nationalism derives its force from its imagined community, because in the minds of each member of that community "lives the image of their communion. . . . [a] fraternity that makes it possible . . . for so many millions of people, not so much to kill, as willingly to die for such limited imaginings" (pp. 6–7).

12

Mary Ward's "Jesuitresses" and the Construction of a Typological Community

LOWELL GALLAGHER

ONE OF THE FEW ECCLESIASTICAL topics on which both Protestant and Catholic authorities in early seventeenth-century England might agree was the career of Mary Ward (1585–1645). Daughter of a prominent Yorkshire family, Ward had gained notoriety by the age of thirty as the founder of a religious community of women, the Schola Beatae Mariae (School of Blessed Mary), which dedicated itself to the education of girls and to the propagation of the Catholic religion on the Continent as well as in England.[1] It was Ward whom George Abbot, Archbishop of Canterbury, had in mind when he made the following comment in 1617: "That woman does more harm to the English Church than many priests. Gladly would I exchange six or seven Jesuits for her" (Hicks 2, p. 323). Ward was also named the perpetrator of "scandal" by William Harrison, Archpriest of the English Catholic mission, in a report sent posthumously to the Agent of the English Secular Clergy in Rome in 1622. Ward's community, Harrison lamented, could be found:

> To manifest such garrulity and loquacity in words, that they are for the most part not only a scorn but a great scandal to many pious people, when they see that many things are done and said by them both unbecoming to their sex and untimely and inconvenient to the Catholic religion, labouring in the midst of heresies.
>
> (Chambers, vol. 2, p. 186)[2]

In this essay I want to give a brief account of the ideological syntax that helped bring together otherwise strange bedfellows—the Archbishop and the Archpriest—in a common ambition, to sink the name and the project of Mary Ward into oblivion.

Harrison's remarks indicate one obvious stumbling block: Ward's school (informally known as the Institute of Mary), violated prevailing gendered schemes of decorum concerning the proper governance of early modern ecclesiastical and social bodies.[3] The general shape of the "scandal" produced by the "unbecoming" behavior of Ward's community can be discerned without much difficulty by surveying the protocol that Ward established in the *Ratio Instituti* (1616), the second of three plans she devised for the community in collaboration with her spiritual advisors.[4] The *Ratio* lays out two principal aims for the Institute: to establish an international network of boarding schools and day schools for girls and to participate in the missionary project of recovering England for Catholicism. Broadly speaking, both aims derived from the educational incentive of early modern humanism and the proselytizing agenda of the Counter-Reformation. What was innovative and unorthodox was Ward's approach to the conceptual boundary maintaining distinctions between male and female agency and vocation in the cultivation of an engaged and informed Christian social practice. Ward's public schools trained female pupils, from both upper and lower social ranks, in "all those liberal exercises which are more suitable for every state of life" (Orchard, p. 37). The "liberal exercises" included "a sense of duty, Christian doctrine, good morals, how to serve God, reading the common [Spanish, French, English] and Latin languages, writing, household management, liberal arts [including mathematics, geography, and astronomy], singing, painting, sewing, spinning, curtain-making" (Orchard, p. 37). Ward's curricula were, one might say, "bi-gendering," in the sense that the Institute fashioned a cadre of "virgins and young girls" equipped not only to "profitably embrace either the secular or the religious state" but to move with ease between prescribed female and male spheres of expertise as well.

Indeed, in several respects the schools of the Institute were legible imitations of Jesuit boys' schools.[5] As the *Ratio* makes clear, the Institute's pedagogical endeavor was itself part of a larger, apostolic ambition exemplified by the Society of Jesus. Ward sought to deploy a female missionary community that would "undertake something more than ordinary" in the "same common spiritual necessity" that had galvanized both religious and secular orders of priests in general and the Jesuits in particular: the "conversion of the kingdom" (England) and "in any place, the propagation of our Holy Mother, the Catholic Church" (Chambers, vol. 2, pp. 373–77).

Like the Society of Jesus, Ward's Institute defined itself as a society governed by an internally elected leader, who was answerable to the "Chief Pontiff" (the Pope) alone (Chambers, vol. 2, p. 376). In this re-

gard, the Institute departed from the administrative protocol of virtually all existing religious orders for women, which by tradition were
placed under local episcopal authority. The Catholic Church did not have
a viable episcopate in place in England, however, when Ward was developing the Institute.[6] Given this circumstance, Ward's choice of the
Jesuit model might have been evaluated on pragmatic grounds. Indeed,
a later era would find Ward's choice eminently reasonable, without regard to any contingencies of diocesan administration: "Lasciate governare
le donne dalle donne" ("Let women be governed by women"), wrote
Clement XI of the Institute, when its Rule finally received papal approval
in 1703 (Chambers, vol. 2, p. 296). But what seemed reasonable to Clement XI in 1703 was viewed as a profound anomaly by most of the church
authorities during Ward's lifetime. The three successive pontiffs whom
Ward sought to convince (Paul V, Gregory XV, Urban VIII) remained
interested in the case but indecisive. Then in 1621 the Bull of Suppression, signed by Urban VIII, dissolved the Institute, declaring it "extinct,
rooted out, destroyed, and abolished" and setting in motion the chain
reaction that would lead to Ward's arrest and imprisonment in Munich
three weeks after the Bull was signed.[7]

Ward was well aware that the survival of the community, at least as
an official organ of the Church, depended on the dispensation of the Holy
See, particularly in view of the fact that the Institute stood in apparent
violation of decrees, enacted at the Fourth Lateran Council (1214) and
the Council of Lyon (1274), which required that all future religious communities declare their spiritual and institutional parentage by adopting
one of four established Rules (St. Basil, St. Augustine, St. Benedict, or
St. Francis) (Orchard, p. 28, note 13). In a memorandum written to the
General of the Society of Jesus in 1622, Ward herself pointed out that
the Council of Trent, which had approved the Jesuit order in 1563, established a precedent for the case of the Institute.[8] Strictly speaking,
Ward's appropriation of certain administrative features of the Jesuit order
amounted to a legal technicality, and it was treated as such in the discussions and reviews conducted by theologians in the months before the
Ratio was to be considered for papal approval.[9] This technicality alone
was not the stuff of "scandal." Two other contested features, however,
were. Ward insisted in the *Ratio* that the Institute could not "exercise
its duties" unless it was freed from two traditional rules governing religious communities of women: the rule of enclosure and the adoption of
a "determined religious habit."[10] In a public letter supporting the Institute, Bishop Blaise of St. Omer, one of Ward's spiritual advisors, argued
that Ward's insistence on these two features demonstrated that her community was not in fact seeking official approbation as a religious order:
"neither by any peculiarity of dress nor by monastic enclosure . . . nor
by any rule, nor by the assumption of the name, have they ever given
themselves out to be nuns or religious women" (Chambers, vol. 1, p. 325).
However well intentioned, this defense underscored the very "peculiar-

ity" that the bishop tried to attenuate: the evidence that Ward's community was carving out an uncharted space between secular and religious states, and between the strict, institutionalized rhythms of the contemplative religious vocation and what Ward called the "time of negociation" in the social world.[11]

In the *Ratio* Ward described the community's practice as a "mixed kind of life" (Chambers, vol. 1., p. 376). The "mixed life," one of "contemplation . . . mixed with action," observed the Pauline missionary ethos (also espoused by the Jesuits), which Ward paraphrased in a set of maxims intended for the sisters of the Institute: "Be all things to all men," she wrote, "that so thou mayest win all for God" (Chambers, vol. 1, pp. 466–67).[12] Freedom from enclosure and from the identifying mark or brand of an institutional garb enabled Ward's community to fulfill this prescription, incarnating the Pauline ideal in the materiality of practice. Thus the Institute, administratively amphibious, produced an itinerant corps of women—itinerant in ways that went beyond the contemplative tradition of the *itinerarium mentis*. The corps disseminated its members across a broad geographical area. By the early 1630s, Ward had founded ten houses and schools throughout Europe, in Belgium, Bohemia, Germany, Austria, and Italy. Ward's third plan (1622) further included a pledge ("a special vow") to participate fully in the Counter-Reformation project of worldwide spiritual colonization, venturing "to carry out whatever the present and future Roman Pontiffs may order," in "whatsoever provinces they may choose to send us— whether they are pleased to send us among the Turks or any other infidels, even to those who live in the region called the Indies" (Orchard, p. 65). This particular ambition remained unrealized in Ward's lifetime. In England, however, the Institute became nomadic, moving primarily between London and Yorkshire and, within London, moving from one residence to another, in order to escape detection by government pursuivants.

From the outset of her mission in England, Ward showed political acumen, surmising that the Institute's best chances of survival in the "sadly afflicted state" of England lay in her community's ability to mime and to exploit the advantages of social prestige and power.[13] The community's first residence in London, in 1609, was in the fashionable district of St. Clement's Churchyard, in the Strand. In 1614 the sisters took up residence in Spitalfields, a fashionable suburb near the Flemish and Venetian embassies, and also a hub of Catholic activity. By 1618 the community was back in the Strand, at Hungerford House. Near capture by pursuivants during her stay at Hungerford House led Ward to relocate to the less reputable, outlying district of Knightsbridge, where she "borrowed of a special friend a garden-house." Here security lay not so much in the outward display of social prominence as in the particular protection afforded by the "special friend," who was "a Protestant, and powerful in regard of the office he held."[14]

The social armature of the Institute partly lay, then, in its capacity to negotiate the boundaries between religious groups and between social classes. One document further indicates how the very definition of community could be quite minimalist, in keeping with the habits of reticence and adaptability that characterized missionary practice in a climate of unpredictable government surveillance. "A relation of one of ours, a lay-sister, one of those that live in villages in England" chronicles the "proceedings and manner of living" of a Sister Dorothea, in Suffolk in the early 1620s.[15] A recusant woman from an apparently privileged background, Dorothea lived incognito "in the house of a poor woman, pretending to be her kinswoman" (Chambers, vol. 2, p. 27). The pretense had in fact two layers. As the narrative makes clear, by the 1620s priests hostile to Ward's enterprise had generated sufficient controversy over the Institute to convince Dorothea that her mission would be more successful if she presented herself as a lay-sister, with no affiliation to the Institute. "So long as I am not suspected to be one of you," she wrote, "I am well beloved, and all I do is exceedingly well liked of. . . . I have no enemies but heretics, whom I fear not at all; but once I be known, my lady bids me look for as many enemies of priests and Catholics as now I have friends of them" (Chambers, vol. 2, pp. 35, 38). It was in this capacity—doubly embedded in the lineaments of Suffolk society—that Dorothea pursued her pedagogical and missionary practice. She established a "floating" school, teaching the Institute's curriculum to children in the homes of their parents.[16] Spending her time "not in one place, but in many," she also persuaded "many from the King his religion," in addition to drawing church-papists (Catholics who chose to obey the government's laws regarding church attendance) into a more active recusancy (Chambers, vol. 2, p. 27). In Dorothea's career, Ward's Institute produced a virtually undocumented "house" with one member only, exemplifying the kind of pragmatic flexibility with institutional codes of identity and rank that the freedom from enclosure and from sartorial definition allowed the sisters. It was precisely this flexibility that earned them the title "Galloping Girls" (Chambers, vol. 2, p. 186).

William Harrison, the Archpriest, probably did not know of Dorothea's career when he prepared his inflammatory account of the Institute in 1621. But the contours of her "manner of living" can be discerned in Harrison's description of the "great scandal." Ward's "religious society," he protests:

> Travels freely hither and thither, changes its ground and habit at will, accommodates itself to the manners and condition of seculars. . . . These Jesuitresses have a habit of frequently going about cities and provinces of the kingdom, insinuating themselves into houses of noble Catholics, changing their habit often, sometimes travelling like some ladies of first consequence, in coaches or carriages with a respectable suite, sometimes, on the contrary, like common servants or women of lower rank, alone and private. (Chambers, vol. 2, p. 185)

Had it found its way into Harrison's account, Dorothea's particular practice might have been granted, minimally, the virtue of consistency: she apparently confined her repertoire of social identities to that of a servant. Other documents, however, corroborate the signs of the "mixed life" that Harrison found obnoxious. The earliest biography of Ward, "A Briefe Relation of the Holy Life and Happy Death of our Dearest Mother" (assumed to be written in 1650 by Winifred Wigmore and Mary Poyntz, Ward's closest friends in the Institute) describes Ward's own palette of social identities during her residence in the elite district of the Strand in 1609. At times she dressed fashionably, "clothed as became her birth for matter and manner," but "when it best suited with present occasions, she put on servants' clothes and mean women's clothes" (Chambers, vol. 1, p. 217).[17] Another source details the "phantastical" attire occasionally adopted by members of the Institute. Barbara Ward (Mary's sister) was seen "dressed in a bright taffeta gown and rich petticoats, trimmed of the newest fashion, and a deep yellow ruff" (Chambers, vol. 1, p. 424).

Mary Chambers, whose nineteenth-century biography of Ward remains an important source of information on Ward's career, notes that "to the eyes of the uninitiated" the women of the Institute easily passed for "ladies accustomed to good society" (Chambers, vol. 1, p. 424). As Harrison's account and Dorothea's personal narrative both indicate, however, the quasi-theatrical practice of the "mixed life" also placed a stigma on the women. Ward's "mixed" society was "observed to have a very bad character, and are very much talked about for petulance and indecorum" (Chambers, vol. 2, p. 186). It is not difficult to imagine what Harrison would have found in Winifred Wigmore's remark concerning the achievment of Ward's house in Rome, which was reputed to be putting the Roman brothels "out of business" (Orchard, p. 71). Wigmore was reporting her sisters' success in carrying out one of Ward's directions for the apostolic work of the community: to "seek out women of doubtful lives and prepare them to receive the grace of the sacraments" (Orchard, p. 64). In Harrison's discursive regime, such work of conversion and purging would be virtually indistinguishable from a process of contamination. While his memorial does not directly impugn the sisters' chastity, the semiotics of restless and errant movement in which he couches his discussion registers the concern that the Institute was introducing courtesanlike habits—a decayed *sprezzatura* of speech and behavior—into the English mission.[18]

Winifred Wigmore preferred a more martial association, one that better fit the notion of "spiritual combat" popular in Counter-Reformation devotional culture.[19] To Wigmore, Mary Ward was a "holy amazon" (Chambers, vol. 1, p. 158).[20] The proactive agency that Wigmore invoked also appeared in Harrison's idiom, in the epithet "Apostolicae Viragines"—apostolic viragoes. Indeed, the Institute's reputation for intellectual discipline and expertise in the "liberal arts" helped promote rumors, in the "familiar speech" of Catholics and Protestants alike, that Ward's "licentious" corps of women was taking over two privileged arenas of male authority: public preaching and the direction of conscience.[21] Ward was reputed to have "preached in a public street before an altar" (Chambers, vol. 1, p. 170).[22] This seems an unlikely event—in view of the political circumstances governing the overt movements of English Catholics at the time—but clearly not an incredible one in the popular imagination. Winifred Wigmore herself observed that Ward would sometimes use "familiar conversation, other times authority . . . amongst the common and poor sort" in order to "put them in doubt of their own error and then lay the light before them" (Chambers, vol. 1, p. 217). It was also rumored that the sisters "pretend to read theology, at least moral theology, in their young ladies' schools, in order, as they say, that they may not be taken in by their confessors."[23] The sisters' reported manipulations of moral theology in their relations with spiritual advisors reinforced the widespread belief that Ward's Institute was in collusion with the Jesuits, who had acquired a reputation for casuistical laxity in the direction of conscience.[24]

Question: What is more dangerous than a Jesuit? Answer: A Jesuitress. This is the shape of the unofficial catechism tacitly rehearsed by Protestant and Catholic populations alike in the pamphlet literature and correspondence concerning the Institute. The ideological work accomplished by this catechism can best be understood as a negotiation or crossing of two semiotic trajectories in the unofficial name for the Institute. On the one hand, the word "Jesuitress" encapsulates the prevailing notion of the proper jurisdiction of female agency in Harrison's culture: Ward's Institute had ventured an "unbecoming" (because female) appropriation of an exclusively male (Jesuit) preserve in the ecclesiastical hierarchy. The single word "Jesuitresses" thus reflects the intent of Ward's male opposition, from both Protestant and Catholic quarters, to secure the identity of the Institute as a category mistake, akin to the mongrel and the chimera. On the other hand, the word "Jesuitress" also conveyed the perception of a suspect kinship between Institute and Society of Jesus, precisely because of the Jesuits' own controversial reputation in Counter-Reformation culture. Indeed, this perceived kinship made the Institute a likely candidate for use as a pawn in the long-standing jurisdictional rivalry between seminary clergy and Jesuits in the English mission.[25] In the protracted course of this rivalry, the seminary clergy, who resented the greater autonomy and latitude of the Jesuit missionaries, cited the Institute as evidence of the Jesuits' willingness to do anything to increase the scope of the Society's influence in England. Thus Matthew Kellison, president of the seminary of the English College at Douay, attributed the very origin of the Institute to the machinations of the Jesuit Roger Lee, who was one of Ward's confessors during her early years in St. Omer, a principal refuge for English Catholic exiles. In Kellison's view, Lee was "a great adept at drawing everything to the

Society under pretence of piety" (Chambers, vol. 1, pp. 50–51).[26] When he called Ward's companions "Jesuitresses," the Archpriest Harrison—the nominal head of the seminary clergy—was at once degrading the Jesuits and maligning the Institute.

For its part, the Society of Jesus was ambivalent toward the "Jesuitresses." John Gerard—one of the most influential English Jesuits—actively supported Ward's enterprise, for example, but his views were not shared by the Society in general. By 1622, according to Kellison, the Institute had been "publicly deserted by all" the Jesuits (Chambers, vol. 2, p. 52).[27] Of course Kellison's report is hardly the most reliable source of information regarding the actions or opinions of the Society. Nevertheless, the remark does convey the climate of escalating internal controversy in the English mission, which made it unlikely that the Jesuit order would officially support a community whose very existence was being served up as evidence not only of female unruliness but also of Jesuit wiles: the Jesuit as pimp.

Such "discord" grew more acute during the 1620s, even as Ward became more determined to secure official sanction for the Institute. She traveled to Rome in 1622 and again in 1624 to present her case to a succession of popes, and in the course of the decade founded new houses in Naples, Perugia, Vienna, Pressburg, and Prague. Ironically, the more her enterprise thrived, the more it seemed indeed to "parallel," as one Jesuit put it, the internationalist scope of the Jesuit mission (Chambers, vol. 2, p. 54). Ward repeatedly called attention to the rapid growth of the Institute as a definitive measure of its value in the "defence and propagation of the faith," but success of this sort only tapped yet another source of anti-Jesuit animus. Consider the Archpriest Harrison's complaint of the sisters' "habit of . . . insinuating themselves into the houses of noble Catholics" (Chambers, vol. 2, p. 185). The complaint registered the seminary clergy's concern that the Institute was draining money away from a crucial source of funds for the English mission ("noble Catholics") and sinking it, just as the Jesuits were suspected of doing, in causes with no discernible bearing on the promotion of an English Catholic nationhood. This concern also informs the accusation that Ward's sisters "squander the dowries of the members and are nevertheless in debt" (Orchard, p. 50).

As the third plan for the Institute (1622) makes clear, Ward's project was not in fact oriented exclusively toward the English mission. Like the Society of Jesus, Ward's Institute intended to promote a universal *societas* "beneath the banner of the Cross" and "under the Roman Pontiff" (Orchard, pp. 64–65). In this regard, Ward's project displayed both the utopian and the nostalgic aspects of the Counter-Reformation apostolic mission. Arguably, the Institute's investment in these very aspects helped produce the imbroglio in which the Institute found itself, caught in the cross fire between the English seminary clergy, the Jesuit mission, and a Vatican hierarchy seeded with anti-Jesuit sentiment.[28] Ward's

Institute was a symptom of the politics of utopian and nostalgic imagining in Counter-Reformation culture, but it also became a symptom of the extreme strain under which another imaginary configuration had been placed in post-Reformation culture generally and in the English mission in particular: the mutual entailment of religious and political allegiances in the formation of national identity.

The wandering movement frequently ascribed to "Jesuitresses" and Jesuits alike in the polemical literature of the period aptly conveys the ambivalent perception of a society prospering without a fixed home, ethos, or identity. With regard to the Institute in particular, there was little doubt, even among those who supported the enterprise, that Ward was mapping an uncharted itinerary through the prevailing ecclesiastical and social orders of the world. As Ward herself observed in a set of instructions written for the Institute in 1617, "all looketh upon you as new beginners of a course never thought before, marvelling at what you intend, and what will be the end of you."[29] This was not naive optimism. Ward was well aware of what, and whom, she was up against. "Men, you know," she wrote, "looketh diversely upon you." Ward urged her sisters to take the diversity of opinion as a sign that the "end" in store for them could not be reliably predicted by male authorities. "Some, thinking we are women, and aiming at greater matters than was ever thought women were capable of, they expect perhaps to see us fall, or come short in many things." Others, she added, "expect to see our fervour decay, and all come to nothing, ourselves to shame and confusion." Having been placed, in effect, in the lower regions of a Picoesque map of human possibility, the Institute, Ward argued, should consider all the options: "Others, I am sure, looketh upon us with another conceit, expecting all the world to be bettered by us!"

Ward's informed utopianism does not translate easily into a unilateral assessment. Her loyalty to the sovereign "Roman Pontiffs"—at least to the *idea* of such sovereignty—and her commitment to a universalist apostolic mission, the "propagation of our Holy Mother, the Catholic Church," indicate that Ward's Institute contributed to the cultural–imperialist legacy advanced by the Counter-Reformation. To insist on the primacy of this feature, however, is to rehearse uncritically the absolutist logic of that very legacy. In the pursuit of her vocation, Ward also showed little compunction in discounting what she believed to be imprudent or harmful advice from confessors and advisors in the hierarchy of the Church. Such apparent pragmatism and independence of thought suggest the emergence of a socially progressive ideology in Ward's enterprise. It is important to recognize, then, that the utopian and nostalgic canopy of Ward's apostolic mission itself enabled Ward to take an instrumental approach to dominant, naturalized aspects of the cultural regime she was nominally propagating.

This feature is particularly notable not only with regard to prevailing gender boundaries but to those of class or social rank as well, as my

brief account of Ward's career has suggested. Indeed, the gendered in-
flection to Ward's "indecorum," as Harrison put it, figured an interre-
lated violation of class and gender boundaries. Consider the entry for
Ward's Institute in *The English Spanish Pilgrime*, an exposé of Catholic insurgence written by the apostate James Wadsworth in 1629. The
"Jesuitrices or wandring Nuns," Wadsworth reports, "goe clad very like
to the Jesuites" (p. 29). The real problem, however, was not that Ward's
sisters adopted the "Ignatian habit" (p. 29) as their calling card, but rather
that they took on a "manner of living" (to recall Sister Dorothea's phrase)
that could be easily construed as Jesuitical in its fluidity. Theirs was
primarily a mimesis of (male) action and agency rather than a visual identification, while the actual cross-dressing permitted by their sartorial
freedom crossed class rather than gender lines. It was this chiasmatic
distribution of identifying marks that gave Ward's companions broad
mobility throughout a diversely stratified social world.

   This is not to say that class distinctions per se had become irrelevant
or unreal to the Institute. Ward and a good number of her earliest companions came from families of genteel and economically comfortable
backgrounds.[30] It would be disingenuous to claim that the financial resources of the families (principally in the form of dowries and charitable
donations) were not crucial to Ward's project. In this regard, the very
inception of the Institute was class-marked. Even so, the combined educational and apostolic habitus built up by the Institute (with the aid of
family endowments) enabled Ward's companions to inhabit a social space
considerably more flexible than the niches assigned to them by virtue
of the contingencies of their social and geographic origin. In this regard,
Ward's three plans for the Institute, the evolving expressions of her
desire to produce "something more than ordinary," produced a performative critique of entrenched class distinctions.[31]

   The most compelling evidence of the extraordinary "end" that Ward
envisioned for the Institute, however, is the way in which Ward taught
her companions to think about gender relations within the institutional
structure of the Church. The text I have in mind is the set of instructions, noted previously, that she wrote for the Institute in 1617. Ward
evidently devised the instructions as a kind of damage control in response
to a contretemps: a public retort made by one of the Institute's own
confessors after he received word of the initial, and favorable, reaction
in Rome to Ward's second plan. "Fervour will decay," the confessor was
heard to say, "and when all is done, they are but women" (Chambers,
vol. 1, p. 408). Ward made the confessor's retort the theme of her instructions. Ward's text provides nothing less than a primer for critiqu-
ing the culturally privileged paternalism that Ward no doubt knew her
companions would have to counter, in both word and action, if the Institute were to survive. Space allows only partial citations, though enough,
I hope, to convey the sense of franchise that informs Ward's discourse
as a whole.

I would know what you all think he meant by this speech of his, 'but women,' and what 'fervour' is. Fervour is a will to do good, that is, a preventing grace from God, and a gift given gratis by God, which we could not merit. It is true fervour doth many times grow cold, but what is the cause? Is it because we are women? No, but because we are imperfect women. There is no such difference between men and women. . . . Heretofore we have been told by men we must believe. It is true we must, but let us be wise, and know what we are to believe and what not, and not to be made to think we can do nothing. If women were made so inferior to men in all things, why were they not exempted in all things, as they are in some? I confess wives are to be subject to their husbands, men are head of the Church, women are not to administer sacraments, nor preach in public churches, but in all other things, wherein are we so inferior to other creatures that they should term us 'but women?' For what think you of this word, 'but women?' but as if we were in all things inferior to some other creature which I suppose to be man! Which I dare to be bold to say is a lie; and with respect to the good Father may say it is an error. . . . There was a Father that lately came into England whom I heard say that he would not for a thousand of worlds be a woman, because he thought a woman could not apprehend God. I answered nothing, but only smiled, although I could have answered him, by the experience I have of the contrary. I could have been sorry for his want—I mean not want of judgment—nor to condemn his judgment, for he is a man of very good judgment; his want is in experience. (Chambers, vol. 1, pp. 408–11)

In certain respects Ward's instructions show a discursive kinship with the printed texts belonging to the gender controversy in contemporary Protestant England: the *Haec Vir* pamphlet and the writings of Rachel Speght and Ester Sowernam, for example. Like these texts, the instructions exploit the rhetoric of syllogistic reasoning; they strategically weigh the force of particular experience over that of customary knowledge; they point up the ironic subtexts to apparently transparent dialogs within a hierarchized social world.[32] In view of these shared frames of reference, Ward's understanding of the architecture of thought and "experience" would not have been unintelligible to the women she hoped to convert in England. It goes without saying, then, that the Institute did not inhabit an insular cultural space. Nevertheless, Ward's humanist and apostolic entrepreneurship conveys her particular response to a group of reading practices she assimilated primarily through the devotional cultures of the Counter-Reformation. The pivot of Ward's thought and experience was an articulation of three devotional patterns: the lives of the saints, typological hermeneutics, and the *imitatio Christi*. Ward's investment in these patterns establishes the vocabulary for what I will call her "conceptual habitat," the discursive and social field in which her promise of "something more than ordinary" could figure not as a radical or trangressive act—not, then, as the kind of "scandal" that Harrison invoked—but instead as a viable extension of the bounds of the normative.[33]

Harrison's memorial itself points up the inaugural theme for the apostolic mission that Ward declared herself ready to carry to "the Indies." Harrison had observed that Ward's enterprise was "untimely" as well as "unbecoming." Indeed, the innovative character of Ward's community turned on its relation to time and to sacred history. In the 1616 *Ratio* Ward argued that what seemed innovative about the "mixed kind of life" was in fact no more than a return to female saintly practice in apostolic tradition. "Such a life," she wrote, "appears to have been led by Saints Mary Magdalen, Martha, Praxedes, Pudentiana, Thecla, Cecilia, Lucy, and many other holy virgins and widows" (Chambers, vol. 1, p. 376).[34] Here Ward was relying on two related schemes of thought common to Catholic and Protestant reformist cultures: hagiographic exemplarity and a kind of performative typology. These schemes provided Ward with an imaginative screen on which to project a future for providential history by remembering the past strategically.[35] Her conciliatory rhetoric notwithstanding, Ward's hagiographic imagination was strategic in the sheer scope of its literalism, which enabled Ward to transform received icons of personal devotion (like Mary Magdalen and Thecla) into personifications of a new institutional ethos—a self-governing apostolic community for contemporary women.

Ward's literalism did not depend on an illusory coincidence of past and present. The organizational profile of the community was "something more than ordinary" precisely because the contemporary cultural scene—as the *Ratio* suggested—posed unprecedented challenges to traditional apostolic practice. The logic here was the narrative logic of typology. Traditionally a mode of scriptural hermeneutics, typology disclosed the deep, unifying structure of Old and New Testaments by positing the retrospective figurality of the Christ-event. In the typological imagination, the Christ-event gave narrative coherence to the sacred book because the event was understood to manifest itself continuously, though differently, in two different temporal schemes, the time of promise and the time of fulfillment. Thus allied to the salvific agency of the Christ-event, typology also consecrated the historicity of the evolving interactions between sacred book and devotional readers.[36] Typology thus provided a conceptual canopy under which a number of phenomena associated with the early modern "experience" of the Christ-event could be understood as typological parsings of what Ward called the "time of negociation." In this time between promise and fulfillment came the technological innovations that disseminated the Word in print culture, the rise of postvernacular sectarianism, and the apostolic programs of the Counter-Reformation—including Ward's Institute. Typology thus provided a way of imagining historical process and change as a therapeutic dynamic of repetition with difference.

It is not surprising, then, that typological arguments should surface in the justifications for the Institute. In 1624, the Archduke Ferdinand of Bavaria, Prince-Bishop of Liège, one of Ward's most ardent supporters, placed the Institute under his sponsorship in a public letter that exploited typology's political utility. The "Institute of these Virgins," the Archduke declared, was "predestined by a particular Providence of God to the conversion of England, alas! altogether lost and depraved, that what a woman has destroyed by woman may be restored" (Chambers, vol. 2, p. 188). Mary Ward had become the new Elizabeth I. Wigmore and Poyntz invoked the same image, rather more elaborately, in their "Briefe Relation." Their chronicle includes the following anecdote to illustrate Ward's heroics while ministering to the Catholic community in London, 1617, under increased government surveillance:

> On a time, tired out with mental employments and other labours, she was importuned to take some recreation. At length yielding thereto, she found out a very unexpected one, of which no one thought, which was to give the Bishop of Canterbury [George Abbott] his wish of seeing her as he had so much desired it, and in effect went to his house at Lambeth, with no small apprehension to her companions who were in terror and alarm at the success of this perilous amusement, but to herself a walk of pleasure and real recreation. God permitted that the Bishop was not at home, but she left her name, and that she had been there to see him, written in the glass window with a diamond. (quoted in Chambers, vol. 1, pp. 425–26)[37]

Wigmore and Poyntz had, in effect, raided the vault of Elizabeth's personal hagiography. The story of Princess Elizabeth's imprisonment at Woodstock in 1555 included the telling detail of her diamond-etched signature, the mark of royal inviolability, left "in a glass window." This detail had been worked up by various hands (notably Holinshed and Camden) into a memory image of the essential narrative logic of the Elizabethan mythology: a harrowing followed by miraculous victory.[38] The "Briefe Relation" reclaimed this memory image typologically, transforming one of the providential signs of Elizabeth's dynastic legitimacy and prestige into a precursory sign of the Institute's own eventual "conversion of the kingdom" (Chambers, vol. 1, pp. 376–77).

In 1650 such an event could not have been thought imminent. For one thing, the immediate readership of the "Briefe Relation" was not large, given that the 1631 Bull of Suppression had virtually abolished the Institute, leaving Ward's surviving companions with few political or financial resources to continue their educational and apostolic projects. Thinking typologically, along with Wigmore and Poyntz, tempers the apparent irony here, however. In addition to memorializing the founder of the Institute, the "Briefe Relation" reenacts Ward's "perilous amusement." The text produces a revisionist history against all odds, for a community whose survival depended on its members' ability to understand the community's evident state of dormancy, not to say its abjection, as the antitype of its future reconstitution.[39]

The central model for this therapeutic revisionism was not typology alone but rather the conjunction of typology and the figure of the abject divinity as construed in Counter-Reformation cultures of the *imitatio*

Christi. This conjunction, principally, is the conceptual habitat for Ward's Institute. Ward's autobiographical fragments and correspondence suggest a reading practice immersed in the diverse *imitatios* in circulation at the time: notably Ignatian Exercises and Salesian devotions, as well as the enduring *Imitatio* of Thomas à Kempis and the more contemporary *Spiritual Combat*, by the Theatine priest Lorenzo Scupoli (Orchard, pp. 38–39). These devotional protocols, while not interchangeable, were guided by a common intuition: that to imitate Christ meant to experience the indwelling of the paradox of the wounded and humiliated god. Set within a typological understanding of historical becoming—a pattern of repetition with difference—the imitation of Christ enabled the experience of the self and of the self's relation to history to be articulated as an ongoing probing into the facets of the Christological paradox.

This pattern can be discerned in Father Roger Lee's exhortation to the community in 1612, which advises the sisters to understand the struggles of the Institute as the living trail of the blood of Christ's circumcision: "But so soon as He began to shed His Blood, His Holy Name was made known, and He was called Jesus, which is in Latin Salvator, Saviour of the World, so that those who truly seek to imitate Him may rightly have their names thus when they begin to suffer and not before" (Chambers, vol. 1, p. 323). Typologically, the gendered aspect of the remembered bloodletting—the ritual practice that identified male membership in the chosen community of Israel—was not a stumbling block for Father Lee's female audience. It was an invitation to enter into the historical arc of a redemptive paradox. To grasp this point we can turn to Ward's retreat notes of 1616. After meditating on her "loathness to suffer," she cites a line from Thomas à Kempis's *Imitation of Christ:* "Lord, let that be made possible to me by grace which seemeth impossible to me by nature" (Orchard, pp. 38–39). As her apostolic career indicates, Ward's experience of "grace," the Pauline mark of spiritual circumcision, enabled her to inhabit an "impossible" regime, one that gave equal place to the devotional conventions of meritorious suffering and to the perceived aberrations (the "scandals") of her particular social practice.[40]

In 1630, in the midst of rumors of the Institute's imminent demise, John Gerard wrote a letter of consolation to Mary Poyntz, reviewing Mary Ward's life in terms that implicitly account for the "scandals" that the Archpriest described. In a passage that seems to yoke the rhetorical exuberance of Christian humanism and baroque mysticism, Gerard describes the pattern of Ward's life as the expression of a sacred oxymoron: "In what can she glory here on earth, except in the Cross of Christ? In toils and sorrows, in pain and contradiction, in adversity and persecution, in affliction and oppression, in sickness and sufferings, finally, in a living death and a dying life, whichever of the two you may like to call it" (Chambers, vol. 2, pp. 316–17). A defense of the Institute written in 1621 by Andrew White, a Jesuit in the English mission, introduces still more suggestive terminology. After invoking various institutional precedents and typological models for the Institute, White describes the "miraculous passages of love" through which "God Himself" has made the Institute "illustrious to the world":

> through infinite crosses, contradictions, pressures, prisons and persecutions, working still by strong, sweet, and prudent patience, heroical acts in the service of God, strange conversions, mutations of manners, change of life, increase of sanctity . . . to the comfort and admiration of all that know them, and glory of Christ Jesus, Whose arms, name and livery they desire to wear. (Chambers, vol. 2, pp. 55–56)

White's text, with its fluid interplay of contrapuntal locutions, captures the "contradictions" and "mutations of manners" in Ward's own social practice. Defending Ward's Institute, White also produces an apologia for a vital aspect of the cultural poetics that Ward inhabited. Reenacting discursively what it sets out to defend, White's text shows how the sacred paradox of the Christ-event, the mark of "infinite crosses," becomes the typological pattern for the enabling contradictions of an apostolic community governed by a woman endowed with what one observer called "the daring of a man" (Chambers, vol. 1, pp. 26–27).

As we have seen, Ward herself admitted her daring, in the 1617 instructions advising her sisters to grasp the sexual politics of paternalist "judgment." Given the context, it is not likely that Ward would have understood her daring to be "that of a man." More likely, she would have understood it to be the daring of a female Christian subject taking literally the paradox of the crucified Corpus and inhabiting it as fully as she could imagine. To the degree that she accomplished this, Ward produced a conceptual habitat for herself and her sisters in which the boundaries between human and divine orders, between male and female attributes, and between dominant and emergent structures of apostolic community were chiasmatically intertwined, in "infinite crosses."

Broadly speaking, Ward's career stands at a point of crossing between two emancipatory figures: the theological figure of "grace" and the pre-Enlightenment one of "reason." Because it speaks to us from this place, Ward's voice occasionally sounds with a doubled accent, channeling divine illumination and rational clarity. Like the enigmatic smile—at once appeasement and critique—that she gave the "Father that lately came into England," Ward's voice presents itself to us, too, as a symptom of the equivocal place that early modern devotional culture occupies in current critical practice, a place at once familiar and strange.

NOTES

1. Publications in English on Mary Ward which I have consulted in preparing this article include Mary Catharine Elizabeth Chambers, *The Life of Mary Ward*, ed. Henry James Coleridge, 2 vols. (London: Burns and Oates, 1882, 1885);

M. Emmanuel Orchard, ed., *Till God Will: Mary Ward Through Her Writings*, intro. James Walsh (London: Darton, Longman and Todd, 1985); Henriette Peters, *Mary Ward: A World in Contemplation,* trans. Helen Butterworth (Leominster: Gracewing, 1994); Marion Norman, "A Woman for All Seasons: Mary Ward (1585–1645), Renaissance Pioneer of Women's Education," *Paedagogica Historica* 23 (1983): 125–43; Leo Hicks, "Mary Ward's Great Enterprise," published in six installments in *The Month* (cited in text as Hicks 1, Hicks 2, and so forth): (February 1928): 137–46; (April 1928): 317–26; (July 1928): 40–52; (September 1928): 231–38; (January 1929): 40–48; (March 1929): 223–36; and Dorothy L. Katz, *'Glow-Worm Light': Writings of 17th-Century English Recusant Women from Original Manuscripts* (Salzburg: Institut für Anglistik und Amerikanistik, 1989), pp. 150–179. Brief mentions of Ward's career are in Patricia Crawford, *Women and Religion in England 1500–1720* (London and New York: Routledge, 1993), pp. 1, 10, 46, 64, 85, 113, 192; and Jo Ann Kay McNamara, *Sisters in Arms: Catholic Nuns through Two Millennia* (Cambridge, Mass.: Harvard University Press, 1996), pp. 462–64.

2. For details concerning the correspondence between Harrison and John Bennet, the Agent of the English Secular Clergy in Rome, see Peter Guilday, *The English Catholic Refugees on the Continent, 1558–1795* (London: Longmans, 1914), p. 183.

3. The history of the nomenclature of the Institute is in Orchard, *Til God Will,* p. 35.

4. The full text of the *Ratio* is in Chambers, *Life of Mary Ward,* vol. 1, pp. 375–85. The three plans of the Institute are described and excerpted in Orchard, *Til God Will,* pp. 34–38, 43–46, 64–65. The collaboration to which I refer may have been more strained than easy. For an account of the apparent tensions between Ward and her spiritual advisors who helped draft the protocol for her community, see Peters, *Mary Ward,* pp. 120–32, 198–203. My use of Ward's name to designate authorship of these documents is not intended to refute Peters' argument. My principal concern here is to emphasize that the very existence of the plans for the Institute testifies to the force of Ward's authorial designs, despite possible difficulties in their construction.

5. Areas of similarity included the daily timetable of the schools, the incorporation of theatrical performances ("French comedies and 'Calderonic' dramas") into the scholars' activities, and the intellectual rigor of the training in "Christian doctrine" and "liberal arts." See Norman, "A Woman for All Seasons," pp. 132–35.

6. The position of Archpriest, held by William Harrison in 1616, had only limited authority over the clergy. Moreover, the position was a source of controversy in the English mission: secular clergy suspected the Archpriest, who was their nominal supervisor, of being the creature of the General of the Jesuit order. For a discussion of the so-called "Archpriest Controversy," see Raymond Stanfield, "The Archpriest Controversy," in *Miscellanea xiii,* vol. 22. Catholic Record Society (London: J. Whitehead, 1921), pp. 132–86.

7. Details of the Bull and Mary's subsequent imprisonment are in Orchard, *Til God Will,* pp. 102–15, and in Chambers, *Life of Mary Ward,* vol. 2, pp. 318–97.

8. "Reasons why we may not alter: First because what we have chosen is already confirmed by the Church and commended in several Bulls, and in the Council of Trent, as a most fit Institute to help souls," cited in Orchard, *Til God Will,* p. 70. The second reason calls on the authority of Ward's own "experience" and the evidence of the "great change of life in all sorts of people in the world" (ibid.). Ward adroitly passed over the inconvenient fact that the Council of Trent had also insisted on the rule of strict enclosure for communities of women. See Chambers, *Life of Mary Ward,* vol. 1, p. 254.

9. For a discussion of the theological debates see ibid., vol. 1, p. 148, with Hicks 1, pp. 142–44.

10. See Orchard, *Til God Will*, p. 45. A further exception was the exemption from ritual practice of "external penances and austerities" (ibid.).

11. The phrase occurs in Ward's description of the period between her departure from the English convent of Poor Clares at Gravelines (which she founded in 1609) and her decision to found the *Schola*; see Chambers, *Life of Mary Ward*, vol. 1, p. 177.

12. Cited in ibid., vol. 1, pp. 466–67. The Pauline apostolic paradigm is 1 Cor. 9:22: "I am made all things to all men, that I might by all means save some." Ward's paraphrase: "Be all things to all men, that so thou mayest win all for God, and be careful as much as thou canst to satisfy all." The expanded definition of the "mixed life" appears in an autobiographical narrative by a member of the Institute known as "Sister Dorothea" (about whom more later), cited in ibid., vol. 2, p. 38. For a discussion of the monastic tradition behind the concept of the "mixed life," see Orchard, *Til God Will*, p. 34.

13. The reference to England is in the *Ratio*, cited in Chambers, *Life of Mary Ward*, vol. 1, p. 375.

14. Details of the Institute's locations in England are in ibid., vol. 1, p. 428. The information concerning the garden-house is from a pamphlet entitled "Godfather's Information about the Jesuitesses" (Archives of the diocese of Westminster).

15. The full text of Sister Dorothea's narrative (1620–21) is cited in Chambers, *Life of Mary Ward*, vol. 2, pp. 27–39.

16. For an account of the tradition of private education in recusant homes, see Norman, "A Woman for All Seasons," pp. 125–9.

17. Where possible, citations from the "Briefe Relation" are from Chambers' transcriptions. Other citations are from the English manuscript in the Archives of the Institute of the Blessed Virgin Mary (I.B.V.M.) in Bar Convent, York. Wigmore and Poyntz, the presumed authors of the "Briefe Relation," wrote the biography as a quasi-hagiographical memorial of Ward for the community; accordingly, they were no doubt more interested than Harrison would have been in depicting Ward's piety. They pointed out that despite her sartorial exuberance Ward "wore underneath a most sharp haircloth, which by continuance did eat into her flesh" (Chambers, *Life of Mary Ward*, vol. 1, p. 217).

18. In their biography of Ward, Poyntz and Wigmore recalled the ambiguous rhetoric in which one woman, recently converted by Ward, couched her assessment of Ward's proselytizing: "Amongst others that were reduced from badd life, one was as famous for her bearth, as enormious for her crimes: this party woud say, she [Ward] had as a bewitching power to draw one from ones selfe, & put them where she would & they ought to be," "Briefe Relation," I.B.V.M. Archives, 20v.

19. One of Ward's favorite books was Lorenzo Scupoli's *Spiritual Combat*, which John Gerard had translated into English in 1598. For a discussion of the importance of this book in Ward's formative years, see Orchard, *Til God Will*, pp. 10, 38.

20. Those who opposed Ward's progress in Rome noted that she was "a woman with the daring of a man" (cited in Chambers, *Life of Mary Ward*, vol. 1, pp. 26–27).

21. A document from 1625 notes that "the sins of pride, licentious life, and talkativeness are to be observed in them" (Vatican MSS. 6922, cited in ibid., vol. 2, p. 170).

22. English polemical literature circulated similar views: "[The Jesuitesses] walke abroad in the world, & preach the Gospell to their sex in England & elsewhere," James Wadsworth, *The English Spanish Pilgrime* (London, 1629), p. 29.

Ward herself acknowledged the traditional restrictions placed on such pastoral activity: "I confess . . . women may not administer sacraments nor preach in public churches" ("Three Instructions," cited in Orchard, *Til God Will*, p. 57).

23. Vatican MSS. 6922, cited in Chambers, *Life of Mary Ward*, p. 170.

24. Relevant accounts of anti-Jesuit mythologies are in Aveling and in Clancy.

25. The central difficulty—the so-called "Archpriest Controversy"—turned on a dispute within the mission over the proper jurisdiction and allegiance of the nominal head of the secular clergy, the Archpriest. The controversy was bound up with the polemic in Counter-Reformation ecclesiastical circles over the relative autonomy enjoyed by the Jesuit order in matters concerning internal government and the deployment of missionary forces. See Guilday, *English Catholic Refugees*, pp. 63–120.

26. Details of Kellison's career are in Orchard, *Til God Will*, p. 49.

27. Cited in Chambers, *Life of Mary Ward*, vol. 2, p. 52.

28. The anti-Jesuit policies of Francis Ingoli, Secretary of Propaganda, were instrumental in the defeat of Ward's petitions to the Vatican; see Hicks 3, pp. 46–47.

29. Ward, "Three Speeches of our Reverend Mother Chief Superior made at St. Omer, having been long absent" (Nymphenburg manuscripts), cited in Chambers, *Life of Mary Ward*, p. 412. See also Orchard, *Til God Will*, p. 59. Further citations in this paragraph are from Chambers, vol. 1, pp. 412–13.

30. For a discussion of Ward's family pedigree, see Peters, *Mary Ward*, pp. 1–27.

31. By "performative" I refer to the capacity of social as well as verbal actions to project world "before" them—a space for future constructions of meaning and value that do not necessarily coincide with the immediate intentions "behind" the actions. The sense of performativity I have in mind here derives partly from Judith Butler's appropriation of speech act theory and partly from Paul Ricoeur's sense of the ontological, world-projecting aspect of hermeneutics. See Judith Butler, *Gender Trouble: Feminism and the Subversion of Identity* (New York: Routledge, 1990), p. 139; and Paul Ricoeur, *From Text to Action: Essays in Hermeneutics II*, trans. Kathleen Blamey and John B. Thompson (Evanston, Ill.: Northwestern University Press, 1991), p. 17.

32. A relevant discussion of the contemporary gender controversy is in Shepherd, 1985.

33. In Raymond Williams's vocabulary, what I am calling a conceptual habitat would be an interactive combination of dominant and emergent "structures of feeling." See Williams, *Marxism and Literature* (Oxford: Oxford University Press, 1977), pp. 132–34. A conceptual habitat is distantly related to Pierre Bourdieu's notion of the "habitus." See Bourdieu, *In Other Words: Essays Towards a Reflexive Sociology*, trans. Matthew Adamson (Stanford, Calif.: Stanford University Press, 1990), pp. 11–14, 77–78. Whereas habitus generally refers to a field of intuitive practices, a conceptual habitat arises through the negotiation of divergent fields of practice, and entails reflective judgments and strategic choices as well as prereflective behavior.

34. Chambers, *Life of Mary Ward*, vol. 1, p. 491, notes that Ward's habitual reading included the "Saints' Lives and Roman Martyrology."

35. Not only the remote but the recent past as well: the life and death of Margaret Clitherow figured centrally as a prototype of Christian heroism in Ward's formative experience. James Walsh (in Orchard, *Til God Will*, p. xi) notes that John Mush, Clitherow's biographer, was Ward's confessor in 1600–4. See also Chambers, *Life of Mary Ward*, p. 51.

36. See A. C. Charity, *Events and Their Afterlife* (Cambridge: Cambridge University Press, 1996); and Jean Danielou, *From Shadows to Reality*, trans. D. Wulstan Hibberd (London: Burns and Oates, 1960).

37. See also Orchard, *Til God Will*, pp. 55–56.

38. See, for example, Raphael Holinshed et al., *Chronicles of England, Scotland, and Ireland*, vol. 4 (London: J. Johnson, 1808), p. 133.

39. Details of the Institute's reconstitution in the eighteenth century and its development in the nineteeth century are in Chambers, *Life of Mary Ward*, pp. 507–59.

40. "Real circumcision," Paul proclaims, "is a matter of the heart, spiritual and not literal" (Romans 2:29). For a discussion of the Pauline ideology of circumcision in the context of rabbinic tradition, see Daniel Boyarin, "'This We Know to Be the Carnal Israel': Circumcision and the Erotic Life of God and Israel," *Critical Inquiry* 18 (Spring 1992): 474–505.

PART IV

· ·

Emerging Alliances

13

The Dearth of the Author

Anonymity's Allies and Swetnam the Woman-hater

VALERIE WAYNE

> And undoubtedly, I thought, looking at the shelf where there are no plays
> by women, her work would have gone unsigned. That refuge she would
> have sought certainly. It was the relic of the sense of chastity that dic-
> tated anonymity to women even so late as the nineteenth century. . . .
> Thus they did homage to the convention . . . that publicity in women is
> detestable. Anonymity runs in their blood.   Virginia Woolf

VIRGINIA WOOLF'S REMARK ABOUT anonymity is valuable not only as
an observation on women's probable condition in early modern print
culture but also as a description of women's recurring position as a subject of indeterminate gender, sexuality, and language, a subject never
fully present or adequately articulated in texts—but not entirely absent,
either. Yet however useful anonymity and pseudonymity might have
been to women authors, those modes of publication prompt a host of
questions for critics doing gender-based analysis. What does it mean,
for instance, that some of the most articulate defenses of women against
misogynist discourse in early modern England were written by authors
whose gender in unknowable? To whom can we attribute agency in those
texts? Can they offer instances of women's alliances if they also represent gender as indefinite and unstable? These are some of the questions
I want to ponder in relation to *Swetnam the Woman-hater Arraigned by*

Women, a play published anonymously as part of the early seventeenth-century controversy provoked by Joseph Swetnam's *Arraignment of Lewd, idle, froward, and unconstant women*. In this inquiry I will draw on the work of Elizabeth Harvey and Diane Purkiss, both of whom have related textual disruptions of gender to issues of authorship by showing that anonymous and pseudonymous publication requires reading strategies that resist reliance on an originary, gendered author who stands outside the work. Their approaches may help us appreciate a play that offers graphic scenes of "women" forging alliances in order to condemn and punish an infamous misogynist, even though all of those who participate in the alliances are not, strictly speaking, women.

In pursuing these issues, I find myself in dialogue with two recent developments in early modern studies. The first is the very welcome proliferation of texts written by early modern women which are appearing in paperback, hardback, facsimile, and electronic editions. Collections like the present one are beneficiaries of this important work, and the opportunity to read and teach women's texts in these new editions has opened up a world of possibilities for us as scholars and educators. At the same time, these developments have occasionally resulted in a polarization between those dedicated to the recovery of women-authored texts and those addressing feminist and other political questions concerning male-authored texts. I think that such polarization is unnecessary, and that it misrepresents the ways in which ideological construction crosses biological boundaries. My approach here is designed to show how difficult it is to maintain that opposition in relation to a gathering of anonymous and pseudonymous texts that might have been written by women or men during the period. A second development in the background of this essay concerns the work that is being done in studies of attribution, especially with reference to the texts of early modern drama and poetry. My subject here addresses problems of attribution as they relate to texts in the early modern controversy about women, and its conclusions have no direct relevance to texts that are not so related. Yet determining whether there is such a relation is part of the problem, and I do want to raise questions about the gendered implications of reading that concern many studies in attribution, because I think there is room to reexamine the presuppositions about gender and authorship on which some of that work proceeds.

Swetnam the Woman-hater was first performed at the Red Bull, a public playhouse, in 1617 or 1618.[1] It was the last entry in the controversy that began in 1615 with Swetnam's *Arraignment* and continued with three prose responses to that text published under the signatures of Rachel Speght, Ester Sowernam, and Constantia Munda in 1617. The genders of these authors have been often discussed. Two of the signatures are probably pseudonyms: Ester Sowernam is a sour imitation of "Swetnam," and Constantia Munda means "elegant constancy." Swetnam's signature was initially pseudonymous as well: *The Arraignment* was first published under the name of Thomas Telltruth until it became so popular that Swetnam signed his name to it in the nine subsequent editions published through 1637. The play called *Swetnam* was published anonymously in 1620.[2] Heywood, Dekker, and Webster have all been proposed as playwrights, but no one has definitively attributed it to an author,[3] and the Brown University Women Writer's Project still carries the play on its list of texts. In some ways this indeterminacy is an advantage: because we do not know who wrote it, we cannot read any author's gender back into the text.

In discussing *Haec Vir*, another anonymous text in the seventeenth-century debate, Elizabeth Harvey shows how an author's indeterminate gender can relate to the transvestism of a text's interlocutors. Rather than reading *Haec Vir* like a text by Ben Jonson, for example, "against a male authorial voice that stands behind it," she says, "it is crucial . . . that we read [it] as anonymous, for, in its refusal to present itself as the property of a (proper) name, it forces us to recognize the role custom plays in fashioning gender, and dressing the voice that speaks it" (Harvey, 1992, p. 49). Harvey's refusal to read with a gynocritical suspicion as if the author were a man or to privilege the author's gender as if she were a woman denies the author any unitary status and also allows her to appreciate "the richly intertextual character of literary production" and the possibilities of literary collaborations (Harvey, 1992, p. 24). Her method appears to draw on the genealogical assumptions of Foucault and Nietzsche that "what is found at the historical beginning of things is not the inviolable identity of their origin; it is the dissension of other things. It is disparity" (Foucault 1986a, p. 79). The anonymous printing of early modern texts was not always a matter of authorial choice but was also a function of specific publishing practices: playscripts in particular often made their way to printers without the knowledge of the playwrights who wrote them or even the companies who performed them, so we need not assume that an author has always refused to sign a text that was published anonymously. She or he may not have had the opportunity to sign it at all. Harvey's approach, therefore, needs to be adapted in light of the material conditions of print culture in general as well as the particular problems posed by the reproduction of a given text.[4] Nevertheless, texts in the medieval and early modern debate very often disrupt the property of the proper name through anonymous and pseudonymous publication. These texts borrow from one another and change each other without regard to who wrote them, and they resist celebrating those alterations as the product of direct imitation or a new author's originality. A genealogical approach as inflected by Harvey thus seems especially appropriate. Just as the texts cannot be grounded in the essentialized gender of an author, they are products of the diffusion of arguments and texts in a popular discourse that extended throughout

Europe for more than three centuries. The play of *Swetnam* has no single origin, then, in several senses of that term, even though it has an identifiable literary source.[5]

Howard Bloch observes that "misogyny as a discourse is always to some extent avowedly derivative; it is a citational mode whose rhetorical thrust is to displace its own source away from anything that might be construed as personal or confessional" (Bloch, p. 6). A worldwide diffusion of misogyny is a possibility envisioned within the play of *Swetnam* by the eponymous character, who goes under the pseudonym of Misogynous and condemns "the deceitfull deuices of a womans crooked conditions":

> which are so many, that if all the World were Paper; the Sea, Inke; Trees and Plants, Pens; and euery man Clarkes, Scribes, and Notaries: yet would all that Paper be scribled ouer, the Inke wasted, Pens worne to the stumps, and all the Scriueners wearie, before they could describe the hundreth part of a womans wickednesse. (*Swetnam*, I.ii.151–58)

Swetnam/Misogynous wants to refashion the world as a misogynist text constructed on a land of paper with the sea of ink wielded by every living man using wooden pens. His inscription of misogyny exhausts all the world's resources in its production and is still inadequate to express the evils of women. Leonato's remark in *Much Ado About Nothing* that, by supposedly being unchaste, Hero has "fallen / Into a pit of ink"[6] implies a related association between ink and misogynist production. Both passages assert the diffusion of misogyny through the inked production of texts and displace any personal agent who might be spilling the ink.[7]

Texts that defended women also engaged in a citational mode, but they had fewer resources on which to draw because there were fewer pro-women texts. Since those defenses were often responses to particular attacks, they also tended to confine themselves to refuting their opponents rather than rewriting the world in their ideological image. Critical discussions of the three defenses written in response to Swetnam usually posit an alliance among the three "women authors,"[8] but the assertion assumes a correlation between the genders of the authors and their pseudonyms that cannot be taken for granted. While there is general agreement that Rachel Speght published under her real name, Simon Shepherd and Ann Rosalind Jones question whether Munda was a woman (Shepherd, 1985, p. 126; Jones, 1990a, p. 58) and Barbara Lewalski has doubts about Sowernam as well (Lewalski, 1993, p. 380 note 17). After reviewing critical treatments of the controversy, Diane Purkiss objects to the "logocentric cycle . . . whereby a female signature prompts a reading strategy designed to uncover female consciousness in texts, and this consciousness in turn is held to manifest the presence of a female author." She proposes instead a "reading strategy which takes account of the function of the pseudonymous signatures as they can be read within the texts themselves, rather than as point-ers to an originary author figure who stands outside the text" (Purkiss, p. 71). For her, names like Ester Sowernam and Jane Anger (an earlier English defender of women presumed to be pseudonymous) suggest not female agency, but "the taking-up of the position of a disorderly woman for the purpose of signifying disorder of some kind." The name Constantia Munda could arise from the allegoric rhetoric of other texts in the debate. Purkiss explains that "none of this by any means rules out the possibility that the authors of the pamphlets may be women, but if so they are women acting women, staging disorderly femininity in a manner which refuses the elision of the symbolic and personal realms sought by modern critics" (Purkiss, p. 85). While this strategy may appear to risk replicating the misogynist assumptions about dis-orderly femininity from which it springs, I read Purkiss's position as being in sympathy with Joan Kelly's observation that, with texts in the debate, "the way beyond that resistance to misogyny had to lie through it" (Kelly, 1984a, p. 94). Purkiss claims that "the placing of a discourse of invective and experience in the mouth of a woman, how-ever fictional, creates a spectacle of female power which displays pre-cisely what Swetnam fears." Instead of offering an essentialist alliance among female authors, the texts celebrate the "theatrical performance of femininity" (Purkiss, pp. 90, 85).

Purkiss's attention to pseudonymity parallels Harvey's concern with anonymity in useful ways. For both critics the absence of certainty about the author's identity throws the emphasis on the movement of the nar-rative, whose discursive disruptions of gender are potentially analogous to disruptions of gendered authorship. Both critics appear to draw on the work of Foucault and Barthes concerning the death of the author as they resist critical readings that are author based. Foucault succinctly summarizes the role that authorial identity is granted in most critical discourse: "The author is the principle of thrift in the proliferation of meaning" (Foucault 1986b, p. 118). Lacking this principle of thrift, anonymous and pseudonymous texts remain ungrounded to an author or gender, but they function differently with respect to their audiences. The pseudonymous texts *purport* to ground themselves in an authorial function that is gendered, but the signature marks a performance that leaves gender open to question and calls more directly for the exposure of the identity beneath the mask, an activity that the "women" of *Swetnam* perform in the course of the play. Pseudonyms mark authorial presence even as they obscure identity. The anonymous text, on the other hand, erases the sign of authorship and thereby opens itself more radi-cally to a proliferation of genders and meanings. The absence of any sig-nature more urgently requires the activities that Foucault advocates for all texts: "we must locate the space left empty by the author's disap-pearance, follow the distribution of gaps and breaches, and watch for the openings that this disappearance uncovers" (Foucault, 1986b, p. 105).

In *Swetnam,* as we shall see, this disappearance prompts an internal fiction about the text's production.

Purkiss's observations about the theatrical performance of femininity are relevant not only to the pamphlets in the Swetnam controversy but to the *Swetnam* play that was an important part of it. Purkiss does not address the play because her concern is with pseudonymous signatures, but, like other critics, she thereby overlooks the most extended staging of the disorderly woman in the Swetnam controversy. The questions raised by the play's anonymity must account for some of its neglect by critics, for its authorship refuses the categories through which most texts claim critical attention. It is dismissed by those using a gynocritical approach because it is assumed to be by a man, and it is ignored by those deploying more conventional approaches because its relation to other contemporary authors and texts is obscured by the erasure of its author. Even those interested in traditional women's alliances have reason to disregard it, since its most active proponent for women is a cross-dressed man. However, it so effectively combines major motifs in the debate literature that Linda Woodbridge uses it as "a satisfying finale" to *Women and the English Renaissance* (1984, p. 301), and Simon Shepherd also positions it as the last chapter in *Amazons and Warrior Women.* As an amazon named Atlanta, Lorenzo in *Swetnam* initiates one of the most impressive series of alliances of women against misogyny in all of Renaissance drama. His/her theatrical performance of femininity also results in the staged ridicule and punishment of the most infamous living misogynist in seventeenth-century England apart from James I. We cannot afford to exclude plays like this in considering women's alliances, because the work's performative mode was a frequent and effective strategy for responding to misogyny in early modern texts.

Performing Alliances

Simon Shepherd offers a helpful reading of *Swetnam's* alliances in relation to other texts of the period:

> The play might seem to compromise itself in the figure of the other "woman," Atlanta. We know it is Prince Lorenzo disguised, and the disguise seems so much a piece of archaic convention, of arty contrivance. It seems to have walked out of Sidney. But in many ways that is what *is* so interesting about it. This type of cross-gender play-acting, especially the use of an Amazon, smacks of the Elizabethan stage more than it does of 1619. But at this period there is a currency of things Elizabethan as a political reference point. (Shepherd, 1981, p. 212)

I will return to the play's evocation of things Elizabethan at the end of this essay. The present point is that Lorenzo/Atlanta's alliance with women in *Swetnam* was often what early modern women's alliances looked like: texts by Sidney and Spenser, as well as those in the debate addressed to a more middle-class readership, used the amazon to defend women.[9] Given the entrenched associations between women and weakness and all the other cultural constraints imposed upon women, the amazon, who combined masculine strength with feminine sympathies, was one of the best available candidates to perform the disorderly woman and mount an effective defense of women against men's physical and verbal attacks. A performative approach, then, which is so in keeping with other disruptions of gender in the period, helps us to recognize one form that those early modern women's alliances often took. They were devised to address immediate, local problems, such as the popularity of Swetnam's *Arraignment*, and they were contingent upon the constraints and opportunities afforded by their own historical occasion. The performance of "woman" was an important way in which women's anonymous or male defenders could affiliate with women in texts of this period.

The main plot of *Swetnam* opens with Atticus, King of Sicily, lamenting the loss of his two sons—he has just buried one and the other, Lorenzo, has been missing for eighteen months—and forbidding his daughter Leonida to marry or have conference with her beloved Lisandro, the Prince of Naples. The play uses the amazonian disguise to enable Lorenzo to "visit the sicke Court, / And free my Sister from captiuitie, / With that good Prince *Lisandro*" (III.ii.19–21), since the lovers have been imprisoned after being discovered together. According to the laws of Sicily, one of these lovers will be condemned to death and the other to banishment. After a contest of generosity in which each claims to be more guilty than the other in a legal proceeding, the judges propose a disputation on "whether the man or the woman in loue commit the greatest offence, by giuing the first and principall occasion of sinning" (III.ii.123–25). The focus thus moves from this pair to more general questions of gender and turns on an ultimately unanswerable question about origins. Advocates for each sex are sought for the purposes of this debate, and Lorenzo appears dressed as an amazon just as the call for advocates is announced. Swetnam/Misogynous volunteers to speak for the men and Lorenzo/Atlanta for the women. This disputation sets up the same opposition that the debate about women depended upon, even drawing on the judicial oration so appropriate to it (Woodbridge, 1984, p. 14), and it addresses one of its primary concerns, the relative sexual guilt of men and women. This is not quite the question posed in the Garden of Eden about who was most responsible for bringing sin into the world; it is a related question posed by a fallen world about which gender seduces the other to sexual activity or desire, and it turns on the suspect assumptions that desire is wrong and responsibility for it can be attributed to one party more than the other. The play's alliances among women are first dramatized in connection with this disputation about who functioned as the "*Primus Motor* that begun the cause" of the lovers' affection (III.i.39).

The women and the amazon present themselves at the disputation as an allied group in opposition to the men. Atlanta begins her speech by apologizing for her position as a woman, effectively imitating female modesty and coy behavior. Her "bashfull weaknesse claymes excuse" (III.iii.54) of her gender so well that one of the lawyers, unaware of her disguise, terms her performance "a quaint insinuation" (III.iii.58). Then the two advocates exchange insults about men and women. Misogynous contends that "Beautie first tempts to lust," but Atlanta retorts that "Lust tempteth Beautie" (III.iii.100), offering a long speech on the seductive wiles of men. At her conclusion the women burst into applause and shout "Atlanta!" three times (III.iii.138–39). This is a gendered contest, and there are cheering sections for each side. Misogynous' reply characterizes women as deceptive and conspiratorial, and his speeches receive a comparable cheer from the men. When he also blames women for "Tyrannies, Oppressions, Massacres," the ruination of cities, "Kingdomes subuerted, Lands depopulated, / Monarchies ended!" (III.iii..202–6), Lorenzo/Atlanta appears to be so sympathetic with women's plight that s/he loses control:

> Base snarling Dogge, bite out thy slandrous tongue,
> And spit it in the face of Innocence,
> That at once all thy rancour may haue end:
> And doe not still opprobriously condemne
> Woman that bred thee, who in nothing more
> Is guiltie of dishonour to her Sex
> But that she hath brought forth so base a Viper,
> To teare her reputation in his teeth,
> As thou hast done. (III.iii..207–15)

In a response reminiscent of Constantia Munda's *The Worming of a mad Dogge* in its imagery and invective, Atlanta evinces such rage that Misogynous calls her a scold. Lorenzo/Atlanta clearly stages the disorderly woman: s/he exhibits his/her emotional affiliation with women's cause by most vehemently opposing the misogynist when s/he cannot control herself. Lorenzo/Atlanta performs woman through acting modest, coy, and angry.

Misogynous concludes the disputation with charges of women's lust, and the judges announce their verdict: "women are the first and worst temptations / To loue and lustfull folly" (III.iii.259–60). Atlanta then objects to the judicial process: "You are impartiall,[10] and we doe appeale / From you to Iudges more indifferent: / You are all men, and in this weightie businesse, / Graue Women should haue sate as Iudges with you" (III.iii.262–65). While the "women" originally bond in opposition to a self-declared misogynist, their continued alliance arises from a sense of injustice due to gender bias in the institution that is supposed to dispense justice (Jordan, 1987, p. 164). Atlanta's radical proposal that the presence of female judges would correct that bias (a correction partially made in the U.S. Supreme Court that does not entirely confirm the gynocritical assumptions behind it) is not the solution pursued by the play, but its being offered by a character first presented as a man is further evidence of his/her affinities with women. The play's resolution instead requires Lorenzo/Atlanta's artful rescue of the condemned lovers, his/her strategic engagement with the women, and the establishment of an all-"women's" court.

Early modern English drama thematizes gender in part because a theater in which all representations of women were performative activates the performative character of masculinity and femininity for actors, audiences, and authors. When, following the disputation, Swetnam tries to seduce the cross-dressed Lorenzo/Atlanta, who is described as "A Masculine Feminine" (IIII.iiii.65), the spectacle evokes what Stephen Orgel describes as the deepest fear about transvestite theater articulated in the antitheatrical tracts, that "what the spectator is 'really' attracted to in plays is an undifferentiated sexuality, a sexuality that does not distinguish men from women and reduces men to women" (Orgel, 1996, p. 29). In this play, the audience witnesses that attraction when Swetnam/ Misogynous arranges an assignation with Lorenzo/Atlanta. As Linda Woodbridge and Constance Jordan have observed, Swetnam/Misogynous gets drunk before meeting her and admits, "Now, methinks / I could performe" (V.ii.38–39). But the performance called for alters when the amazon challenges the misogynist to a duel in defense of women and Misogynous is not up to the fight (V.ii.118–25). Woodbridge remarks, "The play ruthlessly exposes Misogynous's militant masculinity as fraudulent. . . . The implication is clear: it is sexual impotence that has made him a woman-hater" (Woodbridge, 1984, p. 314). When Swetnam/ Misogynous cannot perform as the fencing master he claims to be, the incident evokes the living author who published under the name of Joseph Swetnam, for in 1617 his book on fencing, *The Schoole of the Noble and Worthy Science of Defence,* was published with a dedication to Prince Charles and a reference to Swetnam's serving as tutor to the late Prince Henry "in the skill of weapons" (Swetnam, 1617, A2). Staging the fencing master as inept at his own game when confronted with an amazon was a direct humiliation of a living author. The scene is dramatically analogous to Moll Cutpurse's fight with Laxton in *The Roaring Girl,* where another "masculine feminine" triumphs in a fencing match with a man out to seduce her in order to make the same point against misogynist assumptions about women: "Thou'rt one of those / That thinks each woman thy fond flexible whore" (III.i.72–73). Both incidents displace the antitheatricalists' worst fears about the effect of transvestite theater on the audience by dramatizing the effect of a cross-dressed actor on a character deserving punishment within the fiction.

In both plays, then, the attraction of an unambiguous man for someone performing a role of ambiguous gender results in that man's effeminization, and the effeminized man is ridiculed while the transvestite man/ woman triumphs. Jordan observes that Atlanta is modeled on Zelmane in Sidney's *Arcadia*, the amazon that Pyrocles becomes in order to gain access to and woo Philocleia (Jordan, 1987, p. 152). Pyrocles justifies his performance of the role as a willing imitation of his beloved, and Orgel supposes the imitation would especially have appealed to the many women readers of the romance (Orgel, 1996, p. 80). Lorenzo/Atlanta is created to appeal to the women of *Swetnam*—other characters and members of the audience—for the same reason: they appreciate his performance of woman as an imitation and acceptance of their behavior. His charm for them is related to the appeal Orgel posits for the boy actor:

> For a female audience, in a culture as patriarchally stratified as that of Renaissance England, to see the youth in skirts might be to disarm and socialize him in ways that were specifically female, to see him not as a possessor or master, but as companionable and pliable and one of them—as everything, in fact, that the socialized Renaissance woman herself is supposed to be. (Orgel, 1996, p. 81)

The same argument can apply to a grown man willing to associate with women by donning their skirts. Through the cross-dressed Lorenzo/Atlanta, *Swetnam* presents a companion for women—women, that is, constructed to be disarming but at the same time needing to disarm their adversary because of the misogyny in their culture that constructs them that way. Lorenzo forms an alliance with women by becoming one of them, yet he maintains his "masculine" eloquence and strength. S/he does not lose prowess and power when s/he takes on a female role, whereas Swetnam/Misogynous cannot sustain either. The unstable gender identities introduced into the plot contrast a man's positive imitation of woman with the impotence of women's opponent, thereby disrupting the essentialist assumptions of misogynist arguments against women and redefining gender affiliation in terms of strategic alliance rather than biology. These incidents do not disrupt the culture's higher valuation of masculinity over feminity, or the assumptions that eloquence and power are associated with physical strength; they do, however, present the audience with an exemplary male character whose sympathy for women prompts him to act like one of them.

Punishing Misogyny

After the amazon's victory over Swetnam/Misogynous, all the female characters enter and the greater humiliation of the misogynist begins. Swetnam is horrified at the very sight of the women and cries out, "Murder, murder, murder. I'me betraid" (V.ii.141). He is bound to a stake and muffled. The women gleefully discuss a range of alternatives, from binding his jaws to tearing his limbs joint from joint to torturing him with pincers or bodkins; in the end they take a more moderate vengeance by engaging in a card game called "Post and Paire" (V.ii.167). This game required players to bet on their hands at "post" for cards approaching a total of 21 points, and at "pair" for cards in pairs, such as two queens. Aurelia first proposes that all the knaves (jacks) be left out of the deck when they shuffle the cards, but Atlanta prefers that the knaves be left in at post and taken out at pair (V.ii.169–70). I take this to mean that the knaves remain to count numerically at post but are excluded from any pairings, especially the "pair royal" which would be three cards of any kind.[11] Hence the game refuses to honor alliances among knaves or rogues like Swetnam. Each time the women bet on their hands, they poke Swetnam with a pin, and after a few lines it begins to look as if they are betting in order to be able to prick him rather than because they have been dealt good cards. The rules of the game require a form of ordered play that permits some aggression from the women but contains an expression of chaotic vengeance. Such playful physical assaults by women on misogynists also show up in *The Courtier*, where the women threaten to imitate the fury of the *bacchae* in reacting to Lord Gasper's misogyny (Castiglione, pp. 181–82), and in *The Flower of Friendship*, where Master Gualter is nearly driven out of the arbor for his sexist remarks (Tilney, p. 111). But when Ester Sowernam and her fictional female companions contemplate punishing Joseph Swetnam, they conclude "we would not answere him either with *Achilles* fist, or *Stafford*-law; neither plucke him in pieces as the *Thracian* woman did Orpheus. . . . But as he had arraigned women at the barre of fame and report; we resolued at the same barre where he did vs the wrong, to arraigne him" (Sowernam, p. 27).

The more extended punishment of Swetnam in the play expands on the court proceeding from Sowernam's text. In *Ester hath Hanged Haman*, Swetnam is indicted before two female judges, Reason and Experience, by a jury supposedly consisting of his five senses and the seven deadly sins. He pleads not guilty and then decides not to argue on his own behalf, which leaves him open to the sentence of pressing to death. But the women decline to pursue that sentence because Swetnam could accuse the court of bias since most of its members are women. In place of any judgment against Swetnam, Sowernam ends up delivering a long speech on the wrongs done to women, so that the judicial procedure is truncated and its verdict is deferred "to graunt him longer time to aduice with himselfe whether he would put himselfe to triall or, vpon better deliberation to recall his errours" (Sowernam, p. 31). The play satisfies the expectations aroused by this process more successfully and completes the proceeding by using the counterarraignment to stage a festive mock-trial by the women, which results in a reversal of male justice that is both a projection of male fears about female conspiracy and an appropriation of male judicial authority by women. The scene is so arresting and such a radical departure from early modern courts that it serves as the illustration for *Swetnam's* title page.

Atlanta parcels out roles to the women present, naming Aurelia as the Lady Chief Justice, herself as recorder, Loretta as Notary, and others as crier, keepers, sergeants, and executioners (V.ii.219–25). An old woman is dispatched to call a jury and play the "forewoman" (V.ii.229). Two swords are used for the bar of justice. Swetnam is then brought to the bar and ungagged. He is indicted under the names of *"Ioseph Swetnam, alias Misogynos, / Alias Molastomus, alias the Woman-hater"* (V.ii.255–56), the third name having been provided by Rachel Speght in *A Mouzell for Melastomus*. The very mode of his indictment in this string of monickers replicates the pseudonymous authorship of the controversy. "Thou are here indicted by these names, that thou / . . . / Hast wickedly and maliciously slandred, / Maligned, and opprobriously defamed the ciuill societie / Of the whole Sex of women" (V.ii.259–63). Swetnam pleads not guilty, then denies writing *The Arraignment* and challenges the women to produce it in court, which they do. *The Arraignment* is entered as evidence, but Swetnam still has reason to gloat: "Shew me my name, and then Ile yeeld vnto't" (V.ii.294). The women have presented the pseudonymous first edition, published under the name of Thomas Telltruth. But Aurelia objects to that form of publication: "No, that's your policie and cowardise, / You durst not publish, what you dar'd to write, / Thy man is witnesse to't: [*To* Swash.] sirrah, confesse, / Or you shall eu'n be seru'd of the same sawce" (V.ii.295–98). "Durst" is an archaic form of "dared," and the second line means, "You dared not to publish what you dared to write." It is a descriptive rather than prescriptive statement, and what it describes, in Aurelia's opinion, is Swetnam's cowardice. She advocates publically owning up to the products of one's pen because she wants to hold Swetnam accountable for his text.

This position not only critiques the mode of publication of many texts in the debate; it also critiques the anonymous publication of the play. Aurelia wants to reclaim the property of the proper name because she associates indeterminate authorship with policy, cowardice, or both. Her position is strategically expedient for the women's exposure of Swetnam, just as a gynocritical approach to women's authorship is often a useful form of resistance to the privileging of male writers. In order to confirm that Swetnam is the author, Aurelia requires the "confession" of Swetnam's own man Swash, and since Swash has voiced resistance to his master's misogyny throughout the play, he readily complies. Swash's narrative reconstructs Swetnam's life as a series of dislocations by groups of angry women. Having set up a fencing school in Bristol and written his misogynist book, "the women beat him out the Towne" (V.ii.317), so Swetnam went to London, published it there, "and made a thousand men and wiues fall out. / Till two or three good wenches, in meere spight, / Laid their heads together, and rail'd him out of th'Land, / Then we came hither" (V.ii.320–23). The events in the play are presented as the third time that Swetnam has been denounced by a gathering of women. The "two or three good wenches, in meere spight" have been taken by all critics to refer to the three pamphlets having women's signatures, with "spight" providing a pun on Rachel Speght. The *Swetnam* play presents itself as another defense of women by allying itself with those texts published under women's signatures, and its anonymous publication sustains that association. This text has it both ways: it exposes the author of *The Arraignment* in order to locate the blame for misogyny, but it conceals the author(s) of its own text like the other defenses in the controversy. At the same time it creates such a spectacle of disorderly women and sexual combat that both men and women in the audience can appreciate it. When it comes to locating the voice of misogyny, however, it nails the author.

The play also deliberately elides symbolic and personal worlds in condemning Swetnam. Atlanta sentences him to wear a muzzle as suggested by Speght, to be led through every street in the city, bound to a post in certain places and baited by all the honest women of the parish (V.ii.328–33). This punishment parodies the way in which female scolds and shrews were disciplined during the period, because they too were required to wear bridles or branks that muzzled them and were led through town as a means of shaming them for their insubordinate behavior. The misogynist was the male counterpart to the female shrew, and the sentence that Atlanta announces imposes on him what was required of disorderly women. But when Swetnam in the play retorts that being baited by all the honest women of the parish is no problem because no honest women will be found, Atlanta extends the punishment: he will also be whipped throughout the land and shipped out to live with infidels. Forcing Swetnam to associate with heathens characterizes his misogyny as heresy and polices the borders of European women's alliances by defining them off against foreigners. In the epilogue, Swetnam stands ready to be judged further by the women of the audience, but Leonida pardons him to prove that women are neither tyrannous nor cruel (epilogue, 10–12). He then repents, takes off his theatrical disguise, offers to defend women and to be their ally. Misogyny, too, can be a kind of performance, and this performance is over when the play is done.

Performing the Publication

But the text goes on. One would expect that the scene in which Swetnam was sentenced would end with his punishment, but instead it concludes by attending to the publication of his texts and the play itself. Chief Justice Aurelia maintains her concern about the circulation of misogyny through Swetnam's works: "Call in his Bookes, / And let vm all be burn'd and cast away, / And his Arraignment now put i' the Presse, / That he may liue a shame vnto his Sex" (V.ii.341–44). In addition to burning all copies of *The Arraignment*, Aurelia wants *this* arraignment—the play of *Swetnam the Woman-hater Arraigned by Women*—to be published so that Swetnam can be memorialized as a shame to men. The term "his Arraignment" refers to the text of the play, which is named for the subplot involving Swetnam in order to advertise its connection to the popular controversy even though its main plot concerns the young lovers. In a sense the text misrepresents itself by highlighting its subplot through its title and title page, but the arraignment of Swetnam is the play's main attraction even though it appears in its minor plot. Aurelia's usage reinforces this misrepresentation and links the play further to the printed controversy over Swetnam's text.

Atlanta then designates Swash as the agent for printing the play: "Sirrah, the charge be yours: which if you faile, / You shall be vs'd so too: if well perform'd, / You shall be well rewarded. Break vp Court" (V.ii.345–47). Rarely has a character in a Renaissance play been given the assignment to see it through the press. The emphasis granted the task stresses the play's place in the publications associated with the controversy, and the attribution of the task to Swash tries to create an agent of responsibility for the play within its own fiction. It also implicitly places Aurelia and Lorenzo/Atlanta in the fictional role of authors, for, along with the other women, they have created the scene of the arraignment that Swash is called on to publish as part of the entire text. If, then, this play was written by a man or men, he/they were cross-dressing as authors, ideologically allying themselves with women's cause like the amazon and the cross-dressed boy actor in the play. The assignment to Swash deflects the problem of *Swetnam*'s anonymous authorship even as it marks the publication of the play as a concern separate from its performance. The attention given to the issue points to the "policy" or strategy behind its mode of publication: it problematizes the play's anonymity even as it pretends to resolve it, placing it at a further remove from the living author(s) who wrote about the humiliation of still another author.

The publication of the play also seems to have received more than the usual attention because of the woodcut that appears on its title page, which depicts in careful detail the image of the women's court (Figure 13-1). Andrew Gurr has observed that the "picture probably is not a reproduction of the stage performance, since the room shown has windows, so it cannot represent the tiring-house wall behind the stage" (p. 173). The list of court officials from the play (V.ii.221–25) does not correspond exactly to the drawing, but the woman to the right of the seat of justice may depict the recorder, which was Atlanta's position in the court, and those on either side of Swetnam in the foreground are presumably keepers or sergeants. Swash is not present in this scene, although he is important in the play's arraignment of Swetnam, and no amazon appears anywhere in the illustration. Two swords are said to represent the bar of justice in the text, "One stucke i' the Earth, and crosse it from this Tree" (V.ii.234)—because the play's scene occurs outside in an orchard (V.ii.21), a space beyond the institutionalization of male power— but the illustration is clearly set in an upper-class interior. In short, for all the attention granted to detail in this illustration, it does not tally well

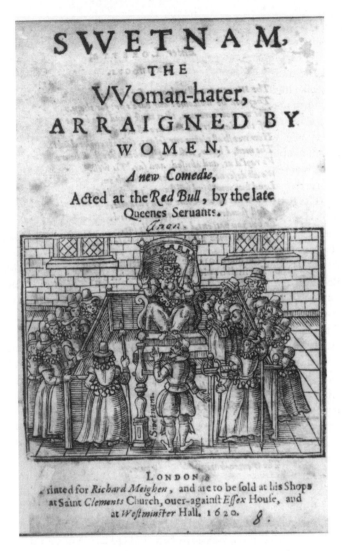

FIGURE 13-1 The title page of *Swetnam the Woman-hater
Arraigned by Women* (1620) showing the women's court.
(Reprinted courtesy of the University of Illinois Library.)

with the women's court in the play and is probably not a representation
of any performance.

What, then, is it? The play was first performed in 1617 or 1618, entered for publication in the Stationers' Register on October 17, 1619, and
printed in 1620. In late January 1620, as is well known, James I required
the London clergy "to inveigh vehemently and bitterly in theyre sermons against the insolencie of our women, and theyre wearing of brode
brimd hats, pointed dublets, theyre haire cut short or shorne, and some

of them stillettaes or poniards," because this apparel was taken as masculine (Chamberlain, vol. 2, pp. 286–87). In the woodcut, all the women except the Chief Justice wear those broad-brimmed hats.[12] We see the front of the doublet only of the Chief Justice, but hers is pointed and she may also have short hair. The women in the illustration thus represent the form of disorderly dress that James specifically objected to, and the play was printed within several months of his admonition. James's misogyny was well established much earlier in his reign: the French ambassador reported around 1605 that "he piques himself on great contempt for women. . . . [T]he English ladies do not spare him but hold him in abhorrence and tear him to pieces with their tongues" (Willson, p. 196). The figure in the woodcut even approaches contemporary likenesses of James.[13] The play was performed by Queen Anne's players when the queen was still alive but living apart from James, and it was published after her death.[14] And like King James and Queen Anne, the royal couple in the play has two sons and a daughter. Simon Shepherd sees a parallel between the oldest son's death announced at the beginning of the play and the death of Prince Henry in 1612, which was felt as a loss by the whole nation. Then he reads Lorenzo as a "Henry-surrogate" who "might have been seen as a spiritual heir to Elizabeth I" because he "dresses as an Elizabethan-type Amazon to fulfil [sic] his political role. On Lorenzo are focused the sort of hopes that were associated with Henry, the restoration of justice and the blessing of true love" (Shepherd, 1981, p. 215). Eventually those hopes come to settle on the second son in both literary and historical narratives.

The woodcut also rekindles memories of Elizabeth I. Gurr explains that "the seat of justice may well have been imitated on stage for the 'state' or throne of a judge or a king" (Gurr, p. 173), and the Lady Chief Justice wears a crown and holds a scepter as symbols of her regal authority while she oversees the women's court. She seems to function both as Chief Judge and as Queen. Given the nostalgia for Queen Elizabeth by 1620, the image of a woman on a throne opposing a misogynist would recall the authority and advocacy of the old Queen. Another defense of women published in 1620, Christopher Newstead's *Apologie for Women,* remembered Elizabeth as "'the Phoenix of her time, our euer to bee renowned Queene, *Elizabeth,* at whose frowne Kings trembled" (Newstead, C2). Although the illustration most directly presents a visual alliance among the women against the figure of Swetnam through the staging of an all-women's court, it may also be read as a confrontation between the misogynist James I and a revived Elizabeth I, who is surrounded by female supporters for the purpose of arraigning the king's retrograde attitudes towards women. This reading would explain the absence of the amazon within the illustration: rather than associate advocacy for women with Lorenzo/Atlanta, the illustration presents that function through the queen and her women dressed in "masculine" apparel. Since the play's title page could have been read by its contemporaries as evoking this politically inflected confrontation, we have still another reason for its anonymous publication. Title-page illustrations probably received less attention from censors than manuscripts themselves,[15] and this illustration could always claim to represent a single scene from the play. The provision of Swetnam's name beside the male figure would protect it from any charge that it was an outright image of the king. But those who perceived the parallels between Swetnam and James—at a time when the latter was especially outspoken against women and when John Camberlain claimed that "our pulpits ring continually of the insolence and impudence of women," as he declared on February 12, 1620 (Chamberlain, vol. 2, p. 289)—could find the title page and the play especially relevant to the current controversy over how women were permitted to appear and behave. That controversy continued with the anonymous publications of *Hic Mulier*, *Haec Vir*, and *Mulde Sack* in the same year, each of which also had a provocative woodcut on its title page.[16]

To acknowledge what Aurelia terms the "policy" behind the absence of *Swetnam*'s author is to find a correlation between the play's textual disruptions of gender—on its title page, in its amazonian prince, through its affiliations between women and a man—and its refusal to present itself as the property of any person or gender. A narrative that gives so much attention to punishing an author is likely to be self-conscious about how it represents its own origins, and this one works quite hard to cover its tracks. It is possible that defending women could occasion even more grief for an early modern author than producing misogyny; hence if Swetnam had cause to disguise his authorship in pseudonymity, the author(s) of the play had even more reason to take shelter in anonymity. After the play was performed and published, Swetnam's *Arraignment*, far from being "burn'd and cast away," was reprinted again and again: following the first four editions, it appeared in 1619, 1622, 1628, 1629, 1633, and 1637, then in six more editions through 1880; it was even translated into Dutch. Each of the four defenses was published only once, although the play may have been staged again around 1633.[17] In a climate that so effectively disseminated misogyny, anonymous and pseudonymous publication enabled alliances with and among women, and textual disruptions of gender offered some resistance to the polarizing effects of the controversy as a whole. So whether or not this "Anonymous" was a woman, s/he did the work of women's ally and remained deeply indeterminate for nearly four hundred years. Here's to the dearth.

NOTES

I am grateful to Susan Frye, Barbara Hodgdon, Karen Robertson, and Valerie Traub for their adroit advice on this essay, and to responses from those in the audience at a conference of the American Historical Association, Pacific Coast Branch, in August 1995, and again at the University of Alabama in March 1997 as part of the Hudson Strode lecture series. Students and faculty at the University of Alabama also participated in a lively reading of the play of *Swetnam the Woman-hater* on March 23, 1997, which taught me just how stageworthy and how funny it could be in performance.

1. Andrew Gurr, *Playgoing in Shakespeare's London* (Cambridge: Cambridge University Press, 1987), p. 174, dates the play in 1617. *The Cambridge Companion to English Renaissance Drama* (Cambridge: Cambridge University Press, 1990), p. 435, and *Annals of English Drama* (London: Routledge, 1989), pp. 112–13, date it in 1618. Coryl Crandall argues in his introduction to *"Swetnam the Woman-hater": The Controversy and the Play* (West Lafayette, Ind.: Purdue University Studies, 1969) that it could not have been written before 1617 because it draws on all of the other texts in the controversy, the last of which, *The Worming of a mad Dogge,* was entered in the Stationers' Register on April 29, 1617, and published later that year. Since Queen Anne died on March 2, 1619, occasioning a dispersal of her players, and the title page attributes the performance to "the late Queenes Seruants," the play was performed before the queen's death. Crandall, Introduction, pp. 26–27, therefore dates the likeliest first performance in 1618.

2. For publication information, see STC entries 23533–23542 (Swetnam's *Arraignment*), 23058 (Speght), 22974 (Sowernam), 18257 (Munda), and 23544 (*Swetnam the Woman-hater*).

3. Crandall, Introduction, pp. 28–30, discusses the possibilities that Heywood and Dekker are the authors, citing Alexander B. Grosart's 1880 edition, "Swetnam the Woman-hater," *Occasional Issues,* 14 (Manchester, 1880), p. xxxiv, and Louis B. Wright, *Middle-Class Culture in Elizabethan England* (Chapel Hill: University of North Carolina Press, 1935), p. 490n. Grosart, Wright, and Crandall favor Heywood. Linda Woodbridge, *Women and the English Renaissance: Literature and the Nature of Woman Kind, 1540–1620* (Urbana: University of Illinois Press, 1984), pp. 320–21, adds Webster as a possible candidate.

4. Michael D. Bristol, *Big-time Shakespeare* (London: Routledge, 1996), pp. 49–58, critiques Foucault's "What is an author?" with reference to early modern print culture and reinterprets the author as "both debtor and trustee of meaning rather than sole proprietor; authority is always ministerial rather than magisterial" (p. 58).

5. The many narratives related to the play begin with Juan de Flores' *Grisel y Mirabella,* a Spanish novella published about 1495 which spread throughout Europe in at least fifty-six known editions, most of them dependent on an Italian translation that was then translated back into Spanish and also published in two-language (Italian–French and Spanish–French), three-language (French, Italian, English), and four-language (Italian, Spanish, French, English) editions that became manuals for language instruction. The initial Italian translation, called *Aurelio e Isabella,* was published under the pseudonym of Lelio Aletiphilo (friend of truth) in 1521. The translators of the multilanguage editions were anonymous. *Swetnam's* author(s) used *The Histoire de Aurelio et Isabelle,* published anonymously in Antwerp in 1556 and in Brussels in 1608, for the English play. The 1608 edition was also licensed in London to E. White in 1586 in a three-language edition and to E. Aggas in 1588 in a four-language edition, so it was probably published in England although no copy is extant. Another version of the narrative appeared anonymously from a London publisher in 1606 under the title, *A Paire of Turtle Doves,* but this text was apparently not adapted for *Swetnam.* The history of these texts and their diffusion appears in Barbara Matulka, *The Novels of Juan de Flores and Their European Diffusion* (New York: Institute of French Studies, 1931), which is still the best treatment of the subject.

6. Shakespeare, *Much Ado About Nothing,* ed. A. R. Humphreys (London: Routledge, 1981), IV.i.137–38.

7. In "Historical Differences: Misogyny and *Othello*," in *The Matter of Difference: Materialist Feminist Criticism of Shakespeare*, ed. Valerie Wayne, pp. 153–70 (Ithaca, N.Y.: Cornell University Press, 1991), I have discussed this problem more directly and tried to distinguish between the highly visible form of misogynist discourse in Renaissance texts, and other misogynist assumptions about women that are obscured through the localized form of discursive misogyny presented by a character like Swetnam.

8. Linda Woodbridge (1984), pp. 92–103, and Elaine V. Beilin, *Redeeming Eve* (Princeton, N.J.: Princeton University Press, 1987) pp. 248–66, treat all three authors as women. Katherine Usher Henderson and Barbara F. McManus, ed., *Half Humankind* (Urbana: University of Illinois Press, 1985), pp. 21–24, argue more directly that Speght, Sowernam, and Munda are women. Ann Rosalind Jones, *The Currency of Eros* (Bloomington: Indiana University Press, 1990), pp. 45–62, discusses the pamphlets as implying an alliance among women. Simon Shepherd edited the same pamphlets under the title *The Women's Sharp Revenge: Five Women's Pamphlets from the Renaissance* (New York: St. Martin's, 1985). Many of the current problems associated with the term "woman writer" are helpfully discussed in Margaret W. Ferguson's essay, "Renaissance Concepts of the 'Woman Writer,'" in *Women and Literature in Britain, 1500–1700*, ed. Helen Wilcox (Cambridge: Cambridge University Press, 1996), pp. 143–68, especially pp. 151–52 and p. 163.

9. For a discussion of Spenser's implicit condemnation of transvestism in *The Faerie Queene*, see Harvey (1992), pp. 32–43.

10. The word "impartial" here means "partial." It is used in connection with "unequal" earlier in the play (III.iii.7) and also appears in *Romeo and Juliet*, the First Quarto, l. 1856 (*OED*, "impartial," a.3) as a misuse for partial. Crandall, Introduction, p. 156, note to III.iii.7, and Shepherd, *Amazons and Warrior Women* (New York: St. Martin's, 1981), p. 211, read the prefix as a possible intensifier.

11. In *The Academy of Armory*, vol. 2 (London: Roxburghe Club, 1905), pp. 73–74, Randle Holme provides a detailed description of the card game of post and pair.

12. Stephen Orgel, *Impersonations* (Cambridge: Cambridge University Press, 1996), p. 84, discusses Paul van Somer's 1617 portrait of Queen Anne in similarly objectionable attire. The hat she wears in this portrait is very like those of the women wearing citizen dress on *Swetnam's* title page, although Anne's hat adds a feather. Those in the title page illustrations to *Hic Mulier* and *Haec Vir* have a feather and even broader brims.

13. See, for example, the engraving of James I by Francis Delaram that appears as plate 126 in Arthur M. Hind's *Engraving in England in the Sixteenth and Seventeenth Centuries*, vol. 2 (Cambridge: Cambridge University Press, 1955), and the images of James by Willem and Simon van de Passe reproduced in David M. Bergeron's *Shakespeare's Romances and the Royal Family* (Lawrence: University Press of Kansas, 1985), frontispiece and p. 34.

14. Marion Wynne-Davies, "The Queen's Masque: Renaissance Women and the Seventeenth-Century Masque," in *Gloriana's Face*, ed. S. P. Cerasano and Marion Wynne-Davis (Detroit, Mich.: Wayne State University Press, 1992), p. 86 observes that "a feminised discourse of political subversion and factional division between King and Queen was as evident in the plays performed before Anne as in those in which she herself participated."

15. John Astington, private communication, June 19, 1996; and Peter Blayney, private conversation, March 26, 1997. Blayney subsequently called my attention to the similarity between the Swetnam illustration and the woodcut to Dekker's *Bellman of London* of 1608, which is reprinted in Blayney's *Texts*

of King Lear and their Origins, vol. 1: *Nicholas Okes and the First Quarto* as woodcut 6 on p. 440. The perspective of the illustrations with the brick wall at the back; the half window of leaded glass in each; the shadings on the floor, on clothing, and on legs; the odd treatment of large hands and the simple treatment of feet in the figures—all these features suggest that the two woodcuts may have been produced by the same artist.

16. *Haec Vir* and *Hic Mulier* also have title pages with woodcuts of women in masculine apparel and men in feminine apparel that were prepared specifically for those texts. The cut on the title page of *Mulde Sacke* copies an elaborate engraving of John Cottington discussed in Hind, *Engraving in England*, vol. 2, pp. 170–71, and it too emphasizes flamboyant dress. The illustrations in all these 1620 publications were probably used to advertise and popularize the controversy at a time when the problem of disorderly apparel was especially heightened by James's prohibitions. I am grateful to John Astington and Adrian Weiss for their advice on these woodcuts.

17. Woodbridge (1984), p. 81, refers to the six editions after 1637 and the Dutch translation. Crandall, Introduction, pp. 27–28, cites Gerald E. Bentley, *The Jacobean and Caroline Stage* (Oxford, 1941–56), pp. v, 1417–18, as discussing the possibility of a 1633 production, because Thomas Nabbes referred to it in his play *Tottenham Court* performed at the Salisbury Court theater in that year.

14

The Erotics of Female Friendship
in Early Modern England

· ·

HARRIETTE ANDREADIS

RECENT INVESTIGATIONS OF EARLY modern texts have begun to refine our understanding of a class of women and behaviors described by their contemporaries in ways that coincide with our modern "lesbian." We have yet to discover how the social and cultural descriptions of these persons and behaviors were formulated, nor do we know how these women themselves—apart from public representations of them—might have negotiated their desires toward each other. In this essay, I demonstrate that as sexual acts between women began to be identified by public discourse in the vernacular as transgressive, "respectable" women— whose connections with each other might be read as "lesbian" today— developed a second, more sexually evasive yet erotically charged language of female friendship to describe female same-sex intimacy. I name this language of female friendship and intimacy a "double discourse" because its emergence parallels the publicly disseminated discourse of overt transgression; for it was the growing acknowledgment of female same-sex sexual behaviors in the public sphere and the corresponding opprobrium directed at them that made this double discourse possible. Those women who were sheltered, privileged, and "respectable," and who were loathe to see themselves or to express their desires in ways considered transgressive, developed more acceptable discursive strategies to contain or to deflect desires that might otherwise have threat-

ened to overwhelm them. This double discourse constitutes a poetic tradition that begins in the impulse to create idealized female communities
in the work of Aemilia Lanyer and Katherine Philips and culminates in
the mid-eighteenth century with the impassioned poems of Mary Leapor.

Much current thought and writing about same-sex female erotics
turns on the indeterminability of sexual definition. Annamarie Jagose,
in *Lesbian Utopics*, for example, describes "the fundamental uncertainty
of the category 'lesbian'" and its "definitional intractability" (p. 9).
Martha Vicinus has commented that "definitional uncertainty is at the
core of lesbian studies"; she describes as "lesbian-like" the murky passions of the Miss Pirie and Miss Scott of Lillian Faderman's *Scotch Verdict* and Lillian Hellman's *The Children's Hour* (pp. 67, 72). Terry Castle,
in *The Apparitional Lesbian* (and also in her work on the historical legacy
of Marie Antionette), describes the "ghosting" of lesbian desire, that is,
the representation of the lesbian and her desire through coded gesture
and oblique reference (especially pp. 1–20, 28–65, 107–49). These are
only a few of the most recent struggles to come to terms with the by
now traditional critical oppositions between Adrienne Rich's assimilation of as many women as possible into a cultural feminist paradigm
of "women-loving women" in a "lesbian continuum" and Catharine
Stimpson's objection that lesbianism concerns sexual desire and that to
diminish the power of sexuality between women reinforces the nega-
tion of female subjectivity.[1]

Given the obstacle of these definitional impasses, there has been a
reluctance to confront the problems of female same-sex sexuality and
eroticism in the period before 1800 in England, long before Freud, the
sexological revolution, and the creation of modern sexual identities.
There has been a refusal even to acknowledge an earlier recognition of
the possibilities for female same-sex erotic activity. However, the work
of Valerie Traub, Katherine Park, Patricia Simons, myself, and others,
demonstrates that the isolation and description of certain behaviors,
following classical precedent for their nomenclature and manifested in
the anatomies and travel narratives of the sixteenth and early seventeenth
centuries, was used to identify and to stigmatize a distinct category of
transgressive woman, albeit one clearly outside the experience and
often the knowledge of "respectable" persons and, especially, beyond
the experience or knowledge of "respectable" women.[2]

"Tribades" (Latin) and *"fricatrices"* (French), occasionally called
"rubsters" in English, were known in the sixteenth century through a
variety of texts available to literate men who read Latin. In the seventeenth century, accounts of the existence of these *"tribades"* and
"fricatrices" became known to a larger literate public (though still mostly
to men) when Latin anatomies were translated into English and vernacular
travel narratives identified the erotic activities of "exotic" (especially
Egyptian) women with each other in harems, baths, and bazaars.[3] Quasi-
medical and folkloric accounts of females with enlarged clitorises which

they could not help but "abuse" seem regularly to have titillated the prurient interests of educated males. Female same-sex eroticism was thus constructed and made explicit in particular restricted discourses as a wantonly transgressive act involving the genital rubbing of one woman against another or the imitation of male penetrative action by an enlarged clitoris or prosthesis. Anatomical accounts and travellers' narratives of "foreign" customs in this way suggest to us the language through which female same-sex sexual behaviors originally entered verbal consciousness in the vernacular.

The trajectory of knowledge about, and consequent representation of, female same-sex sexuality is a complex one during the early modern period. In the sixteenth century, same-sex female erotic behavior was often treated misogynistically, but also with relative matter-of-factness or as a curiosity in texts that were accessible to a largely male readership. In the seventeenth century, this eroticism is presented with increasing ambiguity and self-consciousness on the part of authors and translators. By mid-century, public discourse about these identifiably sexually transgressive women is increasingly relegated to two distinct categories of printed text. On the one hand, it appears in medical treatises, travel narratives, erotica, and other texts that could provoke and satisfy prurient misogynist interests; on the other hand, it becomes evident in allusions by male writers and in literary works by women willing or able to be unconventional.[4] Though the descriptions and allusions by male literary figures provide a discourse that more explicitly describes the nature of sexual activities of women with each other, the presence of clear references to same-sex erotic activity in writing by women is notable at this historical moment.

Just after the middle of the seventeenth century, for example, and coinciding with the increasing availability of vernacular texts that might include identifications and descriptions of same-sex transgressive women, we remark the appearance of literary documents by English women that explicitly portray female same-sex erotic behaviors: the Duchess of Newcastle's play, *The Convent of Pleasure* (1668); Anne Killigrew's poem of erotic flagellation, *Upon a Little Lady Under the Discipline of an Excellent Person* (1686); Aphra Behn's poem *To the Fair Clarinda, Who Made Love to Me, Imagined More than Woman* (1688); and Delarivier Manley's "new Cabal" in her roman à clef *The New Atalantis* (1709) are the best known of these works.[5] Except for Anne Killigrew, whose poem is accompanied by a disclaimer of her authorship, these writers were all in some way considered infamous or associated with scandal.

Margaret Cavendish, the Duchess of Newcastle, was generally regarded as a Tory eccentric whose discourse was described, dismissively, by at least one contemporary as "airy, empty, whimsical and rambling" (Mary Evelyn, quoted in Tomlinson, p. 159) and who "in her rhetoric of dress and behaviour aimed at a blurring of the boundaries between genders similar to that produced by *The Convent of Pleasure*" (Tomlinson,

p. 158). Aphra Behn's notoriety as a spy in Antwerp for Charles II, her incarceration in debtor's prison, her advocacy of education for women, her contributions to the rise of the novel, and her theatrical writings were all well known to her contemporaries; they helped shape her reputation and enhanced her self-fashioning as a woman who consciously transgressed social norms and challenged social values. Like Cavendish, Delarivier Manley was a strong royalist in her political sympathies; however, in the context of contemporary social norms, she was perhaps more than merely eccentric. Manley was involved in a bigamous marriage that she exploited for literary materials on polygamy; moreover, *The New Atalantis*, her "Tory-motivated exposé of the supposed 'secret' lives of rich and powerful Whig peers and politicians of the reigns of the Stuart kings and queens from Charles II to Anne I," was suppressed on publication and she was taken into custody (introduction to Manley, p. v). Creating scandal in her fictions and theatrical productions, she also lived it.

The works of these writers were not generally considered "respectable" since their open articulation of female desire appears to have been an extension of the scandal and notoriety attached to their persons. The willingness of these unconventional women to contribute—at mid-century, just after the Restoration—to a public discourse about the erotic activities of women with each other is evident. Yet this willingness to be transgressive apparently encouraged a more self-protective discourse in other contemporaries, as well as in subsequent writers, who wished to dissociate themselves from transgression.

To summarize: there seems to have been a change in discourse about female same-sex eroticism in England sometime in or around the mid-seventeenth century, in rough coincidence with and following the Restoration. The language of literature and respectable society becomes more evasive as the existence of female same-sex transgressive behaviors was increasingly acknowledged by other dimensions of public discourse. With the approach of the eighteenth century, the definition of female same-sex relations and its expression in public discourse had become more narrowly focused on a specific set of forbidden sexual behaviors. This transgressive sexuality and its discursive articulation appear to have been increasingly circumscribed and split off from representations and understandings of the relations between "respectable" women. Those who were defined as transgressing were over time ever more conclusively ostracized, and in all likelihood relegated to a liminal existence in a subculture analogous to, though probably much less public than, that of London's male "mollies." But the acceptability of the discourses and behaviors of "respectable" women not so relegated is likely to have been unquestioned, and surely regarded as beyond reproach. On the one hand, then, there existed a language of transgressive sexuality by women not unwilling to be seen as flamboyantly overstepping the bounds of convention; on the other hand, there developed an erotically charged yet shadowed language of female same-sex friendship by women seeking the rewards of "respectability" at the same time that they gesture against conventional confinement. This splitting off, or doubling, of discourses created a space for the development, in the mid- to later eighteenth century, of the language of female romantic friendship as the dominant discourse defining "virtuous" and socially impeccable female friends.[6]

What, then, of the erotic expression of "respectable" English women of the *earlier* period of the sixteenth and seventeenth centuries? These women lived in an environment that was mostly homosocial for women as well as for men; they lacked any socially constructed understanding of same-sex erotic relations like that available to their classically educated male peers. In addition, they were culturally dominated by the injunction to marry and have children, and had no opportunities for independence before widowhood might leave them with some financial means to craft lives of their own apart from family exigencies. Literary evidence provides us with possible answers to the nature of the construction of same-sex erotic behavior among women who were literate and of "respectable" social class, and who were unwilling to see themselves as transgressive. This evidence points to a range of sometimes emotionally charged, eroticized discourses and relations between such women that might conceivably have partaken of eroticized behaviors not then defined as sexual, or as transgressive, because they would not have been modeled on valorized male penetrative action.[7]

The writings of women to each other were produced in a society in which a limited range of literary subjects was available to women who sought positive recognition from male peers and the maintenance of their respectability. The kinds of poems written by women to each other fall into several clearly definable categories that appear to have been approved by tradition: poems to a social superior or to the Queen, acknowledging or soliciting patronage; elegiac poems either to a woman friend or to a child who has died, the former admiring a life of strength, courage, and honor, the latter regretting a life too early taken; poems of friendship, either encomia to a beloved friend or invectives on disappointed affections; poems on woman's prescribed social role: virginity, marriage, female vanity, and relations with men; poems on women writing or reading; and dedicatory poems written for other women's plays or poetry. Examples of these abound.[8] Respectable writing women also wrote many kinds of poems that did not entail address to each other or to another woman; however, because they could not utilize the perspectives of political scurrility and explicit sexuality,[9] they usually confined themselves to the genres of meditation, contemplative philosophy, pastoral dialogue, and courtly compliment. Of the kinds of poems written by women to each other, poems of friendship, which often also combined themes from the other categories, offered forms of expression through which an erotically charged poetry of intimacy could and did emerge.

The *consolidation* of possibilities for the production of a poetry of impassioned intimacy between women coincides with the broad social, demographic, and economic changes taking place throughout England (especially in London) during this period. Following the Civil War, the deposition, and the subsequent Restoration, there is not only the permissiveness with respect to sexual matters of the post-1660 period, but a different understanding of sexuality and the body seems to emerge with the confluence of a number of critical social changes in the fabric of English life. Among these were the professionalization of women's writing, the greater dissemination of texts in the vernacular, including medical, travel, and midwifery texts, and the increasing urgency of education and literacy for women. These changes in the production of knowledge existed alongside, and were intimately related to, the pressures of an increasingly populous London, the shifting of class structures to accomodate the development of a bourgeoisie and the rise of a middle class, and the development of ideologies associated with domesticity, including what has been called the "emergent ideology of married love" (Berry, p. 146).[10]

The growing professionalization of literature and the system of patronage for middle-class writers in the early seventeenth century were factors particularly relevant for women writers (Woods, p. xxxiii). The new professionalization is perhaps first clearly recognizable in the unusual, and striking, number of dedicatory poems to women patrons written by Aemilia Lanyer for the prefatory matter of the 1611 edition of *Salve Deus Rex Judaeorum*: she addresses ten women individually, including such eminent personages as the Queen and the Countesses Dowager of Kent, Pembroke, and Cumberland, and concludes with a dedication "To the Vertuous Reader," who is clearly female: "I have written this small volume, or little booke, for the generall use of all vertuous Ladies and Gentlewomen of this kingdome" (Woods, p. 48). Her stated intent is to hold up women for praise and to bring forth their virtues. As her editor Susanne Woods has noted, Lanyer, in reworking her Biblical materials, also introduces "digressions focussing on women" that "interweave the story" (Woods, p. xxxvii). Lanyer's poetry flourishes in and for a community of women, composed both of patrons and peers, that nourishes and sustains her creative efforts.

It is this same impulse to community that we see developed in Katherine Philips's well-known poetic "Society of Friendship."[11] Philips, called the "matchless *Orinda*" after her poetic persona (see Souers), provided in her poetry and letters to the women whom she included in her "Society" the best known example of a charged erotic discourse that evades definition in modern terms. As I have shown elsewhere, Philips' expressions of passion and longing for her female friends—couched in a rhetoric that echoes the fervent emotionalism of male–male platonic friendship and the literary conventions of metaphysical (heterosexual) love poetry—are a model of female same-sex eroticism outside the bounds of contemporary sexual definition and not amenable to American twentieth-century understandings of categories of identity (see Andreadis, 1989, pp. 55–60). Because her discourse and behavior were outside the boundaries of contemporaneous sexual understandings, they were also safe from interpretations that would constrain them. They spoke to a social and literary cult that sustained notions of the purity of women; this was the same impulse that kept from "respectable" women the sexual knowledge purveyed in Latin texts and erased in many translations of the classics and other texts.

Philips established a model of passionate female friendship that set a precedent and was emulated by the female poets and playwrights who followed her in the later seventeenth century.[12] In fact, Philips created more than a precedent; she established a tradition and a discourse for the expression of passions not otherwise given voice. It is clear that the women writers who followed her were mindful that a path had been cleared for the expression of a passionate emotional and discursive attachment between women. Furthermore, it is crucial to recognize that Philips' work, although demonstrably produced by her own emotional and erotic impulses, was grounded in a particular set of circumstances and a particular kind of discourse that were conventional and acceptable in the homosocial culture of the mid-seventeenth century.

Frequent allusions to and emulations of *Orinda*'s poetry of friendship were written by such writers as Aphra Behn and Delarivier Manley in the later seventeenth century. From the often highly self-conscious tributes to *Orinda* we see a "poetry of intimacy" taking shape—even becoming increasingly conventional—in the later seventeenth and early eighteenth centuries in a broad range of poems expressing a variety of intensely intimate emotions by, among others, "Ephelia,"[13] Lady Mary Chudleigh, Anne Finch, Countess of Winchelsea, and Jane Brereton.

These "respectable" poets chose to write after the model established by Philips rather than make any connections between themselves and the synchronous and much more explicitly erotic descriptions of female same-sex activities by Behn, Manley, Newcastle, and Killigrew. It is possible that they did not recognize any connections between their own emotional attachments and those identified by the more explicit discourses of transgressive women like Behn, of libertine men, or of anatomical and travel texts; if they did recognize any connection, they would almost certainly have chosen to suppress such a recognition in the interests of social comfort and safety from ostracism. As others have noted recently in the context of nineteenth- and twentieth-century lesbian studies, the very powerful role played by the unspoken or by the elliptical in literature by women cannot be underestimated. Karla Jay has remarked that, even into the twentieth century, "lesbian eroticism must often be read in the silent spaces in an otherwise heterosexual text. Often, it is the ellipses or breaks in the text that mark the feelings between women that cannot be spoken" (p. 4). Jane Garrity points out that "the sign of lesbian presence is frequently . . . lodged in textual places that expressly demand that we become adept at multilayered readings" (p. 244). In the case of "respectable" women writers of the mid-seventeenth century, we need to remain aware of the possibilities of erotic ellipsis in order to understand the nuances of meaning that inhere in a powerfully charged poetry of friendship.

Erotic in this early modern context, then, describes that spectrum of sometimes diffuse but clearly sensuous feelings and intense emotions found in discourses of passionate engagement between women. While these feelings and emotions may well have included a physiological dimension, they would not necessarily have been genitally focused. By extension, in those instances in which they were genitally focused, they were not likely to have been defined or recognized as sexual. An *erotic ellipsis*, then, may be said to occur when these feelings and emotions are discursively expressed, but not explicitly acknowledged in connection with sexuality or with sexual transgression. Even a cursory examination of the poetry of "Ephelia," Lady Mary Chudleigh, Anne Finch, Countess of Winchelsea, and Jane Brereton—writers who ignored the possibilities offered by the more explicitly sexual discourse of some of their contemporaries—illustrates the strong presence of passionate poems by women to each other in which such erotic ellipsis is apparent.

In "To the Honoured *Eugenia*, commanding me to Write to Her," probably written to her patronness, "Ephelia" explicitly places herself in the tradition of the poetry of intimate friendship and encomiastic gesture associated with Katherine Philips. Like Philips, the poet uses the device of pseudopastoral names both for herself and for her friends; her choice of the pseudopastoral identity of "Ephelia" is a clearly recognizable echo of Philips' assumption of the literary identity of *Orinda*: "Fair Excellence! such strange Commands you lay, / I neither dare Dispute, nor can Obey: / Had I the sweet *Orinda's* happy Strain, / Yet every Line would Sacriledge contain" (1–4). The use of "contain" points to the operations of a shadowed eroticism by suggesting the arrest or inhibition of the threatened "Sacriledge" at the same time as it is conveyed; thus is "Sacriledge," transgression, rejected so that it can be invoked. The erotic charge carried by shadowed discourse here reveals itself explicitly as a threatened pressure against boundaries. "Ephelia" continues:

> Like to some awful Deity you sit,
> At once the Terrour and Delight of Wit:
> Your Soul appears in such a charming Dress
> As I admire, but never can express: . . .
> Pardon, dear Madam, these untuned Lays,
> That have Prophan'd what I design'd to Praise.
> Nor is't possible, but I so must do,
> All I can think falls so much short of you:
>
> (5–8, 27–30)

As does Philips in so many of the poems that established her reputation, "Ephelia" writes with the intense devotion and (dignified) self-deprecation of one certainly awed by and even infatuated with the object of her poetic attentions. The articulation of the inexpressibility of feeling suggests a dimension of intensity that must of necessity remain latent. While the compliment she pays *Eugenia* is in some ways rather conventional, it is also inflected with a more personal emotional cast.[14]

In an encomium "To Madam *Bhen*," "Ephelia" furthers the awareness of a tradition of female poetry and notes the power of emotion, especially the admiration of one woman for another, to silence discursive expression: "Madam! permit a Muse, that has been long / Silent with wonder, now to find a Tongue: . . . / As in your Self, so in your Verses meet, / A rare connexion of Strong and Sweet: . . ." (1–2, 15–16). Expressing unqualified admiration for Behn, "Ephelia" accepts her predecessor's poetic and erotic reputation as "A rare connexion of Strong and Sweet," thereby characterizing Behn's transgressiveness as both complexly configured and attractive. This moment of fascination with Behn's transgression is neatly coterminous with "Ephelia"'s unwillingness to incorporate any similarly overt transgressiveness into her own work.

In "To a Proud Beauty," "Ephelia"'s rage at another woman's scorn is not a simple jealousy in the competition for male attention; instead, the lines are choked by the speaker's conflicted and only semiarticulated passions. She passionately desires the approval of a woman who appears to reject her; she directs condemnation, contempt, and rage at the unresponsive object of her need; and she imagines herself successfully retaliating through the power of language[15]:

> Imperious Fool! think not because you're Fair,
> That you so much above my Converse are,
> What though the Gallants sing your Praises loud,
> And with false Plaudits make you vainly Proud? . . .
> Know too, you stately piece of Vanity,
> That you are not Alone ador'd, for I
> Fantastickly might mince, and smile, as well
> As you, if Airy Praise my mind cou'd swell: . . .
> Since then my Fame's as great as yours is, why
> Should you behold me with a loathing eye?
> If you at me cast a disdainful Eye,
> In biting Satyr I will Rage so high,
> Thunder shall pleasant be to what I'le write,
> And you shall Tremble at my very Sight. . . .
>   (1–4, 13–16, 23–28)

The size of the emotions here is out of proportion to the stated offense, indicating the underlying erotic charge. The speaker's intense anguish and passionate longing vibrate in the interstices between the rage and invective which are her ineffectual gestures of lament for unrequited affection.

Lady Mary Chudleigh, in "To *Clorissa*" (1703), draws on the device of pseudopastoral names and echoes Philips' pastoral themes of a half-century earlier. Opening the poem with an erotic statement both of the speaker's desire and of the seductiveness of her friend, *Marissa* seeks the comforts of *Clorissa*'s "Bosom" as the site of a "sacred Friendship" invited by "ten thousand Charms." The joyfulness expressed by the lines that describe her "gentle Passion" and the "sacred Flames" that "dilate themselves" in every part of her being suggests a most welcome immersion in erotic feeling and the forging of an intense, quasireligious ("sacred"), connection:

> To your lov'd Bosom pleas'd Marissa flies:
> That place where sacred Friendship gives a Right,
> And where ten thousand Charms invite. . . .
> Next these Delights[16] Love claims the chiefest Part,
> That gentle Passion governs in my Heart:
> Its sacred Flames dilate themselves around,
> And like pure Aether no Confinement know:
> Where ever true Desert is found,
> I pay my Love and Wonder too:
>
> (1–3, 45–50)

In the concluding stanza, the speaker represents with exactness the terms of spiritual union and passionate attachment between women initially given voice by Katherine Philips. The speaker describes a kind of emotional fusion ("We'll live in one another's Breast") in which the lives of the "friends" are so comingled that they will find their perfect condition in an afterlife ("in each other there eternally delight"). Their union is characterized by sweetness, by tenderness, by a complete sharing and joining of interests ("be but one"):

> O! let our Thoughts, our Interests be but one,
> Our Griefs and Joys, be to each other known:
> In all Concerns we'll have an equal share,
> Enlarge each Pleasure, lessen ev'ry Care:
> Thus, of a thousand Sweets possest,
> We'll live in one another's Breast:
> When present, talk the flying Hours away,
> When absent, thus, our tender Thoughts convey:
> And, when by the decrees of Fate
> We're summon'd to a higher State,
> We'll meet again in the blest Realms of Light,
> And in each other there eternally delight.
>
> (Uphaus and Foster, pp. 146–48, 66–77)

The terms used to describe this relation are neoplatonic and charged with an emotional intensity that suggests erotic as well as emotional attachment. The tone is erotic, if not sexual, the content sapphic.[17]

In the dialogue "Friendship between *Ephelia* and *Ardelia*" written by Anne Finch, Countess of Winchelsea, and published in 1713, *Ephelia*

presses *Ardelia* for a clear definition of friendship beyond her stated "'Tis
to love as I love you" (2). Winchelsea gives us at once a witty comment
on the limits of what can be spoken and an intense expression of passion between women for which the form of the pastoral dialogue is a
convenient and deceptively conventional vehicle:

> EPH[ELIA]. This indeed, though carried high;
> This, though more than e're was done
> Underneath the rolling sun,
> This has all been said before.
> Can Ardelia say no more?
>
> ARD[ELIA]. Words indeed no more can show:
> *But 'tis to love, as I love you.*
> (Lonsdale, p. 15, 14–20)

Ephelia here scorns *Ardelia*'s earlier description of the generosities of true
friendship as a mere echo of traditional expressions of ideal friendship
by male writers. The exchange in these closing lines of the poem goes
on to delineate the inadequacies of language and the inexpressibility of
erotic emotion between women. In other words, it articulates clearly the
nature of erotic ellipsis.

Conventional form was and continued to be of critical importance to
expressions of same-sex passion, and women writers continued to seek
models in their predecessors. Jane Brereton's "Epistle to Mrs Anne
Griffiths. Written from London, in 1718" (but not published until 1744;
Lonsdale, p. 56), explicitly articulates this deployment of conventional
form. Having raged against the vanities of male critics and their censures
of women writers, she reiterates the standard themes of women's writing, replicating (perhaps because she has internalized them) the judgments of those same misogynistic male critics. The burden of maintaining status as a "respectable" woman writer is apparent in the speaker's
rejection of the sexually tainted female writers represented by Aphra
Behn and Delarivier Manley. In evoking *Orinda*, the architect of respectability for later women poets, Brereton colludes with male authority in
circumscribing acceptable possibilities for women's writing. The poem's
disingenuous closing lines, however, demonstrate Brereton's mastery of
a shadowed discourse. Disdaining the world's opinion and seeking only
to "amuse" herself and "please" her "friend," the poet gestures toward
an elliptically erotic subtext:

> Fair modesty was once our sex's pride,
> But some have thrown that bashful grace aside:
> The Behns, the Manleys, head this motley train,
> Politely lewd and wittily profane;
> Their wit, their fluent style (which all must own)
> Can never for their levity atone.
> But Heaven still, its goodness to denote,
> For every poison gives an antidote:

First, our *Orinda*, spotless in her fame,
As chaste in wit, rescued our sex from shame. . . .
    For me, who never durst to more pretend
Than to amuse myself, and please my friend;
If she approves of my unskillful lays,
I dread no critic, and desire no praise. (18–27, 32–35)

These represent only a sample of the poems written and a partial list of women writing them from the mid-seventeenth century through the first quarter of the eighteenth century. It should be evident from this survey that "respectable" women desiring to express their attachment, however eroticized, to other women gravitated to the shadowed discourse developed by Katherine Philips to articulate her intense passions for her friends. This tradition of a discourse of veiled eroticism, developed in response to a more public language of overt transgression, appears to culminate in the work of the working-class poet Mary Leapor (1722–46), where it points the way for the development of the discourse of female romantic friendship which was to follow shortly thereafter.

In the last months of her life, Leapor was passionately attached to her "friend and mentor" Bridget Freemantle, who saw to it that her poems were published posthumously.[18] In the long "Essay on Friendship," addressed to *Artemisia,* Freemantle's pastoral pseudonym, Leapor echoes Philips and the writers who followed her example in elevating friendship to a "sacred" aspect of the soul: "'Tis not to *Cythera's* Reign nor *Cupid's* Fires,/But sacred Friendship that our Muse inspires" (vol. 1, F5^v).[19] By juxtaposing the "Essay on Friendship" with "David's *Complaint,* ii Samuel, *chap.* I," which precedes it, Leapor revisits almost a century later the impulse that had compelled Katherine Philips to question Jeremy Taylor regarding the religious nature and limits of friendship between women, to which Taylor had responded with his androcentric 1657 work, "A Discourse of the Nature, Offices, and Measures, of Friendship, with Rules of Conducting It, in a Letter to the Most Ingenious and Excellent Mrs. Katharine Philips" (Heber, vol. 11, pp. 299–335). Leapor's "David's *Complaint* . . . ," a passionate lament for Jonathan, takes up the traditional theme of male friendship in the impassioned soul-union of friends and the anguish of survival when one of the pair has died: "He was my Soul's best Pleasure while alive, /And is he blasted?—then do I survive?" (vol. 1, F5).[20] But this then leads Leapor, as it had Philips, to the vexed question in the "Essay on Friendship" of whether women can have similar attachments: "The Wise will seldom credit all they hear, / Tho' saucy Wits shou'd tell them with a Sneer, / That Womens Friendships, like a certain Fly, / Are hatch'd i'th Morning and at Ev'ning die" (vol. 1, F5^v). In response to this denigration of women's higher capacities, the speaker's rhetorical strategy is to detail at length the virtues of moderation, so that "Celestial Friendship with its nicer Rules" becomes "the justly tempered Flame" that "Will glow incessant, and be still the same" (vol. 1, F7). Yet, as in Lady Mary Chudleigh's "To *Clorissa,*" the connection between sacredness ("Celestial Friendship") and passion ("the . . . Flame") is the defining notion on which the poem turns. Finally, Leapor's answer to the scoffers at women's friendship is a description of perfect intimacy, now in its aspect of mutual comforting: "The Soul's Relief, with Grief or Cares opprest, / Is to disclose them to a faithful Breast" (vol. 1, F8^v).

In both "The Beauties of the Spring" (vol. 1, B8-C1^v) and *"Colinetta"* (vol. 1, C5^v–C7^v), Leapor creates female community. In the first of these poems, community emerges through escape to an idyllic sylvan setting with "a Friend" who evokes an erotic response from nature: "At Sight of thee the swelling Buds expand, /And op'ning Roses seem to court thy Hand. . . . / To thee, my Fair, the chearful Linnet sings" (vol. 1, C1–C1^v). The response attributed here to sylvan flora and fauna suggests that the speaker's own feelings towards her "friend" have been displaced, creating a palpably erotic ellipsis. In *"Colinetta,"* a dying old shepherdess lies in the lap of another shepherdess lamenting her passage from a beloved world. She creates a community of women by bequeathing her goods to the other shepherdesses and makes a point of never having envied the heterosexual conquests of other women: "When *Damon* wedded *Urs'la* of the Grange, / My Cheek with Envy ne'er was seen to change" (vol. 1, C7). In both poems, female community is predicated on the absence of heterosexual concerns and on the sharing of an eroticized experience of nature.

"Silvia and the Bee" describes, in the language of the heterosexual lover to his beloved, an erotic allegory in which the bee "Soft humming round the fatal Bow'r" (vol. 1, S8) provokes Sylvia to destroy him. The last stanza is a fancifully erotic compliment to Sylvia who, having been described as the motive for her garden's burst of intensity, now is its most desirable ornament: "Believe me, not a Bud like thee / In this fair Garden blows; / Then blame no more the erring Bee, / Who took you for the Rose" (vol. 1, T). This compliment is familiar as a heterosexual gesture. Ventriloquized by a female poet/speaker who is addressing another woman, it creates a wholly different erotic dynamic, fraught with all the covert sexual implications of bees and stinging. "Song to *Cloe*, playing on her Spinnet" (I4^v–I5^v) is also highly eroticized, thick with "trembling Strings" and *Cloe*'s orphic powers. In "Complaining *Daphne*. A Pastoral" (vol. 2, F4^v–F8), Leapor is even more explicit in conveying a sense of same-sex eroticism in contrast to a damaging heterosexual sexuality. The poem concludes with a sustained "feminine pastoral idyll":

> Her Care convey'd me to a Beechen Shade.
> There with her Hand she press'd my throbbing Head,
> And laid me panting on a flow'ry Bed;
> Then sat beside me in the friendly Bow'r;
> Long Tales she told, to kill the tedious Hour;
> Of lovely Maids to early Ruin led, . . .
> And still howe'er the mournful Tale began,

> She always ended—*Child, beware of Man. . . .*
> Ye Sylvan Sisters! come; ye gentle Dames,
> Whose tender Souls are spotless as your Names!
> Henceforth shall *Daphne* only live for you;
> Content—and bid the lordly Race Adieu;
> See the clear Streams in gentler Murmers flow,
> And fresher Gales from od'rous Mountains blow.
>
> (vol. 2, F7–F8)

The unequivocal rejection of heterosexual relations here opens a space for the implicitly superior intimacies between women, as the narrated perils of heterosexual seduction titillate the present bucolic connection of "gentler Murmurs." In "The Disappointment," which immediately follows "Complaining *Daphne*" in the second volume (vol. 2, F8–G), *Mira* (Leapor's poetic persona) recounts a rejection by a friend which in its bitterness emphasizes the intensity of Leapor's passion for women. *Sophronia*'s seductively "consenting Smile" renders *Mira* nearly prostrate in a language usually reserved for male lovers: her eyes are "dazled"; her brains are "giddy"; her dreams are "golden." But having been disappointed by *Sophronia*'s "imagin'd Favours," *Mira* lashes out to salve the wounds of her unrequited passion:

> When you, *Sophronia,* did my Sense beguile
> With your Half-promise, and consenting Smile;
> What Shadows swam before these dazled Eyes!
> Fans, Lace, and Ribbands, in bright Order rise:
> Methought these Limbs your silken Favours found . . .
> No longer *Mira*, but a shining Belle.
> Such Phantoms fill'd these giddy Brains of mine;
> Such golden Dreams on *Mira*'s Temples shine;
> Till stern Experience bid her Servant rise,
> And Disappointment rubb'd my drowsy Eyes.
> Do thou, *Sophronia*, now thy Arts give o'er,
> Thy little Arts; for *Mira*'s Thoughts no more
> Shall after your imagin'd Favours run,
> Your still-born Gifts, that ne'er behold the Sun.
>
> (vol. 2, F8–F8^v)

The suggestions of transgressive eroticism are palpable in Leapor's work, securely masked by the respectabilities of female friendship and the evasions of conventional literary form, often (as in the case of Katherine Philips) by the uses of pastoralism. Donna Landry has noted "the eroticism of Leapor's textuality" (p. 85) in "An Hymn to the Morning" (vol. 1, C4–C5) in which the female protagonist vies with the poetic and, presumably, with the erotic skills of Sappho:

> Thus sung *Mira* to her Lyre,
> Till the idle Numbers tire:
> Ah! *Sappho* sweeter sings, I cry,

And the spiteful Rocks reply,
(Responsive to the jarring Strings)
Sweeter—*Sappho* sweeter sings.
(C5)

Given the double tradition of Sappho's reputation in early modern England—as the world's preeminent female poet and as an example of prototypical female sexual transgression—it is difficult to avoid the conclusion that *Mira* identifies herself directly with the ambiguities inherent in that tradition.

I have been describing here a historical process in which an eroticized discourse of intimate relations evolved, most often in the guise of patronage or friendship poetry, among literate women; this discourse developed apart from the more explicitly sexualized discourses of male-authored and male-read anatomies, travel narratives, advice manuals, etc., and from purposefully transgressive writing by women around the mid-seventeenth century and after. What we see—with Amelia Lanyer at the end of the sixteenth and the opening of the seventeenth century and Mary Leapor in about the second quarter of the eighteenth century, historically flanking Katherine Philips on either side—is the shaping of a largely poetic discourse of female same-sex intimacy.[21] Distancing themselves, as they were bound to do, from increasingly explicit and more widely acknowledged discourses of transgression, in certain writers this intimacy became erotically charged and expressed an affectional intensity for which the women in question would have had no language of definition.

NOTES

Various drafts of this essay have been presented at conferences: at "Virtual Gender: Past Projections, Future Histories" at Texas A&M University (Spring 1996); at the Pacific Coast Conference on British Studies at UCLA (Spring 1996); at the Sixteenth-Century Studies Conference in San Francisco (Fall 1995); and at the Group for Early Modern Cultural Studies in Dallas (Fall 1995). I would like to thank the many session participants who responded with questions, comments, and caveats for their help in clarifying my argument. The remarks of Kathleen Noonan and Mary Ann O'Farrell have been particularly helpful. But my greatest appreciation and thanks are reserved for the rigorous analyses offered by Karen Robertson and Susan Frye; their encouragement and assistance have represented for me the best meaning of academic women's alliances.

1. See Adrienne Rich, "Compulsory Heterosexuality and Lesbian Existence," *Signs* 5, no. 4 (Summer 1980): 631–60; and Catharine Stimpson, "Zero Degree Deviancy: The Lesbian Novel in English," in *Writing and Sexual Difference*, ed. Elizabeth Abel (Chicago: University of Chicago Press, 1982), pp. 243–59, as well as Bonnie Zimmerman, "What Has Never Been: An Overview of Lesbian Feminist Criticism," in *Feminist Literary Criticism*, ed. Gayle Greene and Coppélia Kahn (New York: Methuen, 1985), pp. 177–210, for the initial delineation of these critical stances.

2. Traub, Park, Simons, and I presented portions of our work in a session on "Early Modern 'Lesbianisms': History, Theory, Representation" at Attend-

ing to Early Modern Women: A Symposium, April 1994 (Center for Renaissance and Baroque Studies, University of Maryland). See Traub, "The Psychomorphology of the Clitoris," *GLQ: A Journal of Lesbian and Gay Studies* 2, no. 1 (1995): 81–113; Park, "The Rediscovery of the Clitoris" in *The Body in Parts*, ed. David Hillman and Carla Mazzio (New York: Routledge, 1996, pp. 170–193); Simons, "Lesbian (In)Visibility in Italian Renaissance Culture," *Journal of Homosexuality* 27 (1994): 81–122; and Andreadis, "Sappho in Early Modern England," in *Re-Reading Sappho*, ed. Ellen Greene, (Berkeley: University of California Press, 1997), pp. 105–121, for published versions of the materials presented at that conference. The work of Emma Donoghue (1993), Theo van der Meer (1992 and 1994), and Randolph Trumbach (1992 and 1994) has also enriched the study of sexual behaviors throughout Europe during this period. Sara Mendelson and Patricia Crawford's presentation of the legal materials in a case of female–female marriage in 1680 provides an interesting, if undertheorized, perspective on the connection between gender and sexuality during this period in England.

3. See Traub, "Psychomorphology," and Andreadis, "Sappho."

4. In "Sappho," I provide extensive documentation for the role played by representations of Sappho in early modern English culture as a kind of barometer of contemporary sexual understandings; she was an exemplar both of the heights of female literary achievement and of depraved, transgressive (heterosexual as well as same-sex female) sexuality. This two-edged, binary reputation sometimes became problematic in encomia to women writers: there is often a repudiation of Sappho the tribade at the same time as her literary exemplarity is asserted. The use of the term "sapphic" to denote "lesbian," however, seems not to have been generally in use before the late nineteenth century, when it apparently replaced, at least in more genteel social strata, the epithets "tribade," "fricatrice," "rubster," "tommy," etc. The *OED* cites the first instance of this usage in 1890 by Billings' *National Medical Dictionary*. It is ironically appropriate that "sapphic" should be first cited in a medical dictionary, since it was in the medical texts of the sixteenth and seventeenth centuries that Sappho was used to exemplify the tribadism of women who "abused" the clitoris.

5. Manley's "new Cabal" is now receiving considerable critical attention, and Behn's works generally have been among the first by women from this period to be included in courses and anthologies, with *To the Fair Clarinda* often anthologized. See, for example, the Penguin edition of Manley (ed. Rosalind Ballaster, 1992) and *The Norton Anthology of Literature by Women* edited by Sandra Gilbert and Susan Gubar (New York: Norton, 1985 and 1996). This interest tells us more about twentieth-century concerns and assumptions than it does about the temper of the period in question: modern feminist critical interest in gender issues and the lives of earlier women writers has often focused, in a sometimes rehabilitative fashion, on apparently transgressive women and on behaviors that elicited negative social attention or notoriety from their contemporaries. More seemingly conforming women have accordingly received less interest, with a consequent distortion of the historical record.

6. See the now-classic studies of Lillian Faderman, *Surpassing the Love of Men* (New York: Morrow, 1981), and Carroll Smith-Rosenberg, "The Female World of Love and Ritual," *Signs* 1, no. 1 (Autumn 1975): 1–29, on female "romantic friendship" in the eighteenth and nineteenth centuries. Marylynne Diggs, "Romantic Friends or 'A Different Race of Creatures': The Representation of Lesbian Pathology in Nineteenth-Century America," *Feminist Studies* 21, no. 2 (Summer 1995): 317–40, furnishes a summary of the critical history of "romantic friendship" as it emerged from the relatively uncomplicated paradigm first proposed by Faderman and Smith-Rosenberg. Though in the 1970s

Faderman and Smith-Rosenberg were loathe to identify the erotics clearly present in the texts they examine, their work does nevertheless identify the problems inherent in our retrospective attempts to comprehend the nature of sexuality and erotics for women in earlier periods. The well-known existence of "Boston marriages," which—as in the case of the Ladies of Llangollen—often also involved gender ambiguity, is perhaps central to the difficulties posed to a modern understanding: these women were "respectable," yet their self-presentations and behaviors *read* like modern lesbianism. With the recovery and publication of the diaries of Anne Lister, it has become clear without a doubt that same-sex erotic behavior was in the later eighteenth and nineteenth centuries consciously enacted in ways that we understand as sexual. See the account of the Ladies of Llangollen by Elizabeth Mavor (London: Penguin, 1973), Helena Whitbread's edition of the diaries of Anne Lister (New York: New York University Press, 1992), and the essays of Jill Liddington (1993) and Anna Clark (1996) exploring the nature of the sexuality presented in Lister's diaries.

7. Bernadette Brooten, *Love Between Women: Early Christian Responses to Female Homoeroticism* (Chicago: University of Chicago Press, 1996), explores the notion of the "unnatural" *(para physin)* and its dependence on an active/passive distinction for sexual behaviors during the early Christian period in the Roman world. The extent to which this distinction might have continued to operate in early modern Europe remains to be researched.

8. See collected poetry in the anthologies edited by Uphaus and Foster (1991); Greer, Hastings, Medoff, and Sansone (1988); Lonsdale (1989); Gilbert and Gubar (1985 and 1996); and others.

9. During the Restoration, however, female reimaginings and rewritings of male libertine poetry appeared. See Warren Chernaik, *Sexual Freedom in Restoration Literature* (Cambridge: Cambridge University Press, 1995), especially the chapter on Aphra Behn (pp. 160–213).

10. The work of Lawrence Manley (1995) on the growth of London, of Richard McKeon (1995) on the rise of domesticity, and of Valerie Wayne (1992) on the ideologies of marriage, has enlarged our perspective on the complex interplay of these multiple social forces in early modern England.

11. Philip Webster Souers, *The Matchless Orinda* (Cambridge, Mass.: Harvard University Press, 1931), postulated that Philips had developed an actual "Society of Friendship" with herself at its center; however, Patrick Thomas, in his edition of her poems and letters (Stump Cross, England: Stump Cross Books, 1990), has questioned the existence of such a community apart from the verbal gestures of Philips and a few of her friends.

12. Richard Barnfield (1574–1627) preceded Katharine Philips in writing *(male)* homoerotic sonnets that use all the witty conventions of heterosexual courtly love poetry (see, for instance, the selection in Stephen Coote, ed., *The Penguin Book of Homosexual Verse*, pp. 162–67). The gracious romanticism of Barnfield's poems furnishes an interesting contrast with, for instance, the later obscenities of Rochester following the Restoration. Barnfield serves as a nice male predecessor for Philips in his similar appropriations of heterosexual convention. But it seems doubtful that his poetry would have been known to her, or that we could find evidence of his direct influence. His example, however, may well have made available poetic possibilities of which she took advantage.

13. "Ephelia" continues to elude scholarly attempts to identify her, most recently by Maureen Mulvihill in the critical essay (pp. 3–88) that accompanies her facsimile edition of "Ephelia"'s *Female Poems on Several Occasions*. Texts of "Ephelia"'s poems cited here are from Greer et al., ed., *Kissing the Rod*, pp. 271–85.

14. We might compare the tone here with that in Philips' letters to the unidentified gentlewoman *Berenice*. "Ephelia"'s poems were published in 1679, while new editions of Philips's poems continued to be published until 1678.

15. The trajectory of "Ephelia"'s emotional expression here may be compared with that in similar poems by Katherine Philips, especially "On Rosania's Apostacy, and Lucasia's Friendship" and *"Injuria amici."* "Ephelia"'s concern with the more abstract ethical and theoretical problems of friendship between women and men, as in her "To *Phylocles*, inviting him to Friendship," echoes Philips in her relations with Sir Charles Cotterell and Sir Edward Dering. And, again like Philips, "Ephelia" emphasizes sex difference and employs ideas of the sexlessness of the soul and Platonic possibility.

16. In the previous stanza, *Marissa* has described the joys of a solitary, contemplative life.

17. See note 4. I use "sapphic" here to suggest the constructedness and perhaps also the fluidity of early modern understandings of female same-sex relations.

18. Leapor's poems were published in two volumes as *Poems upon Several Occasions* (London, 1748–51); her play, *The Unhappy Father. A Tragedy,* was included in vol. 2. Donna Landry, in *The Muses of Resistance* (Cambridge: Cambridge University Press, 1990), remarks that Leapor's poetic voice in the second volume is more "protofeminist" than in the earlier collection of poems (p. 99). Landry also speculates on the degree to which the laboring-class poets she discusses, including Leapor, might have known their poetic predecessors. She concludes, conservatively, that while there is no positive evidence that these poets actually had *read* Philips, Behn or Manley, their poems often take up themes and forms that are already familiar from their writings. Leapor, however, considered herself a student of Pope.

19. I have modernized long ∫s and similar characters in transcribing text from original editions.

20. David and Jonathan were a traditional trope of idealized yet eroticized male friendship. Abraham Cowley (1618–67), a contemporary and admirer of Katherine Philips, had written *Davideis*, a homoerotically charged paean to male friendship that locates erotic ellipsis in an impassioned platonic discourse: "O ye blest One! whose Love on earth became / So pure that still in Heav'en 'tis but the same! / There now ye sit, and with mixt souls embrace, / Gazing upon great *Loves* mysterious Face" (book 2, lines 114–17, cited in Coote, *Penguin Book*, pp. 168–9).

21. While *Orinda's* immediate legacy is for the most part poetic, her articulation of female community also established a positive climate for the theoretical formulations of Mary Astell (see *A serious proposal* [1694]) and the increasingly visible literary presence of an explicitly defined female community in mid-eighteenth-century women's writing—for example, in Sarah Fielding's text for girls, *The Governess, or Little Female Academy* (1749) and in Sarah Scott's *Millenium Hall*, a remarkable testament to the possibilities of female friendship, published in 1762, a brief sixteen years after Leapor's death.

Carol Barash, "The Political Origins of Anne Finch's Poetry," *Huntington Library Quarterly* 54 (Autumn 1991): 327–51, examines "the importance of women's community as a political trope": "For numerous women writers between Philips and [Anne] Finch [1661–1720], the guise of safe, domestic affiliations between women upholds the idea—and figuratively protects the body— of the exiled monarch" (p. 329). This additional dimension complicates and reinforces my more personal and intimate readings by suggesting a politically "respectable" rationale for the impetus to female community.

15

Alliance and Exile

Aphra Behn's Racial Identity

. . . .

MARGO HENDRICKS

[Passing is] hazardous business . . . this breaking away from all that was
familiar and friendly to take one's chance in another environment, not
entirely strange, perhaps, but certainly not entirely friendly. What, for
example, one does about background, how one accounted for oneself.

Nella Larsen

Exilio

In May 1660, Charles II ended a decade-long period of exile, and with
him returned a group of courtiers whose patronage would enable Aphra
Behn not only to embark on a career as a professional writer but also to
sustain that endeavor. Yet this return did not end the psychological effects that exile had on the returning royalists. In spite of a concerted
effort to resume life as if the "rebellion" had never occurred, Charles and
his court were never entirely able to put this moment of alienation and
displacement to rest. In much of the writing produced during the Restoration, exile was a recurring theme or trope. This theme persisted despite the cynicism, secularism, and hedonism that came to be trademarks
of Charles's reign. The irony, of course, is that these writings were not
produced in exile, but in the very space from which the writer was ini-

tially exiled—England. In effect, what transpires is that the formerly exiled subject writes poignantly and tellingly about the experience of exile after the fact. From a psychological perspective, writing about the exile may have functioned as a cathartic exercise for the writer, as well as an attempt to conjure a sense of community with other former exiles. Exilic writing thus serves a strategic political purpose, bringing about unity among those who had shared the King's exile and setting them apart from the rest of the King's court—especially those who had remained in England.

In what follows I will argue that the writings of Aphra Behn contributed to the period's exploration of exile; as a woman writing, she implicitly and explicitly engages exile and the pressure toward community from both a gendered and a racial subject position. For the woman writer, as Behn's pastoral lyric, "Our Cabal," and her poetic epistle, "To Mrs. Price," illuminate, the isolation of exile is intensified as is the need for a community of readers. Deploying gossip as an instrument of community building among the personas within the lyric and poetic epistle, Behn offers a gendered-specific means to resolve the isolation of exile for the woman writer. Yet, when considered in relation to Behn's other work on exile, *Oroonoko*, we realize that the problem of exile is not so easily redressed through the motif of gossip; in using these tropes of exile (isolation and need for community), Behn represents them in extreme forms of slavery and "racial" difference. Strikingly, in this quasi-autobiographical writing the effect of such representations is to direct the reader's gaze to the possibility of racial passing, which demands the most absolute of exiles: an exile where there is no possibility of a return home—an exile chosen to avoid the oppression associated with the color of one's skin. If Maria Rosa Menocal is correct in suggesting that the "lyric is invented in bitter exile. And not just the normal and conventional and essentially metaphoric exile that is, perhaps, the condition of all poetry and of its reading" (pp. 91–92), then intuitively reading Behn's "Our Cabal" and "To Mrs. Price" (as well as *Oroonoko*) as exilic texts may make possible the decryption of a passing subjectivity.

Solace in Exile

A. Bartlett Giamatti notes, in his discussion of the centrality of exile to Petrarch, that exile is less a narrative strategy than an ontological state. Giamatti contends that Petrarch's "sense of identity depended on being displaced, for only in perpetual exile could Petrarch gain the necessary perspective on himself truly to determine, or create, who he was. Only by being eccentric, could he center, or gather in and collect, his self" (p. 13). Only by being "eccentric"—"Other"—can the poet achieve that distance required to embark on the revision of his marginality. Marginality, displacement, alienation, loss, desire, nostalgia—these are the tropes of exilic writing. Aphra Behn's pastoral lyric, "Our Cabal," reflects an engagement of this psychological complexity inherent in exilic writing with its representation of authorial voice and the problem of isolation. The poem opens with a lighthearted exhortation to two friends, "Come, my fair Cloris, come away, / Hast thou forgot 'tis Holyday? / And lovely Silvia too make haste" (Behn, 1993, p. 47). For the remainder of the lyric, the reader is presented with an intimate gaze into a controversial discursive space—gossip.

Behn's use of the pastoral convention to frame her handling of gossip resonates with Patricia Meyer Spacks's suggestion that we think of "gossip as a version of pastoral. Not just any gossip: the kind that involves two people, leisure, intimate revelation and commentary, ease and confidence" (p. 3). In this context, gossip is valued for "the opportunity it affords for 'emotional speculation'" (p. 3). Gossip provides a continuum where exchanges both private and public can be made. These exchanges can, as Spacks contends, have significant effect outside its original context. Yet, because gossip "insists on its own frivolity," it frequently reifies the tendency to view it as a morally or socially suspect form of discourse and thus dismissable. What needs to be iterated here is that gossip also is predicated on the notion of absence and on the creation of an "in-group" (a concept that will become clearer as this essay evolves).

Thomas Parrot's satire "The Gossips Greeting: Or, A new Discovery of such Females Meeting" (1620) illustrates this problematic tendency and the serious social implications of gossip that its "frivolity" masks. "The Gossips Greeting" depicts a conversation between two women (Doll and Bess) who have embarked on a visit to a woman who has just given birth. Their discussion centers on the circumstances of different women in the town or village where Doll and Bess live. In particular, the women's talk focuses on the situation of "gossip Kate," a woman whose husband, "whilst all the weeke at home poore heart she toyle, . . . doth abroad live of the spoyle." According to one of the women, Kate's husband "beates and spurnes her" and "doth keepe a Queane e'ne vnderneath her Nose." While Parrot's purpose in depicting the exchange is to "censure" these "proud, peevish, pavltry, pernicious, she-pot companions, those curious, careless, craft, carping, curtizanicall gossips," his tale engenders a very different portrait than his vituperative comments presuppose.

What becomes obvious in Parrot's characterization of gossip is that the women seem to recognize the importance of alliances and communities generated within, yet distinct from, those instituted by the larger social order, namely marriage and family. Doll and Bess (and others) apparently come together to exchange information, to participate in rituals associated with childbirth (including banquets), and to condemn the antifemale behavior exemplified in Kate's husband. These women's relationships and connections with other women seem to play an important part in not only the social aspect of their lives but also in their individual self-awareness. The alliance of women who form the gossip's network in Parrot's work resists the arbitrary delineation of gossip as trivial. Rather, they illustrate the ways in which this discursive act engenders a range of possibilities for women to function as social agents. For example, upon hearing of Kate's predicament, Doll declares that "were I to chuse againe, I ne're would loue / A ciuill man; a man to all mens sight, Louing and courteous." For, Doll reflects, "I see, and do perceiue it now, . . . / That countenance and conscience seldome gree." Doll's words—even if contradictory to Parrot's intent—attest to the power of the gossips' network; the lesson of Kate's fate, for all women, is to beware of what floats on the surface, for it just may be that— superficial.

Behn's "Our Cabal" similarly reveals the protean quality of gossip, yet with a somewhat different revelation. Transgressing the boundaries between literacy and orality, the poem figuratively "gossips" into existence a complex series of alliances: between reader and poem, reader and speaker, and reader and the women of the poem. As Spacks argues, "gossip speaks in the world's voice and elucidates the world's operation" (p. 8); this world, however, is embodied in one person—the narrator. Images of triviality, solidarity, and self-representation are textured by the readers' knowledge of the writer's isolation and, at the same time, her figurative centeredness in the lyric. As privileged spectators, the reader and the poet's companions thus become implicated in the speaker's act of gossip and the images she creates: "'Tis Philocles, that Proud Ingrate, / That pays her Passion back with Hate" (*Works*, 55–56). Most of the speaker's comments, however, are intended to foster a link between the three women gathered in the room—"yes, Silvia, for sh'l not deny / She loves, as well as thou and I"—or to convey a compassion toward those women abused by a lover, "Poor Doris, and Lucinda too." Even when the narrator sympathetically recounts the difficulties facing one lover, Martillo, there is an absence of condemnation for the object of Martillo's desire. Gossip thus serves not as a malicious force in Behn's lyric, but also as a powerful intervention in the larger world.

In the course of her narrative, the speaker tells Cloris about Philander's "passion" for Lycidas: "So innocent and young he is, / He cannot guess what Passion is. / But all the Love he ever knew, / On Lycidas he does bestow" (183–86). Earlier, Lycidas had been described as a "haughty Swain," who "Barely returns Civility" to the "Beauties" to whom he once vowed "much Love" (149–54). More important, as the speaker confides, Lycidas's fickleness is truly reprehensible because he "pays his Tenderness" to Philander (Mr. Ed. Bed.) in a manner the speaker labels "too Amorous for a Swain to a Swain" (187–88). The frivolous intimacy established at the poem's inception gradually gives way in light of Cloris's disclosure of her affection for Philander. Warming to her account of Lycidas's perfidy, the speaker details his manner and record of abusing women's "hearts." Yet her words appear to be of no avail as, she reveals, she (and others) often have heard Cloris "Vow, If any cou'd your heart subdue, / Though Lycidas you nere had seen, / It must be him, or one like him" (202–4). Her concern prompts the speaker to warn Cloris to "keep your heart at home" (200). Yet, realizing that her efforts are ineffectual, the speaker decides to try another tack and exhorts Cloris to "try thy power with Lycidas; / See if that Vertue which you prize, / Be proof against those Conquering Eyes" (221–22).

The trace of scorn in these words sits uneasy against the sense of alliance that I am suggesting exists between the women in the chamber, yet I would argue that the speaker's challenge resonates with affection and friendship. Our ability to see the bond between the speaker and Cloris is heightened if we take seriously the significance of the poem's title, since the word cabal generally evokes images of secrecy, intrigue, and political coteries, usually comprised by men. Behn's use of the word to describe the group of three women gathered in the chamber, therefore, only serves to heighten the ironic disjunction between the poem's title and its contents, especially since the poem seems concerned not with state affairs but the affairs of women. Even so, by labeling the three women a cabal Behn resists the reification of her poem as merely frivolous. While the orality of the poem's gossip infers its place as part of a private exchange of information, the textuality of the poem emphasizes the importance of gossip to the formation of alliances. The small community of women depicted in the poem functions in the interest of female homosociality. These women gather to share information and offer advice and warnings. Alliance, not competition and rivalry, becomes the frame of reference for the three women who make up Behn's cabal. Gossip and "cabal," as both contradictory terms and social paradigms, work to engender a radical rewriting of the politics of both speech and agency among women.

Amid the seemingly trivial details of contradictory love affairs, heartless men, stunning beauty, and alliances recounted in "Our Cabal" is an image of exile so unassuming that it is easily overlooked: the poet writing. If exile is "a lifelong scenario of estrangement," then what enables the writer to come to terms with exile is her ability to create "not only a new space to exercise one's being but a medium through which to reimagine one's beginnings" (Seidel, p. 5). The idea of the pastoral thus powerfully aids this poetic exercise; its laconic and simple frames of reference (shepherds and shepherdesses, rural topography, and emphasis on the idea of retreat) mark the linguistic intersections where the poet can find, if only temporarily, the means to ease the loss by constituting new alliances. In "Our Cabal," Behn's idealization of alliance conceals the fact that the figure who sits at the center of the alliance, the speaker, is in fact alienated from that which she narrates. Yet the poem itself reminds us that exiles do work in isolation, to create a "psychic space" in order to "weave their web of story." The illusion of conversation, of gossip, is what points to the exile of the represented authorial voice in "Our Cabal." Behn's use of gossip incorporates the writer and reader as speaking and listening subjects, respectively, thereby implicating both as sharers in the communal narrative under construction. Yet, because she is both speaker and writer, Behn mediates the ways this representation can be understood. As Spacks rightfully argues, in gossip the "presence of even a single observer would change the conversation's character: no longer true gossip, only a simulacrum" (p. 8). The creation of a spectorial position that encompasses reader and writer as one masks this fact in Behn's poem.

"Our Cabal" is indeed a simulacrum, one shaped by the self-reflexivity of the writing poet, shadowing its ghostly images of exile in visions of alliance and community. Gossip permits the poet to indulge in a retreat into the idyllic world of the pastoral poem, where loss is defined only in terms of hearts. The poem purposely yet subtly refracts our gaze from its own exilic condition by highlighting the alliance between the three women, thereby concealing the alienated position of the writer who figures herself as simultaneously a member and an outsider of the figurative alliance imagined in "Our Cabal." The lyric is never free of the intrusive presence of its own constitutive moment; there is, after all, the specificity of a woman, Aphra Behn, writing a poetic account of an intimate exchange between friends long after the moment has passed. What "Our Cabal" reveals is the dialectics of writing the defense against the exilic condition; to frame a representation of community, especially through the trope of gossip, the poet must also frame its opposition: isolation and disconnectedness.

Like "Our Cabal," the poetic epistle "To Mrs. Price" figuratively instantiates a pastoral defense against exile, though one which more explicitly elucidates the poet's sense of isolation and her desire to constitute a community to which she can belong. The letter writer begins by celebrating the absence of "noisy Factions of the Court" from the "peaceful Place where [she] gladly" resorts (1). This site is sylvan; the only sounds heard are the "gentle Sighs of Love" as "Nymphs and Swains" prepare for "rural Sports" (6–7). In such a world, the writer notes, any deviation from the norm is quickly redressed: "if by Chance is found a flinty Maid, / Whose cruel Eyes has Shepherds Hearts betray'd," she in "other Climes a Refuge . . . must find, / Banish'd from hence Society of Kind" (9–12). The epistle ends with the writer evoking images of union, of calm, of peace, and exhorting the addressee, "kind Aemilia," to "flie that hated Town, / Where's not a Moment thou canst call thy own," and "share the Pleasures I count only mine" (19–22). What floats to the surface of the epistle is the idyllic, the "retreat" of the poet into what is an acceptable form of exile—the pastoral economy. Yet the poet's own status as a lover (or beloved) in this economy is curiously ambiguous. As in "Our Cabal," the writer alludes to an involvement in an amorous relationship, but the language of the poem and epistles suggests that this relationship is long past and there is no indication that she is involved in a new one. The locus of the writer's attitude is one of detachment;

she is, in effect, the unmarked observer in this tranquil community: part of, yet alien from, the "Society of Kind." Poignantly, she writes that "ev'ry Object adds to our Delight, / Calm is our Day, and peaceful is our Night," even as she sits in solitude penning an epistle to Aemilia.

Benedict Anderson has argued that "communities are to be distinguished, not by their falsity/genuineness, but by the style in which they are imagined" (p. 16). The "imagined community" in "To Mrs. Price" is one where exile is an explicit condition of existence, but it is a condition that is idealized and desirable. In the interstices of the poet's meditation, however, we realize that what seeps to the surface of her exuberance is the emotional and psychic state that the lyric's pastoral conventions cannot entirely obscure. We, as privileged readers, discover what the exile comes to understand as the episteme of exile: there is no adequate replacement for what has been lost. In fact, what makes this epistle more revelatory than Behn's "Our Cabal" is that it paradoxically engages and avoids its own condition of existence. And, in an oft-repeated sign of deferral, the writer seeks not the society that surrounds her but the solace of an already constituted alliance—in effect, seeking the "familiar and friendly."

"To Mrs. Price" illuminates the longing of the subject to resolve the psychic crisis of exile. Despite the pastoral setting, the easy congress among nymphs and swains, the tranquil days and peaceful nights, the writer seems uneasily reconciled with the "Happiness divine" which she claims to have found. Beneath the pastoral language and the air of calm is the suggestive unspoken: the psychic upheaval created by exile. The pastoral world our poet has turned to is a mixture of "tuneful Anger" and "Sighs of Love," of "Cruel eyes," "flinty" maids, and "Nymphs and Swains." The epistle's language is replete with images of death, betrayal, and difference. What we discover upon closer scrutiny is that embedded in the pastoral imagery is a moving plea for succor, for relief from exile. Discord, betrayal, banishment, cruelty, flight, and death are constant reminders of the inadequacy of the pastoral epistle as a defense against exilic loss. As Isis and Thame join, "mixt, embracing, they together flie, / They Live together, and together Die," (15–16) the reader is aware that the joining is temporary, already anticipating its own demise. The word "Die" hovers over the lyric, a sign of mortality and loss, and perhaps despair—a striking contrast to the image of concord that directly follows. In the end, despite the writer's initial praise of the "peaceful Place where I gladly resort," one cannot help but wonder if there isn't a bit of self-mockery in the epistle's final words: "Haste for to meet a Happiness divine, / And share the Pleasures I count only mine" (21–22).

The epistle leaves the reader with an image of a female alliance that is all the more significant when we consider that the epistolary form is an attempt to bridge the disconnectedness and the isolation of the writer, and the loss (even if temporarily) of community or alliances. The epistle is framed in solitude and inflected by the loss of a lover and the potential loss of a friend even as its discourse harkens to an alliance. The epistle's writer makes use of Aemilia's absence to consider the effects of the loss of connection by revisiting the moment in which the connection was engendered. Even so, Behn's epistle reveals none of the sadness or the emotional sorrow associated with exile; for in the moment when the writer must confront her loss, she defers the inevitable reckoning by dealing with another's passions. Exile is deferred but not erased.

"Ego in exilio genitus, in exilio natus sum"

"Was Aphra Behn passing?"[1]

This question was put to me during a brief conversation with African-American scholar Frances Smith Foster concerning Behn's personal and professional history. Foster's question clearly implied color passing and my reply was a decisive "no," for it seemed to me, at the time, that Behn's biographers were quite thorough and the evidence indisputable. However, as I pursued my consideration of Behn's writings and the cultural milieu in which she lived, Foster's softly spoken query haunted my reflections. Questions multiplied, leaving their liminal traces in every opinion, every sentence, every paragraph of what I read.

The word "passing" has a curious and complex sociolexical history in Anglo-American culture. According to *Webster's International Dictionary*, the definition of pass is, "to move or be transferred from one place, state, or condition to another; to change possession, condition or circumstances, to undergo transition or conversion." The word, in both its noun and verb forms, has also come to signify death; that is, rather than say a person died, one might use the verbal phrase "he passed away" or "he passed on" or, simply, "he passed," or "his passing was unexpected." There is another definition of "passing" that has its genesis in all these definitions and yet is distinctive in its own right. This "passing" marks the process whereby a person self-consciously enters into an identity made possible by the instability and uninhabitability of the very ideologies created to prevent such entries. Once entering into this identity, however, the passer must maintain the boundaries of this identity, vigilantly guarding against the slippages, erasures, and exposures that once defined her/him in terms of another identity. The objective is never to be found out.

In one of the most cogent and intelligent discussions of racial and sexual passing, Amy Robinson writes that "sexual preference and race [provide modern racial theorists] . . . with a simple schema of optic dichotomies. That is, subjects were presumed to be either white or black, either straight or gay, as visual paradigms of racial and sexual identity manufactured presumption as a choice between legible social identities" (pp. 717–18). And, she continues, in "such an economy of readable identity, the successful passer only disappears from view insofar as she appears (to her reader) to be the category into which she has passed" (p. 718). Optic knowability, which is rooted in a simple paradigm of either/or identity and is "visible as an epistemological guarantee" to both the passer and the "dupe," is what makes the successful pass. Finally, according to Robinson, what enables passing is "the multiple codes of intelligibility," where an "in-group" ("the group from which one has passed") has intuitive recognition of the "prepassing identity," and a "duped" group sees the "manufactured presumption" of identity in terms of a simple paradigm of social identity. The result, Robinson cogently demonstrates, is a set of "competing rules of recognition," that is, rules predicated upon an opposition to a set of normative standards associated with epidermal, behavioral, or cultural difference.

If Behn was a "passer," from which parent did she inherit her black African ancestry? How did that ancestor end up in Canterbury, if the parish records cited by Behn's biographers are accurate? If she were of "mixed heritage" would there be a cultural necessity for her to engage in "racial passing"? Lastly, what clues, what sort of "evidence," did she leave behind for an inquisitive reader, and can her writings be used to decipher the enigma? What if Behn intended her writings to be read as a "passing" narrative? What if the psychic trauma of conformity to a dominant paradigm of racial identity in early modern English culture engendered in the subject Aphra Behn a hypersensitivity to the contradictions between the passer's ethnicity and the dominant culture into which she assimilates? How would she go about inscribing codes of intelligibility that aid the "reading" of the pass? To explore these and other questions, one would need to argue for a textual and biographical history that if Behn did pass the pass would not be documented—at least not in conventional ways. The reason is obvious: for the individual who engages in color passing, there is always the danger of being found out, of being exposed as a passer. One fears the birth of children, the chance meeting with someone from the old community, the invisible traces of blackness. Passing clearly was not something one did on a whim.

Rather than attempt to prove definitively that Behn may have had a black African ancestor and that, as a result, she was engaged in color passing, I propose to explore the semiotic "machinery" that triggers for an "in-group" the very question Foster asked of me. The problem in the analysis is that in order for a pass to be known there has to be a relationship of complicity between the passer and an "in-group," usually on the part of anyone who knew the passer before the pass. This person (or persons) generally acquiesces to the pass by not revealing it. The epistemological difficulty in my analysis is that Behn and anyone constituted as a contemporaneous member of an "in-group" died three hundred years ago. However, there is another way of "knowing" the pass, of establishing one's status as a member of the "in-group"—intuition. By "intuition," I am invoking Robinson's deployment of the word: "If the action of sight requires a subject, then intuition summons a denotation of unmediated access to a truth whose function is the fortification of the subject who looks. It is thus no accident that the eyes are named as the privileged vehicle of intuitive knowledge" (p. 720). What intuition enables, in Robinson's words, is the "visibility of the apparatus of passing—literally the machinery that enables the performance. What the in-group sees is not a stable prepassing identity but rather the apparatus of passing that manufactures presumption (of heterosexuality, of whiteness) as the means to a successful performance" (p. 721).

Throughout this discussion, the possibility of a "passing" Aphra has stood quietly, a cultural wraith hovering at the margins of my reading and, I would argue, who stood looking over the poet's shoulder, guiding her quill as she embeds the codes of intelligibility and the traces of her passing in her literary writings. In the conflicting signifiers of alliance and estrangement, the question of racial subjectivity dances tantalizingly on the margins in an illusory (and at times elusive) gesture of remembrance until it finds release in the writing subject's most explicit narrative of exile, the novella *Oroonoko*. What I propose to do in the final pages of this essay is to position my reader as a member of the "in-group" that forms part of the triangular condition of Behn's pass, and to guide this reader through an act of intuition to literally discern the pass.

Published in 1688, *Oroonoko* ostensibly recounts the biographical history of an African prince forcibly taken from his homeland and sold into slavery in the English colony of Surinam. The story of Oroonoko's exile is purportedly told to the author, who in turn localizes that narrative in print form. In the telling of Oroonoko's history, the narrator also instantiates her own, producing what Margaret Ferguson notes are complex and multivalent representations of early modern colonial subject positions. In this and other recent feminist discussions of *Oroonoko*, readings of the racial dimension of the novella have centered on the complicated figuration of author and narrative object (Behn and Oroonoko), white woman and black man (again Behn and Oroonoko), and white woman and black woman (Behn and Imoinda). Because the narrator represents herself as a member of the dominant class, and because this representation is taken as "true," the possibility of a third racial paradigm is rarely considered: namely, that the racial triangulation may not be white/black/black, but black/black/black. To explain this provocative hypothesis I want to focus on two often noted yet narrowly read descriptions in the novella. The first is the complicated description of Oroonoko's racial identity. According to the narrator, Oroonoko was:

> pretty tall, but of a shape the most exact that can be fancied; the most famous statuary could not form the figure of a man more admirably turned from head to foot. His face was not of that brown, rust black which most of that nation are, but a perfect ebony, or polished jet. His eyes were the most awful that could be seen, and very piercing; the white of them being like snow, as were his teeth. His nose was rising and Roman, instead of

African and flat. His mouth, the finest shaped that could be seen; far from those great turned lips, which are so natural to the rest of the Negroes. The whole proportion and air of his face was so noble, and exactly formed, that, bating his colour, there could nothing in nature more beautiful, agreeable and handsome. (Behn, 1992, p. 81)

Interestingly, Margaret Ferguson does not make much of this description in her otherwise excellent analysis of *Oroonoko*. Laura Brown, on the other hand, argues that, in describing Oroonoko, "Behn's narrator seems to have only two choices: to imagine the other either as absolutely different and hence inferior, or as identical and hence equal" (Laura Brown, "The Romance of Empire: Oroonoko and the Trade in Slaves," in *The New Eighteenth Century*, ed. Laura Brown and Felicity Nussbaum (New York: Methuen, 1978), p. 48). Thus Brown views the description of Oroonoko as the "failure of Behn's novella to see beyond the mirror of its own culture [that] here raises the question of Behn's relationship with the African slave" (p. 48).

Brown's observation points tantalizingly to what is an intriguing depiction in Behn's novella: the inverse mirroring implied in that relationship when the novella is read as a text of passing. In other words, what the novella may position the "knowing" reader to do is to ignore the optical illusion and "intuit" that Oroonoko is constitutive of the authorial subject, just as the authorial subject contains the black African. To read Behn's novella in this fashion, of course, undermines not only assumptions about Behn's racial identity but also our own complicity in the "false promise of the visible as an epistemological guarantee" (Robinson, p. 716). I want to argue that Behn's novella, coming as it does at the end of her life, schematizes an optic dichotomy whereby the passer reveals herself to an "in-group." It is this suggestive but unexamined possibility, latent but unexamined in any of the recent criticism of *Oroonoko*, that Behn invites "us to see and ponder the fact that we are not seeing the 'whole truth' about her white or non-white characters, including herself" (Ferguson, 1994, p. 189).

Nearly two-thirds into the narrative the narrator remarks:

My stay was to be short in that country, because my father died at sea, and never arrived to possess the honour was designed him (which was lieutenant-general of six and thirty islands, besides the continent of Surinam), nor the advantages he hoped to reap by them, so that though we were obliged to continue on our voyage, we did not intend to stay upon the place. (Behn, 1992, p. 115)

This interjection, of course, serves two purposes: first, it validates the authenticity of the narrative by concretizing the author's presence in both the story and Surinam; and second, it allies the author to the governing structure of the slave society that is Surinam. In addition, the passage also establishes the involuntary exile to Surinam of both narrator and Oroonoko. Both individuals have been brought to an alien world;

the difference is that one enters this world as a slave and the other as, ostensibly, a member of the conquering class.

What is interesting about this "biographical" statement is that nowhere before or after are readers made privy to the Christian names of the narrator or her father. This oversight (?) takes on greater importance when one considers that, since the initial publication of *Oroonoko*, the novella has been used as an evidentiary site in the historical excavation of Aphra Behn's life. One explanation for this absence of patronymic detail is, of course, the fact that Behn is writing a fictional narrative and such details are not necessary for plotting. Another, and more controversial, reason may well reside in the notion that the passage is intentionally ambiguous; that Behn chooses not to name her father or, more relevant to this discussion, her mother. It is this latter possibility that intrigues me. Were we to read *Oroonoko* as the passing subject's "subtle claim of telling in the absence of knowing—[or] 'it takes one to know one'"—we might discover a more complex enunciation of the racial subjectivity of an author in exile. (See Amy Robinson, "It Takes One to Know One: Passing and Communities of Common Interest." *Critical Inquiry* 20 (Summer 1994), pp. 721.)

Central to my reading is the supposition that it is in exilic writing that we find the codes that would reveal the pass. Though not often described as such, the phenomenon of passing is literally a form of exile. As the passage from Nella Larsen's novel *Quicksand and Passing* cited at the opening of this essay indicates, the passing subject breaks away from "all that is familiar and friendly" and constitutes a new identity and a new life "in another environment, not entirely strange, perhaps, but certainly not entirely friendly" (pp. 186–87). Part of this constitution involves replacing old alliances with new ones, finding ways to negotiate the very real possibility that one can never return to the pre-passing environment without revealing the pass. For the passing subject, as this essay's epigram suggests, the pass is not without costs. In writing about the exile, one becomes acutely and often painfully aware of the intricate lability of her or his identity, for exile allows time, ever so much time to reflect on what it means even to conceive of oneself as an individual, as a subject, as an exile.

What deep secrets about her identity would Behn desire to conceal in the fictive anonymity of her genesis? Is there more to her "exile" than she tells? The possibility that there may be a more direct tie linking the novella's author and Oroonoko—a link forged not in Surinam but in that miscegenous space of the early modern European slave trade—has not been explored. What if the narrator's grandmother was of African ancestry and, given the dire situations facing any person of African bloodlines in early modern English colonies, the novella's author was engaged in racial passing? How might the narrator discursively constitute Oroonoko's identity in light of anxiety associated with her own possible pass? To broach these questions (and attempt to address them) is to insist upon a critical awareness that, in the early modern English colonial spaces, not all relations of miscegenation necessarily ended as *Othello* or *Titus Andronicus*. Despite George Best's assertion that "blackeness proceedeth of some natural infection of the first inhabitants of that Countrey, and so all the whole progenie of them descended, are still polluted with the same blot of infection . . . by a lineall discent they have hitherto continued thus blacke" (Hakluyt, vol. 7, pp. 262–63), time proved this assumption a genetic fallacy: within four generations of miscegenation, the "White Ethiop" was a very real possibility, and with it the passing subject. And, it is this porous aspect of genetics, complicating the ideology of race, that marks the narrator's complex and troubling representations of self and Oroonoko.

In his study of writing and exile, *Transgressions of Reading: Narrative Engagement as Exile and Return,* Robert D. Newman argues that what exiled writers do is "continually define themselves in relation to what is absent, their homeland, which they simultaneously embrace and deny. Their recreation of that homeland, necessarily infused with irony, demonstrates memory as a revisionary act and history as an exercise in narrative memory" (pp. 1–2). As a consequence:

> their mental [or, I would posit, poetic] returns are guided by the necessity of making that home, which was once an extension of Self, Other, in part so as to preserve the home that now is. This necessitates alienation from oneself, the Self that was and that still is present as an influence upon and aspect of the present Self. (p. 2)

For Newman, "irony" becomes a "natural vehicle for the writer as exile. The authorial Self is extended into the character functioning within a setting that recalls a previous Self of the author through a present interpretation, and thus must be ironically distanced as Other" (p. 2). And Newman concludes, "readers engaged by a text function much like exiles, viewing the narrative as a type of homeland in which they can no longer live." Persons who engage in racial passing must leave the community of their birth, their families, and, most important, all social and cultural traces of a "pre-passing" identity. What is not discarded (as passing literature demonstrably illustrates) are the "mnemonic traces" of connection, kinship, and belonging, which form the basis of a desire to recreate if not the originary community itself at least a simulacrum. What these exiles discover is that substitute can never stand in for the original. There is no return home.

In the silent space of the poet's room, did the poet's subjectivity come into existence as a memoir of a moment that is a remembrance of a racial past? Did Behn glance out a small window overlooking a busy street in St. Bride's Parish and see a woman of African ancestry struggling to deal with the life of servitude engendered by the color of her skin? Did Behn mentally strip the blouse from the woman's back and see the evidence of a maternal ancestor's resistance to slavery, to rape? Did she see the

African man who had fathered the woman's first child and died trying to prevent both from becoming property of the Portuguese, Dutch, or English slaver? Did Behn unconsciously perceive in the woman the liminal figure of a mother whose *mestizaje* (mixedness) drew the sexual attention of a white planter in Barbados? Are these the constitutive images, the "secret ciphers," along with her own passing, inscribed in the representations of self and Oroonoko, in the depiction of nonroyal black Africans? Is the African prince the self who constitutes Behn's "other"; an abject display of the psychic trauma of passing?

There are no definitive answers to these queries; not enough evidence exists even to establish with absolute certainty Behn's parentage, let alone her ethnicity. What the questions allow me to do is to engage Behn's texts and her position as an authorial subject in early modern England in a manner that permits an epistemological rethinking of the early modern concept of race. It is most often in exile that racial memories can condition the poetics of writing. More significant, it is the resemblances of new alliances to earlier ones that often force the poet to revisit continually the painful memories of what has been lost and, in the process, to return to the moment which triggered the memory. This circularity of remembrance becomes, as it were, a tabula rasa for a "plausible history." Struggling to erase from memory the painful refrains of the *canzoniere di razza*, the *chanson de race*, or the *cantar de raza*, the poet seeks but fails to castigate from her soul the knowledge of her exile.

Writing from and in exile, the passer creates with an aim to "feign telling the truth by feigning to feign" (Derrida, pp. 84–85). The secret cipher of the author's race becomes intelligible when read not only through *Oroonoko* but, more important, through each of Behn's other works as well. However, this intelligibility can only occur when exile ceases to be metaphoric and becomes actual: that is, when alliances and communities fragment, and the narrator can no longer poetically mediate the condition of her exile. Although "Our Cabal," "To Mrs. Price," and *Oroonoko* were published, they resonate as private exchanges, a confidential diary left open for the invading reader, revealing the extraordinary psychic price of exile and passing. The passer must create new alliances and a new identity in an alien world. And although Behn's poetic writings reveal that, for a woman in exile, the creation of alliances with women may somewhat alleviate the sense of loss, the pain of exile never truly disappears. It is not implausible that, in the "secret ciphers" that mark her texts, Aphra Behn has left behind the inscriptions of the genealogy of her exile, her passing, for the intuitive reader. Perhaps, in the figure of Isis (with its dual allusion to the English river near Oxford and the Egyptian goddess, both of which Behn would have known) Behn writes the double histories of her origins and exile. Perhaps, in writing women's alliances into her poetic meditations on exile, Behn came to understand the painful irony that forever escapes women such as Irene

Redfield in Larsen's *Quicksand and Passing:* when passing, a person can never fully account for herself until the two halves of her divided self "live together, and together Die."

NOTE

1. The quote in the heading comes from A. Bartlett Giamatti, *Exile and Change in Renaissance Literature* (New Haven, Conn.: Yale University Press, 1984), p. 12.

16

Aemilia Lanyer and the
Invention of White Womanhood

. . . .

BARBARA BOWEN

"WOMAN," IN THE late-capitalist United States at least, is a racial term. Some of the most powerful work of modern feminism has been devoted to revealing the correlation between race and womanhood that white supremacy must suppress; "all the women are white," the title of a black feminist collection observed in 1982 (Hull et al.). Eve Sedgwick identifies as one of the two great "heuristic leaps" of feminism the recognition that all forms of oppression, though they are structured differently, "must intersect in complex embodiments" (Sedgwick, 1990, p. 33). Where patriarchy coexists and collaborates with white supremacy, "woman" silently encodes at least race, and possibly also class, age, sexuality, ethnicity, physical ability, even weight. Not all women are women. Even as feminists undertake a necessary deconstruction and historicizing of the category "women,"[1] the positioning of some women to reify the womanhood of others persists, with material consequences that become increasingly clear as we enter a global economy.

While women of color and other feminists have made it possible to see the ways in which womanhood is epistemologically complicit with racism, it is perhaps surprising to find that the racialization of "women" was forecast as early as 1611, in one of the first published volumes of original verse by an English woman. Aemilia Lanyer's poem on the passion of Christ, written as England underwent a massive shift in its relation to the world, is an extended meditation on womanhood as a social rather than individual identity, and one at least partly constituted by exclusion. I want to suggest that the grounds for exclusion, as articulated by the poem, are racial ones, with all the complexity that "race" in this period entails. Titled, or as I shall argue mistitled, *Salve Deus Rex Judaeorum* (Hail, God, King of the Jews), Lanyer's poem is actually not one work but many, a series of texts folded in on a disappearing central narrative of the crucifixion. *Salve Deus* stages a dialectic of inclusion and exclusion, with the poet's own status as a woman at stake; of Jewish and Italian descent at a time when both were racialized and "race" was being newly mobilized as a political category, Lanyer writes womanhood as womanhood's Other.[2] My aim is to read the political unconscious of the poem, restoring to its surface the sometimes repressed reality of a gendered and racialized history of struggle,[3] and focusing attention somewhat away from the questions that have so far dominated critical discussion. With a fine modern edition published in 1993 and a substantial body of criticism now in print,[4] *Salve Deus* is poised to become an increasingly central text in evaluations of early modern culture. As it moves into a near-canonical position, if only as "minor" literature, I want to urge that the poem be read for its extraordinary meditation on the racialized process through which early modern women constituted themselves as a group.

In connecting the racialization of womanhood with the beginnings of European hegemony and the distant but real economic relation between European women and the women subjugated by European merchant capitalists in Africa, the Americas, and Asia, I invoke the work of a growing number of scholars who have begun to turn their attention to the gendered history of racism, many of us seeking a basis of collective political agency that does not reinscribe racial domination.[5] To trace what Fredric Jameson calls the "solidarity" of the "forms, structures, experiences, and struggles" of the past with those of the present (p. 18), however, is not to deny the radical differences of history. That both race and gender ordinarily present themselves as unchanging or self-explanatory is a sign of the *success* of patriarchal and white supremacist regimes of knowledge; feminism must intervene to make these categories speak and deliver up their histories. Much of the emphasis of the rapidly developing scholarship on "race" has been on its historicity: not only do notions of race change over time and place, but race itself has no biological basis as a system of human classification—"racism invented race," as Fernand Braudel reminds us. Thus by examining continuities between early modern and late-capitalist formations of womanhood, I do not want to suggest that gender and race are unchanging categories; on the contrary, I hope to retrieve a history that has been systematically forgotten. The work of recovery is already under way by such scholars as Winthrop Jordan, Kim Hall, Ania Loomba, Margo Hendricks, and Lynda Boose, who have made clear the radical instability of the concept of "race" in early modern England, while much of the scholarship on gender in this period has served to complicate the notion of a simple binarism.[6] Nor is "whiteness" exempt from historicization; it needs to be understood as "a complexly constructed product of local, regional, national, and global relations, past and present" (Frankenburg, p. 236). With the concepts of race and gender in particular turmoil in early modern Europe and with both concepts radically bound by their historical moment, we are not going to find any simple origin for what might be called white womanhood. Lanyer's work beckons, however, because it speaks into this turmoil; *Salve Deus* does not so much explain as problematize white womanhood, an ideological formation that continues, in the twentieth century, to limit the possibilities of feminist thought and action.[7]

As a woman publishing a volume of original verse in 1611, Aemilia Lanyer (1569–1645) had almost no precursors[8]; it cannot be coincidental that this early attempt by a woman writer to participate in the literary print culture is also a meditation on the way women are socially defined. *Salve Deus Rex Judaeorum*, Lanyer's only known publication, is a complex plea for readmittance to court circles and resumption of aristocratic financial support; it is also arguably the most important text we have for an understanding of intellectual alliances among literate women in early modern England. One of the very few texts from the period to reflect on class relations among women, or to argue for a change in the poet's own relation to State power through the agency of women, *Salve Deus* is perhaps the only early modern English text to discuss women's communities from the perspective of a racialized outsider. It is now known that Lanyer was the daughter of an Italian Jew who was brought to England in 1541, along with his four brothers, to enhance the quality of the music at the court of Henry VIII.[9] Lanyer was also the discarded mistress of Queen Elizabeth's first cousin Henry Cary, Lord Hunsdon, and later the wife of a French musician, Alphonso Lanyer, who was also at the English court. If she wrote from any of the complicated subject-positions this history would have offered her, Lanyer would be an unusual voice among Jacobean writers. That she saw connections between these positions, and explored their epistemological implications for her as a writer of Christian narrative, makes her unique. But my interest is not so much in her singularity as in the radical impulses her work contains: Lanyer, I would suggest, is of major importance to the feminist project of recovering such initiatives in the texts of early women writers.

Despite its significance for a counterhegemonic reading of the Renaissance, however, *Salve Deus*, as a literary text produced at a time of mass illiteracy, cannot be taken as an expression of all oppositional or marginalized cultures; Jameson is instructive on the problem of the autonomy from history that printed texts project. "Since by definition," he writes, "the cultural monuments and masterworks that have survived tend necessarily to perpetuate only a single voice in [the] class dialogue, . . . they cannot be properly assigned their relational place in a dialogical system without the restoration or artificial reconstruction of the voice to which they were initially opposed" (p. 85). Although there is room for debate here—on the monological nature of canonical texts and on whether Lanyer's poem can be considered a cultural monument merely by having survived—Jameson's formulation provides a historical way of understanding some of the poem's most puzzling formal features: its recursiveness, its tendency to impede its own narrative progress,[10] its strange double-voiced character. *Salve Deus* is both a passionately religious work and a work with the secular position of women at heart. (For Lanyer, as we shall see, these two trajectories are not unconnected.) Her poem is a work of multiple digressions, of anger mixed with longing for aristocratic mothers, of passages demonizing the Jews within a reading of the crucifixion that exculpates at least Jewish women for Christ's death. While Lanyer does not represent the whole range of positions marginalized by early modern English society, she does at least intermittently force a usually silenced voice into the realms of bourgeois high culture. As a woman who was once part of the libidinal economy of the court (like but unlike the men of her family, all court musicians) and who seeks through her poem to win a new position within it, Lanyer is both insider and outsider; her poem speaks alternately in hegemonic and oppositional voices.

Lanyer's importance lies not only in the social position she occupied but in her ability to reconceptualize the master narratives of her culture from within her subject-position. We will be disappointed if we try to resuscitate her as a lyric poet on the order of Jonson or Donne; she needs to be seen outside the masculinist framework these poets and their readers have helped to establish.[11] Although there are lyrical passages in *Salve Deus* and evidence of an impassioned engagement with Jacobean literary culture, Lanyer's contribution is primarily her original critical readings of the world in which she struggled to conduct a public intellectual life. *Salve Deus* is an unapologetic attempt on the part of a Jacobean woman who was denied access to the profession of the male members of her family to be paid for cultural rather than sexual work. (Lanyer's position in the sexual economy is documented by the astrologer Simon Forman, whom she consulted several times in 1597 and whose sensationalized account of her visits provides a crucial, if unreliable, source on her life: "The old Lord Chamberlaine kept her longue She was maintained in great pomp. . . . She hath 40£ a yere and was welthy to him that maried her in moni and Jewells."[12]) It would be hard to overstate the intellectual ambitiousness of Lanyer's poem: this is a work that rewrites both of the major narratives of Christianity from a gendered perspective; that argues for an alternative, matrilinear patronage network in a unique series of dedications exclusively to women; that intervenes directly in a high-stakes legal battle over the right of a woman to inherit property; that invents (as female pastoral) the genre of the English country-house poem[13]; that calls into being, through its sustained address, a community of literate women. Its three sections—dedications, title-poem in *ottava rima*, and the country-house poem "The Description of Cookeham"—rewrite the scripts of patriarchy, in part by defining the collective interests of virtuous womanhood.

The poem's characteristic gesture is to turn from the individual woman to the collective; the gesture occurs in the extraordinary sequence of dedications, but its most vivid appearance is in Lanyer's revision of the story of the Fall. "Eves Apologie," as Lanyer entitles this section, comes halfway through the passion narrative, in which Lanyer gives the largest speaking part to Pilate's wife. The wife's voice displaces Pilate's and even Jesus', as her dream, the subject of one verse in Matthew's gospel,[14] becomes the pretext for an irruption of feminist argument into the mythic narrative. It is Lanyer's brilliant innovation to see that the two central events of Christianity can be linked by gender; if Eve's acceptance of the apple has meant that all women are indicted in the Fall, then guilt for the crucifixion should likewise indict all men. Pilate's wife attempts to clear Eve of blame (interestingly, portraying her as a woman in search of "knowledge") and then makes the poem's crucial leap from the theological to the social:

> Her sinne was small, to what you doe commit;
> . . .
> > This sinne of yours, surmounts them all as farre
> > As doth the Sunne, another little starre.
>
> Then let us have our Libertie againe,
> And challendge to your selves no Sov'raigntie;
> You came not in the world without our paine,
> Make that a barre against your crueltie;
> Your fault beeing greater, why should you disdaine
> Our beeing your equals, free from tyranny?
> > If one weake woman simply did offend,
> > This sinne of yours, hath no excuse, nor end.
> >   (pp. 86–87)

The jump from women's sin to the claim that women should have their liberty restored ("againe") is probably the most idiosyncratic moment in the poem, though humanist defenses of women had already argued for legal rights based on the spiritual equality of the sexes.[15] As it exposes and challenges the theological roots of patriarchy, the passage also hints, via a direct quotation from *The Rape of Lucrece*, that the crucifixion might be understood as a rape. Early in Shakespeare's poem, Tarquin considers whether he should go through with his planned assault on the virtuous Roman matron; he hesitates when he recalls his relation to Lucrece's husband: "But as he is my kinsman, my dear friend, / The shame and fault finds no excuse nor end" (237–38). That Lanyer dares to align the crucifixion with rape (and perhaps the Christian with the

Roman Republican myth of origin, one involving male sacrifice, the other female) suggests the radicalism of imagination that underlies this often conventional poem. The feminized Christ is not an original trope and functions in *Salve Deus* as an analogue to the sufferings of the female patron, but the passage allows Lanyer to voice one of the period's signal assertions of gender equality: "why should you disdaine our beeing your equals?" (Antisemitism had a similar theological basis and could be subject to a similar challenge; if such a connection is implied here, it is never directly made.) Lanyer's vision of prelapsarian Eden necessarily entails freedom from gender hierarchy, as becomes clear in the poem's final section, where gender liberation takes the form of a paradise populated exclusively by women.

My interest in moments like this one—where Lanyer points to the way in which womanhood has been historically created—is in the connection between definitions of women as a collective and the racialized exclusion of some women from womanhood. How much does Lanyer's community of women depend on a shared whiteness? By asking such a question I hope to offer an alternative to what Gayatri Spivak once called the "basically isolationist admiration" for the literature of women writers that "establishes the high feminist norm" (p. 262). Though feminist literary criticism has inched away from this position in the ten years since Spivak wrote "Three Women's Texts and a Critique of Imperialism," discussions of early periods, despite some important exceptions, tend to read women's texts within an analytic based on the English nation-state or at most on Europe.[16] Communities of women, even when formed discursively, seem to me especially subject to isolationist admiration: at the current historical moment they hold out the promise of female agency exercised outside of the privatized world of text or family. But poststructuralist thought has made it clear that communities tend to consolidate their identity through the nomination of an Other; one of the painful lessons of feminist history has been the extent to which white women's communities, even when formed for progressive purposes, have been *constitutive* of white racism. It is urgent, then, at this relatively early stage in the study of Renaissance women's alliances that we pay attention not only to "the complex embodiments" in which different social formations such as sexuality, religion, ethnicity, race, and gender overlap, but to the ways in which they consolidate existing relations of power as female alliances are formed. Particularly in the early modern period, as Europe was embarking on a period of expansionism that would come to be justified by theories of racial superiority, it cannot be taken for granted that alliances among white women were innocent of the ideology that was to emerge as racism.[17]

Toward the end of the fifteenth century Europe became the center of what has been described as the first "world-economy" (Wallerstein, p. 15), and the literature of this period has to be read within an analytic that accounts for that economy just as surely as American literature has

to be read within the context of what Toni Morrison calls a "wholly
racialized society" (Morrison, p. xii). Marx made the connection between
the activities of European merchant capitalism—"the discovery of gold
and silver in the Americas, . . . the beginnings of the conquest and plun-
der of India, and the conversion of Africa into a preserve for the hunt-
ing of blackskins"—and a European commercial war that made the world
into its theater (Marx, p. 915); Immanuel Wallerstein developed Marx's
idea by locating in this period "a kind of social system the world had
not really known before":

> It is an economic but not a political entity, unlike empires, city-states
> and nation-states. . . . It is a "world" system, not because it encompasses
> the whole world, but because it is larger than any juridically-defined
> political unit. And it is a "world-*economy*" because the basic linkage
> between the parts of the system is economic, although this was reinforced
> to some extent by cultural links and eventually . . . by political arrange-
> ments. (p. 15)[18]

While some aspects of Wallerstein's formulation may be open to question, his analysis seems to me a vital antidote to isolationist literary
criticism. Spivak wrote that it should be impossible to read nineteenth-
century British literature without attention to Britain's engagement in
imperialism (p. 262); it should be equally impossible to read sixteenth-
and seventeenth-century English literature outside of an international
context. Trade, colonialism, slavery, and migration impinge everywhere,
even where they are not explicitly at issue.[19] I propose to situate within
the new European world-economy one of the few Renaissance texts in
which a woman writer self-consciously identifies the nature of womanhood and argues for the existence of a women's community. As we shall
see, the text is embedded in a nexus of relations to the colonial enter-
prises of merchant capitalists that are not acknowledged in its exclusive
focus on England.[20] Like all cultural works from this period, *Salve Deus*
will yield new knowledge under the pressure of a reading that does not
serve the interests of nationalism. That the writer in this case occupied
a marginalized position within the English social structure—and that she
seized the margin as a place from which to speak—only makes her poem
a particularly compelling case for a kind of reading all early modern
European literature demands.

IN GROUNDBREAKING scholarship that has begun the development of a
new analytic for early modern literature, Kim Hall shows that "[t]he language of aesthetics is constitutive of the language of race" (Hall, 1994,
p. 179). By the sixteenth century, for instance, the word "fair" had acquired a racial meaning; it began to describe complexion as well as
beauty, and its antonym was now "dark" as well as "foul." This semantic shift, Hall demonstrates, coincided with England's entrance into the
African slave trade and the ideological use of "blackness to privilege

white beauty" (p. 183). Hall argues that women writers, necessarily conscious of the instability of their own subject-position as speakers in a
culture that prescribed silence for women, used the newly racialized
language in distinctive, gendered ways. Hall writes that Mary Wroth
and other literary women demonstrate, in their deployment of the tropes
of light and dark, a "simultaneous recognition of oppression and a will-
to-power" (p. 180), an impulse to consolidate their own tenuous position as authors through reference to women who can be othered. What
happens, though, when the woman writer is herself at least partially
Other, when she not only displays a "heightened sensitivity to difference and to the cultural implications of [her] own investment in the language of racial difference" (p. 179), but suggests that such language
defines her as outside of normative womanhood? Hall groups Lanyer
with Mary Sidney, Elizabeth Cary, and Mary Wroth, and reads the following moment from *Salve Deus* as part of a pattern of references to
Cleopatra by (white) women writers who use her "darkness" to differentiate her from themselves:

> No *Cleopatra*, though thou wert as faire
> As any Creature in *Antonius* eyes;
> Yea though thou wert as rich, as wise, as rare,
> As any Pen could write, or Wit devise;
> Yet with this Lady canst thou not compare,
> Whose inward virtues all thy worth denies:
> > Yet thou a blacke Egyptian do'st appeare;
> > Thou false, shee true; and to her Love more deere.
> > > (p. 112)

Lanyer is contrasting Margaret Clifford, her principal dedicatee, to
women who experience mortal love rather than the love of Christ:
"Great *Cleopatra's* love to *Anthony*, / Can no way be compared unto
thine." For Hall, the lines are evidence that Lanyer "clearly identifies
with the Roman Octavia" (p. 112), the "fair" woman, neglected wife
in Rome. But I am troubled by Lanyer's use of the second person ("*thou
wert as rich . . .*") and the fact that she shifts unexpectedly to direct
address here and the only other time she mentions Cleopatra.

The other reference comes early in the narrative, after an apparent
digression Lanyer calls "An Invective against outward beuty unaccompanied with virtue." In thirty-three stanzas that precede the formal beginning of the passion narrative, Lanyer addresses Margaret Clifford,
reminding her of God's ability to "behold [her] inward cares" (p. 53) and
commending her for withdrawing from court: "Leaving the world, before the world leaves thee" (p. 58). Lanyer catalogues God's powers
through a series of quotations from the Psalms (which in complex ways
address Mary Sidney's translation of the same Psalms), then praises
Clifford's refusal to substitute physical for spiritual beauty. The context
is significant, but consider first the turn to Cleopatra:

Twas Beautie bred in *Troy* the ten yeares strife,
And carried *Hellen* from her lawfull Lord; . . .
    Great *Cleopatraes* Beautie and defects
    Did worke *Octaviaes* wrongs, and his neglects.

What fruit did yeeld that faire forbidden tree,
But blood, dishonour, infamie, and shame?
Poore blinded Queene, could'st thou no better see,
But entertaine disgrace, in stead of fame?
Doe these designes with Majestie agree?
To staine thy blood, and blot thy royall name.
    That heart that gave consent unto this ill,
    Did give consent that thou thy selfe should'st kill.

                                            (p. 60)

The first two lines of this stanza are ambiguous: is Cleopatra the "forbidden tree," whose fruit Antony enjoys, or has Lanyer already begun
the apostrophe to Cleopatra, making adultery the tree and Cleopatra the
Eve-figure who picks the fruit? Given the exoneration of Eve that comes
later in the poem—"Was simply good, and had no powre to see" (p. 84)—
also phrased in terms of blindness, the connection suggested here between Eve and Cleopatra is important. Both are icons of female culpability; the suggestion may be that Cleopatra's story would be as radically
transformed as Eve's if Lanyer were to retell it. Although the poem leaves
the exoneration of Cleopatra as merely a suggestion, and in fact adduces
her as a counterexample to the "virtue" which is its central topic, there
is an intimacy with "the blacke Egyptian" that is unmatched in any of
Lanyer's other discussions of historical female figures. The second-
person address, not used elsewhere in the catalogue of women undone
by beauty, seems to register the pressure the black woman exerts on
Lanyer's text, forcing her to redirect her voice. These two moments may
betray intimacy as well as distance; they may originate in a sense of connection with Cleopatra that must be fended off through accusation.

    Without suggesting that Lanyer was in any simple way either "Jew-
ish" or "black," I want to explore how passages like this one position
her in relation to a racialized Jewishness in early modern England. (A
fuller treatment of Lanyer's position would need to investigate the range
of cultural meanings of Italianness and how they overlap with Jewishness as well as the *differences* between the positions of African and European Jewish women in the seventeenth century. Although the categories "black" and "Jewish" were frequently collapsed in early modern
writing, Lanyer cannot be taken to stand synecdochically for all racialized
women, nor can her voice alone substitute for a whole nonhegemonic
culture that has been obscured. The relation between social groups cannot be reconstructed from one text, even as dialogical a text as this.)
Lanyer presents herself as "dark" almost obsessively in the dedications,
a sequence of eleven texts that simultaneously envision a new kind of
female community and map out Lanyer's own social position. These are

autobiographical texts as well as epideictic ones; like Elizabeth Clinton in her treatise on breastfeeding or Anne Askew in her record of political interrogation, Lanyer finds in the interstices of her subject a space for writing her own life.

The use of multiple dedications exclusively to women is Lanyer's invention; although dedications to individual women were common, especially in the works of women writers, there is no precedent for her choice of nine female patrons. But what Lanyer invents is not just the trick of speaking exclusively to women; as Lorna Hutson has shown, the dedications implicitly show up the language of compliment as a rhetorical traffic in women. Together with the Cookham poem, the dedications—which comprise a full third of *Salve Deus*—make the point that Lanyer seeks an alternative patronage network, one that bypasses the existing structure designed to enable male production of culture. The language of lightness and darkness is highly conventional, especially in dedicatory writing, but Lanyer's reliance on these terms to negotiate a position from which to speak suggests that they had a special potency for her.

The opening poem announces the strategy for much of what follows, as the poet asks Queen Anne:

> From your bright spheare of greatnes where you sit,
> Reflecting light to all those glorious stars
> That wait upon your Throane; To virtue yet
> Vouchsafe that splendor which my meannesse bars:
>   Be like faire *Phoebe*, who doth love to grace
>   The darkest night with her most beauteous face.
>
> (p. 4)

Class, or more accurately social position within her class—what Lanyer calls "my meannesse"—is immediatcly translated into terms of light and dark. In a complex image, Lanyer represents her poem first as "virtue" then as "darkest night" on which the queen is asked to cast her light. Although the reference in the last line is to the poem, not to Lanyer herself, the conjunction of "darkest night" and "beauteous face" brings darkness close to the poet's body in a way that will occur several more times. Darkness and the poet's body are coupled again in the dedication to Margaret Clifford, where Lanyer apologizes for having "neither rich pearles of India, nor fine gold of Arabia" to offer the Countess. She appropriates Peter's description of himself as the healer who offers miraculous restoration rather than silver or gold (Acts 3:2–8), and uses it to position herself as a writer: "having neither rich pearles of India, nor fine gold of Arabia, nor diamonds of inestimable value . . . which were presented by those Kingly Philosophers to the babe Jesus I present unto you even our Lord Jesus himselfe" (p. 34). Lanyer is neither magus nor merchant: in this passage and another, where she is "honey" to Mary Sidney's sugar ("Though sugar be more finer, higher priz'd," p. 30),

Lanyer claims Englishness for herself and suggests that she is not a participant in the world-economy that benefits her patrons. Part of the complexity of the poem is that Lanyer can assert her Englishness and her gender in the same passage that represents her own body as a site of *difference*, for she goes on to compare Christ to a diamond and herself to the foil:

> The sweet incense, balsums, odours, and gummes that flowes from that beautifull tree of Life, sprung from the roote of *Jessie*, which is so super-excellent, that it giveth grace to the meanest & most unworthy hand that will undertake to write thereof; neither can it receive any blemish thereby: for as a right diamond can loose no whit of his beautie by the black foyle underneath it, neither by being placed in the darke . . . so this most pretious diamond . . . can receive no blemish, nor impeachment, by my unworthy hand writing. (pp. 34–35)

Her "hand" is ink, is blackness, is flesh; both her handwriting and her writing hand are the darkness that reveal the brightness of her subject and her patrons.

In her use of the imagery of blackness, Lanyer may be rewriting the topos of authorial humility by way of Mary Sidney, who, at a crucial point in establishing her own literary authority, draws on what Wendy Wall has termed "a debilitating discourse" that aligns the (white) woman writer with darkness. "To the Angell spirit," Sidney's dedication of the *Psalmes* to her brother, comments, "thou art fixed among thy fellow lights: / my day put out, my light in darkenes cast."[21] Wall sees this passage as part of Sidney's effort to invoke the stance of mourner as a legitimation for female authorship; "the powerful emotions of piety and grief" allow Sidney to clear a space for "an alternative poetics of display" (p. 317). Mary Wroth employs the same strategy in her *Urania* (1621), where she becomes, as Kim Hall has suggested, her own "dark lady," frequently comparing herself to night and at one point crying, "Let me be darke."[22] But unlike Sidney and Wroth (whose class and gender position, like that of Lanyer, was complicated by sexual history), Lanyer lives on the fringes of the aristocracy and constantly measures her distance from the world Sidney and Wroth inhabit. The litany of references to her patrons' brightness, together with the dreamlike repeated scene in which she imagines the patrons calling out to her, write her social distance into the poem: "Yet some of you me thinkes I heare to call / Me by my name" (p. 15); "as I wak'd me thought I heard one call" (p. 29)—so end her two allegorical visions of female community. What for Wroth and Sidney may be a gesture of self-erasure that ultimately allows access to poetic voice, for Lanyer becomes a gesture of self-exposure that dramatizes her position on the margins of the community of virtuous womanhood. Lanyer *is* the dark lady, but not in the sense A. L. Rowse maintains; the reluctance among critics to read race in *Salve*

Deus may have been compounded by Rowse, whose misogynistic account of Lanyer seems to have poisoned the topic of her darkness for feminists. The subject needs to be reclaimed from Rowse, however, as it is when we understand authorial darkness as a trope with a specific genealogy in women's writing—and one adapted by Lanyer to negotiate a gender position mediated by both class and sexuality.

If a racialized language of light and dark allows Lanyer to map her distance from the community of women to whom she speaks, the terrain of the erotic allows her to imagine a closeness that might otherwise seem too risky. One of the work's most haunting qualities is its figuration of *collective* female desire—both for the existence of all-women's discursive and physical spaces and for the eroticized male body of Christ. As Wall has shown in *The Imprint of Gender*, Lanyer displaces her own corporality as female poet onto this body; the dedications keep coming back to the image of Christ as bridegroom with the patrons exhorted to accept Christ as their lover. To "all vertuous Ladies in generall," Lanyer writes: "Put on your wedding garments every one, / The Bridegroome stayes to entertaine you all" (p. 12); to Susan Bertie, Countess of Kent, she says: "Receive your Love whom you have sought so farre / . . . Take this fair Bridegroome in your soules pure bed" (pp. 19–20). Lanyer inflects the parable of the wise and foolish virgins from Matthew (25:1–13) with the eroticism of the Song of Songs, the text through which Calvinist passion narratives regularly negotiate the treacherous erotic terrain of representing the body of the crucified Christ.[23] The community of virgins awaiting the bridegroom in Matthew become in Lanyer's text co-spouses of Christ, not merely guests at the wedding. As the poem offers the body of Christ the bridegroom and the crucified Christ as objects of scopophilic desire, an intense female community is established through a shared eroticism. The conventional device of the mirror—which comes to Lanyer through a rich history of Biblical exegesis (the Bible as a mirror reflecting divine truth), ethical exempla literature (the text, as Plutarch proposed, mirroring the reader's virtuous mind), and misogynistic discourse (the glass as the sign of gendered vanity)[24]—becomes in her hands an instrument of female mimetic desire: the imagined longing of each patron for Christ generates a longing for other women. *Salve Deus* offers itself as "the Mirror of a Worthy Mind" (p. 5); the dedications repeatedly signal the poem's connection to the tradition that views the mirror as a site of religious and ethical instruction, while they strive to disconnect the mirror from its association with women's "outward beuty." Seeking Christ in the reflection of their own virtuous reading, the patrons find each other; Lanyer eroticizes the mirror so that both Christ and other women become objects of desire. The poem draws deeply on Ovidian as well as Pauline meanings of reflection, but once again in a way that signals Lanyer's exclusion from the very community she creates. "Let your faire Virtues in my Glasse be seene" (p. 7), she writes to

Queen Anne; looking in the mirror of Lanyer's poem, Anne will become Narcissus, discovering the Other as a self. Only the poet, who cannot be "fair," remains on the dark side of the mirror.

The poem's most explicit comment on the racialized ideology of female beauty occurs in the "Invective against outward beuty unaccompanied with virtue." This is the passage that ends with the reference to Cleopatra as "Poor blinded Queene," and it is worth quoting in full:

> That outward Beautie which the world commends,
> Is not the subject I will write upon,
> Whose date expir'd, that tyrant Time soone ends;
> Those gawdie colours soone are spent and gone:
> But those faire Virtues which on thee attends
> Are alwaies fresh, they never are but one:
>   They make thy Beautie fairer to behold,
>   Than was that Queenes for whom prowd *Troy* was sold.
>
> As for those matchlesse colours Red and White,
> Or perfit features in a fading face,
> Or due proportion pleasing to the sight;
> All these doe draw but dangers and disgrace:
> A mind enrich'd with Virtue, shines more bright,
> Addes everlasting Beauty, gives true grace,
>   Frames an immortall Goddesse on the earth,
>   Who though she dies, yet Fame gives her new berth.
>
> That pride of Nature which adornes the faire,
> Like blasing Comets to allure all eies,
> Is but the thred, that weaves their web of Care,
> Who glories most, where most their danger lies;
> For greatest perills do attend the faire,
> When men do seeke, attempt, plot and devise,
>   How they may overthrow the chastest Dame,
>   Whose Beautie is the White whereat they aime.
>
> (pp. 59–60)

The passage has been subtly analyzed by Lorna Hutson, who reads it as part of an effort to reclaim the disclosure of female beauty from masculinist rhetoric. Refusing to articulate female virtue "as the incriminating display of the female body," Lanyer avoids "the analogical rhetoric through which such a display is produced, the rhetoric which implicitly strives to match 'those matchlesse colours Red and White'" (Hutson, 1992, p. 168). It is important to add to Hutson's analysis, however, that Lanyer's rewriting of the discursive beauty system is enabled by her critique of its fetishization of color.

In directing her (rare) irony towards "those matchlesse colours Red and White," Lanyer takes on the Petrarchan ideal at an especially charged moment in its history. The cult of red and white had a long medieval genealogy, but it was energized by the tradition of representing Elizabeth I in terms of her lily-and-rose beauty. Winthrop Jordan writes that

the English discovery of black Africans at the height of the commodification of "white" complexion in women had an important effect on the
development of racism (Jordan, p. 9) (figure 16-1); Lanyer delays the
passion narrative in order to distance herself from the ideal of beauty as
"fairness." Her repeated allusions to her own darkness, whether intellectual, social, or spiritual, resonate with this attack on the cult of whiteness; by its startling placement in a religious narrative, the "Invective
against outward beuty," in itself a conventional topic, recasts the allusions to darkness in the dedications as references to her own body. Like
Desdemona in a play she may well have seen, Lanyer racializes "fairness"
by recontextualizing the word. Replying to Iago's attempt to praise her
in the traditional terms for female beauty ("If she be fair and wise"),
Desdemona asks, "How if she be black and witty?" switching semantic
fields as she substitutes "black" for "foul." Iago responds: "If she be
black, and thereto have a wit, / She'll find a white that shall her blackness [hit]."[25] Hovering somewhere in this polysemous reply is a pun on
"the white" as the target in archery; this is the same pun Lanyer invokes
in the memorable conclusion of the "Invective": "Beautie is the White
whereat they aime." (She is directly quoting John Lyly here but probably also alluding again to *The Rape of Lucrece*, where Lucrece, a crucial
figure for Lanyer because of her ability to unite virtue with beauty, is
praised by her husband for her "unmatched red and white," p. 11.[26])
Lanyer's invocation of the White is at least as complex as Iago's: a poem
that repeatedly positions its author as black cannot innocently equate
beauty with whiteness, even by way of allusion. She creates a place for
herself inside the circle of virtue that includes the women to whom she
writes, but with the same gesture she places herself outside the ideal of
female beauty to which the patrons, inevitably positioned as "bright,"
still have access. Why does she create a racialized margin moments before she begins the "Preamble of the Author before the Passion"?

Part of the answer lies in the complicated negotiations with Jewishness that are at work in *Salve Deus*. While the poem contains no direct
expression of Jewish belief or historical experience that I have been able
to identify—it is a work squarely within the tradition of Protestant female piety—*Salve Deus* does take on the narrative through which Jewish guilt was constructed and, crucially, it interrogates the discourse of
race through which, in part, Jewish "difference" was expressed. Lanyer's
poem finds that it cannot discuss womanhood without thinking about
race (and class), at just the moment when the terms for "race" across
Europe ("race" in French, *raza* in Spanish, *raça* in Portuguese) began to
be applied to specific groups conceived as physically "different," rather
than to "variously designated notions of lineage or genealogy."[27] *Raza*
in its modern sense is a legacy of the Inquisition, where it was first invoked in order to produce a spiritual difference between Christians on
the one hand and "Moors" and Jews on the other. The metropolitan
concept of race, essentially the Inquisition's *"limpieza de sangre"* or

FIGURE 16-1 Portrait by Pierre Mignard (1612–95) of Louise Renée de Keroualle, Duchess of Portsmouth and mistress of Charles II after 1671. The portrait provides a visual index from late in the seventeenth century of the production of white womanhood through the exclusion of black women. Coral and pearls, evocative of both white female beauty and colonial trade, are offered by an African servant whose posture, hair, and skin are deployed to affirm the beauty of the white woman. Kim Hall's *Things of Darkness* illuminates the "political economy of beauty" in master–servant portraits of the period and includes a full discussion of this work (p. 253). (Courtesy of the National Portrait Gallery, London.)

purity of blood, was transported to the colonies, where it intersected with ideologies of race already in formation and was eventually used to justify both invasion and slavery (Stolcke, pp. 274–76). Although Lanyer may have represented her own darkness out of a sense that her location on the fringes of the ruling class, her public sexual history and, especially, her religious and ethnic heritage could position her as Other, her rhetoric gains power because of its historical situation during the early decades of the racialization of whiteness. In his *Shakespeare and the Jews*, James Shapiro argues that theology, and especially the question of Jewishness, "shaped the way people thought about both racial and national difference in early modern times" (p. 170); my argument is that if the problem of determining Jewish identity had largely defined "race" for the English until the 1550s, England's African and American encounters became definitive afterward, informing English ideas of Jewishness and supplying a new political context for any discourse of "race." Lanyer's poem, if not Lanyer herself, draws on the whole range of meanings blackness was beginning to acquire as she places herself in relation to a (white, Christian) community of women.

There is no question that Jewishness was racialized in early modern England and that a discourse associating Jews with blackness was readily available to the English Renaissance writer. Shapiro provides ample documentation of the "racial" attributes assigned to Jews and the frequency with which Jews were positioned as "dark" to England's "fair." "I knew you to be a Jew," states one 1539 treatise, "for you Jews have a peculiar colour of face different from the form and figure of other men. Which thing hath often filled me with admiration, for you are black and uncomely, and not white as other men."[28] A visitor to a London synagogue reports in 1690 that "they were all very black men, and indistinct in their reasonings as gypsies" (Shapiro, p. 171). And a Portuguese text from 1604 shows how the discourses surrounding Jewishness and Africanness were beginning to overlap: "Who can deny that in the descendants of the Jews there persists and endures the evil inclination of their ancient ingratitude and lack of understanding, just as in Negroes [there persists] the inseparability of their blackness?"[29]

Shapiro shows, however, that such confident pronouncements of the racial status of Jews were often at odds with historical practice, because the Inquisition, the Protestant Reformation, and the growth of merchant capitalism put pressure on definitions of Jewishness in England and gave rise to a new climate of uncertainty about Jewish identity in the sixteenth century (pp. 13–14). While some commentators, notably Thomas Browne, struggled with the question of whether the Jews were "a race" or "a nation," Jews in Europe were successfully passing as Christians and Christians occasionally passing as Jews. For Jewish *women*, the question of identity was even more vexed, as circumcision was the defining mark of "the Jew" for non-Jewish Europe. Lacking the inscription of their religion on their bodies, women were sometimes imagined to have more

cultural mobility than men.[30] We still do not know enough about how
women experienced their Jewishness or how a culture that tended to
feminize Jewish men positioned Jewish women, yet it is clear that the
emerging discourse of race and the new inquiries into the nature of Jewish identity collaborated to produce Jewishness (like Italianness) as at
least potentially marked by darkness.[31]

But would Lanyer have had any sense of herself as a Jew? And if so,
how can we expect to find Jewishness *written* in a literary text, especially one whose title, "Hail, God, King of the Jews," quotes the very
phrase that became a byword for Jewish culpability in Christ's death?
Lanyer's connection to Jewishness comes through her father,[32] in whose
will she is named "Emelia Bassany Daughter of the bodie of Margarett
Bassany also Margarett Johnson my reputed wieff" (Woods, p. xv). The
same document identifies her father as "a native of venice and one of
the Musitions of our Sovereigne Ladye the Quenes majestie" (p. xv).
Baptista Bassano, Aemilia's father, was the youngest of five Jewish brothers who were recruited for the King's Music to bring the practice of playing in consorts to the English court. The Bassano family, as court musicians for several generations, is fairly well documented, and it has been
suggested that the family was drawn to emigrate in part because of the
cultural climate created by the English Reformation.[33] The relation of
the Bassano brothers to Judaism is in itself difficult to ascertain, and even
if Lanyer's father Baptista identified himself as a Jew throughout his life,
his daughter Aemilia, as the child of a non-Jewish mother, would not
usually have been considered Jewish.[34] In addition, Lanyer was baptized
as a Christian, saw her two children baptized, and wrote a Protestant
poem that expresses a vibrant, lived relationship to that religion in a
culture in which the practice of Judaism was officially outlawed: there
is no simple expression of Jewishness in *Salve Deus*.

Although the Bassanos were probably the most assimilated of the
Jewish musical families (as the number of marriage and baptismal records
they left suggests[35]), and Lanyer's own life as the mistress of a powerful
Protestant politician could have worked to interpellate her into the dominant ideology, she was the inheritor of a specific history that may have
sharpened her sense of Jewish identity and its political consequences in
early modern England. In 1541 (immediately after the Bassano family
arrived in England and almost thirty years before Lanyer was born) several Portuguese men, almost certainly including members of the King's
Music and close colleagues of the Bassanos, were arrested and imprisoned on the basis of being "suspected Juis."[36] The arrests were a response
to the forced Inquisition testimony of Gaspar Lopes, who had lived in
London in the 1530s and revealed the presence of a synagogue and Jewish commercial network in England; Henry VIII, eager to consolidate
relations with Charles V of Spain, acted on the testimony. As Italians,
the Bassanos were spared, not being subject to persecution by the Inquisition in the same way the Portuguese were, but they cannot have

been untouched by an event that reversed Henry VIII's policy toward Jews of the professional classes, and marked a watershed in Anglo-Jewish history.[37] Charles V's ambassador to England, who had largely engineered the arrests, wrote in a letter on January 29, 1542: "The King has lately ordered the arrest and imprisonment of the New Christians that came from Portugal. Most likely, however well they may sing, they will not escape from their cages without leaving feathers behind."[38]

The sinister image of caged birds has been read by historians as a reference to the fact that some of the imprisoned were musicians, and the threat of feathers left behind to the expectation that some would not survive prison. A few months after the letter was written, two of the members of the Portuguese viol consort were dead.[39] High-level negotiations, initiated by the sister of the Holy Roman Emperor, succeeded in releasing most of the prisoners, but the uncharacteristic persecution of Jews in England had changed the climate of Jewish life in London. How it affected the Bassanos we cannot know, but to be fellow musicians and fellow Jews and *not* be imprisoned must have put the Bassano brothers in a complicated political and psychological position. When a "mini-expulsion" of Jews from England occurred in 1609, the year before Lanyer's book was entered in the Stationers' Register, would it have evoked this early history of her immigrant family? Already ejected from the inner circle of state power because of a gendered and sexualized class position, Lanyer may have been moved to see herself as an outsider because the 1609 expulsion served as a reminder that Jewishness in England, despite the cachet Judaism was beginning to acquire in intellectual circles,[40] could still be a criminal offense.

Lanyer comes close in this poem to disturbing the central Christian orthodoxy of Jewish guilt. Despite its piety and focus on virtuous womanhood, Lanyer's poem is essentially a polemic: like Rachel Speght's *Mouzell for Melastomus* (1617), *Salve Deus* is a rereading of the Bible, here for the purpose of proving that it was *men* who were guilty in Christ's death. At the heart of *Salve Deus* is the conceit that Christ in his suffering is analogous to Margaret and Anne Clifford in theirs, and that women have historically defended rather than persecuted Jesus. Although Lanyer draws on the antisemitic rhetoric familiar in passion narratives ("The Jewish wolves, that did our Saviour bite," p. 81) and nowhere discusses outright the idea that Jews might not be culpable, her shift from a religious or racial category to a gender category in attributing blame for Christ's death has the effect of repositioning Jews in Christian theology. Jewish women, at least by inference, are exonerated; more tendentiously, non-Jewish men, through the connection Lanyer makes between those guilty of Christ's death and all men who defame women, are implicated. ("[E]vill disposed men . . . doe like Vipers deface the wombes wherein they were bred. . . . Such as these, were they that dishonoured Christ his Apostles and Prophets, putting them to shamefull deaths," pp. 48–49). Lanyer's account of the passion is as a series of episodes in which men—the disciples in Gethsemane, the High Priests, Pilate—fail Christ; and women—Pilate's wife, the Daughters of Jerusalem, the Virgin Mary—comfort, argue for, or mourn him (figure 16-2). This is the reason for the apparently misleading information of her title page, which promises a poem in these four sections: "1 The Passion of Christ. / 2 Eves Apologie in defence of Women. / 3 The Teares of the Daughters of Jerusalem. / 4 The Salutation and Sorrow of the Virgine Marie," and for the emphasis Lanyer gives to such moments as the one where Christ turns to acknowledge the suffering of the Daughters of Jerusalem on his behalf (p. 93). The story Lanyer has to tell is one in which neglected instances of female intervention on Christ's behalf create a new reading of the passion.[41]

FIGURE 16-2 Jacopo Bassano, *The Journey to Calvary* (1543–44). Based on Agostino Veneziano's engraving of a widely known 1517 work by Raphael, this is one example of an iconographic tradition that goes back at least to the twelfth century: women are depicted as witnesses and men as agents of the crucifixion. We do not know how much access to religious painting Lanyer would have had in post-Reformation England, but the unmistakable gender polarity in such scenes provides a tantalizing analogue, perhaps even a source, for her reconceptualization of the passion. The interpretation of the pictorial tradition shown here, with its unusual chiasmic composition, is especially suggestive for *Salve Deus* because the painter himself was a contemporary of Lanyer's father in the Italian city of Bassano del Grappa from which both took their names. (Reproduction by permission of the Syndics of the Fitzwilliam Museum, Cambridge.)

That she called the poem "Hail, God, King of the Jews" may suggest an ambivalence that accompanied her revision of Matthew's gospel. Lanyer appropriates the signal phrase for Jewish (and Roman) *mis*apprehension of Christ's divinity and rewrites it as a hymn of praise for Christ. "Ave rex judaeorum" (or in the odd Geneva translation of Matthew 27:29, "God saue thee kyng of the Iewes"[42]) is the phrase Pilate's soldiers used to mock Christ as they dressed him for the crucifixion; it is also the basis of the inscription on his cross. By inserting "Deus" into the phrase, Lanyer clumsily spells out what is taken in Christian exegesis as a central, elegant irony: the inscription, "Jesus of Nazareth, King of the Jews," designed to mock Christ and record his crime, is seen by Christians as an unintentional acknowledgment of his divinity. Lanyer, however, seems uncomfortable with the irony; it leaves open too much room for misinterpretation, and thus she adds the too-vigorous *Deus*. There is a nervousness in her disassociation from the words of the New Testament Jews that is reminiscent of her nervousness about Cleopatra, and that also shows up in the strange finale to *Salve Deus*, an address to "the doubtfull Reader" owning and disowning her title. It was, she writes, "delivered unto me in sleepe many yeares before I had any intent to write in this maner"; later the phrase became "a significant token, that I was appointed to performe this Worke" (p. 139).[43] Like Pilate's wife, Lanyer is a dreamer: both this dream and an earlier dream vision in which Mary Sidney resolved the contest between Art and Nature allow Lanyer to speculate on the relation between literature and truth; at the same time the identification with Pilate's wife suggests that Lanyer sees her own role as that of truth-teller, a woman whose gendered epistemology gives her salvific insight.

Lanyer's poem ends with her alone, remembering a dreamscape, not embraced by the community of women imagined in every section of the poem. It is significant that female community in *Salve Deus* is always envisioned or remembered, never experienced by Lanyer in the present. The dedications map out the material and cultural potential of a female community; the passion narrative remembers instances of women's collective action on behalf of Christ; the country-house poem laments the loss of an Edenic community of women in retirement from the court. Perhaps *Salve Deus*'s emblematic moment is the story of Lanyer's stealing a kiss from the tree kissed by Margaret Clifford as Clifford departs from Cookham; even when Lanyer comes closest to contact (spiritual and intellectual as much as sexual) with another woman, the connection has to be displaced, secret, at least until it becomes public in the poem.

The female communities on which *Salve Deus* centers are invariably objects of memory or desire: the image of a connection just outside her grasp—whether it be Margaret Clifford's kiss or the community of women who call her by name—defines Lanyer's relation to the collective womanhood she celebrates. Although Lanyer herself may not have connected her writing of her own "darkness" to her exclusion from female community, the political unconscious of the poem ties these two strands together through the emerging discourse of race. Written at the moment when dark-skinned African and Caribbean women were beginning to appear in England, *Salve Deus* speaks from a position of racialized Jewishness—and a position on the margins of the ruling class—in order to suggest that womanhood was beginning to be intertwined with whiteness. Lanyer's poem registers the way in which new discursive formations of collective English womanhood were dependent on a racialized Other. It is not coincidental that Lanyer is always excluded from collective womanhood, nor that collective womanhood is evoked, at the historical moment when it begins to define itself discursively, from a position on the margin. The poem knows that the dark lady is essential to white womanhood; *Salve Deus* captures the historical moment when "womanhood" begins to constitute itself through the exclusion of some women who are not "women." If what we seek as feminists approaching early women writers is something other than a confirmation of the epistemological privilege white, Euro-American women are accustomed to assume, but rather a source of radical knowledge that might help to remake modern feminism, then Lanyer's poem must be one of our points of departure.

NOTES

I wish to thank Jean Howard, who gave me the opportunity to begin research on this topic at the Institute for Research on Women and Gender of Columbia University, and Susan Frye and Karen Robertson, who were exemplary feminist editors. I am grateful also for the deep readings and many suggestions offered by Anthony O'Brien and Marianne Eckardt, for the help of my colleagues Steven Kruger, Michael Sargent, and Alisa Solomon, and for the expert work of my research assistant Jonathan Burton.

1. Important examples include Denise Riley, *"Am I That Name?": Feminism and the Category of "Women" in History* (Minneapolis: University of Minnesota Press, 1988), and Judith Butler, *Gender Trouble: Feminism and the Subversion of Identity* (New York: Routledge, 1990).

2. See Wendy Wall's rich discussion of tropes of absence and otherness in women's poetry: "Dancing in a Net: The Problems of Female Authorship," in Wendy Wall, *The Imprint of Gender: Authorship and Publication in the English Renaissance* (Ithaca, N.Y.: Cornell University Press, 1993), pp. 279–340. I am indebted throughout to the subtlety of Wall's analysis. Ann Baynes Coiro also makes a provocative argument for the importance of Lanyer's political marginality in "Writing in Service: Sexual Politics and Class Position in the Poetry of Aemilia Lanyer and Ben Jonson," *Criticism* 35 (Summer 1993): 357–76. Although I disagree with certain aspects of Coiro's reading, especially her sense that Lanyer is "acutely conscious of those below" her in class (p. 369), her emphasis on Lanyer's *distance* from her patrons has been an important counterpoint to the predominant view that Lanyer offers her patrons unproblematic praise.

3. The phrase is from Fredric Jameson, *The Political Unconscious: Narrative as a Socially Symbolic Act* (Ithaca, N.Y.: Cornell University Press, 1981); Jameson focuses on making visible a repressed history of *class* struggle, with less atten-

tion to race, gender or sexuality, but see pp. 85–87 on recovering marginalized or oppositional cultures.

4. I am indebted to the scholars who first recovered Lanyer's work and made it available in anthologies. Most of these collections also include biographical and critical comment; see Betty Travitsky, ed., *The Paradise of Women: Writings by Englishwomen of the Renaissance* (Westport, Conn.: Greenwood, 1981), pp. 28–29, 97–103; Mary R. Mahl and Helene Koon, eds., *The Female Spectator: English Women Writers Before 1800* (Bloomington: Indiana University Press, 1977), pp. 73–75; and Germaine Greer et al., eds., *Kissing the Rod: An Anthology of Seventeenth-Century Women's Verse* (New York: Noonday Press, 1988), pp. 44–53 (which has particularly good annotations). Until recently, the only complete modern edition of *Salve Deus* was *The Poems of Shakespeare's Dark Lady*, ed. A. L. Rowse (London: Cape, 1978); this has been supplanted by *The Poems of Aemilia Lanyer*, ed. Susanne Woods (New York: Oxford, 1993). All quotations from Lanyer are taken from the Woods edition and followed by page numbers. In addition to the essays by Wall and Coiro mentioned in note 1, critical studies of Lanyer include the following: Elaine V. Beilin, "The Feminization of Praise: Aemilia Lanyer," *Redeeming Eve: Women Writers of the English Renaissance* (Princeton, N.J.: Princeton University Press, 1987), pp. 177–207; Barbara Kiefer Lewalski, "Imagining Female Community: Aemilia Lanyer's Poems," in *Writing Women in Jacobean England* (Cambridge, Mass.: Harvard University Press, 1993), pp. 213–41, which draws on a series of earlier articles on Lanyer by Lewalski; Lynette McGrath, "Metaphoric Subversions: Feasts and Mirrors in Amelia Lanyer's *Salve Deus Rex Judaeorum*," *LIT* 3 (1991): 101–13; Lynette McGrath, "'Let Us Have Our Libertie Againe': Amelia Lanyer's Seventeenth-Century Feminist Voice," *Women's Studies* 20 (1992): 331–48; Lorna Hutson, "Why the Lady's Eyes Are Nothing Like the Sun," in *New Feminist Discourses: Critical Essays on Theories and Texts*, ed. Isobel Armstrong (London: Routledge, 1992), pp. 155–75; Tina Krontiris, "Aemilia Lanyer: Criticizing Men via Religion," in *Oppositional Voices: Women as Writers and Translators of Literature in the English Renaissance* (London: Routledge, 1992), pp. 103–20; and Janel Mueller, "The Feminist Poetics of Aemilia Lanyer's 'Salve Deus Rex Judaeorum,'" in *Feminist Measures: Soundings in Poetry and Theory*, ed. Lynn Keller and Cristanne Miller (Ann Arbor: University of Michigan Press, 1993), pp. 208–36. Jonathan Goldberg's chapter, "Canonizing Aemilia Lanyer," in *Desiring Women Writing: English Renaissance Examples* (Stanford: Stanford University Press, 1997), pp. 16–41, appeared after this chapter was completed. Worth noting also is a web site dedicated to Lanyer: http://www.u.arizona.edu/~kari/lanbib.htm. My essay is indebted in various ways to all of these pioneering studies, even when I take issue with the frameworks in which they read Lanyer.

5. The racialization of womanhood was perhaps first systematically studied in this country by African-American women of the late nineteenth century; see the account of the intellectual tradition they developed in Hazel V. Carby, *Reconstructing Womanhood: The Emergence of the Afro-American Woman Novelist* (New York: Oxford University Press, 1987). This tradition has been recovered and amplified by women of color in the United States and elsewhere, starting in the 1970s; the pathbreaking studies include: bell hooks, *Ain't I A Woman? Black Women and Feminism* (Boston: South End Press, 1981); Cherrié Moraga and Gloria Anzaldúa, eds., *This Bridge Called My Back: Writings by Radical Women of Color* (Watertown, Mass.: Persephone, 1981); Chandra Talpade Mohanty, Ann Russo and Lourdes Torres, eds., *Third World Women and the Politics of Feminism* (Bloomington: Indiana University Press, 1991); and the Hull, Scott, and Smith anthology *But Some of Us Are Brave* (Old Westbury, N.Y.: Feminist Press, 1982). As perhaps the most important intervention in feminist thought, the imperative to racialize gender has been widely discussed, including by

several scholars who have begun to write the history of this intersection: see in particular Elizabeth V. Spelman, *Inessential Woman* (Boston: Beacon, 1988); Vron Ware, *Beyond the Pale: White Women, Racism, and History* (London: Verso, 1982); and Ruth Frankenburg, *White Women, Race Matters: The Social Construction of Whiteness* (Minneapolis: University of Minnesota Press, 1993). In the early modern field, important discussions of race and gender include: Ania Loomba, *Gender, Race, Renaissance Drama* (Manchester: Manchester University Press, 1989); Kim Hall, *Things of Darkness: Economies of Race and Gender in Early Modern England* (Ithaca, N.Y.: Cornell University Press, 1995), Margaret Ferguson, "Juggling the Categories of Race, Class and Gender," *Women's Studies: An Interdisciplinary Journal* 19 (Spring 1991): 159–81; and the revisionary collection edited by Margo Hendricks and Patricia Parker, *Women, "Race," and Writing in the Early Modern Period* (London: Routledge, 1994).

6. Winthrop Jordan, *White Over Black: American Attitudes Toward the Negro, 1550–1812* (Chapel Hill: University of North Carolina Press, 1968) is among the founding works in the field; for Lynda Boose, see her "'The Getting of a Lawful Race': Racial Discourse in Early Modern England and the Unrepresentable Black Woman," in Hendricks and Parker, eds., *Women, "Race," and Writing in the Early Modern Period*, pp. 35–54. For a discussion of the literature on gender and sexuality in early modern England, see Valerie Traub, *Desire and Anxiety: Circulations of Sexuality in Shakespearean Drama* (London: Routledge, 1992).

7. My sense of possible connections between early modern and postmodern periods is influenced by Jonathan Dollimore's formulation; he writes in *Sexual Dissidence: Augustine to Wilde, Freud to Foucault* (Oxford: Clarendon Press, 1991): "I approach the early modern neither as origin of the present nor as that from which the present has declined, but as a range of cultural antecedents which can simultaneously problematize and illuminate their subsequent modern forms, especially the post/modern" (p. 23).

8. Barbara Lewalski identifies Lanyer as "the first Englishwoman to publish a substantial volume of original poems" (*Writing Women in Jacobean England*, p. 213). The only known figure whose achievement is comparable to Lanyer's is Elizabeth Melvill, Lady Culros, whose allegorical poem *Ane Godlie Dreame* was published in Edinburgh in 1606, though Anne Lok Prowse also deserves mention for her poetic meditation appended to a translation of Calvin in 1560 (Woods, *Poems of Aemilia Lanyer*, p. xxxii). Lanyer herself cites the Countess of Pembroke as her predecessor, possibly because she does not make the strict distinction between translation and "original" poetry that arose after the seventeenth century. The Countess of Pembroke's *Psalmes* were prepared for presentation to the Queen in 1599 and circulated in manuscript; Lanyer clearly knew them. Christine de Pizan also wrote a meditation on the passion specifically for women, though it is very unlikely that Lanyer would have known it, because the work has never been published. Christine's *Hours of Contemplation on the Passion of Our Lord* is offered to women readers as "comfort in the misery of endless tribulations." See the preface to this work translated in *The Writings of Christine de Pizan*, ed. Charity Cannon Willard (New York: Persea, 1994), pp. 346–47. I thank Michael Sargent for this reference.

9. A more complete discussion of Lanyer's biography appears later in this essay. The principal sources for her life are: Roger Prior, "Jewish Musicians at the Tudor Court," *The Musical Quarterly* 69 (1983): 253–65; Roger Prior, "A Second Jewish Community in Tudor London," *The Transactions of the Jewish Historical Society of England* 31 (1990): 137–52; David Lasocki, "The Anglo-Venetian Bassano Family as Instrument Makers and Repairers," *Galpin Society Journal* 38 (1985): 112–32; Barbara Kiefer Lewalski, *Writing Women in Jacobean England*; Susanne Woods, introduction to *The Poems of Aemilia Lanyer*; and

Lorna Hutson, "Emilia Lanier" in *The Dictionary of National Biography: Missing Persons*, ed. C. S. Nicholls (Oxford: Oxford University Press, 1993), pp. 388–89. Woods and Lewalski document the primary sources from which a biography can be constructed; these include baptismal and marriage records, records of legal proceedings initiated by Lanyer, documents related to the school she founded in 1617, and the strange accounts by the astrologer Simon Forman of her visits to him in 1597 (Bodleian Manuscript Ashmole 226).

10. This formulation of the poem's structure is offered in Hutson, "Why the Lady's Eyes," p. 162.

11. Both Coiro, "Writing in Service," and Hutson, "Why the Lady's Eyes," make explicit arguments against the masculinist framework in which Lanyer is usually read, while many of the other critical articles make the point implicitly. See Coiro's important discussion of the impact Lanyer would have if fully included in the canon (pp. 357–60), and Hutson's subtle reading of Lanyer against the gendered rhetoric of praise (154–72).

12. Simon Forman, Bodleian, MS Ashmole 226, f. 110v, quoted in Lewalski, *Writing Women*, p. 215. Forman's interaction with Lanyer is discussed in Woods, *Poems of Aemilia Lanyer*, pp. xv–xxiv, and famously in Rowse, *Poems of Shakespeare's Dark Lady*, who bases his identification of Lanyer with the Dark Lady largely on the Forman records.

13. Critics have been reluctant to grant to Lanyer the distinction of inventing the country-house poem in English because of the possibility that Ben Jonson might have written "To Penshurst" first. "To Penshurst," celebrating Robert Sidney's estate, was published in 1616, but written before November 1612, as its reference to Prince Henry's death establishes. "Cooke-ham" was written between February 1609 (as is shown by its reference to Anne Clifford's marriage) and October 1610 (when the book was entered in the Stationers' Register). If "To Penshurst" had indeed been written several years earlier, Lanyer might well have seen it, as she clearly read other manuscript poems of the Sidney circle. But what if Ben Jonson was responding to *her* poem? Coiro points out that our sense of the country-house genre will change once Lanyer is seriously admitted to it ("Writing in Service," pp. 370–74), but the possibilities of reading "To Penshurst" as a rewriting of "Cooke-ham" have yet to be fully explored. See Lewalski's discussion of this point (*Writing Women*, pp. 234–38), and her article, "The Lady of the Country-House Poem," in *The Fashioning and Functioning of the British Country House*, ed. Gervase Jackson-Stops, et al. Studies in the History of Art, no. 25. (London: National Gallery of Art, 1989), pp. 261–75.

14. Matthew 27:19: "Also when he was set downe vpon the iudgement seat, his wife sent to him, saying, Haue thou nothing to do with that iuste man: for I haue suffered many things this day in a dreame by reason of him"; *The Geneva Bible: A Facsimile of the 1560 Edition* (Madison: University of Wisconsin Press, 1969). Pilate's wife's dream is mentioned only in Matthew, which is Lanyer's principal source for the passion narrative.

15. Constance Jordan, *Renaissance Feminism: Literary Texts and Political Models* (Ithaca, N.Y.: Cornell University Press, 1990), p. 5, points out that both Catholic and Protestant doctrine in the early modern period allowed for spiritual equality of the sexes. Religious doctrine, however, did not consider that women's spirtual equality entailed "a correlative political status."

16. See the works by Hall, Loomba, and Ferguson, mentioned earlier, as well as Margaret W. Ferguson, Maureen Quilligan, and Nancy J. Vickers, Introduction to *Rewriting the Renaissance: The Discourses of Sexual Difference in Early Modern Europe* (Chicago: University of Chicago Press, 1986), pp. xv–xxxi. In particular, see the essays in Hendricks and Parker, eds., *Women, "Race," and Writing in the Early Modern Period*, which form a kind of manifesto, though one with many internal debates, for a new, antinationalist criticism of early

modern literature. Margaret Ferguson has written profoundly about the tendency of studies of women's agency in this period to be undertheorized, arguing that it can be connected to "a sense of despair about the possibilities of collective feminist action under the conservative economic and political policies of the 1980s in both Britain and the United States"; Margaret W. Ferguson, "Moderation and Its Discontents: Recent Work on Renaissance Women," *Feminist Studies* 20, no. 2 (1994): 364. For an important critique of the Euro-centric framework of early modern studies, see Walter D. Mignolo, *The Darker Side of the Renaissance: Literary, Territoriality, and Colonization* (Ann Arbor: University of Michigan Press, 1995).

17. Categories of gender, religion, and class all were mediated both by each other and by the imperialist enterprise: English notions of Jewishness, for instance, were informed by the emerging discourse of "race" even as they derived primarily from local pressures, while the poor laws in England from the seventeenth century were directly connected to merchant capitalism in the New World. See Emily C. Bartels, "Malta, the Jew, and the Fictions of Difference: Colonial Discourse in Marlowe's *The Jew of Malta*," *ELR* 20 no. 1 (1990): 1–16, for an important discussion of links between colonialism and the treatment of the oppressed at home in England. She reads Marlowe's representation of Jewishness through the colonial context of Malta. Bartels cites Steven Mullaney, *The Place of the Stage: License, Play, and Power in Renaissance England* (Chicago: University of Chicago Press, 1988), p. 71, on the connection between English poor laws and English imperialism.

18. As the capital necessary for the emerging capitalist mode of production was acquired from Europe's colonies at an astonishing rate—for instance when Drake's first expedition was launched with £5,000 and brought £600,000 in profit—European women were cast in a new role as the "consumers and demonstrators" of wealth, as Maria Mies has shown in *Patriarchy and Accumulation on a World Scale: Women in the International Division of Labour* (London: Zed, 1986), p. 101. While slave women in the Caribbean were being forbidden to marry or have children (it was cheaper to import slaves than to support slave families), European women were being interpellated into the ideology of domesticity and affective motherhood. The story of the relation between European and non-European women is more complex and nuanced than I can suggest here, but it is important to see both that gender in the early modern period was configured within a new international economy and that the economy itself was already gendered. See Mies's important discussion of the "housewifization" of European women concurrent with the subordination of non-European women (pp. 100–11).

19. Ania Loomba, "The Color of Patriarchy: Critical Difference, Cultural Difference, and Renaissance Drama," in Hendricks and Parker, eds., *Women, "Race," and Writing*, p. 26, makes this point when she writes of reading Shakespeare: "[t]he notion of 'race' must transcend the black presence in the plays and inform understandings of gender, the state, political life, and private existences." For related "racialized" analyses, see Edward Said, *Culture and Imperialism* (New York: Vintage Books, 1993) and Toni Morrison, *Playing in the Dark: Whiteness and the Literary Imagination* (New York: Vintage Books, 1992).

20. There is evidence that *Salve Deus* was implicated in the financial arrangements that subtended England's rise to imperial power. Lanyer's need for funds probably arose from her husband's loss of money in the Essex expedition to the Azores in 1597 and later in his campaigns to subjugate Ireland. A copy of the poem was presented by Lanyer's husband to the powerful Archbishop of Dublin only a month after the title was entered in the Stationers' Register (October 2, 1610). See Lewalski, *Writing Women*, pp. 321–22, on the history of this copy, and Woods, *Poems of Aemilia Lanyer*, p. xlix, on the presentation to

the Archbishop. The copy now in the Chapin Library at Williams College bears an inscription on the title page in a contemporary hand: "guift of Mr. Alfonso Lanyer .8.No 1610" and the signature "Tho: Jones." Thomas Jones was Archbishop in 1610, and Alphonso Lanyer had served with him in the Irish campaigns. Both Lewalski and Woods feel that the omission of the most feminist of the dedications, "To the Vertuous Reader," from this copy is significant.

21. Cited in Wall, *Imprint of Gender*, p. 317, from "To the Angell spirit of the most excellent Sir Philip Sidney," *The Triumph of Death and Other Unpublished and Uncollected Poems*, ed. Gary Waller (Salzburg: Universität Salzburg, 1977).

22. Kim Hall, "Acknowledging Things of Darkness: Race, Gender, and Power in Early Modern England," (Ph.D. diss., University of Pennsylvania, 1990), p. 63. The passage from Wroth occurs in Sonnet 100, line 6; *The Poems of Lady Mary Wroth*, ed. Josephine Roberts (Baton Rouge: Louisiana State University Press, 1983). Both Hall and Wroth are cited in Wall, *Imprint of Gender*, p. 332. See also Hall's discussion of Wroth in *Things of Darkness: Economies of Race and Gender in Early Modern England* (Ithaca: Cornell University Press, 1995).

23. See Debora Shuger's detailed and sensitive account of Calvinist passion narratives in *The Renaissance Bible: Scholarship, Sacrifice, and Subjectivity* (Berkeley: University of California Press, 1994), where she comments, "Pictures of desirable and powerful manhood replace the shameful body in an anamorphic sequence—the bruised and deformed figure of Christ suddenly reconfigured as beautiful and virile. The images of the grotesque and erotic bodies are very closely juxtaposed" (p. 97).

24. On the association of the mirror with the practice of reading Scripture, see Steven F. Kruger, *Dreaming in the Middle Ages* (Cambridge: Cambridge University Press, 1992), p. 138. Kruger cites Ritamary Bradley, "Backgrounds of the Title *Speculum* in Medieval Literature," *Speculum* 29 (1954): 100–15. On the overlap between traditions of ethics and misogyny in the trope of the mirror, see Karen Newman, *Fashioning Femininity and Renaissance Drama* (Chicago: University of Chicago Press, 1991), pp. 7–8, cited in Wall, *Imprint of Gender*, p. 322. Lynette McGrath, in "Metaphoric Subversions," has an important commentary on Lanyer's use of the mirror; she argues that *Salve Deus* uses the image "to reinforce alliances of women with women and women with a feminized, maternal Christ" (p. 108). McGrath cites Luce Irigaray, *Speculum of the Other Woman*, trans. Gillian C. Gill (Ithaca, N.Y.: Cornell University Press, 1985), in a suggestive discussion of Lanyer's eroticism.

25. *Othello* (II.i.132–33); William Shakespeare, *The Riverside Shakespeare*, ed. G. Blakemore Evans (Boston: Houghton Mifflin, 1974). This edition uses the Q1 reading, "hit," which is suggestive of the pun on "the white" as a target; the F1 reading, "fit," seems more consistent with a pun on "wight" and "white."

26. John Lyly, *Euphues and His England* (1580), in *John Lyly. The Anatomy of Wit . . . Euphues and His England . . .* , ed. Edward Arber (London, 1869), p. 406. The quotation is from a dialogue that has just defined beauty as a "white and read [red] complection." Camilla, the female speaker, refutes the man's argument "that where beautie is, there is also vertue" (p. 405) and recommends instead such qualities as temperance and chastity in both women and men. By citing this text, Lanyer takes a position vis-à-vis the masculinist literature for women; how she envisions the alternative she offers becomes clear as she revises her source. The passage is part of Camilla's argument that male desire, not female beauty, has agency in love; it plays on the newly double meaning of the word "fair": "The similitude you brought in of the arrowe, flewe nothing right to beautie, wherefore I must shute [shoot] that shafte at your owne brest. For if the eye of man be the arrow, and beautie the white (a faire mark for him that draweth in cupids bow) then must it necessarily ensue, that the archer

desireth with an ayme to hitte the white, not the white the arrowe, that the marke allureth the archer, not the shooter the marke" (p. 407, modernizations in Arber's text). On the ways Lyly had capitalized on the popularity of his first book among women readers, see Suzanne Hull, *Chaste, Silent, and Obedient: English Books for Women, 1475–1640* (San Marino, Calif.: Huntington Library, 1982), p. 11.

27. Margo Hendricks and Patricia Parker, Introduction to *Women, "Race," and Writing*, p. 2. My discussion here closely follows theirs; on the controversial history of the origins of the Spanish word *raza* and the development of modern notions of "race" from the needs of the Inquisition, see the important essay by Verena Stolcke, "Invaded Women: Gender, Race, and Class in the Formation of Colonial Society," in Hendricks and Parker, eds., *Women, "Race," and Writing in the Early Modern Period*, p. 276.

28. Sebastian Munster, *Messias Christianorum et Judaeorum* (Basel, 1539), sig. A5v, as translated in Paul Isaiah [Eleazar bar Isaiah, pseud.], *The Messiah of the Christians, and the Jewes* (London, 1655), Sig. B3v, p.2. The text is cited in James Shapiro, *Shakespeare and the Jews* (New York: Columbia University Press, 1996), p. 170; my discussion closely follows Shapiro's pioneering archival work on the subject. Note that the passage from Munster deliberately reverses the language of the Song of Songs—"I am blacke, o daughters of Ierusalem, but comelie"—the text that is to be the basis of the most jubilant passages in *Salve Deus*.

29. The 1690 text is by Robert Kirk, in Donald MacLean, ed., "London in 1689–90," *Transactions of the London and Middlesex Archeological Society* n.s. 7 (1937): 151, cited in Shapiro, *Shakespeare and the Jews*, p. 171. The 1604 Portuguese text is by Prudencio de Sandoval, in Jerome Friedman, "Jewish Conversion, the Spanish Pure Blood Laws, and Reformation: A Revisionist View of Racial and Religious Antisemitism," *The Sixteenth Century Journal* 18 (1987), 16–17 (cited in Shapiro, p. 36). One measure of the prevalence of the association of Jewishness with blackness is that it began to be denied in late seventeenth-century writing; Shapiro cites Francois Maximilien Mission's 1691 discussion of the "vulgar error that the Jews are all black" (Shapiro, p. 171).

30. The best known example of this pattern is *The Merchant of Venice*, where Jessica is imagined as able to "cross the religious boundaries that divide [her] stigmatized father . . . from the dominant Christian community" (Shapiro, *Shakespeare and the Jews*, p. 120). See Shapiro's discussion of this topic, pp. 120–21. See also Boose, "'The Getting of a Lawful Race,'" on the coupling of "the Turk and the Jew" in early modern drama as "oppositional examples of some kind of similar Otherness." "Might the implied alienation of this pair," Boose asks, "be likewise grounded in bodily difference—not the difference of 'nature' signified by skin color but the difference that religion and culture had carved upon the (male) *body*?" (p. 40).

31. Dympna Callaghan's essay on Elizabeth Cary (in *Women, "Race," and Writing*) is an important beginning to this work. I am grateful for her example in formulating my argument about Lanyer's expression of her own Otherness. Callaghan writes, "I want to argue here that suppression of 'race' not only erases important thematic issues, but also impairs our understanding of gender within [*The Tragedie of Mariam*] and the position of Cary as a Renaissance woman writer" (p. 164).

32. Baptista Bassano's Jewishness has been established on the basis of his name, his association with other known Jews, his profession as a maker and player of recorders, and his probable origin in the northern Italian town of Bassano del Grappa (which was itself founded by an Ashkenazi Jew). See Prior, "Jewish Musicians," pp. 253–59, and Prior, "Second Jewish Community,"

pp. 138–41 and 145–50; also Lasocki, "Anglo-Venetian Bassano Family," pp. 114–15; both Shapiro and Katz include the Bassanos in their discussions of the London Jewish community in the mid-sixteenth century; see Shapiro, *Shakespeare and the Jews*, pp. 68–70; David S. Katz, *The Jews in the History of England* (Oxford: Oxford University Press, 1994), p. 7.

33. This is an argument made by Roger Prior, in his groundbreaking article on the subject, "Jewish Musicians at the Tudor Court." In "A Second Jewish Community in Tudor England," Prior has developed his argument. He speculates that they had fled Bassano for the relative safety of Venice in the 1520s or 1530s, a time when the presence of Spanish armies in Northern Italy made life particularly dangerous for Jews who had to pass as Christians, as musicians would have been required to do in order to work outside the Jewish community. Venice offered the relative safety of the Ghetto, and the freedom to practice their religion, but no opportunity to participate in the range of musical life beyond the walled Jewish quarter. England, especially under Henry VIII, who had already consulted Jewish scholars on the question of divorce and adopted a deliberate policy of cultivating enemies of the Pope, promised freedom from persecution by the Inquisition and access to the high European musical culture. Ironically, it also provided contact with other Jews, for Henry had recruited Sephardic Jews from Portugal to form a viol consort at the same time the Bassanos came to England. Before the decline of the financial value of a court position in the early seventeenth century, the Bassanos trained their sons (apparently no daughters became professional musicians) for the family profession, and by 1630 thirteen of the nineteen court wind players were Bassanos (Lasocki, "Anglo-Venetian Bassano Family," p. 115).

34. The law regarding the religion of children of mixed marriages is from Mishnah and Talmud [Kid. 3:12] and was firmly in place by this time, but we do not know how it was observed by Jews living in England. There is evidence, for instance, that a the *son* of a non-Jewish mother in England may have identified more with his Jewish heritage than the *daughter* of one of the other Bassano brothers, a woman who was Lanyer's cousin (Prior, "Second Community," p. 146). On the sources for the law determining the religion of children, see "Jew," in *Encyclopedia Judaica* (Macmillan: Jerusalem, 1971), which also cites Yad, Issurei Bi'ah 15:3–4. On the complicated relation of Mishnah and Rabbinic Judaism to the Greco-Roman legal system of Palestine, see David Biale, *Eros and the Jews: From Biblical Israel to Contemporary America* (New York: Basic Books, 1992). We get a sense of how difficult it was for the small Jewish community in England to observe their religion from the Inquisition testimony of Thomas Fernandes in 1557, which recounts that Simon Ruiz, a Jew living in London, would secretly send other Jews the dates of Passover (Katz, *Jews in the History of England*, p. 11).

35. We do not know how long Lanyer lived with her family as part of the community of Jewish musicians, for her father died when she was seven and she spent some time in the household of the Countess of Kent. We do know that the family retained some of its "foreignness," being on record as still speaking Italian in the 1590s and owning land in Venice as late as 1635, and that they continued to live in close contact with London's Jewish community until at least the mid-seventeenth century. The Bassanos left more records than any of the other musical families; there is evidence of marriages and baptism; of wills, including Lanyer's father's, witnessed by Christians; of a series of petitions to Queen Mary from the Bassano brothers; and of one member of the family's boasting to John Spencer, the sheriff of London, when threatened with arrest, "We have as good friends in the court as thou hast and better too" (Prior, "Second Community," p. 148). By 1634, when Lanyer was in her sixties, several of

her nephews had obtained a family coat of arms, and even during her child-hood her father would have had the title "gentleman," a courtesy extended to all court musicians (Lasocki, "Anglo-Venetian Bassano Family," p. 116).

36. *The Acts of the Privy Council* i.76, January 17, 1542/3: "the matter betwene his Majestie and certeyne marchawntes strawngers, probably suspected to be Juis," cited in Katz, *Jews in the History of England*, p. 8. This is the record of one of several Privy Council discussions of the 1541 imprisonment case. On March 9, 1542/3, the matter was finally resolved, when the Privy Council recorded its intention "to restore the goods of certain Portuguese (seized because of their being charged with Judaism), in whose favour [Mary, regent of the Netherlands] has twice written during these past months, as also have the King and Queen of Portugal" (cited in Katz, p. 9). Roger Prior was the first to make the claim that the prisoners included Portuguese musicians, as well as merchants. His argument has been accepted by David Katz, the leading historian of Anglo-Jewry (Katz, p. 7), and receives serious consideration in Shapiro, *Shakespeare and the Jews*, p. 69. See also Prior's article, "More (Moor? Moro?) Light on the Dark Lady," *Financial Times*, October 10, 1987, P1, p. 17, where important information on the Bassano family coat of arms (and a possible pun it contains on the Italian word "moro") is offered in service of a defense of A. L. Rowse's reading of Shakespeare's *Sonnets*.

37. Katz, *Jews in the History of England*, sees the imprisonment as a turning point: "The testimony of Gaspar Lopes before the Inquisition was part of the change in attitude towards the Jews which would lead to their flight from England during this period" (p. 6).

38. Eustace Chapuys to Granvelle, January 29, 1542, in Great Britain, Public Record Office, *Letters and Papers, Foreign and Domestic, of the Reign of Henry VIII, 1509–1547*, ed. James Gairdner and R. H. Brodie (London: Her Majesty's Stationery Office, 1900), vol. 17, no. 64 (cited in Katz, *Jews in the History of England*, p. 7). The remainder of this short letter, part of which was originally in code, discusses the Genovese ambassadors at the English court and the Bishop of London. In a letter written the same day to Charles V, Chapuys describes "the King's [Henry's] frequently expressed wish for a closer reliance with the [Holy Roman] Emperor [Charles V]," and Henry's "fear of making an alliance with France, to thwart which has been his continual study" (G.B., PRO, *Letters and Papers*, vol. 17, no. 63).

39. Prior gives the names of those who died: Romano of Milan and Anthony Moyses ("Second Community," p. 141). Moyses, a sackbut player, had his will witnessed by four members of the viol consort, including one, Ambrose Lupo, who used what seems to be the Hebrew spelling of his name in the legal document (ibid., p. 140). Immediately after the release from prison was negotiated in the Privy Council, all but one of the six Jewish viol players at Henry's court left England, although most returned the following year.

40. The major work on this topic is David S. Katz, *Philo-Semitism and the Readmission of the Jews to England, 1603–1655* (Oxford: Clarendon, 1982). "It was during the early seventeenth century, " Katz writes, "that a positive philo-semitic view of contemporary Jewry developed in England" (p. 7). The sources of English philosemitism are complex; they include an interest in Hebrew as a possible universal language, a belief that the lost tribes of Israel had been found in the New World and thus that they could be converted to Christianity, and a movement toward religious toleration that began to be extended to Jews. But Katz points out that seventeenth-century England wanted "Judaism without Jews," and Shapiro, *Shakespeare and the Jews*, shows that there was often little ideological distinction between antisemitism and philosemitism (p. 11).

41. Mueller, "Feminist Poetics," also comments on the aptness of the title-page headings, and discusses the significance of Lanyer's timing in issuing a

challenge to orthodox readings of the passion just as the Authorized Version of
the Bible was being published. Its publication in 1611, the same year as *Salve
Deus*, marked the intersection of "court culture, humanist scholarship, and
vernacular biblicism" (p. 215).

42. The phrase "Ave rex judaeorum" is at the center of a modern controversy on whether the gospels attempt to shift the blame for Christ's death from
the Roman authorities to an instance of "mob violence" by the Jews; see William Foxwell and C. S. Mann, intro., transl. and notes to *The Anchor Bible:
Matthew* (Garden City, N.Y.: Doubleday, 1971), p. 335. The phrase appears in
all four gospels—in Mark 15:32 and Matthew 27:42 it is used by "the chief
priests of the Jews" as well as the Roman authorities—and almost certainly is a
parody of the form "Ave Caesar!" the greeting of the emperor (Foxwell and
Mann, p. 336). It is almost always translated "*Hail*, King of the Jews!" and occurs
in this form in the Wyclif (1380), Tyndale (1534), Cranmer (1539), Rheims (1582),
and King James (1611) versions of Matthew 27:29. The Geneva Bible translates
the passage from Matthew "*God saue thee* kyng of the Iewes," whereas it translates the occurrences of the phrase in the other Gospels "*Hail* kyng of the Iewes"
(with some variation in spelling). I have not been able to explain the idiosyncracy
of the Geneva translation of Matthew, but it seems clear that Lanyer was using
this version, and that her reading of *Salve* back into the Biblical text is a result
of her adherence to the Geneva Bible, coupled with an imperfect knowledge of
Latin. She may also have been influenced by the popular opening of hymns,
"Salve," although I have not been able to find a contemporary hymn beginning "Salve Deus."

43. For an extended discussion of what she calls "the mystique of salutation in Lanyer's religious poetics," see Mueller, "Feminist Poetics," pp. 222–77,
who also comments on Lanyer's addition of "Deus" to the phrase from Matthew. Mueller illuminates a pattern of salutations in *Salve Deus* and describes
the form as "a speech act uniquely expressive of the capacity to apprehend truth
that distinguishes women and the feminized Christ" (p. 224).

Afterword

Producing New Knowledge

. . . .

JEAN E. HOWARD

THE TIME SEEMS RIGHT for this volume, focusing as it does on women's alliances in the early modern period, partly because it allows us to mark the distance we as feminists have come since we unself-consciously embraced the slogan: "Sisterhood is powerful." Sisterhood *is* powerful, of course, but it is also often achieved by some women at the expense of others and is notoriously unstable, because "woman" is not in any simple sense a unitary social category. What is particularly bracing about the present volume is its hardheaded acknowledgment of the many things that separate women from one another—status and class, age, race, marital status, geographical location—and at the same time its optimism about the ways in which such knowledge opens possibilities for forging more adequate collectivities.

That we should turn now from individuals—the individual woman writer, the individual woman ruler, the individual literary character—toward a renewed focus upon collectivities and alliances seems important for several reasons. First, it marks a new stage in literary–historical research in this field. Exceptional women have always stood out, as have the isolated heroines of Jacobean tragedy; but now the collective process of feminist scholarship has made it possible to speak of a wider range of early modern women and their relations to one another, both in social and textual worlds. Whether discussing the working maids of London, the religious followers of Mary Ward, or the fictitious city wives of *Westward Ho*, the contributors to this volume are investigating social actors and practices that have as yet been insufficiently explored. The volume thus demonstrates that feminist work in the early modern field continues to develop as more texts and more archives are opened and as new questions are asked of more familiar materials. As a result of this new scholarship, networks are appearing where individuals once stood in splendid isolation—networks of women linked by kinship circles, by conditions of work, by religious commitments, and even by the misogynous outbursts of a figure like Joseph Swetnam.

The focus on networks and collectivities is also important for political reasons. While individual women can negotiate systems of oppression and exploitation, they can rarely change them, at least those women not lucky enough to inherit a throne. If we want to examine the agency of women as political actors, it is often of collectivities that we must speak. Taken together, the essays in this volume suggest that women in the early modern period recognized gender, along with other social categories, as the basis for affiliation and alliance, and sometimes for political action. Discursive evidence such as the poems of Isabella Whitney or Aemilia Lanyer show that gender, as well as class, family connections, and religion, provided a well-understood language for defining identity and elaborating commonalities of experience and social positioning. In the case of those people who opposed Joseph Swetnam's misogyny, gender also became the basis for an imagined collective punishment of an enemy to women.

The Swetnam affair, in fact, raises several important issues, one having to do with how social groups become politicized and transform largely implicit affiliations into the basis for political undertakings. I find it significant that those who "arraigned" Swetnam were responding directly to the offensiveness of his woman-hating pamphlet. Predictably, an attack on "women" produced a defense of "women," in the process allowing the category to become a staging ground for political contestation. In his discussion of Mary Ward's activities in establishing a religious community of women, informally known as the Institute of Mary, Lowell Gallagher points to a similar instance of politicization. Mary Ward's most outspoken defense of her right, *as a woman*, to establish her order of "Jesuitresses" was a rejoinder to one of the confessors of her Institute who asserted that fervor for the project would wane because those involved were "but women." Ward obviously occupied several subject positions, and her identity as a Catholic and an imitator of Christ was at least as powerful as her identity as a woman. Nonetheless, when gender figured as a trope of disability in attacks upon her work, those attacks solidified her gender identification. Bonds between women in the early modern period were often only implicitly or tacitly acknowledged, although research reveals they did exist. The essays in this volume suggest that the politicization of those implicit bonds and their transformation into the basis for collective action *for and in the name of women* frequently occurred when gender became the articulated ground for denigration or for the curtailment of women's activities. In these instances, repression spawned its own counterforce. Mary Wack suggests that this was true not only for the fictitious women of *Swetnam the Woman-hater Arraigned by Women*, but also for the alewives of Chester whose anger at sixteenth-century restrictions of their rights as brewers and their role in public life may have led to changes and additions to the Chester cycle plays that spoke to the new social circumstances of these women. This volume offers impressive evidence of the many kinds of affiliative bonds among women in this period, and it begins to consider the ways in which those bonds could become the basis for resistance and social change.

The Swetnam affair is also important because, as Valerie Wayne suggests, it raises questions about who is part of "women's alliances." There is a nice ambiguity in this volume's title. It obviously points primarily to alliances *of* women, in which women figure as the primary subjects of analysis as well as the primary social actors. But "women's alliances" can also mean alliances *for* women, that is, alliances that serve the interests of women. In either case, the question arises: who is woman? And who stands with woman? Gender essentialism haunts such questions, and it is a danger we should confront, perhaps more strenuously than much of this volume does. Barbara Bowen makes a strong case in her essay on Aemelia Lanyer that woman is not a self-evident category, in the sense that it was the early modern period that first made whiteness and English womanhood synonymous. Dark women implicitly did not fit the category. In talking about women's alliances, one has to delineate carefully who, in a given circumstance, gets to be a woman.

Valerie Wayne's interesting discussion of the uncertain authorship of *Swetnam the Woman-hater* further complicates the issue of the gender basis for inclusion in women's alliances. Wayne argues that the unknowability of the gender of the author(s) of *Swetnam the Woman-hater* does not affect its political utility, any more than does the fact that it may have been written primarily to make a profit rather than to further women's social position. For her, anonymous authorship starkly reveals the performativity of gender. In the course of the "gender wars" resulting from Swetnam's initial tract, femininity and masculinity get elaborated as discursively constructed positions, but ones differentially linked to and entangled with various social structures and institutions such as the law or the university. Rather than a self-evident foundation, gender is a performative act with real social consequences, and as such it is an occasion for mobilization for and against social institutions and other social actors. Men can perform femininity, for progressive or reactionary ends, or, as men, they can ally themselves with or against feminist positions in gender struggles. What the Swetnam affair makes problematic is the claim to gender authenticity.

What it further obscures is any clear link between the intentions of actors and social outcomes. We do not know exactly who penned this play or why, whether the motive was profit, the eradication of misogyny, or the incitement of further misogyny. Paradoxically, social outcomes may have involved *both* the production of further antifeminist discourse *and* the articulation of gender as a category of social identification and mobilization from which to press for feminist agendas having very little to do with Swetnam himself or his crude brand of woman-baiting. Undeniably, one of the gains of recent feminist work about the early modern period, including much of the work in this volume, has been to reclaim the individual and collective agency of women in articulating and forwarding what they understand to be their interests. Whether it be Sir Walter Ralegh's wife, Elizabeth Throckmorton, attempting to use networks of aristocratic women to secure the property claims of herself and her son; or the privileged and anonymous needlewomen of the period who by their choice of subject matter turned needlework into assertions of their claims to various kinds of power; or female writers of the seventeenth century who mobilized the legacy of Queen Elizabeth to articulate their authority as writing subjects—in all these cases and many others, women tacitly or explicitly united with other women in the purposeful pursuit of their gendered interests. In recognizing the variety of strategies by which early modern women made discursive and material alliances with other women to get what they individually and collectively desired, scholars are rewriting the narratives that construct women, especially women in past eras, as victims pure and simple.

Nonetheless, any rigorous account of social change and gender struggle will also need to take account of unanticipated outcomes and of changes that result from social transformations that are not willed or controlled by any social group. In a trivial sense the anonymity of the play arraigning Swetnam and its complex social effects simply make evident what is more generally true: that actors act in conditions not primarily of their own making, that stated and actual intentions may differ, and that outcomes of action are unpredictable. There are many large-scale phenomena, such as the advent of capitalism, that make the analysis of agency even more complicated. As Alice Clark argued at the beginning of this century, the material conditions circumscribing women's lives changed markedly in the seventeenth century, particularly as the work place and the home began to be separate spaces and as women's roles in production changed. The endless debate about whether things got worse or better for women as a result of these changes may be unanswerable if posed in such monolithic terms, precisely because "women" is not a unified category and because change occurred unevenly across a range of practices and spheres. Nonetheless, women's alliances and women's collective agency both affected the material world around them and were affected by it. To understand fully how women were social agents in the early modern period, and the limits of their agency, it is necessary to take account of the complicated economic and social structures in which they functioned. Before the advent of the public theater and the printing press, the Swetnam affair could not have unfolded as it did, with print and the market lending notoriety both to a misogynist and his adversaries, and making gender a complicated point of identification and politicization. There is much more work of a systematic sort to be done in exploring the complex relationship between material change and women's collective agency, but this volume points the way toward such large-scale studies.

The value of this volume, however, lies not only in the way it marks a fresh moment in the development of feminist work on early modern texts, but also in the new knowledge it gives us. There is no sense in recapitulating the contents of the essays here. Suffice it to say that work on understudied texts such as *Westward Ho* and the writings of Bathsua Makin and Diana Primrose is valuable, as is work on understudied social practices such as needlework and understudied social actors such as the female vagrant or the "female Jesuit." Though most of these essays are written by literary critics, historians are also represented. The fascinating essay by historian Kathleen Brown, for example, explores the complex relations among women on a Virginia plantation, demonstrating both how divided the women were from one another by factors such as race and class and also how gossip functioned as a social practice that disciplined women more than it united them.

I wonder, however, how many historians will read this book and avail themselves of the new knowledge it contains, as compared to the number of literary critics who eagerly devour the latest historical monographs on every aspect of early modern life from guild structures to religious practices? In recent years, the two-way street between literature and history increasingly has felt like a one-way thoroughfare. In part, this has to do with the reaction to new historicism within both literary and historical studies. New historicism's lasting impact is apparent everywhere. Few literary critics speak of the universal values embodied in the period's texts, and it is now mainstream critical practice to provide historical contextualization for canonical and noncanonical works alike.

At the same time, as a critical practice new historicism has limitations, and these have been detailed at exceeding length—a sure sign that new historicism has been important. Those alert to developments in the field have known for ten years that questions have been raised about the status of the anecdote in new historical practice, the relationship posited between historical particulars and general claims, the new practice's early commitment to the binaries of subversion and containment, its predominant interest in texts by and about men and social elites, its possible status as a new formalism, and, conversely, its insufficient attention to the formal properties of texts. Again, those alert to the field's development have seen changes in historicist work that implicitly or explicitly respond to many of these critiques. We are no longer living in a critical world in which "Invisible Bullets" can be taken as the vanguard of historicist work.

But in some literary and historical circles the nuanced debate about new historical practice has been reduced to the mantra: "new historicism isn't historical enough." Unpacking just what this means is not easy. To historians it sometimes seems to mean that literary work of an historicist stripe simply does not look enough like work done in history departments. This can be merely a defensive reaction to the unfamiliar. Sometimes it means that literary people are ignorant of the knowledge history departments produce and use words such as *class*, *the state*, *capitalism*, or *Puritanism* without understanding the rich historical debates about these phenomena as they apply, or do not apply, to the early modern period. This second category of critique is important and has to be addressed by literary scholars. We will not be producing adequate accounts of early modern culture if we choose to speak about phenomena that have interested historians and yet do so in ignorance of their work. It seems to me, however, that there has been a stampede to redress that problem. At Columbia University where I teach, literature graduate students are eagerly enrolling in history courses (though the traffic never goes in the opposite direction), and literary conferences in the early modern period have reached out to include historians on programs and panels. I hardly know a literary scholar who does not regularly read the latest historical monographs in our field.

I am much less certain that the same can be said of historians' knowledge of literary criticism. The problem here is a complex one. The cry that "new historicism isn't historical enough" has made some literary scholars think that perhaps they should simply *become* historians in their work, that they should aspire to be like historians and learn their knowledges and their techniques of inquiry. This establishes the dynamic whereby the historian is constructed as the authority who corrects and instructs—surely a tempting subject position. But new historicism at its most promising was not about turning literary scholars into historians, but about producing new forms of historical knowledge in which all kinds of cultural texts, including poems, plays, and humanist prose, but also popular pamphlets, diaries, travel narratives, court cases, maps, and pictures, would be read for evidence of the ideological struggles, the social logics, and the shaping narratives that gave meanings to early modern life.

Historically minded literary scholars should not aspire, in my view, to *be* historians; rather, they should be informed about historians' work and then go do their own work, with their own tools, which above all include well-developed strategies for reading texts in complex ways. Symptomatic readings of both the Marxist and the psychoanalytic variety have developed ways of reading the unsaid of narratives; for connecting latent and manifest content; and for dealing with displacements, repressions, contradictions, and elisions. Formalist and structuralist readings provide strategies for grouping texts into genres, for relating particular texts to categories of texts, and for discussing the politics of form and the way the formal features of texts structure and construct meaning. Discursive analyses provide strategies for reading across generic and formal boundaries to map the operation of dominant, residual, emergent categories of thought. In practice, literary scholars are defined partly by the kinds of texts they read, and new historicism has expanded notions of what those texts can be. But the field is defined as well by the techniques used to approach those texts, and those techniques of reading are various, rigorous, and highly developed. Using those strategies to read early modern texts produces knowlege about dimensions of early modern life not necessarily attended to by historians. Literary critics read texts not necessarily to map "the way it was" in an empirical sense, but to expose conflicting constructions of the real, to read the fantasy life of a culture, or to chart the anticipatory and compensatory functions of narrative. Fantasies, narratives, discourses, and genres—these are all historical phenomena. Is it presumptuous to assume that the knowledge literary critics produce about them should be of as much interest to historians as their monographs ought to be to us?

In this volume, Jodi Mikalachki's essay on female vagrants does a fine job in showing what historians can learn from literary scholars. Warning literary critics against the unproblematic borrowing from social and cultural history to ground their own readings of texts, she skillfully shows the limitations in historians' constructions of the female vagrant, limitations springing in large part from inadequate reading strategies and sometimes from a blindness to gender stereotyping. Mikalachki's account of the female vagrant, and her reading of the texts through which this figure comes into view, should certainly be of interest to historians as well as to literary critics, demonstrating how a two-way traffic in the sharing of knowledge can lead to more adequate historical narratives on the part of historians as well as literary scholars.

Maids and Mistresses, Cousins and Queens: Women's Alliances in Early Modern England provides plenty of material, then, for thinking again about the relationship of history to literature, about more adequate strategies for reading texts historically, and, above all, about the material and political nature of women's alliances in this period. As an example of the various ways in which critical practice can be both feminist and historicist, it shows how far we, collectively, have come from the early days of feminist work, even as its concluding section points ahead to the work still to be accomplished in expanding our understanding of who is to be included in these alliances.

Bibliography

Abrams, Philip, and E. A. Wrigley, eds. *Towns in Societies: Essays in Economic History and Historical Sociology*. Cambridge: Cambridge University Press, 1978.

Adams, Simon. "Eliza Enthroned? The Elizabethan Court and Its Politics." In *The Reign of Elizabeth I*, ed. Christopher Haigh, pp. 55–77. London: Macmillan, 1984.

Adelman, Janet. "Male Bonding in Shakespeare's Comedies." In *Shakespeare's "Rough Magic": Renaissance Essays in Honor of C. L. Barber*, ed. Peter Erikson and Coppélia Kahn, pp. 73–103. Newark: University of Delaware Press, 1985.

———. *Suffocating Mothers: Fantasies of Maternal Origin in Shakespeare's Plays, Hamlet to The Tempest*. New York: Routledge, 1992.

Aers, David. "*Piers Plowman*: Poverty, Work, and Community." In *Gender, Community, and Individual Identity*, 1988.

Alexander, Michael van Cleave. *The Growth of English Education: 1348–1648*. Pennsylvania State University Press, 1990.

Amussen, Susan Dwyer. "Elizabeth I and Alice Balstone: Gender, Class, and the Exceptional Woman in Early Modern England." In *Attending to Women in Early Modern England*, ed. Betty S. Travitsky and Adele F. Seeff, pp. 219–40. Newark: University of Delaware Press, 1994.

———. "Gender, Family, and the Social Order, 1560–1725." In *Order and Disorder in Early Modern England*, ed. Anthony Fletcher and John Stevenson, pp. 196–217. Cambridge: Cambridge University Press, 1985.

———. *An Ordered Society: Gender and Class in Early Modern England*. Oxford: Basil Blackwell, 1988.

Anderson, Benedict. *Imagined Communities: Reflections on the Origin and Spread of Nationalism*. London: Verso, 1991.

Anderson, Mary Desiree. *Drama and Imagery in English Medieval Churches*. Cambridge: Cambridge University Press, 1963.

Anderson, Patricia Anne. "Gossips, Ale-Wives, Midwives, and Witches." Ph.D. diss., SUNY-Buffalo, 1992.

Andreadis, Harriette. "The Sapphic-Platonics of Katherine Philips, 1632–1664." *Signs* 15 no. 1 (Autumn 1989): 34–60.

———. "Sappho in Early Modern England: A Study in Sexual Reputation." In *Re-Reading Sappho: Reception and Transmission*, ed. Ellen Greene, pp. 105–21. Berkeley: University of California Press, 1997.

Anonymous. *Westward For Smelts*, ed. James Orchard Halliwell. London: The Percy Society, 1848.

Arthur, Liz. *Embroidery 1600–1700 at the Burrell Collection*. London: John Murray, 1995.

Ashley, Kathleen. "Divine Power in Chester Cycle and Late Medieval Thought." *Journal of the History of Ideas* 39 (1978): 387–404.

Ashley, Sir Francis. *The Case Book of Sir Francis Ashley J.P., Recorder of Dorchester, 1614–1635*, ed. J. H. Betty. Dorset Record Society, 1981.

———. *The Case Book of Sir Francis Ashley*. British Library, Harleian MSS 6715.

Aske, James. "Elizabetha Triumphans." In *The Progresses and Public Processions of Queen Elizabeth*. Vol. 2, ed. John Nichols, pp. 545–82. London, 1788–1805.

Assembly Books of Southampton, 1602–1616. 4 vols., ed. J. W. Horrocks. Southampton: Cox & Sharland, 1917–1925. [ABS]

Astell, Mary. *A serious proposal to the ladies, for the advancement of their true and greatest interest*. London, 1694.

Auerbach, Nina. *Communities of Women*. Cambridge, Massachusetts: Harvard University Press, 1978.

Aveling, Hugh. *The Jesuits*. New York: Stein and Day, 1981.

Awdeley, John. "The Fraternity of Vagabonds." In *The Elizabethan Underworld*, ed. A. V. Judges, pp. 51–60. London: Routledge, 1930.

Axton, Marie. *The Queen's Two Bodies: Drama and the Elizabethan Succession*. London: Royal Historical Society, 1977.

Aydelotte, Frank. *Elizabethan Rogues and Vagabonds*. Oxford: Clarendon, 1913.

Babcock, Barbara A. *The Reversible World: Symbolic Inversion in Art and Society*. Ithaca, N.Y.: Cornell University Press, 1978.

Barash, Carol. "The Political Origins of Anne Finch's Poetry." *Huntington Library Quarterly* 54 (Autumn 1991): 327–51.

Barlow, William. *Magneticall Advertisements*. 1616. Reprint, Amsterdam and New York: Theatrum Orbis Terrarum and Da Capo Press, 1968.

Barnfield, Richard. In *The Penguin Book of Homosexual Verse*, ed. Stephen Coote, p. 166. New York: Viking Penguin, 1986.

Bartels, Emily C. "Malta, the Jew, and the Fictions of Difference: Colonial Discourse in Marlowe's *The Jew of Malta*." *English Literary Renaissance* 20, no. 1 (1990): 1–16.

Barthes, Roland. "The Death of the Author." In *Image, Music, Text*, trans. Stephen Heath, pp. 142–48. New York: Hill and Wang, 1977.

Bassnett, Susan. *Elizabeth I: A Feminist Perspective*. New York: St. Martin's Press, 1988.

Beckwith, Sarah. *Christ's Body: Identity, Culture, and Society in Late Medieval Writings*. New York: Routledge, 1993.

Beek, Pieta van. "'One Tongue is Enough for a Woman': The Correspondence in Greek between Anna Maria van Schurman and Bathsua Makin." *Dutch Crossing: A Journal of Low Country Studies* 19, no. 1 (Summer 1995): 24–48.

Behn, Aphra. *Oroonoko, The Rover, and Other Works*, ed. Janet Todd. Columbus: Ohio State University Press, 1992.

———. "To the Fair Clarinda, Who Made Love to Me, Imagined More than Woman (1688)." In *The Norton Anthology of Literature by Women*, ed. Sandra Gilbert and Susan Gubar. New York: W. W. Norton & Company, 1985.

———. *The Works of Aphra Behn*, ed. Janet Todd. Columbus: Ohio State University Press, c.1992–c.1996.

Beier, A. L. *Masterless Men: The Vagrancy Problem in England, 1560–1640*. London: Methuen, 1985.

Beier, A. L., and Finlay, Roger. *London 1500–1700: The Making of the Metropolis*. London and New York: Longman, 1986.

Beilin, Elaine V. *Redeeming Eve: Women Writers of the English Renaissance*. Princeton, N.J.: Princeton University Press, 1987.

Belsey, Catherine. "Disrupting Sexual Difference: Meaning and Gender in the Comedies." In *Alternative Shakespeares*, ed. John Drakakis, pp. 166–90. New York: Methuen, 1985.

Bennett, Judith. *Ale, Beer, and Brewsters in England: Women's Work in a Changing World, 1300–1600*. New York: Oxford University Press, 1996.

———. "Conviviality and Charity in Medieval and Early Modern England." *Past and Present* (February 1992): 19–42.

———. "Medieval Women, Modern Women: Across the Great Divide." In *Culture and History, 1350–1600: Essays on English Communities, Identities and Writing*, ed. David Aers, pp. 147–75. Detroit, Mich.: Wayne State University Press, 1992b.

———. "Misogyny, Popular Culture, and Women's Work." *History Workshop Journal* 31 (1992): 166–88.

———. "The Village Ale-Wife: Women and Brewing in Fourteenth-Century England." In *Women and Work in Pre-Industrial England*, ed. Barbara Hanawalt, pp. 20–36. Bloomington: Indiana University Press, 1986.

Bennett, Judith, Elizabeth Clark, and Sarah Westphal-Wihl, eds. *Working Together in the Middle Ages; Perspectives on Women's Communities*. Signs 14 (Winter 1989).

Bergeron, David M. *Shakespeare's Romances and the Royal Family*. Lawrence: University Press of Kansas, 1985.

Berry, Philippa. *Of Chastity and Power: Elizabethan Literature and the Unmarried Queen*. London and New York: Routledge, 1989.

Bevington, David. *Medieval Drama*. Boston: Houghton Mifflin, 1975.

Biale, David. *Eros and the Jews: From Biblical Israel to Contemporary America*. New York: Basic Books, 1992.

Bieber, Margarete. *Ancient Copies: Contributions to the History of Greek and Roman Art*. New York: New York University Press, 1977.

Blain, Virginia, Isobel Grundy, and Patricia Clements, eds. *The Feminist Companion to Literature in English*. New Haven, Conn.: Yale University Press, 1990.

Blayney, Peter W. M. *The Text of King Lear and their Origins, Vol. 1: Nicholas Okes and the First Quarto*. Cambridge: Cambridge University Press, 1982.

Bloch, R. Howard. "Medieval Misogyny." In *Misogyny, Misandry, and Misanthropy*, ed. R. Howard Bloch and Frances Ferguson, pp. 1–24. Berkeley: University of California Press, 1989.

Boccaccio, Giovanni. *Concerning Famous Women*, trans. Guido A. Guarino. London: George Allen and Unwin, 1964.

Bono, Barbara. "Mixed Gender, Mixed Genre in Shakespeare's *As You Like It*." In *Renaissance Genres: Essays on Theory, History, and Interpretation*, ed. Barbara Keifer Lewalski, pp. 189–212. Cambridge, Mass.: Harvard University Press, 1986.

Boose, Lynda. "'The Getting of a Lawful Race': Racial Discourse in Early Modern England and the Unrepresentable Black Woman." In *Women, "Race," and Writing in the Early Modern Period*, ed. Margo Hendricks and Patricia Parker, pp. 35–54. London: Routledge, 1994.

———. "Scolding Brides and Bridling Scolds: Taming the Woman's Unruly Member." *Shakespeare Quarterly* 42, no. 2 (1991): 179–213.

Bourdieu, Pierre. *In Other Words: Essays Towards a Reflexive Sociology*, trans. Matthew Adamson. Stanford, Calif.: Stanford University Press, 1990.

Boyarin, Daniel. "'This We Know to Be the Carnal Israel': Circumcision and the Erotic Life of God and Israel." *Critical Inquiry* 18 (Spring 1992): 474–505.

Bradbrook, Muriel. "Dramatic Role as Social Image: A Study of *The Taming of the Shrew*." *Shakespeare-Jahrbuch* 94 (1958): 132–50.

Bradley, Ritamary. "Backgrounds of the Title *Speculum* in Medieval Literature." *Speculum* 29 (1954): 100–15.

Bradstreet, Anne. "In Honor of that High and Mighty Princess, Queen Elizabeth, of Most Happy Memory." In *The Complete Works of Anne Bradstreeet*, ed. Joseph R. McElrath, Jr., and Allan P. Robb. Boston: Twayne, 1981.

Brathwaite, Richard. *The English Gentlewoman*. 1631. In *Daughters, Wives, and Widows: Writings by Men about Women and Marriage in England, 1500–1640*, ed. Joan Larsen Klein. Urbana and Chicago: University of Illinois Press, 1992.

Braunmuller, A. R., and Michael Hattaway, eds. *The Cambridge Companion to English Renaissance Drama*. Cambridge: Cambridge University Press, 1990.

Bray, Alan. *Homosexuality in Renaissance England*. Boston: Gay Men's Press, 1982.

Bredbeck, Gregory. *Sodomy and Interpretation: From Marlowe to Milton*. Ithaca, N.Y.: Cornell University Press, 1991.

Brink, Jean R. "Bathsua Makin: Educator and Linguist." In *Female Scholars: A Tradition of Learned Women before 1800*, ed. Jean R. Brink, pp. 86–100. Montreal: Eden Press Women's Publications, 1980.

———. "Bathsua Reginald Makin: 'Most Learned Matron.'" *Huntington Library Quarterly* 54, no. 4 (1991): 313–26.

Bristol, Michael D. *Big-time Shakespeare*. London: Routledge, 1996.

Broe, Mary Lynn, and Angela Ingram. *Women's Writing in Exile*. Chapel Hill and London: University of North Carolina Press, 1989.

Brooten, Bernadette. *Love Between Women: Early Christian Responses to Female Homoeroticism*. Chicago: University of Chicago Press, 1996.

Brown, Judith. *Immodest Acts: The Life of a Lesbian Nun in Renaissance Italy*. New York: Oxford University Press, 1978.

Brown, Kathleen. *Good Wives, Nasty Wenches, and Anxious Patriarchs: Gender, Race, and Power in Colonial Virginia*. Chapel Hill: University of North Carolina Press, 1996.

Brown, Laura. "The Romance of Empire: *Oroonoko* and the Trade in Slaves." In *The New Eighteenth Century*, ed. Laura Brown and Felicity Nussbaum, pp. 41–61. New York and London: Methuen, 1978.

Brownstein, Oscar. "Revision in the 'Deluge' of the Chester Cycle." *Speech Monographs* 36 (1969): 55–65.

Bruto, Giovanni. *The Necessarie, Fit, and Convenient Education of a Yong Gentlewoman*. London: Adam Islip, 1598. Ann Arbor: University Microfilms, Pollard Reel No. 181.

Bullough, Geoffrey. *Narrative and Dramatic Sources of Shakespeare*. 8 vols. New York: Columbia University Press, 1957–1975.

Burns, Jane. *Bodytalk: When Women Speak in Old French Literature*. Philadelphia: University of Pennsylvania Press, 1993.

Butler, Judith. *Gender Trouble: Feminism and the Subversion of Identity.* New York: Routledge, 1990.

Calendar of Dorset Wills Proved in the Prerogative Court of Canterbury, Somerset House, London, 1383–1700, ed. George S. Fry. London: Edward Fry and George Fry, 1911.

Callaghan, Dympna. "Re-reading Elizabeth Cary's *The Tragedie of Mariam, Faire Queene of Jewry.*" In *Women, "Race," and Writing in the Early Modern Period,* ed. Margo Hendricks and Patricia Parker, pp. 163–77. London: Routledge, 1994.

The Cambridge Companion to English Renaissance Drama, ed. A. R. Braunmuller and Michael Hattaway. Cambridge: Cambridge University Press, 1990.

Camden, Carroll. *The Elizabethan Woman.* Mamaroneck, N.Y.: Paul P. Appel, 1975.

Camden, William. *Annales: The True and Royall History of the famous Empresse Elizabeth queene of England,* trans. A. Darcie. London, 1625. STC 4497.

———. *The History and Annals of Elizabeth, Queen of England,* trans. Richard Norton. London, 1630. STC 4500.

Canham, Roy. *2000 Years of Brentford.* London: HMSO, 1978.

Capp, Bernard. *English Almanacs: Astrology and the Popular Press.* Ithaca, N.Y.: Cornell University Press, 1979.

Carby, Hazel V. *Reconstructing Womanhood: The Emergence of the Afro-American Woman Novelist.* New York: Oxford University Press, 1987.

Carlson, Susan. "Women in *As You Like It.*" *Essays in Literature* 14, no. 2 (Fall 1987): 152–69.

Caroll, Berenice A. *Liberating Women's History.* Urbana: University of Illinois Press, 1976.

Carr, Lois Green, and Lorena S. Walsh. "The Planter's Wife: The Experience of White Women in Seventeenth-Century Maryland." *William and Mary Quarterly,* 3rd ser., 25 (October 1977), 542–71.

Cary, Elizabeth, The Lady Falkland. *The Tragedie of Mariam, The Fair Queen of Jewry.* 1613. ed. Barry Weller and Margaret W. Ferguson. Berkeley: University of California Press, 1994.

Castiglione, Baldassare. *The Book of the Courtier,* trans. Sir Thomas Hoby. 1561. Reprint, ed. J. H. Whitfield. New York: E. P. Dutton, 1975.

Castle, Terry. *The Apparitional Lesbian: Female Homosexuality and Modern Culture.* New York: Columbia University Press, 1993.

Chamberlain, John. *The Letters of John Chamberlain.* 2 vols., ed. Norman Egbert McClure. Philadelphia: American Philosophical Society, 1939.

Chambers, Mary Catherine Elizabeth. *The Life of Mary Ward.* 2 vols., ed. Henry James Coleridge. London: Burns and Oates, 1882, 1885.

Chandler, Frank Wadleigh. *The Literature of Roguery.* Boston: Houghton Mifflin, 1907.

Charity, A. C. *Events and Their Afterlife: The Dialectics of Christian Typology in the Bible and Dante.* Cambridge: Cambridge University Press, 1996.

Cheal, David. *The Gift Economy.* London: Routledge, 1988.

Chernaik, Warren. *Sexual Freedom in Restoration Literature.* Cambridge: Cambridge University Press, 1995.

Christine de Pizan. "The Hours of Contemplation on the Passion of Our Lord." In *The Writings of Christine de Pizan,* ed. Charity Cannon Willard, pp. 346–47. New York: Persea, 1994.

Cioni, Maria I. *Women and Law in Elizabethan England with Particular Reference to the Court of Chancery.* New York: Garland, 1985.

Clancy, Thomas H. *Papist Pamphleteers: The Allen–Parsons Party and the Political Thought of the Counter-Reformation in England, 1572–1615.* Chicago: Loyola University Press, 1964.

Clark, Alice. *The Working Life of Women in the Seventeenth Century*. 1919. Reprint, London: Routledge & Kegan Paul, 1982.

Clark, Anna. "Anne Lister's Construction of Lesbian Identity." *Journal of the History of Sexuality* 7, no. 1 (July 1996): 23–50.

Clark, Peter. *The English Alehouse: A Social History, 1200–1830*. London: Longman, 1983.

———. "The Migrant in Kentish Towns 1580–1640." In *Crisis and Order in English Towns, 1500–1700*, ed. Peter Clark and Paul Slack, pp. 117–63. London: Routledge & Kegan Paul, 1972.

Clark, Peter, and Paul Slack, eds. *Crisis and Order in English Towns, 1500–1700*. London: Routledge & Kegan Paul, 1972.

Clifford, Anne. *The Diary of Anne Clifford 1616–1619: A Critical Edition*, ed. Katherine O. Acheson. New York: Garland Publishing, 1995.

———. *The Diary of Lady Anne Clifford*, ed. Vita Sackville-West. London: William Heinemann, 1924.

———. *Lady Anne Clifford*, ed. George C. Williamson. Kendal: Titus Wilson, 1922.

Clopper, Lawrence. "The History and Development of the Chester Cycle." *Modern Philology* 75 (1978): 219–46.

———. "Lay and Clerical Impact on Civic Religious Drama and Ceremony." In *Contexts for Early English Drama*, ed. Marianne Briscoe and John Coldewey, pp. 102–36. Bloomington: Indiana University Press, 1989.

———, ed. *Records of Early English Drama: Chester*. Toronto: University of Toronto Press, 1979.

Coiro, Ann Baynes. "Writing in Service: Sexual Politics and Class Position in the Poetry of Aemilia Lanyer and Ben Jonson." *Criticism* 35 (Summer 1993): 357–76.

Coldewey, John. "Some Economic Aspects of the Late Medieval Drama." In *Contexts for Early English Drama*, ed. Marianne Briscoe and John Coldewey, pp. 77–101. Bloomington: Indiana University Press, 1989.

Coote, Stephen, ed. *The Penguin Book of Homosexual Verse*. New York and Harmondsworth: Penguin, 1983.

Copland, Robert. "The Highway to the Spital-house." In *The Elizabethan Underworld*, ed. A. V. Judges, pp. 1–25. London: Routledge, 1930.

Cornwallis, Jane. *The Private Correspondence of Jane, Lady Cornwallis, 1613–1644*, ed. Lord Baybrooke. London, 1842.

Coulton, George Gordon. *Medieval Panorama: The English Scene from Conquest to Reformation*. Cambridge: The University Press, 1938.

Crandall, Coryl. Introduction to *Swetnam the Woman-hater*. West Lafayette, Ind.: Purdue University Studies, 1969.

Crawford, Patricia. *Women and Religion in England 1500–1720*. London and New York: Routledge, 1993.

———. "Women's Published Writings 1600–1700." In *Women in English Society 1500–1800*, ed. Mary Prior, pp. 211–82. London: Methuen, 1985.

Crawford, Patricia, and Sara Mendelson. "Sexual Identities in Early Modern England: The Marriage of Two Women in 1680." *Gender & History* 7, no. 3 (November 1995): 362–77.

Cressy, David. "Kinship in Early Modern England." *Past and Present* 113 (1986): 38–69.

Crompton, Louis. "The Myth of Lesbian Impunity: Capital Laws from 1291 to 1791." *Journal of Homosexuality* 6 (1980–81): 11–25.

Danielou, Jean. *From Shadows to Reality: Studies in the Biblical Typology of the Fathers*, trans. D. Wulstan Hibberd. London: Burns and Oates, 1960.

Daston, Lorraine, and Katherine Park. "The Hermaphrodite and the Orders of Nature: Sexual Ambiguity in Early Modern France." *GLQ: A Journal of Gay and Lesbian Studies* 1 (1995): 419–38.

Davies, John Silvester. *A History of Southampton.* Southampton: Gilbert & Co., 1883.

Davis, Natalie Zemon. *Fiction in the Archives: Pardon Tales and their Tellers in Sixteenth-Century France.* Stanford, Calif.: Stanford University Press, 1988.

———. "Women's History in Transition: The European Case." *Feminist Studies* 3, nos. 3–4 (1976): 82–103.

de Grazia, Margreta, Maureen Quilligan, and Peter Stallybrass, eds. *Subject and Object in Renaissance Culture.* Cambridge: Cambridge University Press, 1996.

Deimling, Hermann, ed. *The Chester Plays, Part 1.* EETS ES 62. London: Oxford University Press, 1892.

Dekker, Thomas. *The Bellman of London.* In *The Elizabethan Underworld,* ed. A. V. Judges, pp. 303–11. London: Routledge, 1930.

———. *Northward Ho.* Vol. 2, ed. Fredson Bowers. Cambridge University Press, 1958.

———[?]. *O per se O.* In *The Elizabethan Underworld,* ed. A. V. Judges, pp. 366–82. London: Routledge, 1930.

———. *Penny-Wise, Pound-Foolish,* ed. E. D. Pendry. Cambridge, Mass.: Harvard University Press, 1968.

Dekker, Thomas, and Thomas Middleton. *The Roaring Girl.* Vol. 3, ed. Fredson Bowers. Cambridge: Cambridge University Press, 1958.

Dekker, Thomas, and John Webster. *Westward Ho.* Vol. 2, ed. Fredson Bowers. Cambridge: Cambridge University Press, 1958.

de Lauretis, Teresa. *Alice Doesn't: Feminism, Semiotics, Cinema.* Bloomington: Indiana University Press, 1984.

———. *Technologies of Gender: Essays on Theory, Film, and Fiction.* Bloomington: Indiana University Press, 1987.

Derrida, Jacques. *The Postcard: From Socrates to Freud and Beyond,* trans. Alan Bass. Chicago and London: University of Chicago Press, 1987.

DiGangi, Mario. "Asses and Wits: The Homoerotics of Mastery in Satiric Comedy." *English Literary Renaissance* 25 (Spring 1995): 179–208.

Diggs, Marylynne. "Romantic Friends or 'A Different Race of Creatures': The Representation of Lesbian Pathology in Nineteenth-Century America." *Feminist Studies* 21, no. 2 (Summer 1995): 317–40.

Dolan, Frances. *Dangerous Familiars: Representations of Domestic Crime in England 1550–1700.* Ithaca, N.Y.: Cornell University Press, 1994.

Dollimore, Jonathan. *Sexual Dissidence: Augustine to Wilde, Freud to Foucault.* Oxford: Clarendon Press, 1991.

Donoghue, Emma. *Passion Between Women: British Lesbian Culture 1668–1801.* London: Scarlet Press, 1993.

The Dorset Protestation Returns Preserved in the House of Lords, 1641–2. Vol. 12, ed. Edward A. Fry. London: Edward Fry and George Fry, 1912.

Dorset Record Office. *Dorset Quarter Sessions Order Book.* QSM 1/1. [DQSM]

Dunn, Leslie C., and Nancy A. Jones, eds. *Embodied Voices: Representing Female Vocality in Western Literature.* Cambridge: Cambridge University Press, 1994.

Durant, David. *Bess of Hardwick: Portrait of an Elizabethan Dynast.* New York: Atheneum, 1978.

Edwards, Edward. *The Life of Sir Walter Raleigh.* 2 vols. London: Macmillan, 1868.

Elizabeth I. "The Golden Speech." London, 1601. STC 7578.

———. "Her MAIESTIES most Princely answere, delivered by her selfe at the Court at White-Hall, on the last day of November 1601." (Taken down by "A. B.") London, 1601.

———. *The Letters of Queen Elizabeth,* ed. G. B. Harrison. London: Cassell & Co., Ltd., 1935.

————. *The Poems of Queen Elizabeth I*, ed. Leicester Bradner. Providence, R.I.: Brown University Press, 1964.

————. *The Public Speaking of Queen Elizabeth*, ed. George Rice. New York: Columbia University Press, 1951.

Elliott, John. "Medieval Acting." In *Contexts for Early English Drama*, ed. Marianne Briscoe and John Coldewey, pp. 238–51. Bloomington: Indiana University Press, 1989.

Elliott, Vivien Brodsky. "Single Women in the London Marriage Market: Age, Status, and Mobility, 1598–1619." In *Marriage and Society: Studies in the Social History of Marriage*, ed. R. B. Outhwaite, pp. 81–100. New York: St. Martin's Press, 1982.

Erickson, Amy Louise. *Women and Property in Early Modern England*. London and New York: Routledge, 1993.

E. T. *The Lawe's Resolution of Women's Rights*. London: John More, 1632.

Evans, John T. *Seventeenth-Century Norwich*. Oxford: Clarendon, 1979.

Ezell, Margaret J. M. *The Patriarch's Wife: Literary Evidence and the History of the Family*. Chapel Hill and London: University of North Carolina Press, 1987.

Faderman, Lillian. *Surpassing the Love of Men: Romantic Friendship and Love Between Women from the Renaissance to the Present*. New York: Morrow, 1981.

Farge, Arlette. *Fragile Lives: Violence, Power, and Solidarity in Eighteenth-Century Paris*. Cambridge, Mass.: Harvard University Press, 1993.

Fehrenbach, R. J. "Isabella Whitney, Sir Hugh Plat, Geoffrey Whitney, and 'Sister Eldershae.'" *English Language Notes* 21 (September 1983): 7–11.

————, ed. "A Letter Sent by the Maydens of London (1567)." *English Literary Renaissance* 14 (Autumn 1984), 3: 28–47.

Ferguson, Margaret W. "Juggling the Categories of Race, Class and Gender: Aphra Behn's *Oroonoko*." *Women's Studies: An Inter-disciplinary Journal* 19 (Spring 1991): 159–81.

————. "Moderation and Its Discontents: Recent Work on Renaissance Women." *Feminist Studies* 20, no. 2 (1994): 349–66.

————. "News from the New World: Miscegenous Romance in Aphra Behn's *Oroonoko* and *The Widow Ranter*." In *The Production of English Renaissance Culture*, ed. David Lee Miller et al., pp. 151–89. Ithaca, N.Y.: Cornell University Press, 1994.

————. "Renaissance Concepts of the 'Woman Writer.'" In *Women and Literature in Britain, 1500–1700*, ed. Helen Wilcox, pp. 143–68. Cambridge: Cambridge University Press, 1996.

Ferguson, Margaret W., Maureen Quilligan, and Nancy J. Vickers. Introduction to *Rewriting the Renaissance: The Discourses of Sexual Difference in Early Modern Europe*, ed. Margaret W. Ferguson, Maureen Quilligan, and Nancy J. Vickers, pp. xv–xxxi. Chicago: University of Chicago Press, 1986.

Fergusson, Francis. *The Human Image in Dramatic Literature*. 1957. Reprint, Glouceste, Mass.: Peter Smith, 1969.

Fielding, Sarah. *The Governess, or Little Female Academy*. 1749. Reprint, with introduction by Mary Cadogan. London and New York: Pandora Press, 1987.

Fineman, Joel. "Fratricide and Cuckoldry: Shakespeare's Doubles." In *Representing Shakespeare: New Psychoanalytic Forms*, ed. Murray M. Schwartz and Coppélia Kahn. Baltimore: Johns Hopkins University Press, 1980.

Fisher, F. J. "The Development of the London Food Market, 1540–1640." *The Economic History Review* 5, no. 2 (1935): 46–64.

Fisher, Sheila. "Taken Men and Token Women in *Sir Gawain and the Green Knight*." In *Seeking the Woman in Late Medieval and Renaissance Writings:*

Essays in Feminist Contextual Criticism, ed. Sheila Fisher and Janet E. Halley, pp. 71–105. Knoxville: University of Tennessee Press, 1989.

Fisher, Sheila, and Janet E. Halley, eds. *Seeking the Woman in Late Medieval and Renaissance Writings: Essays in Feminist Contextual Criticism*. Knoxville: University of Tennessee Press, 1989.

Fitz, Linda T. "'What Says the Married Woman?': Marriage Theory and Feminism in the English Renaissance." *Mosaic* 13 (1980): 1–22.

Fletcher, Anthony, and John Stevenson, eds. *Order and Disorder in Early Modern England*. Cambridge: Cambridge University Press, 1985.

de Flores, Juan. *The Historie of Aurelio and of Isabell*. Antwerp: Juan Steelsio, 1556. STC 11092.

Foeken, Ingrid. "A Ritual a Day Keeps the Therapist Away: The Merger Process in a New Perspective." In *Homosexuality, Which Homosexuality?*, ed. Dennis Altman, Carole Vance, Martha Vicinus, Jeffrey Weeks et al., pp. 83–95. London and Amsterdam: GMP Publishers and Schorer, 1989.

Ford, John. *Tis Pity She's A Whore*. In *Drama of the English Renaissance II: The Stuart Period*, ed. Russell A. Fraser and Norman Rabkin, pp. 651–80. New York: Macmillan, 1976.

Forman, Simon. *Casebooks*. Bodleian Manuscript Ashmole 226.

Foucault, Michel. *The History of Sexuality*, vol. 1: *An Introduction*, trans. Robert Hurley. New York: Vintage Books, 1980.

———. "Nietzsche, Genealogy, History." In *The Foucault Reader*, ed. Paul Rabinow, pp. 76–100. Harmondsworth: Penguin, 1986a.

———. "What Is an Author?" In *The Foucault Reader*, ed. Paul Rabinow, pp. 101–20. Harmondsworth: Penguin, 1986b.

Foxwell, William, and C. S. Mann, eds. *The Anchor Bible: Matthew*. Garden City, N.Y.: Doubleday, 1971.

Frankenburg, Ruth. *White Women, Race Matters: The Social Construction of Whiteness*. Minneapolis: University of Minnesota Press, 1993.

Frantis, Wayne E. *Paragons of Virtue: Women and Domesticity in Seventeenth-Century Dutch Art*. New York: Cambridge University Press, 1993.

Fraser, Antonia. *The Weaker Vessel*. New York: Knopf, 1984.

Fraser, Nancy. "Rethinking the Public Sphere: A Contribution to the Critique of an Actually Existing Democracy." In *Habermas and the Public Sphere*, ed. Craig Calhoun, pp. 109–42. Cambridge, Mass.: MIT Press, 1992.

Friedman, Jerome. "Jewish Conversion, the Spanish Pure Blood Laws, and Reformation: A Revisionist View of Racial and Religious Anti-semitism." *Sixteenth Century Journal* 18 (1987): 3–30.

Frye, Susan. *Elizabeth I: The Competition for Representation*. New York: Oxford University Press, 1993.

———. "The Myth of Elizabeth I at Tilbury." *Sixteenth Century Journal* 23 (1992): 95–114.

Furman, Nelly. "The Politics of Language: Beyond the Gender Principle?" In *Making a Difference: Feminist Literary Criticism*, ed. Gayle Greene and Coppélia Kahn, pp. 59–79. London and New York: Routledge, 1985.

Garber, Marjorie. *Vested Interests: Cross-Dressing and Cultural Anxiety*. New York: Routledge, 1992.

Garrity, Jane. "Encoding Bi-Location: Sylvia Townsend Warner and the Erotic of Dissimulation." In *Lesbian Erotics*, ed. Karla Jay. New York and London: New York University Press, 1995.

Garvin, Katherine. "A Note on Noah's Wife." *Modern Language Notes* 49 (1983): 88–90.

Giamatti, A. Bartlett. *Exile and Change in Renaissance Literature*. New Haven, Conn.: Yale University Press, 1984.

Gibson, Gail McMurray. *The Theater of Devotion: East Anglian Drama and Society in the Late Middle Ages.* Chicago: University of Chicago Press, 1989.

Gilbert, Sandra, and Susan Gubar, eds. *The Norton Anthology of Literature By Women: The Traditions in English.* 1985 2nd ed. New York and London: Norton, 1996.

Girouard, Mark. *Hardwick Hall.* 1989. Reprint, London: The National Trust, 1992.

Godin, Karin S. "'Slander in an Allow'd Fool': *Twelfth Night*'s Crisis of the Aristocracy." *Studies in English Literature* 33, no. 2 (Spring 1993): 309–25.

Goldberg, Jonathan. *Desire Women Writing: English Renaissance Examples.* Stanford, Calif.: Stanford University Press, 1997.

———. *Sodometries: Renaissance Texts, Modern Sexualities.* Stanford, Calif.: Stanford University Press, 1992.

Goldberg, P. J. P. *Women, Work, and Life Cycle in a Medieval Economy: Women in York and Yorkshire c. 1300–1520.* Oxford: Clarendon Press; New York: Oxford University Press, 1992.

———. "Women's Work, Women's Role in the Late-Medieval North." In *Profit, Piety, and the Professions in Later Medieval England*, ed. Michael Hicks, pp. 34–50. Gloucester: Alan Sutton, 1990.

Great Britain. *Public Record Office. Letters and Papers, Foreign and Domestic of the Reign of Henry VIII*, volume 17, ed. James Gairdner and R. H. Brodie. London: HMSO, 1900.

Greenblatt, Stephen. *Shakespearean Negotiations: The Circulation of Social Energy in Renaissance England.* Berkeley: University of California Press, 1988.

Greene, Gayle, and Coppélia Kahn. "Feminist Scholarship and the Social Construction of Woman." In *Making a Difference: Feminist Literary Criticism*, ed. Gayle Greene and Coppélia Kahn, pp. 11–36. London and New York: Routledge, 1985a.

———, eds. *Making a Difference: Feminist Literary Criticism.* London and New York: Routledge, 1985b.

Greene, Richard. *Mary Leapor: A Study in Eighteenth-Century Women's Poetry.* Oxford: Clarendon Press, 1993.

Greene, Richard Leighton, ed. *A Selection of English Carols.* Oxford: Clarendon Press, 1962.

Greene, Robert. "The Conversion of an English Courtezan." In *The Elizabethan Underworld*, ed. A. V. Judges, pp. 226–47. London: Routledge, 1930a.

———. "A Disputation Between a He-Cony-Catcher and a She-Cony-Catcher." In *The Elizabethan Underworld*, ed. A. V. Judges, pp. 206–26. London: Routledge, 1930b.

———. *A Quippe for an Upstart Courtier: The Life and Complete Works of Robert Greene.* Vol. 11, ed. A. B. Grosart, pp. 205–94, 323–37. New York: Russell and Russell, 1964.

Greer, Germaine, Susan Hastings, Jesyln Medoff, and Melinda Sansone, eds. *Kissing the Rod: An Anthology of Seventeenth-Century Women's Verse.* New York: Noonday Press, 1988.

Grossberg, Lawrence, Cary Nelson, and Paula A. Treichler, eds. *Cultural Studies.* New York: Routledge, 1992.

Guilday, Peter. *The English Catholic Refugees on the Continent, 1558–1795.* London: Longmans, Green, 1914.

Gunew, Sneja. *Feminist Knowledge: Critique and Construct.* London: Routledge, 1990.

Gurr, Andrew. *Playgoing in Shakespeare's London.* Cambridge: Cambridge University Press, 1987.

Habermas, Jurgen. *The Structural Transformation of the Public Sphere: An Inquiry into a Category of Bourgeois Society.* Cambridge, Mass.: MIT Press, 1989.

Haigh, Christopher. *Elizabeth I*. London: Longman, 1988.

Hakluyt, Richard. *The Principall Navigations: Voyages, Traffiques and Discoveries of the English Nation* 1598–1600. 12 vols., ed. Walter Raleigh. Glasgow: James Maclehose & Sons, 1903–5.

Hall, Kim. "Acknowledging Things of Darkness: Race, Gender, and Power in Early Modern England." Ph.D. diss., University of Pennsylvania, 1990.

———. "'I Rather Would Wish To Be A Black-Moor': Beauty, Race, and Rank in Lady Mary Wroth's *Urania*." In *Women, "Race," and Writing in The Early Modern Period*, ed. Margo Hendricks and Patricia Parker, pp. 178–94. London: Routledge, 1994.

———. "Sexual Politics and Cultural Identity in *The Masque of Blackness*." In *The Performance of Power: Theatrical Discourse and Politics*, ed. Sue-Ellen Case and Janelle Reinelt, pp. 3–18. Iowa City: University of Iowa Press, 1991.

———. *Things of Darkness: Economies of Race and Gender in Early Modern England*. Ithaca, N.Y.: Cornell University Press, 1995.

Halley, Janet E. "Textual Intercourse: Anne Donne, John Donne, and the Sexual Poetics of Textual Exchange." In *Seeking the Woman in Late Medieval and Renaissance Writings: Essays in Feminist Contextual Criticism*, ed. Sheila Fisher and Janet E. Halley, 188–206. Knoxville: University of Tennessee Press, 1989.

Hanawalt, Barbara A. "Lady Honor Lisle's Networks of Influence." In *Women and Power in the Middle Ages*, ed. Mary Erler and Maryanne Kowaleski, pp. 188–212. Athens: University of Georgia Press, 1988.

Hannay, Margaret, ed. *Silent but for the Word: Tudor Women as Patrons, Translators, and Writers of Religious Work*. Kent, Ohio: Kent State University Press, 1985.

Happe, Peter et al. "Thoughts on 'Transvestism' by Divers Hands." *Medieval English Theatre* 5, no. 2 (1983): 110–22.

Harbage, Alfred, S. Schoenbaum, and Sylvia Stoler Wagonheim, eds. *Annals of English Drama, 975–1700*. London: Routledge, 1989.

Harman, Thomas. "A Caveat or Warning for Common Cursitors, Vulgarly called Vagabonds." In *The Elizabethan Underworld*, ed. A. V. Judges, pp. 60–118. London: Routledge, 1930.

Harris, Barbara J. "Property, Power, and Personal Relations: Elite Mothers and Sons in Yorkist and Early Tudor England." *Signs* 15, no. 3 (1990): 606–32.

Harris, John Wesley. *Medieval Theatre in Context: An Introduction*. London: Routledge, 1992.

Harty, Kevin. "The Unity and Structure of the Chester Mystery Cycle." *Mediaevalia* 2 (1976): 137–58.

Harvey, Elizabeth. "Ventriloquizing Sappho: Ovid, Donne, and the Erotics of the Feminine Voice." *Criticism* 31 (1989): 115–38.

———. *Ventriloquized Voices: Feminist Theory and English Renaissance Texts*. London: Routledge, 1992.

Hay, Robert. "Addenda to Shakespeare's Bawdy: *As You Like It*, IV.1.201–208." *American Notes & Queries* 13, no. 4 (December 1974): 51–53.

Haywood, Louise M. "*Gradissa*: A Fictional Female Reader in/of a Male Author's Text." *Medium Aevum* 64, no. 1 (1995): 85–99.

Hearn, Karen. *Dynasties: Painting in Tudor and Jacobean England*. Peterborough: Tate, 1995.

Heber, Reginald, ed. *The Whole Works of the Right Rev. Jeremy Taylor*. 15 vols. London: Ogle, Duncan and Co., 1822.

Heisch, Allison. "Queen Elizabeth I: Parliamentary Rhetoric and the Exercise of Power." *Signs* 1, no. 4 (Autumn 1975): 31–55.

———. "Queen Elizabeth and the Persistence of Patriarchy." *Feminist Review* 4 (1980): 45–56.

Helm, James L. "Bathsua Makin's *An Essay to Revive the Art of Antient Educa-tion of Gentlewomen.*" In *The Canon of Seventeenth-Century Educational Reform Tracts. Cahiers Elisabethains* 44 (October 1993): 45–55.

Henderson, Katharine Usher, and Barbara McManus, eds. *Half Humankind: Contexts and Texts of the Controversy about Women in England, 1540–1640.* Urbana: University of Illinois Press, 1985.

Hendricks, Margo, and Patricia Parker, eds. *Women, "Race," and Writing in the Early Modern Period.* London: Routledge, 1994.

Hening, William Waller, ed. *The Statutes at Large.* 5 vols. Richmond, Va.: S. Shepherd, 1809–23.

Herman, Peter. "Leaky Ladies and Droopy Dames: The Grotesque Realism of Skelton's *The Tunnynge of Elynour Rummynge.*" In *Rethinking the Henrician Era: Essays on Early Tudor Texts and Contexts,* ed. Peter Herman, pp. 145–69. Urbana: University of Illinois Press, 1994.

Heywood, Thomas. *England's Elizabeth Her Life and Troubles During Her Minorities from the Cradle to the Crown.* London, 1631. STC 13313.

————. *If You Know Not Me, You Know Nobody.* Part 1. 1605. Reprint, ed. Philip R. Ryder. New York: Garland, 1982.

————. *If You Know Not Me, You Know Nobody.* Part 2. 1605. Reprint, ed. Madeline Doran. London: Malone Society, Oxford University Press, 1934.

Hibbert, Christopher. *The Virgin Queen: Elizabeth I, Genius of the Golden Age.* Reading, Mass.: Addison-Wesley, 1991.

Hicks, Leo. "Mary Ward's Great Enterprise." Serialized in *The Month* (Febru-ary 1928): 137–46; (April 1928): 317–26; (July 1928): 40–52; (September 1928): 231–38; (January 1929): 40–48; (March 1929): 223–36.

Hill, Christopher. "Censorship and English Literature." In *The Collected Essays of Christopher Hill,* pp. 32–71. Amherst: University of Massachusetts Press, 1987.

Hind, Arthur M. *Engraving in England in the Sixteenth and Seventeenth Centu-ries,* vol. 2. Cambridge: Cambridge University Press, 1955.

Hindley, Charles. *Tavern Anecdotes and Sayings.* London: Chatto and Windus, 1875.

Hirshberg, Jeffrey Alan. "Noah's Wife on the Medieval English Stage: Icono-graphic and Dramatic Values of Her Distaff and Choice of the Raven." *Stud-ies in Iconography* 2 (1976): 25–40.

Historical Manuscripts Commission. *Calendar of the Manuscripts of the Most Honorable the Marquess of Salisbury Preserved at Hatfield House.* 14 vols., ed. Edward Salisbury. London: HMSO, 1883–1923.

————. *Calendar of the Manuscripts of the Most Honorable, the Marquess of Salisbury Preserved at Hatfield House.* Vol. 15, ed. M. S. Giuseppe. Lon-don: HMSO, 1930.

————. *Report on the Laing Manuscripts Preserved in the University of Edinburgh.* Vol. 1, ed. Henry Patom. London: HMSO, 1914.

————. *Report on the Manuscripts of Allan George Finch, Esquire. Called Burley-on-the-Hill, Rutland.* Vol. 1, ed. S. C. Lomas. London: HMSO, 1913.

————. *Report on the Manuscripts of Lord De L'Isle and Dudley Preserved at Penshurst Place.* 6 vols., ed. C. L. Kingsford. London: HMSO, 1888–1905.

Hobby, Elaine. "'My affection hath an unknown bottom': Homosexuality and the Teaching of *As You Like It.*" In *Shakespeare and the Changing Curricu-lum,* ed. Lesley Aers and Nigel Wheale, pp. 125–42. London: Routledge, 1992.

————. *Virtue of Necessity: English Women's Writing 1646–1688.* London: Virago Press, 1988.

Hoby, Mary Margaret. *The Diary of Lady Margaret Hoby 1599–1605,* ed. Dor-othy M. Meads. New York: Houghton Mifflin, 1930.

Hodges, Laura F. "'Noe's Wife': Type of Eve and Wakefield Spinner and 'Re-
    calcitrant Wife' in the Ramsey Abbey Psalter." In *Equally in God's Image:
    Women in the Middle Ages*, ed. Julia Bolton-Holloway, Joan Bechtold, and
    Constance S. Wright, pp. 30–45. New York: Peter Lang, 1990.
Holinshed, Raphael et al. *Chronicles of England, Scotland, and Ireland*. Vol. 4.
    London: J. Johnson, 1808.
Holme, Randle. *The Academy of Armory, or A Storehouse of Armory and Blazon*.
    Vol. 2. London: Roxburghe Club, 1905.
Holstun, James. "'Will you rend our ancient love asunder?': Lesbian Elegy in
    Donne, Marvell, and Milton." *ELH* 54 (1987): 835–67.
hooks, bell. *Ain't I A Woman? Black Women and Feminism*. Boston: South End
    Press, 1981.
Hopkins, Lisa. *Elizabeth I and Her Court*. New York: St. Martin's Press, 1990.
Howard, Jean E. *The Stage and Social Struggle in Early Modern England*. New
    York: Routledge, 1994.
Howard, Jean E., and Phyllis Rackin. *Engendering a Nation: A Feminist Account
    of Shakespeare's English Histories*. London: Routledge, 1997.
Howe, Elizabeth. *The First English Actresses: Women and Drama, 1660–1700*.
    Cambridge: Cambridge University Press, 1992.
Howell, Martha. "Fixing Moveables: Gifts by Testament in Late Medieval Douai."
    Past and Present 43, no. 150 (1996): 3.
Hoy, Cyrus. Introductions, notes, and commentaries to texts in *The Dramatic
    Works of Thomas Dekker*. Vols. 2 and 3. Cambridge: Cambridge Univer-
    sity Press, 1980.
Hughes, Thomas. "On the Inns and Taverns of Chester, Past and Present, Part
    1." *Chester Archaeological Society Journal* 2 (1856): 91–110.
Hughes-Hallett, Lucy. *Cleopatra: Histories, Dreams, and Distortions*. New York:
    Harper Perennial, 1990.
Hull, Gloria T., Patricia Bell Scott, and Barbara Smith. *All the Women Are White,
    All the Blacks Are Men, But Some of Us Are Brave: Black Women's Studies*.
    Old Westbury, N.Y.: Feminist Press, 1982.
Hull, Suzanne. *Chaste, Silent, and Obedient: English Books for Women, 1475–
    1640*. San Marino, Calif.: Huntington Library, 1982.
Hunt, Margaret. "Report of a Conference on Feminism, Sexuality, and Power:
    The Elect Clash with the Perverse." In *Coming to Power: Writings and
    Graphics on Lesbian S/M*, ed. by the Members of Samois. 3rd ed., pp. 81–
    89. Boston: Alyson Publications, 1987.
Hunt, William. *The Puritan Moment: The Coming of Revolution in an English
    County*. Cambridge, Mass.: Harvard University Press, 1983.
Hutson, Lorna. "Emilia Lanier." In *The Dictionary of National Biography: Miss-
    ing Persons*, ed. C. S. Nicholls, pp. 388–89. Oxford: Oxford University Press,
    1993.
————. "Why the Lady's Eyes Are Nothing Like the Sun." In *New Feminist
    Discourses: Critical Essays on Theories and Texts*, ed. Isobel Armstrong,
    pp. 155–75. London: Routledge, 1992.
Hutton, Laurence. *Literary Landmarks of London*. London: Osgood, McIlvaine,
    1892.
Iles, C. M. "Early Stages of English Public House Regulation." *Economic Jour-
    nal* 13 (1903): 251–62.
Irigaray, Luce. *Speculum of the Other Woman*, trans. Gillian C. Gill. Ithaca, N.Y.:
    Cornell University Press, 1985.
————. *This Sex Which Is Not One*, trans. Catherine Porter. Ithaca, N.Y.: Cornell
    University Press, 1985.
Isaiah, Paul [Eleazar bar Isaiah, pseud.]. *The Messiah of the Christians and the
    Jewes*. London, 1655.

Jagose, Annamarie. *Lesbian Utopics*. New York and London: Routledge, 1994.

James, Mervyn. "Ritual, Drama, and Social Body in the Late Medieval English Town." *Past and Present* 98 (1983): 3–28.

James, T. B. *Southampton Sources 1086–1900*. Southampton: University of Southampton Press, 1983.

Jameson, Fredric. *The Political Unconscious: Narrative as a Socially Symbolic Act*. Ithaca, N.Y.: Cornell University Press, 1981.

Janeway, Elizabeth. *Man's World, Woman's Place: A Study in Social Mythology*. New York: Morrow, 1971.

Jankowski, Theodora A. "'As I Am Egypt's Queen': Cleopatra, Elizabeth I, and the Female Body Politic." In *Assays, Critical Approaches to Medieval and Renaissance Texts*, ed. Peggy A. Knapp, pp. 91–109. Pittsburgh: University of Pittsburgh Press, 1989.

———. "Historicizing and Legitimating Capitalism: Thomas Heywood's *Edward IV* and *If You Know Not Me, You Know Nobody*." *Medieval and Renaissance Drama in England* 7 (1995): 305–37.

———. *Women in Power in the Early Modern Drama*. Urbana: University of Illinois Press, 1992.

Jardine, Lisa. "Twins and Travesties: Gender, Dependency, and Sexual Availability in *Twelfth Night*." In *Erotic Politics: Desire on the Renaissance Stage*, ed. Susan Zimmerman, pp. 27–38. New York: Routledge, 1992.

Jay, Karla. "On Slippery Ground: An Introduction." In *Lesbian Erotics*, ed. Karla Jay, pp. 1–11. New York and London: New York University Press, 1995.

Jeafreson, John Cordy. "The Manuscripts of the Corporation of the City of Chester." In *Historical Manuscripts Commission: Appendix to the Eighth Report*. London: HMSO, 1908.

Jinner, Sarah. *An Almanack or Prognostication for the year of our LORD 1658*. London, 1658.

Johnson, Paul. *Elizabeth I: A Biography*. New York: Holt Rinehart, 1974.

Jones, Ann Rosalind. "Assimilation with a Difference: Renaissance Women Poets and Literary Influence." *Yale French Studies* 62 (1981): 135–53.

———. "Counterattacks on 'the Bayter of Women': Three Pamphleteers of the Early Seventeenth Century." In *The Renaissance Englishwoman in Print: Counterbalancing the Canon*, ed. Anne M. Haselkorn and Betty S. Travitsky, pp. 45–62. Amherst: University of Massachusetts Press, 1990a.

———. *The Currency of Eros: Women's Love Lyric in Europe, 1540–1620*. Bloomington: Indiana University Press, 1990b.

———. "Inscribing Femininity: French Theories of the Feminine." In *Making a Difference: Feminist Literary Criticism*, ed. Gayle Greene and Coppélia Kahn, pp. 80–112. London and New York: Routledge, 1985.

———. "Surprising Fame: Renaissance Gender Ideologies and Women's Lyric." In *The Poetics of Gender*, ed. Nancy K. Miller, pp. 74–95. New York: Columbia University Press, 1986.

Jonson, Ben. *Ben Jonson*. 11 vols., ed. C. H. Herford, Percy Simpson, and Evelyn Simpson. Oxford: Clarendon Press, 1925–1952.

———. "Discoveries." In *Ben Jonson: The Complete Poems*, ed. George Parfitt. Appendix 1, pp. 373–458. London: Penguin, 1988.

———. *Epicoene*. In *Drama of the English Renaissance: The Stuart Period*, eds. Russell A. Fraser and Norman Rabkin, pp. 101–42. New York: Macmillan, 1976.

———. *The Magnetic Lady*. In *Ben Jonson*. Vol. 6, ed. C. H. Herford, Percy Simpson, and Evelyn Simpson, pp. 499–597. Oxford: Clarendon Press, 1938.

———. *The Masque of Beauty*. In *Ben Jonson*. Vol. 7, ed. C. H. Herford, Percy Simpson, and Evelyn Simpson, pp. 181–94. Oxford: Clarendon Press, 1941.

————. *The Masque of Blackness.* In *Ben Jonson.* Vol. 7, ed. C. H. Herford, Percy Simpson, and Evelyn Simpson, pp. 169–80. Oxford: Clarendon Press, 1941.

————. *The Sad Shepherd.* In *Ben Jonson's Plays and Masques,* ed. Robert M. Adams, pp. 275–310. New York and London: W. W. Norton, 1979.

Jordan, Constance. "Gender and Justice in *Swetnam the Woman-Hater.*" *Renaissance Drama* n.s. 18 (1987): 149–69.

————. *Renaissance Feminism: Literary Texts and Political Models.* Ithaca, N.Y.: Cornell University Press, 1990.

Jordan, Winthrop. *White Over Black: American Attitudes Toward the Negro, 1550–1812.* Chapel Hill: University of North Carolina Press, 1968.

Judges, A. V., ed. *The Elizabethan Underworld.* London: Routledge, 1930.

Kahn, Coppélia. *Roman Shakespeare: Warriors, Wounds, and Women.* London: Routledge, 1997.

————. "Whores and Wives in Jacobean Drama." In *In Another Country: Feminist Perspectives on Renaissance Drama,* ed. Dorothea Kehler and Susan Baker, pp. 246–60. Metuchen, N.J.: Scarecrow Press, 1991.

Kantorowicz, Ernst. *The King's Two Bodies: A Study in Medieval Political Theology.* Princeton, N.J.: Princeton University Press, 1957.

Katz, David S. *The Jews in the History of England.* Oxford: Oxford University Press, 1994.

————. *Philo-Semitism and the Readmission of the Jews to England, 1603–1655.* Oxford: Clarendon, 1982.

Katz, Dorothy L. *"Glow-Worm Light": Writing of the 17th-Century English Recusant Women from Original Manuscripts.* Salzburg: Institut für Anglistik und Amerikanistik, 1989.

Keel, Gilchrist. "'Like Juno's Swans': Celia and Rosalind in *As You Like It.*" *Conference of College Teachers of English Studies* 56 (September 1991): 5–11.

Kelly Gadol, Joan. "Early Feminist Theory and the *Querelle des Femmes.*" In *Women, History, and Theory: The Essays of Joan Kelly,* pp. 65–109. Chicago: University of Chicago Press, 1984.

————. *Women, History, and Theory: The Essays of Joan Kelly.* Chicago: University of Chicago Press, 1984.

Kettering, Sharon. "The Patronage Power of Early Modern French Noblewomen." *The Historical Journal* 32, no. 4 (1989): 817–41.

King, John N. "Patronage and Piety: The Influence of Catherine Parr." In *Silent But for the Word: Tudor Women as Patrons, Translators, and Writers of Religious Works,* ed. Margaret P. Hannay, pp. 43–60. Kent, Ohio: Kent State University Press, 1985.

King, Walter. "Regulation of Alehouses in Stuart Lancashire: An Example of Discretionary Administration of the Law." *Transactions of the Historic Society of Lancashire and Cheshire* 129 (1979): 31–46.

Kolve, V. A. *The Play Called Corpus Christi.* Stanford: Stanford University Press, 1966.

Kowaleski, Maryanne, and Judith M. Bennett. "Crafts, Gilds, and Women in the Middle Ages: Fifty Years After Marian K. Dale." *Signs* 14, no. 2 (1989): 474–501.

Krieger, Elliot. *A Marxist Study of Shakespeare's Comedies.* New York: Barnes & Noble, 1979.

Krontiris, Tina. *Oppositional Voices: Women as Writers and Translators of Literature in the English Renaissance.* London: Routledge, 1992.

Krueger, Roberta L. "Double Jeopardy: The Appropriation of Woman in Four Old French Romances of the 'Cycle de la Gageure.'" In *Seeking the Woman in Late Medieval and Renaissance Writings: Essays in Feminist Contextual Criticism,* ed. Sheila Fisher and Janet E. Halley, pp. 21–50. Knoxville: University of Tennessee Press, 1989.

Kruger, Steven F. *Dreaming in the Middle Ages*. Cambridge: Cambridge University Press, 1992.

Kussmaul, Ann. *Servants in Husbandry in Early Modern Europe*. Cambridge: Cambridge University Press, 1981.

Lacey, Robert. *Sir Walter Raleigh*. New York: Atheneum, 1974.

Lancaster Orders 6. Virginia State Library and Archives, Richmond, Virginia.

Landry, Donna. *The Muses of Resistance: Laboring-Class Women's Poetry in Britain, 1739–1796*. Cambridge: Cambridge University Press, 1990.

Lanyer, Aemilia. *The Poems of Aemilia Lanyer*, ed. Susanne Woods. New York: Oxford University Press, 1993.

———. *The Poems of Shakespeare's Dark Lady: Salve Deus Rex Judaeorum by Emilia Lanier*, ed. A. L. Rowse. London: Cape, 1978.

Larsen, Nella. *Quicksand and Passing*, ed. Deborah E. McDowell. New Brunswick, N.J.: Rutgers University Press, 1986.

Lasocki, David. "The Anglo-Venetian Bassano Family as Instrument Makers and Repairers." *Galpin Society Journal* 38 (1985): 112–32.

Latt, David. "Praising Virtuous Ladies: The Literary Image and Historical Reality of Women in Seventeenth-Century England." In *What Matter of Woman: Essays on English and American Life and Literature*, ed. Marlene Springer, pp. 39–64. New York: New York University Press, 1977.

The Lawe's Resolution of Women's Rights. London: John More, 1632.

Leapor, Mary. *Poems Upon Several Occasions*. 2 vols. London: J. Roberts, 1748–1751.

Leinwand, Theodore B. *The City Staged: Jacobean Comedy 1603–13*. Madison: University of Wisconsin Press, 1986.

———. "Spongy Plebs, Mighty Lords, and the Dynamics of the Alehouse." *Journal of Medieval and Renaissance Studies* 19, no. 2 (1989): 159–84.

Lerner, Gerda. *The Creation of Feminist Consciousness: From the Middle Ages to Eighteen-seventy*. Oxford: Oxford University Press, 1993.

"A Letter Sent by the Maydens of London." London: 1567.

Levin, Carole. *The Heart and Stomach of a King: Elizabeth I and the Politics of Sex and Power*. Philadelphia: University of Pennsylvania Press, 1994.

Levin, Richard A. *Love and Society in Shakespearean Comedy: A Study of Dramatic Form and Content*. Toronto: Associated University Presses, 1985.

Levine, Laura. *Men in Women's Clothing: Anti-theatricality and Effeminization, 1579–1642*. Cambridge: Cambridge University Press, 1994.

Lewalski, Barbara Kiefer. "The Lady of the Country-House Poem." In *The Fashioning and Functioning of the British Country House*, ed. Gervase Jackson-Stops et al., pp. 261–75. Studies in the History of Art. Vol. 25. London: National Gallery of Art, 1989.

———, ed. *The Polemics and Poems of Rachel Speght*. Oxford: Oxford University Press, 1996.

———. "Typological Symbolism and the 'Progress of the Soul' in Seventeenth-century Literature." In *Literary Uses of Typology, from the Late Middle Ages to the Present*, ed. Earl Miner, pp. 79–114. Princeton, N.J.: Princeton University Press, 1977.

———. *Writing Women in Jacobean England*. Cambridge, Mass.: Harvard University Press, 1993.

Liddington, Jill. "Anne Lister of Shibden Hall, Halifax (1791–1840): Her Diaries and the Historians." *History Workshop: A Journal of Socialist and Feminist Historians* 35 (Spring 1993): 45–77.

Lindon, Robin Ruth, ed. *Against Sadomasochism: A Radical Feminist Analysis*. San Francisco: Frog in the Wall Press, 1982.

Lonsdale, Roger, ed. *Eighteenth Century Women Poets*. Oxford and New York: Oxford University Press, 1990.

Loomba, Ania. "The Color of Patriarchy: Critical Difference, Cultural Differ- ence, and Renaissance Drama." In *Women, "Race," and Writing*, ed. Margo Hendricks and Patricia Parker, pp. 17–34. London: Routledge, 1994.

———. *Gender, Race, Renaissance Drama*. Manchester: Manchester University Press, 1989.

Luke, Mary M. *Gloriana, The Years of Elizabeth*. New York: Coward, McCann & Geoghegan, 1973.

Lumiansky, Robert M. "Comedy and Theme in the Chester Harrowing of Hell." *Tulane Studies in English* 10 (1960): 5–12.

Lumiansky, Robert M., and David Mills, eds. *The Chester Mystery Cycle*. Vol. 1: Texts. EETS SS 3. London: Oxford University Press, 1974.

———, eds. *The Chester Mystery Cycle*. Vol. 2: Commentary and Glossary. EETS SS 9. London: Oxford University Press, 1986.

———. "Concerning Sources, Analogues, and Authorities." In *The Chester Mystery Cycle: Essays and Documents*, ed. Robert M. Lumiansky and David Mills, pp. 87–110. Chapel Hill: University of North Carolina Press, 1983.

Lyly, John. *The Anatomy of Wit. Editio Princeps 1579*. In *Euphues and His England*. Editio Princeps 1580. Reprint, ed. Edward Arber. London: 1869.

———. *Gallathea and Midas*, ed. Anne Begor Lancashire. Lincoln: University of Nebraska Press, 1969.

MacLean, Sally-Beth. *Chester Art: A Subject List of Extant and Lost Art Includ- ing Items Relevant to Early Drama*. EDAM Reference Series. Vol. 3. Kalama- zoo: Western Michigan University, 1982.

Magnusson, Lynne. "The Elizabethan Woman as Suitor: Epistolary Rhetoric and Shakespearean Intertexts." First Plenary Session, Rocky Mountain Medieval and Renaissance Association Conference. Banff, Alberta, May 15, 1997.

Maguire, Laurie E. "'Household Kates': Chez Petruchio, Percy, and Plantagenet." In *Gloriana's Face: Women, Public and Private, in the English Renaissance*, ed. S. P. Cerasano and Marion Wynne-Davies, pp. 129–66. New York: Harvester Wheatsheaf, 1992.

Mahl, Mary R., and Helen Koone, ed. *The Female Spectator: English Women Writers before 1800*. Bloomington: Indiana University Press, 1977.

Makin, Bathsua. *An Essay to Revive the Antient Education of Gentlewomen in Religion, Manners, Arts and Tongues: with An Answer to the Objections against this Way of Education*. 1673. Reprint, ed. Paula L. Barbour. Los Angeles: Augustan Reprint Society, 1980.

———. *Musae Virginea*. London, 1616.

———. "Upon the Much Lamented death of the Right Hounourable, the Learned Lady Langham." 1664. Ms., HA 8799, Huntington Lib.

Malcolmson, Cristina. "'What You Will': Gender and Social Mobility in *Twelfth Night*." In *The Matter of Difference: Materialist Feminist Criticism of Shakespeare*, ed. Valerie Wayne, pp. 29–57. Ithaca, N.Y.: Cornell Univer- sity Press, 1991.

Manley, Delarivier. *The New Atlantis (1709)*, ed. Rosalind Ballaster. New York and London: Penguin, 1992.

Manley, Lawrence. *Literature and Culture in Early Modern London*. Cambridge: Cambridge University Press, 1995.

Marcus, Leah S. *Puzzling Shakespeare: Local Reading and Its Discontents*. Berkeley: University of California Press, 1988.

Marshall, John. "Modern Productions of Medieval English Plays." In *The Cam- bridge Companion to Medieval English Theatre*, ed. Richard Beadle, pp. 290– 311. Cambridge: Cambridge University Press, 1994.

Martin, Lynn. *The Jesuit Mind: The Mentality of an Elite in Early Modern France*. Ithaca, N.Y.: Cornell University Press, 1988.

Marx, Karl. *Capital: A Critique of Political Economy*. Vol. 1, trans. Ben Fowkes. New York: Vintage Books, 1976.

Massinger, Philip. *The City Madam*, ed. T. W. Craik. London: Ernest Benn, 1964.

Matchinske, Megan. "Legislating 'Middle-Class' Morality in the Marriage Market: Ester Sowernam's *Ester hath hang'd Haman.*" *English Literary Renaissance* 24, no. 1 (1994): 154–83.

Matthew. In *The Geneva Bible: A Facsimile of the 1560 Edition*, pp. AA.ii–EE.i. Madison: University of Wisconsin Press, 1969.

Matulka, Barbara. *The Novels of Juan de Flores and Their European Diffusion: A Study in Comparative Literature*. Comparative Literature Series. New York: Institute of French Studies, 1931.

Maurer, Margaret. "Reading Ben Jonson's Queens." In *Seeking the Woman in Late Medieval and Renaissance Writings: Essays in Feminist Contextual Criticism*, ed. Sheila Fisher and Janet E. Halley, pp. 233–63. Knoxville: University of Tennessee Press, 1989.

Mavor, Elizabeth. *The Ladies of Llangollen: A Study in Romantic Friendship* 1971. London: Penguin, 1973.

McGrath, Lynette. "'Let Us Have Our Libertie Againe': Amelia Lanier's Seventeenth-Century Feminist Voice." *Women's Studies* 20 (1992): 331–48.

———. "Metaphoric Subversions: Feasts and Mirrors in Amelia Lanier's *Salve Deus Rex Judaeorum.*" *LIT: Literature Interpretation Theory* 3 (1991): 101–13.

McKeon, Michael. "Historicizing Patriarchy: The Emergence of Gender Difference in England, 1660–1760." *Eighteenth-Century Studies* 28, no. 3 (1995): 295–322.

McKewin, Carole. "Counsels of Gall and Grace: Intimate Conversations Between Women in Shakespeare's Plays." In *The Woman's Part: Feminist Criticism of Shakespeare*, ed. Carolyn Ruth Swift Lenz, Gayle Greene, and Carol Thomas Neely, pp. 117–32. Chicago: University of Illinois Press, 1980.

McLaren, Angus. *Reproductive Rituals: The Perception of Fertility in England from the Sixteenth Century to the Nineteenth Century*. New York: Methuen, 1984.

McLuskie, Kathleen E. *Dekker and Heywood: Professional Dramatists*. New York: St. Martin's, 1994.

McNamara, Jo Ann Kay. *Sisters in Arms: Catholic Nuns Through Two Millenia*. Cambridge, Mass.: Harvard University Press, 1996.

Meese, Elizabeth. *(Sem)erotics: Theorizing Lesbian Writing*. New York: New York University Press, 1992.

Melvill, Elizabeth. *Godlie Dreame, compiled by Elizabeth Melvill, Ladie Culros younger*. Edinburgh, Andro Hart, 1620.

Menocal, Maria Rosa. *Shards of Love: Exile and the Origins of the Lyric*. Durham: Duke University Press, 1993.

Merrell, Floyd. *Sign, Textuality, World*. Bloomington: Indiana University Press, 1992.

Mertes, Kate. *The English Noble Household 1250–1600*. London: Basil Blackwell, 1988.

Middleton, Thomas. *A Chaste Maid in Cheapside*, ed. Bryan Loughrey and Neil Taylor. London: Penguin, 1988.

———. *Women Beware Women*, ed. Roma Gill. New York: W. W. Norton, 1968.

Middleton, Thomas, and Thomas Dekker. *The Roaring Girl*, ed. Paul A. Mulholland. Manchester: Manchester University Press, 1987.

Middleton, Thomas, and Nicholas Rowley. *The Changeling*. In *Drama of the English Renaissance II: The Stuart Period*, ed. Russell A. Fraser and Norman Rabkin, pp. 339–430. New York: Macmillan, 1976.

Mies, Maria. *Patriarchy and Accumulation on a World Scale: Women in the International Division of Labour.* London: Zed, 1986.

Mignolo, Walter D. *The Darker Side of the Renaissance: Literacy, Territoriality, and Colonization.* Ann Arbor, Mich.: University of Michigan Press, 1995.

Miles, Margaret R. *Image as Insight: Visual Understanding in Western Christianity and Secular Culture.* Boston: Beacon Press, 1985.

Mill, Anna Jean. "Noah's Wife Again." *PMLA* 56 (1941): 613–26.

Millard, Barbara C. "'An Acceptable Violence': Sexual Contest in Jonson's *Epicoene.*" *Medieval & Renaissance Drama in England* 1 (1984): 143–58.

Mills, David. "The Chester Cycle." In *The Cambridge Companion to Medieval English Theatre,* ed. Richard Beadle, pp. 109–33. Cambridge: Cambridge University Press, 1994.

———. "Theories and Practices in the Editing of the Chester Cycle Play-manuscripts." In *The Chester Mystery Cycle: A Casebook,* ed. Kevin Harty, pp. 3–17. New York: Garland, 1993.

Minutes of the Norwich Court of Mayoralty 1630–35. Vols. 15 and 36, ed. William L. Sachse. Norwich: Norfolk Record Society, Number 942, 1967. [NCM]

Mohanty, Chandra Talpade, Ann Russo, and Lourdes Torres, eds. *Third World Women and the Politics of Feminism.* Bloomington: Indiana University Press, 1991.

Montrose, Louis Adrian. "The Elizabethan Subject and the Spenserian Text." In *Literary Theory, Renaissance Texts,* ed. Patricia Parker and David Quint, pp. 303–40. Baltimore: Johns Hopkins University Press, 1986.

———. "'The Place of a Brother' in *As You Like It*: Social Process and Comic Form." *Shakespeare Quarterly* 32 (1981): 28–54.

Moraga, Cherríe, and Gloria Anzaldúa, eds. *This Bridge Called My Back: Writings by Radical Women of Color.* Watertown, Mass.: Persephone, 1981.

Morris, Helen. "Queen Elizabeth I Shadowed in Cleopatra." *Huntington Library Quarterly* 32 (1969): 271–78.

Morris, Rupert. *Chester in the Plantagenet and Tudor Reigns.* Chester, ca. 1895.

Morrison, Toni. *Playing in the Dark: Whiteness and the Literary Imagination.* New York: Vintage Books, 1992.

Mueller, Janel. "The Feminist Poetics of Aemilia Lanyer's 'Salve Deus Rex Judaeorum.'" In *Feminist Measures: Soundings in Poetry and Theory,* ed. Lynn Keller and Cristianne Miller, pp. 208–36. Ann Arbor: University of Michigan Press, 1993

———. "Troping Utopia: Donne's Brief for Lesbianism." In *Sexuality and Gender in Early Modern Europe,* ed. James Grantham Turner, pp. 182–207. Cambridge: Cambridge University Press, 1993.

Muir, Kenneth. *Shakespeare's Comic Sequence.* New York: Barnes & Noble, 1979.

Mullaney, Steven. *The Place of the Stage: License, Play, and Power in Renaissance England.* Chicago: University of Chicago Press, 1988.

Mullany, Peter F. "Topographical Bawdy in Shakespeare." *American Notes & Queries* 12, no. 4 (December 1973): 51–53.

Mulvihill, Maureen E. *Poems by Ephelia (c. 1679).* Facsimile reprint of *Female Poems on Several Occasions.* 1679. Delmar, N.Y.: Scholars' Facsimiles & Reprints, 1993.

Munda, Constantia. *The Worming of a Mad Dogge: Or, A Soppe for Cerberus the Jaylor of Hell.* In *The Women's Sharp Revenge,* ed. Simon Shepherd, pp. 125–57. New York: St. Martin's Press, 1985.

Munster, Sebastian. *Messias Christianorum et Judaeorum.* Basel, 1539.

Myers, Mitzi. "Domesticating Minerva: Bathsua Makin's 'Curious' Argument for Women's Education." *Studies in Eighteenth Century Culture* 14 (1985): 173–92.

Neale, J. E. *Essays in Elizabethan History.* London: Cape, 1958.

Nevinson, J. L. "Embroidered by Queen and Countess." *Country Life,* pp. 217–35. January 22, 1976.

Newman, Karen. *Fashioning Femininity and English Renaissance Drama.* Chicago: University of Chicago Press, 1991.

Newman, Robert D. *Transgressions of Reading: Narrative Engagement as Exile and Return.* Durham, N.C.: Duke University Press, 1993.

Newstead, Christopher. *An Apology for Women: Or, Womens Defence.* 1620. Reprint, Ann Arbor: University Microfilms, Pollard Reel, 1967.

Nicoll, Allardyce. *Stuart Masques and the Renaissance Stage.* New York: Harcourt, Brace, 1938.

Nichols, John. *The Progresses and Public Processions of Queen Elizabeth I.* 3 vols. 1823. Reprint, New York: Burt Franklin, 1966.

Norman, Marion. "A Woman for All Seasons: Mary Ward (1585–1645), Renaissance Pioneer of Women's Education." *Paedagogica Historica* 23 (1983): 125–43.

Oldys, William. *Life of Sir Walter Raleigh.* London, 1740.

Orchard, M. Emmanuel, ed. *Till God Will: Mary Ward Through Her Writings.* London: Darton, Longman, and Todd, 1985.

Orgel, Stephen. *Impersonations: The Performance of Gender in Shakespeare's England.* Cambridge: Cambridge University Press, 1996.

———. "Nobody's Perfect: Or Why Did the English Stage Take Boys for Women?" *South Atlantic Quarterly* 88 (1989): 7–29.

Osborne, Laurie E. "Dramatic Play in *Much Ado About Nothing:* Wedding the Italian *Novella* and English Comedy." *Philological Quarterly* 69, no. 2 (1990): 167–88.

———. "Letters, Lovers, Lacan: Or Malvolio's Not-So-Purloined Letter." *Assays* 5 (1989): 63–89.

Palmer, John. *Comic Characters of Shakespeare.* London: Macmillan, 1947.

Park, Clara Claiborne. "As We Like It: How a Girl Can Be Smart and Still Popular." In *The Woman's Part: Feminist Criticism of Shakespeare,* ed. Carolyn Ruth Swift Lenz, Gayle Greene, and Carol Thomas Neely, pp. 100–16. Chicago: University of Illinois Press, 1980.

Park, Katharine. "The Rediscovery of the Clitoris: French Medicine and the Tribade, 1570–1620." In *The Body in Parts: Discourses and Anatomies in Early Modern Europe,* ed. Carla Mazzio and David Hillman, pp. 170–93. New York: Routledge, 1996.

Park, Katharine, and Lorraine Daston. "The Hermaphrodite and the Orders of Nature: Sexual Ambiguity in Early Modern France." *GLQ: A Journal of Lesbian and Gay Studies* 1, no. 4 (1994): 419–38.

Parker, Rozsika. *The Subversive Stitch: Embroidery and the Making of the Feminine.* 1984. Reprint, London: The Women's Press, 1989.

Parrot, Thomas. *The Gossips Greeting: Or, A new Discovery of such Females Meeting.* London: 1620.

Partridge, Eric. *Shakespeare's Bawdy.* New York: Dutton & Co., 1969.

Paster, Gail Kern. *The Body Embarrassed: Drama and the Disciplines of Shame in Early Modern England.* Ithaca, N.Y.: Cornell University Press, 1993.

Pearson, Lu Emily. *Elizabethans at Home.* Stanford, Calif.: Stanford University Press, 1957.

Pequigney, Joseph. *Such Is My Love: A Study of Shakespeare's Sonnets.* Chicago: University of Chicago Press, 1985.

———. "The Two Antonios and Same-Sex Love in *Twelfth Night* and *The Merchant of Venice.*" *English Literary Renaissance* 22 (1992): 201–22.

Peters, Henriette. *Mary Ward: A World in Contemplation,* trans. Helen Butterworth. Leominster: Gracewing, 1994.

Phythian-Adams, Charles. *Desolation of a City: Coventry and the Urban Crisis of the Late Middle Ages*. Cambridge: Cambridge University Press, 1979.

Platt, Colin. *Medieval Southampton: The Port and Trading Community, A.D. 1000–1600*. London: Routledge & Kegan Paul, 1973.

Plutarch. *Makers of Rome: Nine Lives by Plutarch*, trans. Ian Scott-Kilvert. London: Penguin, 1965.

Ponzio, Augusto. *Man as Sign: Essays in the Philosophy of Language*, trans. Susan Petrilli. Berlin: Mouton de Gruyter, 1990.

Pound, John F. "An Elizabethan Census of the Poor: the Treatment of Vagrancy in Norwich, 1570–80." *University of Birmingham Historical Journal* 8 (1962): 135–61.

———. *Poverty and Vagrancy in Tudor England*. London: Longman, 1971.

Poyntz, Mary, and Winifred Wigmore. "A Briefe Relation of the Holy Life and Happy Death of our Dearest Mother." York: Archives of the Institute of the Blessed Virgin Mary, The Bar Convent.

Prescott, Ann Lake. "The Pearl of the Valois and Elizabeth I: Marguerite de Navarre's Miroir and Tudor England." In *Silent But for the Word: Tudor Women as Patrons, Translators, and Writers of Religious Work*, ed. Margaret Hannay. Kent, Ohio: Kent State University Press, 1985.

Primrose, Diana. *A Chaine of Pearle. or A Memoriall of the peerles Graces, and Heroick Vertues of Queen Elizabeth of Glorious Memory*. London: 1630. STC 20388.

Prior, Roger. "Jewish Musicians at the Tudor Court." *The Musical Quarterly* 69 (1983): 253–65.

———. "More (Moor? Moro?) Light on the Dark Lady," *Financial Times*, October 10, 1987, Sec. P1, p. 17.

———. "A Second Jewish Community in Tudor London." *The Transactions of the Jewish Historical Society of England* 31 (1990): 137–52.

Prouty, Charles. *The Sources of "Much Ado About Nothing": A Critical Study Together With the Text of Peter Beverley's "Ariodanto and Ieneura."* New Haven, Conn.: Yale University Press, 1950.

Prowse, Anne Lok, trans. *Sermons upon the songe that Ezechias made after he had bene sicke*, John Calvin. London, 1560.

Purkiss, Diane. "Material Girls: The Seventeenth-Century Woman Debate." *Women, Texts, and Histories 1575–1760*, ed. Clare Brant and Diane Purkiss, pp. 69–101. London: Routledge, 1992.

Quaife, G. R. *Wanton Wenches and Wayward Wives*. New Brunswick, N.J.: Rutgers University Press, 1979.

Rackin, Phyllis. "Androgyny, Mimesis, and the Marriage of the Boy Heroine on the English Renaissance Stage." *PMLA* 102 (January 1987): 29–41.

Rastall, Richard. "Music in the Cycle." In *The Chester Mystery Cycle: Essays and Documents*, ed. Robert M. Lumiansky and David Mills, pp. 111–64. Chapel Hill: University of North Carolina Press, 1983.

Ribton-Turner, C. J. *A History of Vagrants and Vagrancy and Beggars and Begging*. Montclair, N.J.: Patterson Smith, 1972.

Rich, Adrienne. "Compulsory Heterosexuality and Lesbian Existence." *Signs* 5, no. 4 (Summer 1980): 631–60.

Ricoeur, Paul. *From Text to Action: Essays in Hermeneutics II*, trans. Kathleen Blamey and John B. Thompson. Evanston, Ill.: Northwestern University Press, 1991.

Rid, Samuel [?]. "Martin Markall, Beadle of Bridewell, His Defence and Answers to the Bellman of London." In *The Elizabethan Underworld*, ed. A. V. Judges, pp. 383–422. London: Routledge, 1930.

Riley, Denise. *"Am I That Name?": Feminism and the Category of "Women" in History*. Minneapolis: University of Minnesota Press, 1988.

Rinehart, Keith. "Shakespeare's Cleopatra and England's Elizabeth." *Shakespeare Quarterly* 23 (1972): 81–86.

Robbins, Russell Hope. "John Crophill's Ale-Pots." *Review of English Studies* 20 (1960): 182–89.

Robertson, Karen. "A Revenging Feminine Hand in *Twelfth Night*." In *Reading and Writing in Shakespeare*, ed. David Bergeron, pp. 116–30. Newark: University of Delaware Press, 1996.

Robinson, Amy. "It Takes One to Know One: Passing and Communities of Common Interest." *Critical Inquiry* 20 (Summer 1994): 715–36.

Rose, Mary Beth, ed. *Women in the Middle Ages and the Renaissance: Literary and Historical Perspectives.* Syracuse, N.Y.: Syracuse University Press, 1986.

Rosenthal, Joel T. *Patriarchy and Families of Privilege in Fifteenth-Century England.* Philadelphia: University of Pennsylvania, 1990.

———. *The Purchase of Paradise: Gift Giving and the Aristocracy, 1307–1485.* London: Routledge & Kegan Paul, 1972.

Roth, Cecil, and Geoffrey Wigoder, eds. *Encyclopedia Judaica.* 16 vols. Jerusalem: Macmillan, 1971.

Rowse, A. L. *Ralegh and the Throckmortons.* London: Macmillan, 1962.

Rubin, Gayle. "Thinking Sex: Notes for a Radical Theory for the Politics of Sexuality." In *Pleasure and Danger: Exploring Female Sexuality*, ed. Carole Vance, pp. 267–319. London: Routledge & Kegan Paul, 1984.

———. "The Traffic in Women: Notes on the 'Political' Economy of Sex." In *Toward an Anthropology of Women*, ed. Rayna R. Reiter, pp. 157–210. New York: Monthly Review Press, 1975.

Rubin, Miri. *Corpus Christi: The Eucharist in Late Medieval Culture.* Cambridge: Cambridge University Press, 1991.

Said, Edward W. *Culture and Imperialism.* New York: Vintage Books, 1993.

Salgado, Gamini, ed. *Cony-Catchers and Bawdy Baskets: An Anthology of Elizabethan Low Life.* Harmondsworth: Penguin, 1972.

Samaha, Joel. "Gleanings from Local Criminal Court Records: Sedition Amongst the 'Inarticulate' in Elizabethan Essex." *The Journal of Social History* 8 (1975): 61–79.

Scattergood, John, ed. *The Complete English Poems of John Skelton.* New Haven, Conn.: Yale University Press, 1983.

Schleiner, Louise. "Ladies and Gentlemen in Two Genres of Elizabethan Fiction." *Studies in English Literature, 1500–1900* 29 (1989): 1–20.

———. *Tudor and Stuart Women Writers.* Bloomington: University of Indiana Press, 1994.

Schochet, Gordon J. "Patriarchalism, Politics, and Mass Attitudes in Stuart England." *Historical Journal* 12 (1969): 413–41.

Scott, Joan Wallach. "The Problem of Invisibility." In *Retrieving Women's History*, ed. S. Jay Kleinberg, pp. 5–29. Oxford: Berg Publishers Ltd/ UNESCO Press, 1988.

Scott, Sarah. *Millenium Hall.* 1762. Reprint, ed. Gary Kelly. Ontario and New York: Broadview Press, 1995.

Sedgwick, Eve Kosofsky. *Between Men: English Literature and Male Homosocial Desire.* New York: Columbia University Press, 1985.

———. *Epistemology of the Closet.* Berkeley: University of California Press, 1990.

Seidel, Michael. *Exile and the Narrative Imagination.* New Haven, Conn.: Yale University Press, 1986.

Shakespeare, William. *Antony and Cleopatra*, ed. Maynard Mack. Baltimore: Penguin, 1960.

———. *As You Like It*, ed. Agnes Latham. The Arden Shakespeare. London: Methuen, 1975.

————. *Much Ado About Nothing*, ed. A. R. Humphreys. London: Routledge, 1981.

————. *Othello, the Moor of Venice*. In *The Riverside Shakespeare*, ed. G. Blakemore Evans, pp. 1198–1248. Boston: Houghton Mifflin, 1974.

————. *The Rape of Lucrece*. In *The Riverside Shakespeare*, ed. G. Blakemore Evans, pp. 1720–1744. Boston: Houghton Mifflin, 1974.

————. *The Riverside Shakespeare*, ed. G. Blakemore Evans. Boston: Houghton Mifflin, 1974.

————. *The Tempest*, ed. Frank Kermode. New York: Methuen, 1964.

————. *Twelfth Night*, ed. J. M. Lothian and T. W. Craik. The Arden Shakespeare. London: Methuen, 1975.

Shammas, Carole. "Black Women's Work and the Evolution of Plantation Society in Virginia." *Labor History* 26 (Winter 1985): 5–28.

Shapiro, James. *Shakespeare and the Jews*. New York: Columbia University Press, 1996.

Sharpe, J. A. *Crime in Seventeenth-Century England*. Cambridge: Cambridge University Press, 1983.

————. "The History of Crime in Late Medieval and Early Modern England: A Review of the Field." *Social History* 7 (1982): 187–203.

Shaw, Fiona, and Juliet Stevenson. "Celia and Rosalind In *As You Like It*." In *Players 2: Further Essays in Shakespearean Performance by Players with the Royal Shakespeare Company*, ed. Russell Jackson and Robert Smallwood, pp. 55–71. Cambridge: Cambridge University Press, 1988.

Shell, Marc. *Elizabeth's Glass*. Lincoln: University of Nebraska Press, 1993.

————. *Money, Language, and Thought: Literary and Philosophical Economies from the Medieval to the Modern Era*. Berkeley: University of California Press, 1982.

Shepherd, Simon. *Amazons and Warrior Women: Varieties of Feminism in Seventeenth-Century Drama*. New York: St. Martin's, 1981.

————. *The Women's Sharp Revenge: Five Women's Pamphlets from the Renaissance*. New York: St. Martin's, 1985.

Shields, Rob. *Places on the Margin: Alternative Geographies of Modernity*. London: Routledge, 1991.

Shuger, Debora. *The Renaissance Bible: Scholarship, Sacrifice, and Subjectivity*. Berkeley: University of California Press, 1994.

Sidney, Mary Herbert. *The Triumph of Death and Other Unpublished and Uncollected Poems*, ed. Gary Waller. Salzburg: Universität Salzburg, 1977.

Sidney, Philip. *The Poems of Sir Philip Sidney*. Vol. 1, ed. William A. Ringler, Jr. Oxford: Clarendon Press, 1962.

Simons, Patricia. "Lesbian (In)Visibility in Italian Renaissance Culture: Diana and Other Cases of *donna con donna*." *Journal of Homosexuality* 27, nos. 1–2 (1994): 81–122.

Skelton, John. *The Complete English Poems*, ed. John Scattergood. New Haven, Conn.: Yale University Press, 1983.

Slack, Paul. "Poverty and Politics in Salisbury 1597–1666." In *Crisis and Order in English Towns, 1500–1700*, ed. Peter Clark and Paul Slack, pp. 164–203. London: Routledge & Kegan Paul, 1972.

————. "Vagrants and Vagrancy in England, 1598–1664." *Economic History Review*, 2nd ser. 27 (1974): 360–79.

Smith, Bruce R. *Homosexual Desire in Shakespeare's England*. Chicago: University of Chicago Press, 1991.

Smith-Rosenberg, Carroll. "The Female World of Love and Ritual: Relations Between Women in Nineteenth-Century America." *Signs* 1, no. 1 (Autumn 1975): 1–29.

Somerset, Anne. *Ladies in Waiting From the Tudors to the Present Day*. New York: Knopf, 1984.

Souers, Philip Webster. *The Matchless Orinda*. Cambridge, Mass.: Harvard University Press, 1931.

Southampton Court Leet Records 1550–1624. 4 vols. ed. F. J. C. Hearnshaw and D. M. Hearnshaw. Southampton: H. M. Gilbert & Son, 1905–8. [SCLR]

Sowernam, Ester. *Ester Hath Hang'd Haman*. In *The Women's Sharp Revenge*, ed. Simon Shepherd, pp. 85–124. New York: St. Martin's Press, 1985.

Spacks, Patricia Meyer. *Gossip*. Chicago and London: University of Chicago Press, 1986.

Speght, Rachel. *A Mouzell for Melastomus*. In *The Women's Sharp Revenge*, ed. Simon Shepherd, pp. 57–83. New York: St. Martin's Press, 1985.

———. *A Mouzell for Melastomus*. In *The Polemics and Poems of Rachel Speght*. Ed. Barbara Kiefer Lewalski. New York: Oxford University Press, 1996.

———. *The Polemics and Poems of Rachel Speght*. Ed. Barbara Kiefer Lewalski. New York: Oxford University Press, 1996.

Spelman, Elizabeth V. *Inessential Woman: Problems of Exclusion in Feminist Thought*. Boston: Beacon, 1988.

Spenser, Edmund. *The Faerie Queene*. 1596. Reprinted in *Spenser, Poetical Works*, ed. J. C. Smith and E. de Delincourt, pp. 1–407. Oxford: Oxford University Press, 1975.

Spivak, Gayatri Chakravorty. "Three Women's Texts and a Critique of Imperialism." In *"Race," Writing, and Difference*, ed. Henry Louis Gates, Jr., pp. 262–80. Chicago: University of Chicago Press, 1985.

Spufford, Margaret. *Small Books and Pleasant Histories: Popular Fiction and its Readership in Seventeenth-Century England*. Cambridge: Cambridge University Press, 1981.

Stallybrass, Peter. "Patriarchal Territories: The Body Enclosed." In *Rewriting the Renaissance: The Discourses of Sexual Difference in Early Modern Europe*, ed. Margaret Ferguson, Maureen Quilligan, and Nancy Vickers, pp. 123–42. Chicago: University of Chicago Press, 1986.

———. "The World Turned Upside Down: Inversion, Gender, and the State." In *The Matter of Difference: Materialist Feminist Critiques of Shakespeare*, ed. Valerie Wayne, pp. 201–20. Ithaca, N.Y.: Cornell University Press, 1991.

Stanfield, Raymund. "The Archpriest Controversy." In *Miscellanea XII*. Vol. 22. Catholic Record Society, pp. 132–86. London: J. Whitehead & Son, 1921.

Starkey, David, ed. *Rivals in Power: Lives and Letters of the Great Tudor Dynasties*. London: Macmillan, 1990.

Steen, Sara Jayne. *The Letters of Arbella Stuart*. New York: Oxford University Press, 1994.

Steen, Sara Jayne, and Elizabeth Hageman. "Teaching Judith Shakespeare." *Renaissance Quarterly* (Winter 1996): entire issue.

Stephen, Leslie, and Sidney Lee. *Dictionary of National Biography*. London: Smith, Elder, 1885–1901.

Stiebel, Arlene. "Not Since Sappho: The Erotic Poems of Katherine Philips and Aphra Behn." *Journal of Homosexuality* 23 (1992): 153–84.

Stimpson, Catharine. "Zero Degree Deviancy: The Lesbian Novel in English." In *Writing and Sexual Difference*, ed. Elizabeth Abel, pp. 243–59. Chicago: University of Chicago Press, 1982.

Stolcke, Verena. "Invaded Women: Gender, Race, and Class in the Formation of Colonial Society." In *Women, "Race," and Writing in the Early Modern Period*, ed. Margo Hendricks and Patricia Parker, pp. 272–86. London: Routledge, 1994.

Stone, Lawrence. *The Family, Sex, and Marriage in England 1500–1800*. New York: Harper & Row, 1979.

Strickland, Agnes. *Lives of the Queens of England from the Norman Conquest*. Vol. 4. London: Henry Colburn, 1854.

Strong, Roy. *The Cult of Elizabeth: Elizabethan Portraiture and Pageantry*. Berkeley: University of California Press, 1977.

Sussman, Charlotte. "The Other Problem with Women: Reproduction and Slave Culture in Aphra Behn's *Oroonoko*." In *Rereading Aphra Behn: History, Theory, and Criticism*, ed. Heidi Hutner, pp. 212–31. Charlottesville: University of Virginia Press, 1993.

Sutherland, Sarah. "'Not or I see more neede': The Wife of Noah in the Chester, York, and Towneley Cycles." In *Shakespeare and Dramatic Tradition: Essays in Honor of S. F. Johnson*, ed. W. R. Elton and W. B. Long, pp. 181–93. Newark: University of Delaware Presss, 1990.

Swain, Margaret. *Figures on Fabric: Embroidery Design Sources and Their Application*. London: Adam & Charles Black, 1980.

———. *The Needlework of Mary Queen of Scots*. London: Van Nostrand Reinhold, 1973.

———. *Scottish Embroidery Medieval to Modern*. London: B. T. Batsford, 1986.

Swetnam, Joseph. *The Arraignment of Lewd, Idle, Froward, and Unconstant Women*. In *Half Humankind: Contexts and Texts of the Controversy about Women in England, 1540–1640*, ed. Katherine Usher Henderson and Barbara F. McManus, pp. 189–216. Urbana: University of Illinois Press, 1985.

———. *The Schoole of the Noble and Worthy Science of Defence*. London: Nicholas Okes., 1617.

Swetnam the Woman-hater: The Controversy and the Play, ed. Coryl Crandall. West Lafayette, Ind.: Purdue University Studies, 1969.

Taylor, John. *The Praise of the Needle*. London, 1631.

Teague, Frances. "New Light on Bathsua Makin." *Seventeenth-Century News* 44, nos. 1–2 (1986). 16.

———. "Woman of Learning: Bathsua Makin." In *Women Writers of the Seventeenth Century*, ed. Katharina M. Wilson and Frank J. Warnke, pp. 285–94. Athens: University of Georgia Press, 1989.

Thomas, Keith. *Religion and the Decline of Magic*. New York: Charles Scribner's Sons, 1971.

Thomas, Patrick, ed. "An Edition of the Letters and Poems of Katherine Philips, 1632–1664." Ph.D. diss., University College of Wales, Aberystwyth, 1982. (Published as *The Collected Works of Katherine Philips: The Matchless Orinda*. Stump Cross, England: Stump Cross Books, 1990–92.

Thompson, Roger. *Women in Stuart England and America*. London: Routledge & Kegan Paul, 1978.

Tilney, Edmund. *The Flower of Friendship: A Renaissance Dialogue Contesting Marriage*, ed. Valerie Wayne. Ithaca, N.Y.: Cornell University Press, 1992.

Tomlinson, Sophie. "'My Brain the Stage': Margaret Cavendish and the Fantasy of Female Performance." In *Women, Texts, and Histories 1575–1760*, ed. Claire Brant and Diane Purkiss, pp. 134–63. New York: Routledge, 1992.

Tourneur, Cyril. *The Revenger's Tragedy*. In *Drama of the English Renaissance II: The Stuart Period*, ed. Russell A. Fraser and Norman Rabkin, pp. 21–54. New York: Macmillan, 1976.

Transcript of the Registers of the Company of Stationers of London, 1554–1640 A.D, ed. Edward Arber. 1875. Reprint, New York: Peter Smith, 1950.

Traub, Valerie. *Desire and Anxiety: Circulations of Sexuality in Shakespearean Drama*. New York: Routledge, 1992.

————. "The (In)Significance of 'Lesbian' Desire in Early Modern England." In *Queering the Renaissance*, ed. Jonathan Goldberg, pp. 62–83. Durham, N.C.: Duke University Press, 1994.

————. "The Perversion of 'Lesbian Desire.'" *History Workshop Journal* 41 (1996): 23–49.

————. "The Psychomorphology of the Clitoris." *GLQ: A Journal of Lesbian and Gay Studies* 2, nos. 1–2 (1995): 81–113.

Traub, Valerie, M. Lindsay Kaplan, and Dympna Callaghan, ed. *Feminist Readings of Early Modern Culture: Emerging Subjects*. Cambridge: Cambridge University Press, 1996.

Travis, Peter. *Dramatic Design in the Chester Cycle*. Chicago: University of Chicago Press, 1982.

Travitsky, Betty, ed. *The Paradise of Women: Writings by Englishwomen of the Renaissance*. 1989. Reprint, Westport, Conn.: Greenwood, 1991.

————. "The 'Wyll and Testament' of Isabella Whitney." *English Literary Renaissance* 10 (1980): 76–94.

Trumbach, Randolph. "Sex, Gender, and Sexual Identity in Modern Culture: Male Sodomy and Female Prostitution in Enlightenment London." In *Forbidden History: The State, Society, and the Regulation of Sexuality in Modern Europe*, ed. John C. Fout, pp. 89–106. Chicago: University of Chicago Press, 1992.

————. "London's Sapphists: From Three Sexes to Four Genders in the Making of Modern Culture." In *Third Sex, Third Gender: Beyond Sexual Dimorphism in Culture and History*, ed. Gilbert Herdt, pp. 111–36. New York: Zone Books, 1994.

Twycross, Meg. "'Transvestism' in the Mystery Plays." *Medieval English Theatre* 5, no. 2 (1983): 123–80.

Uhl, Sarah. "Forbidden Friends: Cultural Veils of Female Friendship in Andalusia." *American Ethnologist* 18, no. 1 (1991): 90–105.

Underdown, David. *Fire From Heaven: Life in an English Town in the Seventeenth Century*. New Haven, Conn.: Yale University Press, 1992.

————. *Revel, Riot, and Rebellion*. Oxford: Oxford University Press, 1985a.

————. "The Taming of the Scold: The Enforcement of Patriarchal Authority in Early Modern England." In *Order and Disorder in Early Modern England*, ed. Anthony Fletcher and John Stevenson, pp. 116–36. Cambridge: Cambridge University Press, 1985b.

Uphaus, Robert W., and Gretchen M. Foster, eds. *The "Other" Eighteenth Century: English Women of Letters 1660–1800*. East Lansing, Mich.: Colleagues Press, 1991.

Utley, Francis Lee. "The Devil in the Ark." In *Internationaler Kongress der Volserzählungsforscher in Kiel und Kopenhagen; 19.8–29.8: 1959, Vorträge und Referate*, pp. 446–63. Berlin: de Gruyter, 1961.

————. "Noah, His Wife, and the Devil." In *Studies in Biblical and Jewish Folklore*, ed. Raphael Patai, Francis Lee Utley, and Dov Noy, pp. 59–91. Bloomington: Indiana University Press, 1960.

van Beek, Pieta. "'One Tongue Enough for a Woman': The Correspondence in Greek Between Anna Maria van Schurman (1607–1678) and Bathsua Makin (1600–167?)." *Dutch Crossing: A Journal of Low Countries' Studies* 19, no. 1 (1995): 24–48.

van der Meer, Theo. "Tribades on Trial: Female Same-Sex Offenders in Late Eighteenth-Century Amsterdam." In *Forbidden History: The State, Society, and the Regulation of Sexuality in Modern Europe*, ed. John C. Fout, pp. 189–210. Chicago: University of Chicago Press, 1992.

————. "Sodomy and the Pursuit of a Third Sex in the Early Modern Period."

In *Third Sex, Third Gender: Beyond Sexual Dimorphism in Culture and History*, ed. Gilbert Herdt, pp. 137–88. New York: Zone Books, 1994.

Vicinus, Martha. "Lesbian History: All Theory and No Facts or All Facts and No Theory." *Radical History Review* 60 (1994): 57–75.

Virgil. *The Aeneid*, trans. H. Rushton Fairclough. The Loeb Classical Library, rev. ed. Cambridge, Mass.: Harvard University Press, 1965–66.

"Virginia State Papers: Resignation of John Tayloe from the Council." *Virginia Magazine of History and Biography* 17 (1909): 369–70.

Vives, Juan. *A very frutefull and pleasant boke called the Instruction of a Christen Woman . . .*, trans. Rycharde Hyrd (London, 1540). STC 24856, reel 158.

Wadsworth, James. *The English Spanish Pilgrime, or, A New Discovery of Spanish Popery, and Jesuiticall Strategems, With the Estate of the English Pentioners and Fugitives under the King of Spaines Dominions, and Elsewhere at the Present. Also Laying open the New Order of the Jesuitrices and Preaching Nunnes.* London, 1629. STC 24926.

Wall, Wendy. "Dancing in a Net: The Problems of Female Authorship." In *The Imprint of Gender: Authorship and Publication in the English Renaissance*, pp. 279–340. Ithaca, N.Y.: Cornell University Press, 1993.

————. *The Imprint of Gender: Authorship and Publication in the English Renaissance.* Ithaca, N.Y.: Cornell University Press, 1993.

Waller, Marguerite. "The Empire's New Clothes: Refashioning the Renaissance." In *Seeking the Woman in Late Medieval and Renaissance Writings: Essays in Feminist Contextual Criticism*, ed. Sheila Fisher and Janet E. Halley, pp. 160–83. Knoxville: University of Tennessee Press, 1989.

Wallerstein, Immanuel. *The Modern World-System I: Capitalist Agriculture and the Origins of the European World-Economy in the Sixteenth Century.* San Diego, Calif.: Academic Press, 1974.

Walsh, Lorena S. "The Experiences and Status of Women in the Chesapeake, 1750–1775." In *The Web of Southern Social Relations: Women, Family, and Education*, ed. Walter J. Fraser et al., pp. 1–18. Athens: University of Georgia Press, 1985.

Ware, Vron. *Beyond the Pale: White Women, Racism, and History.* London: Verso, 1982.

Watt, Tessa. *Cheap Print and Popular Piety, 1550–1640.* Cambridge: Cambridge University Press, 1991.

Wayne, Valerie. "Historical Differences: Misogyny and Othello." In *The Matter of Difference: Materialist Feminist Criticism of Shakespeare*, ed. Valerie Wayne, pp. 153–79. Ithaca, N.Y.: Cornell University Press, 1991.

————. Introduction to *The Flower of Friendship: A Renaissance Dialogue Contesting Marriage*, ed. Valerie Wayne. Ithaca, N.Y.: Cornell University Press, 1992.

————. "Refashioning the Shrew." *Shakespeare Studies* 17 (1985): 159–87.

Webster, John. *The Duchess of Malfi.* In *Drama of the English Renaissance II: The Stuart Period*, ed. Russell A. Fraser and Norman Rabkin, pp. 475–515. New York: Macmillan, 1976.

Whitbread, Helena, ed. *I Know My Own Heart: The Diaries of Anne Lister 1791–1840.* New York: New York University Press, 1992.

Whitney, Isabella. "A Modest meane for Maids." In *A sweet nosegay or pleasant posye. Contayning a hundred and ten Phylosophicall flowers.* In *"The Floures of Philosophie" (1592) by Sir Hugh Plat and "A Sweet Nosgay" (1573) and "The Copy of a Letter" (1567) by Isabella Whitney*, ed. Richard Panofsky. Delmar, N.Y.: Scholars' Facsimiles and Reprints, 1982.

Wickham, Glynne. *The Medieval Theatre.* 3rd ed. Cambridge: Cambridge University Press, 1987.

Wiesner, Merry. *Women and Gender in Early Modern Europe*. Cambridge: Cambridge University Press, 1993.

Wigmore, Winifred, and Mary Poyntz. "A Briefe Relation of the Holy Life and Happy Death of our Dearest Mother." York: Archives of the Institute of the Blessed Virgin Mary, The Bar Convent.

Williams, Neville. *All the Queen's Men*. London: Weidenfeld & Nicholson, 1972.

Williams, Raymond. *Marxism and Literature*. Oxford: Oxford University Press, 1977.

Willis, Deborah. *Malevolent Nurture: Witch-Hunting and Maternal Power in Early Modern England*. Ithaca, N.Y.: Cornell University Press, 1995.

Willson, D. Harrison. *King James VI and I*. Oxford: Alden, 1956.

Wilson, Adrian. "The Ceremony of Childbirth and Its Interpretation." In *Women as Mothers in Pre-Industrial England: Essays in Memory of Dorothy McLaren*, ed. Valerie Fildes, pp. 68–107. London: Routledge, 1990.

Wilson, Edward. "Local Habitations and Names in MS Rawlinson C 813 in the Bodleian Library, Oxford." *Review of English Studies* n.s. 41, no. 161 (1990): 12–44.

Wilson, K. P. "The Port of Chester in the Fifteenth-Century." *Transactions of the Historic Society of Lancashire and Cheshire* 117 (1965): 1–15.

Wilson, Violet. *Society Women of Shakespeare's Time*. Port Washington, N.Y.: Kennikat Press, 1970.

Wiltenburg, Joy. *Disorderly Women and Female Power in the Street Literature of Early Modern England and Germany*. Charlottesville: University of Virginia Press, 1992.

Woodbridge, Linda. "Palisading the Elizabethan Body Politic." *Texas Studies in Language and Literature* 33, no. 3 (1991): 327–54.

———. *Women and the English Renaissance: Literature and the Nature of Womankind, 1540–1620*. Urbana: University of Illinois Press, 1984.

Woods, Susanne. Introduction to *The Poems of Aemilia Lanyer*, ed. Susanne Woods, pp. xv–xlii. New York: Oxford University Press, 1993.

Woolf, Rosemary. *The English Mystery Plays*. Berkeley: University of California Press, 1972.

Woolf, Virginia. *A Room of One's Own*. New York: Harcourt, Brace, 1929.

Woolley, Hannah. "To all Maidens, who desire to be Chamber-maids to persons of Quality." In *The Gentlewomans Companion, or a Guide to the Female Sex . . . whereunto is added a Guide for Cook-maids, Dairy-maids, Chamber-maids, and all others that go to Service*. London: Edmund Thomas, 1675.

Wright, Pam. "A Change in Direction: the Ramifications of Female Household, 1558–1603." In *The English Court: From the War of the Roses to the Civil War*, ed. David Starkey et al., pp. 147–72. New York: Longman, 1987.

Wrightson, Keith. *English Society, 1580–1680*. New Brunswick, N.J.: Rutgers University Press, 1982.

———. "The Nadir of English Illegitimacy in the Seventeenth Century." In *Bastardy and Its Comparative History*, ed. Peter Laslett, Karla Oosterveen, and Richard M. Smith, pp. 176–91. Cambridge, Mass.: Harvard University Press, 1980.

Wroth, Lady Mary. *The Countesse of Mountgomeries Urania*. London, 1621. STC 26051.

———. *The Poems of Lady Mary Wroth*, ed. Josephine Roberts. Baton Rouge: Louisiana State University Press, 1983.

Wynne-Davies, Marion. "The Queen's Masque: Renaissance Women and the Seventeenth-Century Court Masque." In *Gloriana's Face*, ed. S. P. Cerasano and Marion Wynne-Davies, pp. 79–104. Detroit, Mich.: Wayne State University Press, 1992.

Yost, John K. "The Value of Married Life for the Social Order in the Early English Renaissance." *Societas* 6 (1976): 25–40.

Zimmerman, Bonnie. "What Has Never Been: An Overview of Lesbian Feminist Criticism." In *Feminist Literary Criticism*, ed. Gayle Greene and Coppélia Kahn, pp. 177–210. New York: Methuen, 1985.

Index